History of East Asia

A Captivating Guide to the History of China, Japan, Korea and Taiwan

Free Bonus from Captivating History (Available for a Limited time)

Hi History Lovers!

Now you have a chance to join our exclusive history list so you can get your first history ebook for free as well as discounts and a potential to get more history books for free! Simply visit the link below to join.

Captivatinghistory.com/ebook

Also, make sure to follow us on Facebook, Twitter and Youtube by searching for Captivating History.

Contents

Introduction

It has long been said that history repeats itself. However, that is a convenient and hasty dismissal of the stark differences that characterize the histories of the Far Eastern countries: China, Korea, Japan, and Taiwan. Each of these countries is utterly unique. And each of these countries treasures its own past. Among the gleaming glassy skyscrapers are ancient shrines, which grow in well-manicured gardens where water trickles over small stones, dancing in dappled sunlight.

China

China is the largest out of the lot, and in a way, it was the father to the people who inhabit Korea, Taiwan, and Japan. China is known as the "Land of the Red Dragon," who left his footprints in the soils that have been trodden by the many dynasties of his children. The dragon is considered to be a powerful but gentle and noble beast. According to the traditional creation myth, China was born from his union with the divine.

Mighty rivers flow over China's topography, namely the great Yangtse and Yellow Rivers. The Yellow River is not a misnomer; it is truly yellow due to the silt from rice paddies. China was also home to the Silk Road, which carried printed silken fabrics to an astonished Europe.

The Han Chinese remain the largest ethnic segment of China, and they have been since the early days of Chinese civilization. They were ethnically somewhat different from those Chinese who came from the north. The northern Chinese were (and still are) generally taller than the Han Chinese.

The Han gave birth to gifted mathematicians and were the very first to call mathematics an art. Herbal medicine found its origins in China, as did gunpowder and fireworks. It has been said that experiments with gunpowder even blew up the home labs of foolhardy alchemists. The Han also invented the hot air balloon and Chinese finger puzzles!

Chinese emperors carried the Mandate of Heaven, meaning they were granted the divine right to rule. However, the people eventually eliminated those whom they felt lost that sacred mandate. For instance, the Mandate of Heaven was forcibly taken from Zhao Bing, the last emperor of the great Song dynasty. It was also taken away by the notable Mongol Genghis Kahn in 1206 CE. In 1260 CE, his grandson, Kublai Kahn, feasted upon the laurels left to him by the Xia, the Shang, the Han, the Song, the Tang, the Jin, the Yan, and the Sui. Not to be outdone, Kublai Khan started his own dynasty—the Yuan. This was followed by the great Ming dynasty, which yielded some of the world's greatest artistic treasures.

Both the Ming dynasty and the Joseon dynasty of Korea shared knowledge of agricultural techniques. As a result of this partnership, the two countries developed new seed varieties that were resistant to drought, and they also conferred on scientific inventions as well.

The Manchu people were responsible for the creation of the Qing dynasty, which followed the Ming. They forced the Ming dynasty to vanish from history in 1644. The Qing was the last dynasty of China, and it became just another artifact of history by 1912 when the young Puyi, the last emperor of China, was forced to give up his crown.

Trade is the door that opens up most countries to ideas and culture from other nations, but it is fraught with problems. So, when people with strange-sounding names from strange places beyond the horizon trampled their shores, the Chinese shut down their ports. This was short-lived. The Dutch East India Company came with goods that the Chinese craved, and since China had goods Europeans wanted, the idea of trade became more appetizing to the Chinese. The British came with their grand sailing ships, as well as the Americans and Portuguese. As a result of this, pirates and smugglers reared their ugly heads, attempting to turn the trade with other nations to their advantage. In the 16th century, the Chinese tried to stop the influx of ideas reaching their shores, but they had to be satisfied with limiting it.

In the beginning, China was fairly isolated, but despite this, it still had enemies to face. At first, wars weren't fought between deities, as the myths say. Rather, they were fought between mortal men who thought of themselves as deities. Dynasties rose and fell throughout the many dusty years, with battle-hardened warriors stumbling upon the crumbled bloody stones that the dynasties built before them. Before long, more enemies from within sprung up, such as the Red Turbans, the Yellow Turbans, the Taipings, and the Boxers.

Like other nations, China had its fair share of wars. In 1894, the First Sino-Japanese War broke out between China and Japan, and it was later followed by yet another war between the two parties in 1937. China faced Western powers as well, such as the British and French in the First Opium War in 1839 and the Second Opium War in 1856.

Despite being a formidable power, China lost all these aforementioned wars except for the Second Sino-Japanese War. In 1895, after the conclusion of the First Sino-Japanese War, China was forced to surrender its interests in Korea and hand over Taiwan to the Japanese. China was sucked into World War I by Japanese interference in an internal affair, and China joined the Allies in World War II, which helped lead to their resounding victory in the Second Sino-Japanese War.

The Chinese have always honored their age-old traditions and customs. Although China progressed in many ways, they didn't get rid of their last emperor until 1912, with the aforementioned Puyi. Puyi would later come back to the throne for a short stint, reigning, in the loosest sense of the word, for around twelve days in 1917. China's first president was Sun Yat-sen, who became the provisional president in early 1912. Political parties now gripped China. Sun Yat-sen up his own party, the Kuomintang, but shortly after, another party was formed: the Communist Party of China. The two entities joined up during Sun Yat-sen's administration. However, this changed when the reins of government were handed to Chiang Kai-shek, who ruled via the National Revolutionary Army. He was strictly anti-Communist and purged members of the Communist Party within the government and military.

The rising star of the Communist Party, Mao Zedong, later known as Chairman Mao, and Chiang Kai-shek waged war over control of China. At the end of their conflict, two Chinese governments emerged. In 1949, Chiang Kai-shek resigned, and his government, now known as the Republic of China, retreated to Taiwan. Mainland China became the People's Republic of China. It governs from Beijing and is still a communist government today.

Korea

According to Korea's creation myth, a tiger and a bear competed to determine who would become human and visit the valleys of Earth. The bear won, and it stands as a solid symbol of strength.

The competition of the tiger and the bear can be said to symbolize the early history of Korea, which was besieged by competition for dominance among the early tribes who first migrated to this humble peninsula. The winters are colder there than in most countries in the temperate zone, as it is subject to a Siberian high-pressure system. From early on, these people produced heat in their pit dwellings through a clever floor plan. The country also enjoyed the waters of the Yellow Sea, which flow from China.

Korea is a country of immigrants, whose earliest ancestors came 9,000 years ago. They did not originate from China but rather from frigid North and Southeast Asia.

When the Koreans arrived, they came in clans with a preset system of social stratification in place. They set up three kingdoms for themselves: Goguryeo, Baekje, and Silla.

Goguryeo was intensely interested in expansion. Likewise, the southern kingdom of Silla was interested in expansion, as it was hemmed in on both sides by the sea. Baekje, in the meantime, was vulnerable, as it lay in the middle of the peninsula. As would be expected, the three kingdoms went to war with each other throughout the 6th century.

During the 7th century, the Tang dynasty of neighboring China allied with Silla, and they conquered Baekje and later Goguryeo. The population then shifted north to avoid the many conflicts. They intermingled and intermarried with the Mohe people, who are thought to be ancestors of the Manchu.

By that point, the people of Korea were strong enough to shed the Tang dynasty's overwhelming influence. With the help of their newfound alliance with the early Manchu, the Koreans in the north repelled the Tang. Their territory expanded as a result. They absorbed Baekje and created a huge new northern territory, which they called Balhae. By the 8th century, there were two states: Balhae and Silla.

In 936 CE, the kingdoms were united under King Wang Geon, and he created the Goryeo dynasty. This created the foundation for the country of Goryeo or, as it is known today, Korea.

However, things did not remain peaceful in Korea, as the Koreans had to fight off incursions. In the 13th century, they were in a weakened condition, and the Mongols invaded them. Consequently, Korea became their tributary state. The Mongols under Kublai Khan also annexed mainland China, creating the Yuan dynasty. After the death of Kublai in 1294 CE, the Yuan dynasty slowly began to fall apart. By 1368, it had given way to the

Ming dynasty, and Korea was freed from its vassalage to the Mongols.

Under King Taejo of Korea, good relations were established with the Ming dynasty. Taejo created the Joseon dynasty, and the country became a monarchy, which promulgated an isolationist policy. Despite this policy, Buddhism and Confucianism flourished during that time.

During the reign of King Seonjo in the mid-16th century, the military was built up, and fortifications were created to stave off attacks by the nomadic tribes of the Khitans and Jurchens. The large territory of Balhae virtually disappeared, as it was swallowed up little by little by these nomads.

In 1590, the island of Japan, under Toyotomi Hideyoshi, was desirous of conquering Ming China and asked Seonjo for permission to cross Korea on the way there. King Seonjo suspected that might lead to Korea's annexation because Japan had a powerful navy and ground force. He adamantly refused, notified Ming China, and allied himself with them. The Ming tried to help the Koreans, but they had been weakened over the years by internal conflicts and were forced to withdraw. The Japanese handily took Seoul, Korea's capital.

Realizing the threat that Japan exercised in the region, China sent in reinforcements. Nearly 100,000 Chinese and Koreans were slaughtered, but the Japanese were forced to retreat. On their way out of the country, the Japanese deliberately destroyed Korean farmlands and threw the country into a famine.

Although Korea did win, the government was blamed for the aftermath of the war. Upheavals occurred between political factions. The ultra-conservatives took the reins of power, but Korea was extremely vulnerable. In 1627, an aggressive division of their perennial nemesis, the Jurchens, migrated into Manchuria, and the Manchu invaded Joseon. They won, and Korea was coerced into paying annual tributes.

Commerce thrived between Korea and China, but Korea continued to keep themselves isolated from other foreign intrusions. Much of the activity Korea wanted to avoid was involvement in the illegal opium trade in the 19th century. The profitability of that trade brought in foreign pirates from Britain and France, only to be followed by foreigners trying to control the trade.

In 1853, Commodore Matthew Perry, an American sea captain, opened up Japan to American trade. This move shook up the Asian world, and both Japan and Korea took notice of the advanced armaments and the formidable warships America had. Japan scrambled to improve its own navy and armaments because they still harbored an interest in Korea. In 1875, Japan forced themselves into the harbor of Pusan in the south. Korea was unable to repel them, and Japan forced the Koreans to sign the Treaty of Ganghwa. This granted the Japanese free access to the port of Pusan. To increase support, Korea signed a treaty with China in 1882, and in the same year, they created relations with America and Russia.

In 1894, the Chinese sent in supportive troops to Korea, as they had long been trading partners and likewise needed to push the Japanese out of the area. The Japanese and Chinese engaged each other on Korean soil, triggering the First Sino-Japanese War. It was a short war, and by April 1895, China had been defeated.

Russia then jumped on the opportunity to use Korea as a base, as they could utilize their ports and repel the Japanese threat in the area. In 1897, Russia revised its trade and amity treaty with Korea, sent in aid, and even trained Korean troops.

In 1905, war broke out between Russia and Japan. Korea decided to step away from the conflict and declared neutrality. Most of the battles were fought at sea, with Russia using various Korean ports, while Japan used Incheon in southwestern Korea. Japan was victorious in the war, and it annexed Korea in 1910.

During World War I, Korea played an ancillary role. However, the Japanese troops who were stationed there were abusive and abducted Korean women. Protests erupted everywhere, calling for independence, but it was all to no avail.

During World War II, Korea was tasked by their Japanese overlords to manufacture weapons for Japanese soldiers. In 1944, 200,000 Koreans were inducted into the Japanese military.

The war ended shortly after in 1945, with the bombing of Nagasaki and Hiroshima. Japan was defeated. It had been decided earlier that Korea should be an independent country, but the future does not always go according to plan. Korea became independent, but it was no longer just one country: it was two. North Korea was under Russia's protectorate, while South Korea was overseen by the United States of America. The northern portion, known as the People's Republic of Korea at the time, was heavily influenced by communist principles, which the US objected to. The issue was brought to the United Nations, but it wasn't resolved to the satisfaction of both Russia and the US.

In 1948, elections were held in South Korea, while North Korea had none. Syngman Rhee was elected as the first president of South Korea, while communist North Korea established the Democratic People's Republic of Korea and appointed Kim Il-sung as its president.

In 1950, North Korea invaded South Korea. The issue was presented to the United Nations, which condemned the attack and sent in an international force. In 1951, General George MacArthur and his American troops forced the North Koreans to withdraw to the border. A neutral area, called the Korean Demilitarized Zone, was established. Although peace talks continued, no resolution was reached that would result in the reunification of Korea. Therefore, it was just a ceasefire agreement.

In North Korea, Kim Jong-un succeeded Kim Il-sung. In 2017, North Korea launched an intercontinental ballistic missile capable of carrying a nuclear warhead. Two nuclear bombs were also tested underground. China suspended oil shipments to North Korea, and food aid from the US was suspended until the International Atomic

Energy Commission could verify that the manufacturing of gas centrifuges, which are needed for nuclear weapons, had ceased.

Over the years, South Korea converted from an agricultural community to a highly profitable industrial economy. They manufacture cars, ships, and sophisticated technological products such as semiconductors. Their business sector is intensely involved in financing.

Taiwan

Taiwan, an island located off the eastern coast of mainland China, is a country composed of immigrants, even from its earliest days. The earliest immigrants didn't come from China, as one might suspect, but from the South Pacific.

The Chinese came in the 3rd century CE during the Qin dynasty and set up states of their own. They were an ethnic group known as the Han. They settled in the north, where the climate was similar to that of mainland China. One of the subgroups was the Hakka people, who were outcasts in China. Throughout its early years, Taiwan became a haven for refugees from other countries.

Although the Chinese immigrants held on to some of their ancient beliefs, they brought in more recently developed religious beliefs, especially that of Taoism. They also believed in a pseudo-religious system of orderly living called Confucianism. It basically promulgated adherence to the proper authorities.

Taiwan was originally called Formosa, which means "beautiful island." It is separated from mainland China by the Taiwan Strait, which allowed for the trafficking of these displaced peoples.

Iron was discovered in the mountains, which provided their Chinese neighbors with the much-needed element, which they used for farming tools and weapons. Thus, trade flourished between the two nations.

The Dutch East India Company—known for its engagement in worldwide trade—established a huge trading post called Fort Zeelandia in southwestern Taiwan in 1634. The Taiwanese people rebelled against them, as the fort was basically used for Dutch international trade, and they competed with the Taiwanese in the trade market. Ming Chinese arrived to help the Taiwanese expel the Dutch. In 1662, the Chinese succeeded in driving out the Dutch, but they stayed and created their own settlements.

In 1683, the Qing dynasty of China took over the western and coastal areas of Taiwan. With the steady arrival of the Chinese, the original settlers of Taiwan fled to the highland areas to escape.

There was much piracy at sea, which gave rise to the heavy trafficking of opium in Taiwanese ports. The opium trade attracted even more foreign intruders. This time, it was the Portuguese who made a lot of money transporting opium from India into China and even Taiwan. China was the largest importer of opium, but its government wanted opium curbed since it affected so much of its population.

The First and Second Opium Wars were fought between 1839 and 1860, and it involved China, Great Britain, and France, although its impact was felt worldwide. Since Britain and France essentially won the wars, opium was legalized for a short time, which allowed any country to partake in the trade. The opium trade was suppressed in the 20th century, but opium derivatives are still illegally sold around the world.

In 1894, Japan and China engaged in the First Sino-Japanese War. Taiwan, with its deepwater ports, was a prize both Japan and China craved. To protect their assets in Taiwan, the Qing dynasty declared that all of Taiwan was a part of China. However, this was merely an exercise in futility because the Qing wasn't strong enough to preserve China.

Therefore, at the end of the First Sino-Japanese War, the Qing lost its control over Taiwan, and it was ceded to the Japanese. Japan colonized Taiwan and put Goto Shinpei in charge of civilian affairs. Under his leadership, Taiwan became industrialized.

World War I broke out in 1914. Both Taiwan and Japan provided supportive roles for the Western Allies by keeping the sea lanes open.

World War II found Japan on the opposing side of the Allies, and the Japanese occupiers of Taiwan conscripted the Taiwanese into their armed forces. Japan assigned many of them to China and the islands in the South Pacific. Taiwan's indigenous population was accustomed to the sub-tropical temperature, and they were a great asset in the Japanese war effort.

The Taiwanese were involved throughout the war effort, but their heaviest involvement occurred in 1944 during the Formosa Air Battle. The skies of Taiwan were constantly darkened by fighter planes, and the seas around Taiwan were full of battleships and aircraft carriers. The Japanese airbase was in Taipei, located in northern Taiwan, and there were frequent American bombing runs on the base.

In 1945, America dropped the atomic bomb on Nagasaki and Hiroshima, which abruptly ended the war in favor of the Allies. Due to the Treaty of San Francisco (1951) and the Treaty of Taipei (1952), Japan surrendered its annexed lands in Taiwan, Korea, and other islands and sectors controlled by them during the war. However, the treaties that ended World War II stopped short of declaring Taiwan as a sovereign country.

In 1948, China underwent internal turmoil. Chiang-Kai-shek was forced out of mainland China, and he soon established the Republic of China on the island of Taiwan. Over time, Taiwan transformed from an authoritarian state into a democracy. However, Taiwan is still known as the Republic of China today, although there have been calls on both sides of the aisle to either unify with China or become an independent country.

Japan

The early settlers of the island of Japan were the Ainu. A later migration was made by the Yayoi culture of East Asia. The Yayoi and Ainu were ethnically very different from each other. The Yayoi brought with them the knowledge of rice paddies and metallurgy as early as 1000 BCE.

Shintoism was Japan's first religion, and it remains the most popular religion amongst the people today. Buddhism was transplanted there from Korea, which spread to China and Taiwan as well.

Many Asian cultures depended upon familial clans, and Japan was no different. These clans were often enemies of each other, as each clan wanted to be the dominant one. For many years, the Fujiwara clan was the most powerful, to the point where they could influence the emperor by raising him in their own household.

From its nascent days, Japanese society was divided into social classes, which were characterized by occupations. This was feudal Japan—a time when upward mobility wasn't possible. In the interest of self-defense and expansionism, Japan was organized into districts run by daimyos, or "lords." Over time, powerful rulers known as shoguns appeared, who held more power than the emperor himself.

Perhaps one of the most iconic images of Japan is that of the samurai wielding his katana. Samurais were warriors hired by the daimyos to protect their estates. They followed a sacred code called Bushido, which were honorable principles a samurai must abide by.

Kamakura Japan was one of its most notable eras, which lasted from the 12th to the 14th century. The Mongolian invasion under the famous warrior Kublai Khan occurred during that time, and the Japanese fiercely fought him off.

Just like Kublai, the great warriors of Japan craved expansion. To the west of Japan lay the huge country of China, which was ripe for conquest. Japan attacked Korea in 1592 with the intention of moving into Ming China. China sent over reinforcements continually, knowing the threat Japan posed. The Koreans and Chinese fought courageously and managed to reduce the Japanese forces from 150,000 to a meager 53,000. Japan underwent the humiliation of defeat and was unable to defeat the Ming or subjugate Korea.

The Japanese, tired of the battles and bloodshed, turned inward and isolated themselves from the world at large. China and Korea soon followed suit. It wasn't until 1853, when Commodore Matthew Perry arrived, that their isolation ended.

In 1868, feudal Japan, which was ruled by shogunates, was brought to its knees. The Meiji Restoration followed. During that era, the entire political structure of Japan transformed.

In 1939, the Western world became embroiled in World War II. Japan craved an empire that spanned the globe, although their main focus at the time was on East Asia and the islands in the southwestern Pacific. In 1941, Japan attacked the American base at Pearl Harbor, Hawaii, which led to the US entering the war.

Japan was a powerhouse in the East. At the beginning of World War II in 1939, the Japanese already occupied Korea, Taiwan, French Indochina, Cambodia, Thailand, Vietnam, and sectors of China. Hong Kong and Malaysia surrendered to the Japanese in 1941. In 1942, Japan conquered the Bataan Peninsula and controlled the Philippines. Japan captured Borneo, Guam, Indonesia, Burma (Myanmar), Singapore, Shanghai, and Guadalcanal. As one can see, Japan did very well in the war, and they were well on their way to creating the empire they so desired.

However, the war turned in favor of the Allies in 1942, with Allied victories in the Coral Sea off Australia's east coast and at Midway Island, north of Hawaii. This was followed by the recapture of the Philippines, Guadalcanal, Malaysia, Guam, and Borneo. The Americans dropped the atomic bomb in 1945, and Japan had no other choice but to surrender. As a result of the Paris Peace Treaties of 1947, Japan had to withdraw from its occupied territories, and the United States occupied Japan from 1947 to 1952, with the exception of Okinawa.

In 1952, the Treaty of San Francisco granted sovereignty to Japan, and arrangements were made to release Allied prisoners of war from Thailand, the Philippines, Malaysia, Singapore, Taiwan, Borneo, Burma, China, Indonesia, and some South Pacific islands. The Japanese prisoners of war were released from Australia, Canada, the US, France, Germany, and England. Okinawa was returned to Japan in 1971 by virtue of the Okinawa Reversion Agreement.

After the war, Japan grew leaps in and bounds with its economy, which is still running strong today. Although Japan still has an emperor today, the country has a constitutional monarchy, meaning the emperor is more of a figurehead than a ruler with power.

Part 1: History of China

A Captivating Guide to Chinese History, Including Events Such as the First Emperor of China, the Mongol Conquests of Genghis Khan, the Opium Wars, and the Cultural Revolution

Introduction

The history of China is complex—perhaps more complex than that of other nations. The ethnic groups that compose China go back to prehistoric times, and each group lent its own color to the enormous nation. It is not like a diluted mixture of all its cultures; rather, it is a collage.

Yet there are immutable elements still present today. Rice originated in China, and so did stir-frying. Anyone who has enjoyed a snack or two from a delightful swimming pool imitates the same practice in the water towns of China from times past. Brocade and printed silk fabrics were first created in China. Iridescent porcelain is a product of the Ming dynasty. The Chinese were among the first to develop blast furnaces. They were the first to invent fireworks and gunpowder. And the list goes on and on.

As you read this, you will note that history tends to repeat itself in the rise and fall of the many dynasties of China. However, you will also notice that there are clear distinctions between one era and the next.

In an analysis of maps showing the expansion and decline of the many dynasties throughout Chinese history, one can readily see that the smaller kingdoms frequently relocated. Some were by nomadic societies, but others were forced to do so through the fortunes or misfortunes of war. Emperors lived and died, but one can see the characteristics of their reigns as being propelled by power and expansionism, avarice, self-defense, intellectualism, altruism, wickedness, or simply by chance.

The culture of China is rich. The poetry and writing of China are permeated with feelings and are read and respected throughout the world. The Chinese have always had a reverence for their own history, which was meticulously recorded throughout the long and dusty years. Their artwork speaks with the simplicity of nature itself, and a common theme one can find is that the individual expresses himself as a part of the whole.

This idea can be found in Sinification, the spread of Chinese culture, namely the Han Chinese culture, which is a two-pronged dilemma. Practically speaking, it creates a blending of different peoples and can yield a peaceful co-existence and a semblance of harmony, but it can also condemn the richness that comes from diversity. The various cultures of Asia prize their own heritage and way of life, but Sinification tends to eliminate that. Over time, many cultures that had been Sinicized managed to find their old traditions and bring them back to the forefront. However, their lives had been inextricably changed due to Chinese involvement, and it was not always in a bad way, as the Chinese brought agricultural advancements and more forward-thinking to some cultures.

It is impossible to describe the impact China has made on all of humankind, but this book will attempt to do so by diving into its rich history.

Chapter 1 – The Land of the Yellow Emperor

The Legend of P'an Ku

From out of the chaos, the deep profoundness of the origin of life, rose Nu Kua Shih. It is said in the ancient texts that she took yellow clay in her hands and molded a man and a woman. It was up to them to keep their world healthy and whole. But they didn't always perform well, and their failure to protect the earth had ramifications.

In the world, which was composed of China, repairs were needed because of flooding. The people believed that this flooding was caused by Huang Di, the mythical "Yellow Emperor," who was displeased when his people misbehaved. The Yellow Emperor was so named because he was made of the soil, which had a distinctive yellow tinge. When the wise Nu Kua Shih saw that, she took mercy upon the people and stopped the floods. Thus, the land was saved from total destruction. China has two great rivers, the Yellow River and the Yangtze, and even to this day, flooding is a perennial problem because of the periodic flooding of those rivers.

The descendants of the first ancient people of China were farmers who dwelt in city-states. Emigration was forbidden, as their leaders realized that strength resided in numbers. Defense depended upon the population, and so did the cultivation of crops. There were peasant farmers, but there were also higher-class farmers who ran estate-like farms. Later on, the peasants worked outside walled cities, and the inner areas fostered merchants, scholars, and artisans.

The first dynasty of China was called the Xia dynasty. The foundations of the Xia lay in myths, so some scholars believe that this dynasty might not have existed at all. The establishment of the Xia dynasty is credited to a man named Yu the Great. Although Huang Di was said to have curbed the floods of the Yellow River, the Xia people believed that Nu Kua Shih was the one who actually stopped the floods, and so, they deified her.

The Xia dynasty is believed to have ruled between 2100 and 1600 BCE, if it even existed at all. The problem of its authenticity lies in the fact that are no contemporary written records of it; in fact, the earliest mention of it dates to around the 13th century BCE.

Shang and Zhou

Around 1600 BCE, the Shang dynasty came about. It had a vassal state called the Zhou. The staple food for the people of the Shang and the Zhou was rice, an ideal crop for a country that is covered in water. According to an ancient legend, rice was discovered when a dog ran through the floodwaters with mysterious seeds attached to his tail. When the people were starving, they heated the seeds in water. The seeds then expanded and became soft enough to eat. The rice saved the people, and they considered it a gift from Huang Di. The people grew rice in paddies, and they created terraces for the rice to prevent erosion. The original rice they grew was a variety of long-grain brown rice.

The upper classes enjoyed meat from cows, chickens, pigs, sheep, and deer. The lower classes and the slaves mostly lived on fish. It is interesting to note that the Chinese developed their traditional method of cutting food up into small tasty bits in ancient times. As early as the year 1000 BCE, during the Zhou dynasty, they mastered the techniques of stir-frying, steaming, and deep-frying food. It was felt that cooked food was the mark of civilization.

During the Shang dynasty, a script was developed, which consisted of a series of pictographs. In a short period of time, many of these "pictures" became less complex and more symbolic. They even had symbols to indicate phonetic pronunciation to help avoid confusion. The inscriptions spoke of births, harvests, wars, human sacrifices, and threats of war from neighboring tribes. Archeologists and linguists have isolated as many as 3,000 characters from the writings discovered from the Shang dynasty.

The great philosopher Confucius was born in 551 BCE during the Zhou era. His beliefs have inspired people for generations. The Confucian code taught obedience to proper authorities and added much to promoting a sense of self-generated integrity to the people.

Other aspects of culture of this time can be found in the various decorations they created. Most of the Shang dynasty took place during the Bronze Age, and as such, they used bronze for bowls, incense containers, ceremonial masks, wine vessels, and weapons. As the Shang dynasty faded away, so, too, did the use of bronze. Iron metallurgy wasn't fully developed until the 10th and 9th centuries BCE. As soon as that occurred, iron quickly replaced bronze for use in warfare because bronze could easily be broken in battle.

The people of the ancient Shang and Zhou dynasties mostly settled between the Yangtze and Yellow Rivers. The Yellow River was aptly named, as it does have a yellow tinge due to the sediment it picks up on its way to the sea.

The Battle of Muye

The ruler of the Zhou, King Wu, was looked upon as the chief leader of the Chinese people. In the year 1046 BCE, Di Xin, the ruler of the Shang, strongly craved the throne and even told his people that he had the Mandate of Heaven, the idea that a ruler was selected by the deities to lead the people. Natural disasters were seen as a definitive sign that a ruler had lost the Mandate of Heaven. However, when it came to war, when one side won, everyone accepted the belief that the Mandate of Heaven was on the winner's side.

According to legend, the people of the Shang were displeased with Di Xin after he married an evil woman named Daji. Di Xin, they said, became ruthless after he married her. At the Battle of Muye, located in eastern China, the warriors used pikes, spears, crossbows, and halberds. Chariots were also used, and the craftsmen designed special war chariots that were pulled by two horses and manned by two warriors.

Battles were fought in strict formation, and it was dishonorable to take advantage of an opponent's mishaps, like a broken chariot wheel. Battlefields were designated in advance, and they were placed at a distance from villages so the civilian population would be protected.

The Battle of Muye was bloody, and Di Xin had many defections from among his army, which included both soldiers and slaves. Because he lost the confidence of his people, he lost the throne, and the Shang dynasty ended with him. In the ancient narrative, the *Commentary of Zuo*, it says, "Calamity shall arise when officials lack credibility. Without supporters, one is sure to perish." After the battle, it is said that Di Xin adorned himself with jewels and set himself on fire. The Zhou then became the ruling dynasty in China, with Wu as its first king.

Societal Structure

King Wu set up a feudal structure in the country. It separated the people into classes:

1. The king
2. The royal household and its courtesans
3. The sheriffs
4. The soldiers
5. The common people
6. The slaves

When Wu died, his oldest son, Cheng, hadn't come of age yet (he would have been around thirteen years old_, so China was run by a regent, his uncle Duke Wen. Over the years, the various village complexes battled against one another to gain greater control. There was also an impetus to use stronger weapons, and the workers started using bog iron taken from the swamps. It was melted in furnaces and molded to create iron swords and even farming implements.

Jealousies and hegemony predominated during the Warring States period, which took place between 475 and 221 BCE. When the Zhou dynasty began to fall in the 5th century, they had to rely on armies from their allies. These states saw a chance to become the one true power of the Chinese people, and constant wars broke out between them, with alliances shifting often. Once the Jin state was broken up, three major competitors emerged—the Zhao, Wei, and Han states. Over time, though, seven states fought for the control of China: Qin, Han, Wei, Zhao, Qi, Chu, and Yan. This will be touched on a bit more in the next chapter with the rise of the Qin state and dynasty, but suffice to say, there was a lot of turmoil between the seven states.

Culture

While warriors were competing for political dominance, philosophy flourished among the people.

Confucius, who lived from 551 to 479 BCE, inspired the masses with his humanistic approach to life. He eschewed scrupulous adherence to a list of rules and regulations and instead favored a philosophy that was practical and compassionate. He was, however, very demanding in terms of respect for authority. He believed in loyalty to the state and to one's parents. The cultivation of virtue was vital to a successful life, as was unselfishness.

Taoism came into being when it was promoted by Laozi in the 4th century BCE. He taught a belief in the "Way," which is a harmonious process of living. It means that one needs to traverse the "path" of righteousness and free oneself from selfish desires. In a harmonious society, unhappiness results from wanting that which one cannot have. Unlike Confucius, Laozi didn't stress obedience but taught that one should live a life that was natural, one that coincided with the tempo of life.

The early priests were often fortune-tellers. They used small animal bones that would be thrown into a fire until they cracked. When that happened, the oracle presented his or her answer to questions their clients asked. The bones they used for divination were called "oracle bones."

The use of *Tao Te Ching*, an important text in Taoism, has a divination function and is still popular today for fortune-telling. The ancient version used sayings from Laozi. They were written in pictographs on bamboo strips. The client would ask the question, and then the strips would be thrown down, after which the fortune-teller would interpret it. Today, cards are used instead of bamboo.

Before the invention of paper, bamboo was used for writing. It was cut into strips, attached at the back, and opened out like an accordion.

Chapter 2 – Imperial China Emerges

The Qin Dynasty

As time moved on, seven states emerged as forces to be reckoned with, and each warred with the others for dominance.

Fate Foretold

The people of the states of Wei, Han, Chu, Qi, Yan, and Zhao were horrified by the ruthlessness of the Qin state that emerged in the west. The priest Bo Yangfu prophesied about the end time for the Zhou dynasty when that happened. He said, "The Zhou is coming to an end! The qi [life force] of heaven and earth is never disorderly. It is people who introduce chaos to it." And he was not wrong, for the Zhou was indeed coming to an end. In 256 BCE, the Zhou dynasty disintegrated after its defeat by the Qin state.

Qin was different from the other Warring States. They didn't follow the code of honor on the battlefield, instead striking when the opportunity was ripe. Their army was also large and well-trained, headed by competent generals who believed in the goal they were pursuing: the dominance of the Chinese states. One such general was the domineering and legalistic philosopher Shang Yang, who, in 341 BCE, successfully led the Qin army against the Wei.

With that win, the two major states left to fight for dominance was Qi and Qin.

By 247, it was clear that Qin was the strongest of the lot. If the other states had united with each other, they might have been able to stand against the powerful Qin soldiers. They did not do this, and so, Qin began to swiftly conquer all seven states, starting with the Han state in 230 BCE. Next, Wei fell in 225 BCE, followed by the Chu state in 223. In 222 BCE, Zhao and Yan were conquered. Qi, knowing that its time was up, surrendered its cities without a fight. In 221 BCE, a new dynasty was born: the Qin dynasty.

Although the Qin state was able to overcome these states fairly easily, difficulties did arise. In 227 BCE, Jing Ke and Qin Wuyang of Yan planned to present King Zheng of Qin with a map of their chief city. However, within the rolled-up map was a dagger—the two were actually assassins who wanted to take the Qin state out with one swipe of a blade. However, they were not very good assassins, as Qin Wuyang was so scared that he couldn't even present the map to the king. This left the plot in Jing Ke's hands alone. As soon as the king unrolled the map, Jing Ke grabbed the dagger and attacked. The king attempted to pull his sword out but was unable to do so easily due to its length. After one of the Qin officials managed to distract Jing Ke long enough, the king drew his sword and stabbed Jing Ke nine times.

The King Zheng of this story changed his name to Qin Shi Huang when he became China's first emperor. And to ensure that the nation remained as one, the Qin sought uniformity everywhere. They introduced a detailed standardization of weights and measures. For example, carts that were pulled on the roads always left ruts after it rained, which would later harden when the mud dried. The emperor's solution was to regulate the width of axles. That way, all the ruts were in the same place, and the carts would be able to travel at an efficient speed.

The Qin was a totalitarian regime. Threatened by principles and words from the past, Qin Shi Huang burned whatever tomes and writings he could find.

The Unseen Emperor

The emperor virtually "disappeared" during his reign. He didn't want to be observed by the common people because that might make him vulnerable when he traveled, so he inaugurated a massive transportation network with a tree-lined elevated road for only himself and his entourage. It was called the Qin Direct Road, and it spanned the entire length of the states under his control.

Qin Shi Huang was also an unseen power. Signs of his changes were seen everywhere, but people weren't permitted to touch him. One of the first projects Qin Shi Huang undertook was to register the entire population. But perhaps the greatest accomplishment of the Qin dynasty was the Great Wall of China.

The Great Wall

To protect his empire from the interference of neighboring feudal lords, whose ideas might inspire disunity, the emperors had a massive wall constructed. Several walls had already been made prior, some as old as the 7th century, and Qin Shi Huang decided to have them connected in 221 BCE. As time went on, the different dynasties that ruled China repaired and added to it, creating what we know as the Great Wall today. It was maintained over the centuries to help protect the country from barbarian hordes, such as the Huns, Turks, Mongols, Khitan, Jurchens, and the Xiongnu.

The Fall of the Qin Dynasty

After the reign of Qin Shi Huang, his son, Qin Er Shi, was named the new emperor, but he was only a puppet in the hands of his eunuch, Zhao Gao. Qin was only nineteen years old, and as such, he was malleable to Zhao's domineering influence. Zhao also learned that Qin Er Shi was very gullible and created a laughing stock out of the boy by conspiring with other courtiers to convince the emperor that a horse he gave him for dinner was actually a deer.

Unfortunately, that sort of naïve behavior on the emperor's part opened up opportunities for peasant rebellions. Qin had a tendency to micromanage, and he punished people for minor infractions. Zhao made Qin become a hidden emperor, like his father, which allowed Zhao to gain more power and blinded Qin to the gravity of the revolts that broke out during his reign. Qin Er Shi ruled for only three years. He was killed in a coup led by Zhao Gao, and the next ruler would be Ziying, who took the title of king rather than emperor.

In 207 BCE, the Qin were beaten in the Battle of Julu. After the battle, one of the rebel generals, Xiang Yu, buried 200,000 Qin soldiers alive! However, he spared the three major generals, who would go on to become kings during the Eighteen Kingdoms period. Ziying was forced to capitulate to Liu Bang, another rebel leader, thus ending the Qin Empire.

The Eighteen Kingdoms

Between 206 and 202 BCE, China became engaged in an all-out war. After the Qin Empire dissolved into eighteen various states, Xiang Yu and Liu Bang realized that China needed unification; however, they couldn't both be the supreme leader of a unified China. So, the two waged war against each other, with the other sixteen kings choosing a side.

Xiang Yu was ruthless and warlike, and he attempted to assassinate Liu. Liu, on the other hand, was a man who engendered intense loyalty among his followers. After conquering a number of states, in addition to the ones he was entitled to within the Chu state, Xiang Yu assembled a huge army and pursued Liu Bang, who controlled the Han state, with a hateful vengeance. He defeated Liu Bang after three major battles, after which Liu Bang called for an armistice.

Liu Bang initially adhered to the conditions of the agreement. However, Liu's followers knew that Xiang Yu couldn't be trusted and strongly urged their leader to break the agreement. Liu wasn't in a good position to win the war against Xiang Yu but was finally able to convince two powerful local leaders to help by bribing them with a promise of titles. It worked, and Liu Bang defeated Xiang Yu at the Battle of Galaxia in 202 BCE.

Xiang Yu was a man unaccustomed to defeat, but he stood strong with the few men he had left. However, they were soon killed, and after Xiang Yu became mortally wounded, he decided to take his own life. China was now Liu Bang's.

The Han Dynasty

Liu Bang became the emperor of the Han dynasty in 202 BCE, and he took the regnal name of Emperor Gaozu. As demonstrated throughout the period of the Eighteen Kingdoms, he was a principled man. Although he didn't like the principles of Confucius initially, he later became dedicated to the Confucian belief that moral leadership was essential to create a stable country.

As one of his first actions as emperor, Gaozu rewarded those who had helped him win. He also realized that the most important aspect of leading a country was its economy. He thus appointed Xiao He, who had helped him tremendously during the war with Xiang Yu, to be in charge of the food supplies to feed the people during times of famine. Cao Shen, another one of the men who fought on the side of the Han state, was made the chancellor, who was expected to organize and run an efficient government.

Cao Shen was a scholarly man and consulted experts in various aspects of governing. Following Confucian ideals, Cao selected leaders of the administration based on competence, honesty, and their obedience to authority, not on heredity, as it had been done in the past.

Having experienced the heavy tax burden thrust upon the people during the Qin dynasty, Cao lowered the taxes on the peasants. However, he did raise the taxes on the merchants, as they had been benefiting quite well during the wars. He nationalized the iron and salt industries when he noted that a handful of people were making an enormous fortune from it while others were being exploited.

This was called the "Golden Age of Ancient China." Gaozu created an atmosphere of creative freedom so that the country would be successful, and the economy was stimulated by Gaozu's efforts to open the Silk Road routes, which connected the East to the West, to facilitate trade. Because of the desirability of silk, one of the most important inventions was that of a primitive loom, which gave Chinese craftsmen the ability to produce patterned clothing to sell via the Silk Road. Archeologists have discovered models of that loom in Laojunshan in Shu province that date back to the Han dynasty.

The Han-Xiongnu War, 133 BCE–89 CE

In 133 BCE, Emperor Wu of the Han dynasty attacked the nomadic and fierce Xiongnu. The Xiongnu were very aggressive and skilled horsemen, originating in the steppe regions north of today's China. The Xiongnu made enemies of many nearby tribes by raiding their farms, destroying their granaries, and confiscating their lands. Emperor Wu created an alliance between his people and the Yuezhi people, who were also nomadic, as well as excellent warriors and horsemen. Some of Wu's warriors were infantrymen and had to fight on foot.

Around the year 114 BCE, the Silk Road, a network of trade routes that connected the East and the West, was expanded by the Han dynasty. Wu used the Silk Road to transport his forces to fight the Xiongnu. He was assisted by General Huo Qubing, who led the cavalry forces. By the year 110, they had forced the Xiongnu to retreat into the Gobi Desert.

Chapter 3 – The Supremacy of the Han, 202 BCE–220 CE

In 53 BCE, the Xiongnu Empire was in turmoil. Huhanye had rebelled in 59 BCE with the hopes of becoming the ruler, but his brother, Zhizhi, still stood in the way. Zhizhi was stronger than Huhanye, who decided to go to the Han for help. In order to gain their assistance, Huhanye made peace with the Han, and Xiongnu became a tributary state. In those days, it was customary to send someone of royal blood as a hostage to the dominant power. Along with a caravan of gifts, precious cloth, and jewels, Huhanye sent his son, Shuloujutang, to live at the Han court. In response, the Han sent a bronze plaque that read, "To Han obedient, friendly and loyal chief of Xiongnu of Han." It was to be displayed prominently and served as a pledge of loyalty to the Han emperor.

Zhizhi also sent his son to the Han in 53 BCE, and while he sent envoys in the following years with tribute, he failed to come in person to present them, as was expected. This was considered to be a great insult, and since his brother, Huhanye, had respectfully followed protocol, the Han backed him. In 36 BCE, the Han surrounded Zhizhi's fortress and proceeded to kill over 1,000 of the Xiongnu, along with Zhizhi and his wives. The victorious Han general, Chen Tang, took the severed head of Zhizhi to Emperor Yuan of Han.

Beginning of the Strife

The Han dynasty, too, was besieged with jealousies, internal conflicts, and revolts. This cost the empire money, and the imperial treasury was slowly depleted to keep pace with the cost of these wars.

In the year 9 CE, Wang Mang usurped the throne. He had no royal blood in him, but he still declared to the people that he and he alone had the Mandate of Heaven. Some historians view his grab for power as just that, while others believe he had great plans for social reforms. While Wang Mang believed his rule to be separate from the Han dynasty, naming it the Xin dynasty, most historians consider it to be an interregnum period, as the Xin dynasty ended with Wang Mang's death.

The unrest only grew under Wang Mang's rule, triggering uprisings and wars, especially in the lands of the Eastern Han. While Wang Mang's reforms were progressive at the beginning of his rule, which included the abolition of slavery, they didn't please the people, and he ended up reverting back to the old ways. His plans for the economy didn't pan out well either, and by 17 CE, the imperial coffers were empty, which wasn't helped by the rampant corruption taking place. As the taxes increased and the corruption in government remained, the belligerent peasants united and rebelled. Wang fought against them but lost more and more support. After that, the populace surrendered to the authority of the rightful Han heir, Liu Xiu, who became Emperor Guangwu.

The Good Emperor Guangwu

Emperor Guangwu faced many pretenders when he ascended the throne in 25 CE. For instance, Gongsun Shu formed the Cheng dynasty the same year, which grew to cover a large area of China. Guangwu was a man of peace and detested the bloodshed of Han against Han, but there was no other option but to fight the Cheng.

However, the Cheng dynasty was not the only threat that Guangwu had to defeat in order to unify the empire. Several regional powers popped up, and Guangwu spent many years in defeating them. Guangwu preferred the diplomatic approach, which worked in some cases. Wei Xiao of the Xizhou and Dou Rong of Liang province submitted to the emperor. Guangwu appointed Dou Rong as the prime comptroller of his region. Guangwu often awarded titles and honors to the warlords who submitted but never sufficient enough power to overtake the empire.

Not all so easily acquiesced to the Han. Liu Yong, who claimed to be the actual Han emperor and controlled the Jiangsu area (current-day Henan province), attacked the Han. In 29 CE, he and his son were killed by Emperor Guangwu's forces. By the year 30 CE, the Han had united all of eastern China.

However, Emperor Guangwu still had Gongsun Shu and the powerful Cheng dynasty to deal with. In 33, Guangwu was able to place all of his attention on Gongsun. After several battles, Guangwu had his warriors surround Gongsun in his capital in 36. Gongsun was tricked into believing that Guangwu's soldiers were weaker than they appeared, and in the battle that followed, he was mortally wounded. His entire family was massacred, as were members of other prominent officials of the Cheng dynasty. Once the Cheng dynasty fell, all of China was united once again.

Contributions of the Han

The Chinese people were gifted mathematicians, and the Han invented the system of Gaussian Elimination, which is a process in linear algebra used to eliminate all but one variable in an equation. Gaussian Elimination would permit a numeric solution in determining measurements and quantities. It was part of the *Nine Chapters on the Mathematical Art* and predated mathematics in Europe.

In the year 105 CE, Cai Lun perfected the invention of paper. It was made from hemp, tree bark, and rags and fabrics that were formed by splitting up old fishing nets. In the year 132, Zhang Heng invented the first seismometer, a device that measures earthquakes. He was also a gifted astronomer and astonished the scientific community by saying that the moon doesn't shine with its own light but rather the reflected light of the sun. Zhang Heng was also the first to create an accurate map of the stars in the celestial hemisphere.

The Han developed many other things that we take for granted today. The wheelbarrow, the magnetic compass, the loom, and the hot air balloon were all invented by the great minds of the Han dynasty. The earliest versions of the blast furnace and the steering wheels of ships can also be contributed to Chinese civilization.

The Yellow Turban Rebellion, 184–205

Taoist traditions were constantly practiced throughout these trying times. Many holy priests, magicians, and practitioners of early Chinese herbal medicine helped the less fortunate, sick, and vulnerable. The founder of the Yellow Turbans, Zhang Jue, was a devotee of Taoism. He announced to the people that the Han domination was coming to an end. He stated that a new time awaited and pronounced, "The Azure Sky is already dead; the Yellow Sky will soon rise. When the year is jiazi [184 CE], there will be prosperity under Heaven!" The "Azure Sky" refers to the Han dynasty.

According to the legends, people reported that they saw the sacred signs, which included a plume of black smoke in the imperial audience chamber that was in the shape of a dragon and an earthquake, which occurred in a distant province. Due to the earthquake, which people claimed occurred in 184 CE, a fissure broke the earth open, and warriors emerged. The warriors wore yellow turbans to proclaim their fellowship.

However, the real truth is not so much in the realm of the supernatural. Zhang Jue and his brothers, Zhang Bao and Zhang Liang, were faith healers. They taught the art of Chinese herbal medicine to their pupils. The religious aspect of these leaders seemed to serve as a justification for the violence that accompanied this revolt.

Sima Qian, a Chinese historian and a contemporary under the Han regime, wrote that many military feats were attributed to the Zhang brothers. In one transcript written by Sima Qian, it said that Zhang Bao "spread his hair and held out his sword, summoning spirits with magic arts. Suddenly a tempest sprung up, and the air became a black mist." From that mist, the tale goes on to say that the numerous troops emerged from the mist and went into battle.

The Yellow Turban Rebellion was widespread, and they even recruited non-Chinese to participate in it. Some joined to bring down the Han Empire, but many who joined were warlords seeking to expand their own petty little kingdoms.

There were many factions that split off from the initial membership of the Yellow Turbans, who battled for control of various provinces. Little by little, the factions were suppressed. When the infamous warrior Cao Cao waged against the Yellow Turbans in Yu province in 205, it finally fizzled out. After this was accomplished, Cao Cao had successfully united northern China and then proceeded to the south.

The Battle of Red Cliffs, 208

The northern warlord Cao Cao decided to conquer the lands south of the Yangtze River: Zhouzhuang, Wuzhen (Wuhan), Xitang, and Tangli. They were ancient water towns, networked with canals. Today, many tourists and residents can travel by boat and dine at the seaside stands, enjoying some of the culinary delicacies the vendors create. Today's great city and seaport of Shanghai is also within this area.

Cao Cao invaded those picturesque and important cities in 208. Although he was a formidable warlord, he made a mistake that other invaders often make—he didn't familiarize himself with the environmental characteristics of the area. The Yangtze, like the Yellow River, overflowed several times during the seasons, and Cao Cao didn't know this. So, even though he and his troops outnumbered the home forces, his horses, his warriors, and their weapons became stuck in the muck and mud of the water towns. Cao Cao's soldiers were forced to wade through the swamps and were sometimes victimized when they reached patches of quicksand. In fact, Liu Bei, one of the leaders of the defenders of the water towns, laughed and said to Cao Cao's warriors, "After passing through hell, like quicksand, not even a blade of grass has grown. You will definitely die here!"

Some historians have called the Battle of Red Cliffs a naval battle, and, in a way, it was. When the enemy in the south launched fire ships across the Yangtze, those who hadn't got stuck in the mud leaped into what water they could find. Cao Cao was then forced to retreat.

Through the centuries, the figure of Cao Cao carries with him a legacy of power that attracts the egotistical of any age. Of him, it was said, "You're wise enough to rule the world and perverse enough to destroy the world."

The Three Kingdoms, 220–280

Cao Cao's son, Cao Pi, created his own state called Wei in 220. When Emperor Xian of the Han abdicated, Cao Pi took the throne, ending the Han dynasty once and for all. Soon after this, two rivals, Liu Bei and Sun Quan, created the Shu Han and Wu states, respectively.

Wei, Shu, and Wu created the foundation for today's most popular video games. These games are historically based and feature the figures that are highlighted in this book. Cao Pi, for instance, is the questionable hero of the evil, dark worlds that permeated the Han Chinese in these turbulent times.

The emperors of the three kingdoms were young and inexperienced, so their courtiers, who were castrated eunuchs, manipulated the country and gained power. Those were dark days, but homegrown leaders rose from among the people. These leaders rose up and, according to an ancient storyteller, announced, "We vow to stand by each other and be blood brothers forever. Let us agree to protect the people of our homeland!" This tale was written in the *Romance of the Three Kingdoms* by Luo Guanzhong. It is a story about the warlords of legend and lore loosely based on the history of this chaotic period. It is a tale about subterfuge and treason and talks of courage against cowardice.

The three kingdoms were eventually unified in 280, with Sima Yan conquering the last-standing kingdom of Wu. Sima Yan then established the Jin dynasty and was known to posterity as Emperor Wu.

The Jin Dynasty, 266–420

Although the Jin dynasty united the areas of what now is eastern China, the government split the districts up into a complex system of smaller administrations. As many as eleven existed in the year 400, but it eventually increased to sixteen. Territorial expansions occurred, and the original Jin state was then divided into regions to the north and northwest—South Yan, North Yan, Wei (named after the original Wei state), Xia, and Liao.

While the officials busied themselves with administrative affairs, the artisans of the area developed fine porcelain pottery called celadon, also known as greenware. The artifacts were finely hewn and are quite valuable today. Greenware was the precursor of the fine tri-colored glazes created during the following Tang dynasty.

Murder and Assassinations

Cruelty spawned from the jealousies and the evil-doings of the last ruler of the Jin dynasty, which ultimately led to its demise. Emperor An was the legitimate heir when he came to the throne in 397, but he was developmentally disabled. Because of his disability, he was strangled in 419 at the age of 37 by order of his own regent, Liu Yu. Liu Yu was one of the many regents that Emperor An had, as it was a highly coveted position. Liu Yu then proclaimed the boy's brother, Sima Dewen, to be the new emperor. However, Emperor Gong (Sima Dewen's regnal name) yielded to Liu Yu's power a year later, surrendering the throne to him. Liu Yu was concerned that Sima would eventually regain the position, so he decided to take matters in his own hands and had the 35-year-old Sima asphyxiated with a blanket. With the death of Sima Dewen, the Jin dynasty met its end.

The Northern and Southern Dynasties, 386–589

The evil that had been kindled during the Jin dynasty spread throughout the country, giving rise to many divisions and sub-divisions in order to satisfy the petty rulers of the smaller provinces.

Power was divided between the northern and southern kingdoms, with the kingdoms falling and rising to new kingdoms as time went by. At times, kingdoms existed simultaneously with another, such as the northern kingdoms of Western Wei (535–557) and the Northern Qi (550–577).

Since the Northern and Southern dynasties lasted for a little over 200 years, many rulers rose up, and this book will examine one such ruler. In 561, Emperor Wu of Northern Zhou came to power. In the early part of his reign, he let his cousin, Yuwen Hu, do much of the ruling, as Yuwen Hu was essentially the man who placed Emperor Wu on the throne. Over time, though, the emperor amassed more personal power, and he successfully attacked Yuwen Hu in 572. The rest of his reign was spent on the idea of uniting China under one ruler, but Emperor Wu suddenly died in 578, leaving the throne to his son, Yuwen Yun.

Sadly, Yuwen Yun, who became known as Emperor Xuan upon ascending the throne, was a poor leader. His father's attempts at unifying China were thrown out the window, as Emperor Xuan sought to return to traditionalist values instead of attending to more important matters. Less than a year after assuming the throne, Xuan passed it onto his son, Emperor Jing. In 580, after the death of Emperor Xuan, Emperor Jing's father-in-law, Yang Jian took power and established his own dynasty, the Sui dynasty, in 581. His royal name was Emperor Wen.

Throughout the time of the Northern and Southern dynasties, people sought refuge in Buddhism, Taoism, and Confucianism. Although Buddhism was introduced much later than the other two religions, it quickly rose in popularity. While these three religions vied for dominance, the holy priests still recognized the importance of all three belief systems. In the 6th century, the people erected glorious temples for worship within the Hanging Monastery, an elegant structure carved into the cliffs in northeast China. According to legend, it was designed by a monk named Liaoran, and it contains exquisite carvings, pillared balconies, multiple staircases, and painted statues of Buddhist priests and worshippers. The marvelous structure is a tourist site today.

The Sui Dynasty, 581–618

Although the Sui dynasty didn't last for very long, Emperor Wen was able to unite all of China under one rule. Besides this great accomplishment, the Sui Dynasty also constructed the Grand Canal. Until that time, soldiers on long campaigns had to stop to grow their own vegetables and grain for food. Once food could be sent to them by boat, it was far more convenient and less time-consuming.

The Grand Canal was and still is the longest canal in the world. It is 1,776 miles long, and it starts in Beijing and runs northwest to Hangzhou. The Grand Canal connects the Yellow River with the Yangtze, as well as four other minor rivers. After the canal was built, trading flourished among the provinces. Trade was vital to the empire because its ships carried grain to the imperial court and to the eastern coast.

Emperor Wen of the Sui knew that the area under his control was frequently being flooded by the Yellow and Yangtze Rivers. So, in 584, he hired engineer Yuwen Kai to alleviate the problem. Yuwen Kai and his engineers created smaller canals to divert the water. They built the Guangtong Canal to stem off the overflow from the Grand Canal, and they also dug the Shanyang Canal to allow for increased traffic between the Yangtze and Huai Rivers. Many scientific studies are currently being conducted on the Grand Canal regarding its environmental impact, and the most promising results are being implemented.

In 594, there was a severe drought. To cut back on food, the emperor and his court abstained from meat for a year. When Yang Guang, Wen's son and future heir, asked that his father to establish an elaborate festival to the gods to relieve the drought, Wen did so. However, Wen was extremely frugal, and he didn't give much money toward the festival.

In the spring of 604, the emperor made preparations to move to Renshou Palace, where he customarily spent the summers after it was built in 593. A sorcerer, however, warned him that if he went there, he would not return. Ignoring that warning, Wen went to Renshou anyway and died there from an illness. He was revered for generations to come.

His son, Yang Guang, assumed the throne, taking the regnal name Emperor Yang. According to interpretations of an ancient plaque designed between 604 and 617, scholars indicate that Yang was hedonistic and overworked his laborers, who were recruited to make his life pleasurable. History seems to bear that out because peasant rebellions were frequent during his rule. In addition, Yang made the futile attempt to conquer Korea and parts of what is Vietnam today.

One of his generals and governors, Li Yuan, began to amass personal power. In 617, Li managed to capture the capital and placed Yang's grandson on the throne. Once Emperor Yang died in 618, Li removed the young emperor and declared himself to be the new ruler of China. He created one of the most influential Chinese dynasties: the Tang dynasty.

Chapter 4 – The Golden Age: The Tang Dynasty, 618–907

In 618, Li Yuan took the royal name Emperor Gaozu. He adopted many of the wise practices of Emperor Wen. Adult males were granted lots of land on which they paid taxes. Gaozu also established a monetary system using copper coins and wrote a code of law. Unfortunately, he met the same fate as former Emperor Yang of the Sui dynasty. In 626, one of his three sons, Li Shimin, killed his brothers. His father, afraid of what his son's next actions might be, abdicated and left the throne to him. Shimin was then known as Emperor Taizong. Despite his criminal ways, he was an effective emperor. Life as a royal was, at best, extremely risky for siblings and close relatives. As such, these were not the kindest of times.

In 657, Taizong annexed the Eastern Turkic Khaganate and expanded the empire. The Turkic Khaganate, located in current-day Kyrgyzstan, was good for growing pomegranates, grapes, and rice. In addition, the Turks in that region were rather compliant and adjusted well to their tributary status.

Taizong did much good for his country by creating storage granaries in case of famine, and he also inaugurated a civil examination to ascertain administrative ability for those who served in governmental offices. The Tang dynasty expanded its sphere of influence into the Persian Empire in Central Asia and today's Afghanistan.

The "Wicked" Empress

Taizong died in 649. His son, Gaozong was the next in line. However, Gaozong was in love with one of his father's concubines, Wu Zetian. Wu was very anxious to gain control of the matters of the state.

In 660, her wish came true when Gaozong began to suffer from an illness, allowing Wu to seize the opportunity to gain a lot of power. She was essentially able to rule in his stead, but to do so safely, she needed to eliminate her competition. She found excuses to put Gaozong's other wives under house arrest, and she didn't just target these influential women. In 652, Wu gave birth to a son, Li Hong. Four years later, he became the crown prince, and as time went by, he became more assertive and outspoken against his mother's actions. According to contemporary historians, she poisoned him in 675. Considering the things she did to keep power, it is entirely possible that she was the one behind his death.

In 683, Emperor Gaozong died and was succeeded by Wu's other son, Li Zhe, who became Emperor Zhongzong. All was well until Zhongzong tried to appoint his father-in-law, Wei Xuanzhen, as chancellor. Wu swiftly fired him and exiled her son. Obviously, Wu did not hide her ambitions or power. She then placed her youngest son, Li Dan (Emperor Ruizong), on the throne.

Although she still held all of the power, with her son ruling as a figurehead, she wanted more. In 690, Wu announced a new dynasty, the Zhou dynasty, and attempted to rule it herself. To bolster her authority, she wrote the *Great Cloud Sutra*, which foretold a female emperor would be responsible for eradicating problems such as famine, worry, and illness from the world. She also claimed to be an incarnation of Maitreya, the successor to Buddha.

To this day, Wu Zetian has been the only female emperor of China. Although it was novel for a woman to rule, she honestly was not much different from other male emperors. She introduced some new reforms, but she overall kept things the way they had been, bringing about a period of stability to the nation. However, the people did not recognize her proclaimed new dynasty and did not care for her methods of gaining power (some of which were most likely exaggerated—this book only skims the surface of what she was accused of doing). In 705, a large palace coup took place. Wu Zetian was forced to surrender her position, and Zhongzong was restored as emperor. Unfortunately for Zhongzong, he made the fatal error of marrying someone much like his mother.

In 710, Zhongzong died. Most historians agree that he was murdered by his scheming wife, Empress Wei, who craved a life similar to Wu Zetian's. Conspiracies and counter-conspiracies overtook the court, as the various courtesans and court officials attempted to gain more power in the empire. To frighten Wei, the conspirators murdered her two nephews and cousin. Wei then fled to a camp of palace guards. However, they were also disgusted by her nefarious behavior, and Wei was beheaded! Her body and those of her associates were displayed in public on the streets of Chang'an.

In 710, Zhongzong's brother, Ruizong, ascended to the throne once more. However, after hearing some dire predictions from his astrologers, he retired and passed the throne to his son, Emperor Xuanzong, in 712. Xuanzong was a wise man who surrounded himself with capable chancellors. He steeped himself in Chinese philosophy and paved the way for prosperity and peace in the realm.

The Cultural Achievements of the Tang

The Tang dynasty is noted in the world of art and literature for its treasures. Many of these works of art were transported on the Grand Canal and the Silk Road to be sold to other countries.

Yi Xing was an engineer who developed uses for hydraulic power, which farmers incorporated into devices similar to the waterwheel to use on their farms. Yi adopted that same movement to create a celestial globe with toothed gears to measure the planets' movements. In 725, he invented a kind of clock that operated on the movement of water into different-sized scoops, which were divided into measurements that marked the hours and days in a five-day cycle. It was equipped with bells and drums to ring the hour and quarter-hours.

Li Bai was one of the most noteworthy poets during the Tang dynasty. His works reflect nature and are filled with compassionate, deep, and thoughtful reflections. However, he used simple words. The Taoist nature of his work is clear: "We sit together, the mountain and me, until only the mountain remains." Between 779 and 831, another fine writer, Yuan Zhen, wrote the *Yingying's Biography*, which was later used in Chinese operas. Contemporary histories also wrote during this period, providing future scholars with a wealth of material on the politics, practices, and culture of the Tang.

Woodblock printing was one of the Tang's most notable accomplishments, as it was a way that the Chinese could print their sacred histories, stories, and poetry. Not only that, but the technique was applied to fabrics as well. This helped seamstresses create beautiful patterns on their clothing.

Printing was a rather tedious process, as it required many wooden blocks to be carved. The pictographs that formed Chinese characters also had to be cut in relief. Letters, of course, needed to be printed as if in a mirror image in order to be read. Then the layout of the words was pressed on silk. The Chinese are very artistic and used many motifs to decorate their fabrics. Flowers and plants were the most common themes. They liked bright colors, so a technique of reproducing color was invented. Crushed berries or minerals were mixed with water to produce the colors. In cases where more than one color was needed, a picture was separated into colors, and multiple woodblocks would be used. Prior to the computer, artists utilized color separation to create a cohesive and attractive design.

Sancai is a form of earthenware pottery characteristic of the Tang period. Tri-color vases and figures, mostly used in Tang tombs, were very popular. The Taoists of Tang believed in an afterlife and likewise believed that a person's tomb should include all the items necessary in life. Statues of hunters, servants, and horses were found inside many of these tombs.

Sancai was composed of bauxite, a valuable resource even today. Today, China is the world's second-largest producer of bauxite. It is used for making abrasives, cement products, and aluminum. For the Tang pottery and ceramics, the bauxite figure needed two firings in the kiln in order to create a tri-color statuette. Predominant colors found in Tang China were brown, green, and red. Since bauxite is very versatile, glazes could be made from it as well. The application of these glazes added to the unusual beauty of the works.

The Tang also oversaw the expansion of the Longmen Grottoes. They had been carefully carved into the side of a mountain. In the mountain, which supports the grottoes, there are over 2,000 caves with figures, nearly 2,500 stelae, and 100,000 statues. Empress Wu, despite her failings, had an appreciation of art and respect for Buddhism, so she contributed to its upkeep.

Metalwork was also produced by the gifted artisans of the period. They used precious metals, such as silver and gold. Bronze was also used to make mirrors and cups.

Perhaps one of the lesser-known inventions of the Chinese is something called sticky rice mortar. It was first used around 500 CE, which was before the time of the Tang dynasty, but it became widely used during the Tang. So, in essence, waterproofing was made possible due to the use of rice! When sticky rice soup was mixed with flaked, heated, and moistened lime from limestone, it created a mortar suitable for bricklaying and patching up gaps in houses. It was even used to repair holes in the Great Wall.

Gunpowder!

The Chinese alchemists were well known as healers and magicians. They spent many hours experimenting with elements found from rocks and plants. When sulfur, charcoal, and saltpeter are combined and heated, the mixture explodes. No doubt this was discovered by accident when the substance was placed in a closed container with one end open. Chinese alchemists were well known as a risk-taking group of people, with their singed beards, missing eyebrows, and burns on their faces from the many different chemicals they mixed together. After many attempts, they were able to achieve proto-fireworks. They were used at festivals as primitive firecrackers or simply to impress a crowd of admirers. It wasn't until the 10th century that gunpowder was used in warfare. The Chinese were the first to invent the substance, and it wouldn't spread throughout Eurasia until the 13th century.

In 858, a Taoist text printed a recipe for it as six parts sulfur, one-part birthwort root, and six parts saltpeter. "Birthwort root" is a related genus to the beautiful clematis plant. The rhizomes (horizontal roots) of the plant were used in this formula, but they aren't necessary to create the mixture that makes gunpowder.

The Chinese text that delineated the chemical recipe for gunpowder went on to warn the readers that the resulting product could cause burns on one's skin and could even burn down houses if mixed inside one's laboratory. The early version of gunpowder was called *huo yao*, meaning "fire medicine."

Government

The administration of the Tang had three departments that were tasked with the job of issuing and reviewing policies and seeing to it that the people were aware of the latest pronouncements. Six ministries handled a wide assortment of duties, including finances, military, and justice. Many of the emperors had careful tallies made of the populations in their various provinces and tributary states so that proper taxes could be collected and tax regulations enforced. The Tang also had a postal service with routes that were about 20,000 miles long altogether.

The An Lushan Rebellion

To mar an otherwise peaceful time, a disgruntled general named An Lushan persuaded his warriors to rebel in 755. He declared himself to be the emperor of northern China, and the new Yan dynasty was formed, which existed at the same time as the Tang dynasty. An Lushan's first move was to capture Luoyang, which became his capital. The forces then planned to move on the Chinese capital of Chang'an (today's Xian). It took some time to capture it, but by 756, it belonged to An Lushan and his forces.

The Seven-Year Yan Dynasty

Emperor Xuanzong of the Tang hired as many as 22,000 mercenaries, some of whom were from the northwestern area of China. Many of them were Uyghurs, who were reportedly Muslims of Turkish origin. Originally, they lived in the Tarim Basin (north-central China) but had been supplanted throughout the centuries. Currently, they reside in diaspora communities in Kazakhstan, **Kyrgyzstan**, Uzbekistan, and throughout Europe and the Americas.

During the An Lushan Rebellion, there were murders and conspiracies among the rebel generals, who craved lucrative positions in the new Yan dynasty. In fact, An Lushan was murdered by his own son, An Qingxu, after he became enraged by his father's threats directed at his friends. One of the powerful generals, Shi Siming, then killed An Qingxu. Shi Siming's son, Shi Chaoyi, killed his father and proclaimed himself Emperor Suzong. This all took place within four years, between 757 and 761. As a result, a number of the generals became incensed by this internecine turmoil and abandoned the Yan cause. By 763, the cause was lost, and Shi Chaoyi committed suicide to avoid capture.

The Ebbing of the Tang Dynasty

The An Lushan Rebellion was not the cause of the fall of the Tang. Under Emperor Xuanzong's guidance, art, literature, and learning permeated the land. However, toward the end of his reign, Xuanzong took an even greater interest in his concubines, especially his favorite, Yang Guifei. He paid less attention to ruling, leaving it in the hands of his advisors.

Emperor Xuanzong gave Yang Guifei anything she wanted, whether it was gowns, jewels, or elaborate parties. However, she then started asking the emperor to appoint her family members to important positions in the administration. He passed that duty to one of his chancellors, Li Linfu, with instructions to do so. Li Linfu assigned the Yang family to lucrative governmental posts, and he even put some of his own personal friends in these positions as well. As a result, the civil service system of administering tests to prospective administrators was neglected. Hence, many vital positions were held by virtual incompetents. In addition, many of these officials weren't even Chinese. They were foreign nationals who had other interests closer to heart than China.

The emperor's closest friends told him that Yang and her family were harmful to the empire. He reluctantly gave his assent for her to be taken care of. In 756, the year after the An Lushan Rebellion had started, she was strangled, and her body was buried in a simple manner. The emperor felt much remorse, although he knew that such matters were often handled violently. Emperor Xuanzong was also saddened by her nearly anonymous burial and sent his eunuchs to rebury her properly in 757. Unfortunately, Yang's body had decomposed, but the eunuchs found a bag of fragrances and dried flower petals in her coffin and brought it to him. Upon seeing it, he wept uncontrollably and was consumed with guilt and loss.

In 806, the Taoist poet Bai Juyi wrote the *Song of Everlasting Regret* about Xuanzong's tragic experience. One stanza reads: "On one night in Longevity Hall, let's be two birds flying side by side.

Let's be two branches on the earth inseparably tied. The sky and the earth will not be eternal, however. Only this regret remains and lasts forever and ever."

By 757, Xuanzong was no longer emperor. When he fled from the An Lushan Rebellion in 756, his son, Li Heng, had taken the throne. The rule of Emperor Suzong (Li Heng) was marked by internal power struggles and the An Lushan Rebellion. After the death of Suzong in 762, Emperor Daizong took the throne. While the rebellion was put down during his reign, other rebellions broke out from various warlords, and they essentially ruled as separate states, barely pledging any sort of loyalty to the emperor. The succeeding emperors were unable to unite China effectively, which eventually led to the disintegration of the Tang dynasty.

Back to the Beginning

The Tang had risen at a time when warlords ruled kingdoms and spent their regimes either gratifying themselves or defending their mini-kingdoms. And it was clear that history was repeating itself once again. The last Tang emperor, Ai, was only fourteen years old when he was forced off the throne. With that move, the Tang dynasty died—not with the blast of gunpowder nor with the blow of a sword but with the plaintive sigh of a boy. The year was 907.

Chapter 5 – The Song Dynasty, 960–1279

Following the Tang Dynasty, there was a period of continuing chaos in the leadership of China and its administration. After 907, when the Tang dynasty collapsed, the chaos existed for 53 more years. The period known as the Five Dynasties and Ten Kingdoms took place between 907 and 960. Eight land segments in the southeast were occupied by the Wu, Min, Shu, the later Zhou, Liang (or Liao), Wuyue, the northern Han, and the southern Han, Jingnan and Annam states. The larger portions of China were settled by the Khitans (Mongols), the North Jan, the Shatuo (a Sinicized Turkic tribe), the state of Da Chang Hi, Tufan (Tibetans), and the Uyghurs.

A Prophecy Initiates the Song Dynasty

The emperor-to-be of the Song dynasty was foretold by an unknown prophet who told military leaders and chancellors that Zhao Kuangyin had received the Mandate of Heaven, meaning that he had the approval of the deities to rule as emperor. He actually became emperor during a coup, although the prophecy most likely helped to launch him on the throne. He was then known as Emperor Taizu. He wanted to unite all of the small kingdoms into one large one. He began his rule in 960, but his dream would not come true during his reign, although he did manage to unify a good chunk of China.

During the first year of his reign, he reduced threats to his unity plan by awarding the high-ranking military commanders with a grand buffet, as well as generous estates and money for retirement. After some negotiations, the plan worked. Taizu initiated his plan of uniting the kingdoms, and a period of peace followed. After that, the Song territory expanded.

The "Shadows by the Candle and Sounds from an Axe"

One night, when he was 49 years old, Taizu was ill and retired to his chamber. No one was permitted to enter, as he was sleeping. However, in the middle of a dark night, observers reported that they looked up into the window of the emperor's chamber and saw the light of a candle dancing on the wall. Then they saw a tall black shadow leaning over the emperor's bed. The next thing they heard was the sound of an ax falling on the wooden floor and then nothing more.

In the morning, the emperor was found dead. No concrete evidence has arisen to confirm this story, but it has remained popular nonetheless. It is certainly suspicious that his younger brother, Zhao Kuangyi (Emperor Taizong), took the throne in 976 instead of Taizu's sons.

Taizong conquered the lands of the Northern Han and Wuyue. Although he attempted to conquer the Liao lands, he didn't succeed, having lost miserably at the Battle of the Gaoliang River in 979. Taizong's forces also ventured outside his territory to try to capture Dai Viet (today's Vietnam). That, too, was unsuccessful. However, it led to the introduction of Champa rice, which had been grown only in Dai Viet. It is a rice hybrid that matures faster and can be harvested twice in one season.

Taizong's successor, Emperor Zhenzong, was irritated by the failure of the Chinese to conquer the Liao dynasty of the Khitans back in 979. He felt he could conquer them and attempted to do so in the year 1004. The Song lost, and as a consequence, the emperor became subservient to them. This entailed the paying of annual tributes. On several occasions, Zhenzong added Champa rice to his tributes, and that served to mellow the disposition of the Khitan people.

Emperor Renzong succeeded Zhenzong in 1022. Although he was admired by the Chinese as being fair-minded and tolerant, the emperor was an incurable pacifist. In a questionable effort to prevent the Western Xia state in the west from attacking, Renzong paid hefty bribes to their enemy, the Liao state, so as to maintain a balance of power. While it wasn't an unwise decision considering the odds, it did create a hole in the country's treasury. Renzong reigned until 1063. Not unexpectedly, the head of the Liao dynasty paid his respects at Renzong's funeral.

The Artist Emperor

The earlier Song emperors focused upon the expansion of the Song dynasty. However, Emperor Huizong, who ruled from 1100 to 1126, was in a different category. His contribution wasn't one of military might or conquest; it was to the preservation and prolongation of Chinese culture and art. Huizong was a master calligrapher and rendered beautiful and delicate silk paintings of birds and flowers. His calligraphy style, called "Slender Gold," opened up a whole new way of artistic expression for other artists and calligraphers. He also wrote elegant poetry.

Huizong knew his limitations and admitted that he was not a man of might. He neglected the military, and when the Jurchen nomads of the Jin dynasty from the north invaded Liao, Huizong allied with them. This got rid of the Liao state, but it also meant that the Jurchen had no other enemy in the area but the Song. Huizong wanted to flee, but his advisors begged him to abdicate first. His son, Emperor Qinzong, became the ruler of a tumultuous period.

Sadly, Emperor Qinzong was not a strong military leader either. Although the Jurchens gave up the siege of Bianjing in 1126, the Song capital, the Song was forced to sign a treaty, agreeing to send the Jin dynasty tributes every year. The treaty only placated the Jurchens for so long, and they came back in 1127 and finally entered the capital. Huizong was sent to a distant region for the last eight years of his life, where he was forever isolated from the people he loved. Tragically, he died there in poverty.

In 1127, the Song dynasty retreated south of the Yangtze River. This is why historians break the Song dynasty into two parts: the Northern Song and the Southern Song.

In 1206, the Song again went to war against the Jin, who ruled the north, under the urging of Chancellor Han Tuozhou. Emperor Ningzong felt that the Jin had been weakened by a string of natural disasters, so he took advantage. It didn't work, though, and the Song lost their bid to regain their northern lands. A peace treaty was signed in 1208, and to make matters worse, the Song government was forced to reinstate their tribute payments.

The Mongols' Attack against the Jin Dynasty

In 1211, the great Genghis Khan of the Mongols attacked the Northern Song region, which was held by the Jin. The Mongols were able to make the Jin into a vassal state. However, the Jin made some moves that the Mongols did not like; namely, they moved the capital from Beijing to Kaifeng. The Mongols retaliated and conquered the Jin dynasty entirely in 1234.

The Song had been allied with the Mongols during this, but when they stepped out of bounds and took over some important cities, such as Kaifeng and Chang'an, the Mongols reacted with force. In 1259, the Mongols moved in to invade the Song, and they did so in the typical Mongol style, with brute force and swift maneuvers.

While the Song won some battles, mainly due to the sudden death of Ogedei Khan, Genghis Khan's son, who took over after his father had died, the Mongols often had the upper hand. One of the most important battles, the Battle of Xiangyang, took place between 1267 and 1273. Kublai Khan, Genghis Khan's grandson, who was now the leader of the Mongol Empire, and his brother, Hulagu

Khan, partook in this battle. Kublai and Hulagu both had an interest in the town of Xiangyang because it was near the great trading center in Hangzhou just to the west. Xiangyang had an impressive fort there, so the Mongols employed their trebuchets and the Chuangzi-Nu, a clever wooden and metal device that could shoot volleys of burning arrows at the enemy. They also used what were called "thunder crash bombs," metal cylinders filled with gunpowder. The Mongols were successful in this battle, and they were ultimately successful in the war against the Song. By 1279, the Song dynasty was no more.

The "Last" Song Emperor

The moral character of Emperor Lizong, who assumed the throne in 1224, was deplorable. He was self-indulgent and blind to the growing threat of the Mongols, who had already attacked and conquered some of the Jin lands to the north.

Lizong had no sons of his own, so he decided to adopt his nephew, Duzong, and ready him to be the heir to the throne. However, Duzong had developmental difficulties and limited intelligence because his mother had tried to abort him when she was pregnant, and the medical procedures she underwent were crude.

Duzong held the throne from 1264 to 1274. Courtiers felt pity for Emperor Duzong, as he was physically and mentally incapable of his role. In fact, Duzong heard about the Mongols and the Battle of Xiangyang from a palace maid. When Duzong asked a Song chancellor, Jia Sidao, about the attack, the man tried to hide it from him in a misguided effort at compassion.

Duzong was not technically the last emperor of the Song dynasty. However, many historians view him as the last one because he was the last emperor who could have made a real change in stopping the Mongols' advancement.

Chapter 6 – Kublai Khan: The Yuan Dynasty, 1271–1368

Kublai Khan was the grandson of Genghis Khan. When he was younger, he had studied Chinese philosophy and Buddhist teachings from Haiyun, a Buddhist monk, as well as a more advanced form of Buddhism under Drogon Chogyal Phagpa, a revered teacher of Buddhism. In 1252, Kublai was in charge of the territories in northern China that the Mongols had captured. While there, he learned mathematics and astronomy from the well-known Zhao Bi who lived there. In 1260, after the death of Mongke Khan, Kublai became the new ruler of the Mongol Empire.

Kublai Khan was not only a great leader and fighter, but he was also an excellent writer and poet. His narrative, *Ascent to Spring Mountain*, contains fascinating nature motifs and deep thoughts, such as, "Flowers shone bright rays and auspicious colors gleamed like a rainbow. Incense smoke wafted like mist and a blessed light emanated."

In 1271, the year the Mongols overran the Song dynasty, Kublai Khan announced the advent of a new dynasty known as Yuan. In the city of Shangdu, also known as Xanadu, Kublai built his summer palace, which is located in present-day Inner Mongolia. In

1275, the Italian explorer Marco Polo described it as "the palace of the Great Khan, [is] the most extensive that has ever been known. The sides of the great halls are adorned with dragons in carved wood and gold, figures of warriors, of birds and of beasts. On each of the sides of the palace are grand flights of marble steps."

There were parks and grazing lands, on which Kublai kept a herd of special white horses, the Mongolian horse, a recognized breed today. It is a very hardy horse, accustomed to frigid temperatures and hard travel. These horses were ideal for battle. Mongolian cavalrymen could ride these horses without saddles by gripping the animal's sides with their legs alone.

Kublai Khan was fond of great feasts and enjoyed the entertainment of magicians from other lands. Marco Polo tried to figure out their act, saying that they were carried out by the use of helpers in the crowd. These magicians could raise glasses in the air without being held.

Religious tolerance was practiced throughout the realm. Kublai Khan respected the practices of Christians, Jews, Buddhists, shamans, Taoists, and Muslims.

War against Japan

The great Khan had an intense interest in widening his empire and sent out military expeditions with the purpose of invading Japan, Vietnam, Java, and Burma.

In 1281, Kublai Khan invaded Japan. He had an excellent Mongol navy, which he utilized by sending out 3,500 ships from southern China into the harbors of Japan. He sent out two fleets, with one fleet taking an easterly route and the other taking a southern one. However, the eastern fleet failed to follow orders and wait for the southern fleet to join up with them. Instead, the eastern fleet attacked mainland Japan alone.

As one might expect, their attempt to invade Japan went terribly. Many Mongols were either killed, wounded, or ended up in slavery. Japan was able to stay isolated, as they kicked the Mongols out of the waters surrounding their islands.

Battles in Dai Viet (Vietnam)

There were three great battles initiated by the Yuan dynasty to gain control of Dai Viet. In 1257, the Mongols subdued the Tran clan of Dai Viet, and it became a vassal state that had to pay tribute. However, when the Yuan asked to march through Tran territory in order to gain access to the south (South Vietnam), the Tran king refused. Insulted, the Mongolians demanded their surrender, which the Tran refused. So, in 1284, the Yuan attacked Dai Viet and won. After the Tran surrendered, they decided not to go ahead with a peace treaty. Instead, the Tran attacked the Mongols, and they proved to be victorious.

In 1285, the Mongols attacked again. This time, the soldiers of Dai Viet obtained the help of a neighboring khan, Duwa of the Chagatai Khanate. He assisted the Dai Viet soldiers and defeated Kublai's soldiers at a garrison in the Tarim Basin.

In 1287, the Mongols attempted to invade Dai Viet once more. This time, they achieved a partial victory and occupied some land near Ha Long Bay. However, the Tran general, Tran Khanh Du, destroyed the Mongolian supply ships. Bereft of supplies, the Mongols were forced to retreat the following year.

Invasions of Burma

The battles between the Yuan dynasty and Burma dragged on and off for nearly ten years, between 1277 and 1287. While the Mongols had been able to subdue them early on, they had a difficult time collecting tributes and had to return frequently to demand them. Unknown to the Mongols, the tiny kingdoms of the land were constantly restive. In addition, the Burmese were mostly farmers who had endured several droughts.

In 1287, when a treaty was drawn up, the king of Burma was assassinated. He had been accused of abandoning his people to the Mongols. In their histories, King Narathihapate was then called "the king who fled from the Taruk."

Society and Welfare Programs

Kublai Khan organized society according to ethnic groups. He did so to keep Mongolians in the top positions of power during his reign. The order would have gone something like this: 1) Mongols, 2) central Asians (non-Chinese), 3) northern Chinese, and 4) southern Chinese.

However, he was merciful and believed in fairness. After he conquered the country of Burma, he discovered that there was great poverty, especially among those who were ill or unable to support their families. To the regions with the greatest need, he sent grain and cloth for making clothing. He also had construction workers from his lands help repair homes in cases of disasters, such as floods and wars. In addition, he asked that farmers donate their time and skills if farms in those afflicted areas had needs like sowing, harvesting, or digging irrigation channels.

Death of Chabi and Kublai

Some of Kublai's imperial princes joined together in rebellion, and they attempted to gain land and wealth for themselves. Corruption crept into the government, and Kublai was powerless to control it, as large parts of the empire in the 13th century defied central control.

In 1281, Kublai's favorite wife, Chabi, died, and he became despondent. As Kublai reflected on his past life, his failures to subjugate Japan and Dai Viet occupied his mind, making him even more depressed. Likewise, he was unable to control the corruption in the government and the resentment of the peasants, as they were being overtaxed.

In 1287, Nayan's Rebellion triggered constant unrest in the Manchuria districts, and variations of that revolt haunted him for years. In 1294, Kublai Khan died at the age of seventy-eight.

Ma Zhiyuan (pen name: Dongli), a Yuan poet, wrote of Kublai Khan, saying, "A withered vine, an ancient tree, crows at dusk. A little bridge, a flowing stream. An old road, wind out of the west, an emaciated horse. On the horizon at sunset is a broken-hearted man."

The Decline of the Yuan

Unlike the Chinese emperors before him, Kublai Khan's rise wasn't marred with fratricide and murder. However, the strife and challenges of managing China tore away at the fabric of society. Despite the lack of internecine violence, discrimination against the Han Chinese by Kublai Khan and the Mongolian overlords made its mark, as vital governmental positions were always given to Mongolians, while the Chinese held lesser posts. Because the Han was the major ethnic group in mainland China, this prejudice eventually bred violence.

The Red Turban Rebellions

Many of the Han Chinese turned to their religious roots in Buddhism, seeking solace from the growing prejudice of the Mongols. In the 13th century, the White Lotus movement, which followed the belief in the coming of a savior, Buddha Maitreya, triggered revolts against Mongolian rule. When the White Lotus organization was banned, they went underground.

In 1351, the White Lotus movement spawned what was called the Red Turban Rebellion. They were so-named because they wore red scarves and red turbans. The Red Turbans formed an official army and attacked Mongol officials indiscriminately. A powerful leader by the name of Zhu Yuanzhang rose from this movement, and he would go on to found the next dynasty of China.

While the infrastructure of the Yuan dynasty was crumbling due to the rebellions, plague struck. Millions of people died; it is estimated that in the 14th century, 30 percent of the population of China died from the disease. Thus, the Yuan dynasty lost its support, and it succumbed to the ravages of violence and disease.

Chapter 7 – The Great Ming Dynasty, 1368–1644

The Hongwu Emperor

In 1368, Zhu Yuanzhang, the hallowed victor of the Red Turban Rebellion, became the first emperor of the Ming dynasty. He took on the era name of "Hongwu," meaning "vastly martial." The use of era names had been used since 140 BCE, but the Hongwu Emperor introduced the tradition of having only one era name for each ruler; before this, rulers could change their era name as many times as they pleased.

So far, Chinese history had been characterized by a repetitious pattern of conspiracies, murders, betrayals, and corruption. Hongwu was a man familiar with all of that, and these aspects manifested under his own rule. He conducted frequent purges of his administration and even his own staff of servants. Some historians report that Hongwu's paranoia resulted in as many as 30,000 executions. The country had many military garrisons, especially along its borders, but Hongwu didn't give his generals much authority to make independent decisions. Hongwu also adopted a legal code fashioned after Confucian philosophy. Confucius was noted as being a leader who placed a heavy emphasis on obedience to authority, so a Confucian legal code was a logical outcome of such thinking.

The Mongols, who had ruled prior to the Ming dynasty, were scrupulously controlled. During the Yuan era, the Han Chinese were the victims of prejudice, so this might be considered a case of reverse discrimination.

The Miao Revolts

Southern China, in the 1370s, was a rebellious area, especially Yunnan province, just north of Burma. The native people there resisted the Ming-style of governance, and in doing so, they represented a threat to the emperor's authoritarian regime. In order to control these violent outbreaks, which were referred to as the Miao revolts, Hongwu recruited the Uyghur people from the northwestern provinces of China. The Uyghur forces suppressed these rebellions, but revolts later broke out again in the 15th century. The Ming emperor was able to put the rebellions down again, albeit doing so in cruel ways. For instance, in 1460, the Ming emperor called for the castration of over 1,500 Miao boys, some of whom died in the process. Those that survived were turned into eunuch slaves.

Eventually, many of the Uyghurs migrated to Hunan in central China. These people were referred to as Hui Chinese, the majority of whom practiced Islam.

The Manchurian Sector

In Manchuria, in north-central China, most of the people were descendants of the Jurchens, who were troublesome nomads. The Hongwu Emperor didn't desire close relations with them, and his administration had little political presence in the area, with the exception of posted guards and garrisons to quell local unrest. This would change over time, with later Ming emperors interested in controlling the area more fully.

The Tibetans

In Tibet, the Hongwu Emperor granted the people semi-autonomy. They were (and still are) fervent Buddhists, ranging among four different Buddhist sects. The predominant sect is the Gelug, "Yellow Hats," which is led by a leader called the Dalai Lama. Today's head of Tibetan Buddhism, Tenzin Gyatso, is the 14th Dalai Lama. Historically, the Tibetans had the protection of the Mongols, which tended to dissuade the Hongwu Emperor and other Ming emperors from creating close relations with them.

The Yongle Emperor

Although the Hongwu Emperor named his grandson, Zhu Yuwen, as his successor, his son, Zhu Di, was consumed with jealousy and set off a three-year civil war during which he had his nephew, his nephew's wife, his aunt, and the palace courtiers killed. Zhu then proclaimed himself to be the Yongle Emperor in 1402.

The Forbidden City

The Forbidden City is a complex of imperial palaces, administrative buildings, worship areas, and residences for the palace personnel and widowed empresses from prior years.

The Yongle Emperor established the capital at current-day Beijing in 1420, which was where he started building the Forbidden City in 1406. It is the crowning achievement of his reign. The Forbidden City is so named because only the emperor, his immediate family, and his eunuch servants were supposedly allowed to enter unless the emperor had given his express permission otherwise. The ancillary outer buildings served administrative functions, so those were places where other officials and state visitors could enter and perform their duties.

This magnificent structure has 980 rooms. There is a 171-foot moat around it, as well as a myriad of thick defensive walls. The artisans imitated the building styles they saw in the silk paintings of the Song dynasty. There are elaborate gateways on all four sides bearing the names "Gate of Divine Might," "East Glorious Gate," West Glorious Gate," "Dongan Gate," "East and West Chang'an Gates," and "Meridian Gate." Many of the inner buildings carry inspirational names like "Hall of Supreme Harmony," "Palace of

Heavenly Purity," "Hall of Earthly Tranquility," and "Hall of Universal Happiness."

The roofs in the Forbidden City were made with yellow-glazed tiles and decorated with lines of statuettes with imperial dragons, phoenixes, and the like. The walls are punctuated with reliefs, mandalas, paintings, and icons. Themes are derived from Taoism, but there are some areas manifesting shamanism or Buddhist beliefs.

Treasure Voyages

The Yongle Emperor wanted to impress the countries near China with the wealth of the Ming dynasty in order to discourage invasions and project the enormous power of the Ming. Starting in 1403, he had his admiral, Zheng He, order the construction of fleets of impressive ships. They were heavily armored and carried artistic creations, silks, clothing with gold brocade, and a collection of supplies. The Chinese gave these treasures as gifts to the heads and representatives of foreign governments. They then invited dignitaries and ambassadors from various countries to visit them in China. Because of this unexpected generosity, some of the other countries were willing to become tributary states in exchange for military defense.

On their first voyage in 1405, they went to Champa (Vietnam), Java, Malacca (Malay), Aru (Indonesia), Semudera (Sumatra), Ceylon (Sri Lanka), and other islands and lands in the South Pacific. On their way back to China, Zheng He and his crew had to confront the pirate Chen Zuyi. For years, the pirates had monopolized the seas around Sumatra and raided ships of other island countries. The Chinese attacked the pirates' vessels and took Chen Zuyi and three other pirates back to China, where they were executed in 1407. The people of Sumatra, in particular, were grateful. That encounter opened up navigation channels south of Indonesia and its environs.

In 1407, the Yongle Emperor continued his treasure voyages. Most of the time, relations were cordial. However, on their second expedition to Java, some Chinese ambassadors were killed. The people of western Java were insulted that the Chinese first paid respects to their enemies in eastern Java, and they took it out on the visiting Chinese. The two were at a crossroads because of a civil war that hadn't been entirely resolved. After the civil war had ended, the king of western Java sent envoys to China on an apology tour, and relations were reestablished.

On their third voyage in 1409, the Chinese visited many of the islands they had seen before, but they also toured Ceylon (Sri Lanka) and ports in southern India. Ceylon and its ruler, King Alagakkonara, had a local reputation for threatening small neighboring island regimes that had diplomatic relations with China. As might be expected, Alagakkonara attacked the Chinese fleet. Zheng. He responded by disembarking troops at their capital city of Kotte and captured it. They then kidnapped the king and carried him back to China. The Yongle Emperor decided to release him. The event was recorded by the chronicler Yang Rong, who called the people of Ceylon "insignificant worms" and wrote, "the august emperor spared their lives, and they humbly kowtowed, making crude sounds, and praised the sage-like virtue of the Ming ruler."

The Yongle Emperor freed the king of Ceylon, not to show his magnanimity but rather his power and influence. In 1411, he had King Alagakkonara deposed and placed a pro-Chinese king on the throne.

On the fourth voyage, which took place between 1413 and 1415, Zheng He and his men meddled in the affairs of the island of Sumatra. They deposed a man who had usurped the throne of Sumatra and had him transported back to China, where he was executed. Following that, Sumatra made generous annual tributes to China in gratitude.

During the fourth journey, there are records, which are backed up by archeological evidence, that indicate the Chinese treasure voyages traveled as far as the Strait of Hormuz in the Persian Gulf.

In 1419, the fifth treasure voyage sailed to the Gulf of Aden in Yemen near the Red Sea. The tributes the Chinese received after their voyages there included exotic animals such as leopards, rhinoceroses, camels, zebras, and even ostriches.

On their sixth voyage in 1421, the Chinese fleet left with envoys from Aden and Siam (Thailand). They most likely saw a small portion of the noteworthy Grand Canal before arriving at the imperial court in Beijing. The Yongle Emperor had recalled the treasure fleet to protect Beijing because hostilities were heating up between Ming China and the Mongols.

The Yongle Emperor died in 1424. After his death, China progressively started to withdraw from the world stage and became increasingly isolated.

The Tumu Crisis

After having lost their power in China, the Mongols were resentful. This continued to spur hatred and violence.

In 1449, things came to a head. The Yongle Emperor's great-grandson and descendant, the Zhengtong Emperor, who came to power in 1435, was captured by Mongol rebels at a battle outside the Tumu Fortress, which abutted Mongol territories. Although emperors didn't usually lead troops into battle, his eunuch advisor, Weng Zhen, encouraged him to do so. It was a disaster.

Esen Taishi, the leader of the Mongols, planned on getting a hefty ransom for the emperor's release and some profitable arrangements in terms of trade. The Ming officials refused to pay the ransom or negotiate, and so, Esen's efforts failed. Esen antagonized his forces with that failure, and they assassinated him in retaliation. The Mongols held the Zhengtong Emperor for a year, during which time the Zhengtong Emperor abdicated in favor of his younger brother, who became the Jingtai Emperor. Regardless of the fact that there was no trade deal and no ransom, the Mongols still fared quite well, having purloined many weapons and gear from the dead Chinese warriors.

When the Mongols released Zhengtong, Chinese officials immediately placed him under house arrest, and he stayed there for almost seven years. In 1457, Zhengtong deposed the Jingtai Emperor and assumed the role of emperor once more, now calling himself the Tianshun Emperor.

Retaking the imperial throne wasn't an easy move for the Tianshun Emperor. Because the imperial forces under General Cao Qin had failed to prevent the kidnapping of the emperor, Cao was afraid he himself might be executed. After all, Cao's non-Chinese forces were Mongols who were loyal to the Ming. Even though those Mongols were aligned with the Ming, their ethnicity alone made them look guilty.

On account of the incident, Lu Gao of the imperial house was sent to investigate the role of Cao Qin. Cao couldn't let that happen, so he decapitated Lu Gao and dismembered his body. He then took Lu's severed head to the grand secretary of the regime, Li Xian, and lied to him, saying that it was Lu Gao himself who was planning the rebellion. Li Xian didn't believe him, so Cao stole some paper from Li Xian's office and wrote a message to the emperor, claiming Cao was innocent. No one allowed that note to go through to the emperor. No doubt they felt it was a subterfuge. Cao now felt he had only one option: unseat the Tianshun Emperor in a coup.

Cao Qin's Rebellion

In 1461, Cao and his men entered the Forbidden City, attacked Dongan Gate and East and West Chang'an Gates. They set fire to the two Chang'an Gates and raced inside. General Sun Tang of the Imperial Guard and his soldiers stormed in. Cao's forces killed two of them and fled outside the walls to Dongan Gate. The imperial soldiers killed some of Cao's men, including his brother. He and his men then retreated and tried to escape through the gate on the outer wall. Many of his men escaped into the city.

Like a frightened boy, Cao ran to his own home and threw up makeshift defensive walls and objects. Once the imperial troops under Sun Tang broke in, Cao threw himself down a deep well on his property and died. The warriors hoisted up his body, dismembered it, and put it on public display in Beijing.

Cao's men were eventually rounded up. Some seemed to have been coerced into the rebellion or were misled into believing it was something else. These men were released or given lesser sentences, while others involved were sentenced to death. From that point on, any Mongols who served in the army were given desk posts elsewhere or were forced to retire. A program was then started to relocate the Mongols living inside the empire. Many were sent to remote places with uncomfortable climatic conditions.

From Exploration to Isolation

In 1479, the Ministry of War burned the written records of Zheng He's treasure voyages. Regulations spewed forth from the administration, restricting the sizes of new ships to be built and specifying the military functions of such vessels. Ships were docked until they rotted from disuse.

This seems like a radical thing to do. After all, the huge, well-armed Chinese ships decreased incidents of piracy, especially in the South Pacific. Zheng He and his sailors had annihilated pirate vessels and discouraged others from raiding the cities of defenseless island nations. This all changed, though, when China started to withdraw from the world stage.

After the treasure voyages of the Yongle Emperor, there was a great backlash in China against the rise of international trade and goodwill missions to neighboring countries. For years, historians and political commentators have argued about the possible causes for that.

One theory has to do with social class rivalry. The nobles and elites within the top circles of the administration were overprotective of their influence. The increase of trade was a threat to them because it brought wealth and importance to the rising merchant class. Instead of allowing free trade, the government monopolized foreign trade. As a result, the mercantile class objected to governmental control. They did yield some power because shipping and mercantilism have a nearly symbiotic relationship. In the 15th century, China had 3,500 ships—more than that of the US Navy today!

The costs of Zheng He's treasure voyages between 1407 to 1433 was another possible reason for the cessation of regular voyages. They were expensive and required many funds from the nation's treasury to supply and maintain the ships. Some argue that they weren't that profitable, as the net income was negligible.

In addition, there was internal strife caused by the rebellions related to the Mongols. The Chinese navy was useless in those struggles since they occurred within the country itself.

Competition also existed between court officials and the eunuchs who were close to the emperor. The eunuchs preferred international trade, but the reasons for that preference is vague. Some historians indicate that it gave the eunuchs an opportunity to siphon profits for themselves.

The Ming rulers were sometimes called xenophobes, but they did pull back on some of the "alien" cultural practices that existed during the former Yuan dynasty. The first emperor—the Hongwu Emperor—required Muslim women to marry Han Chinese men in order to become more Sinicized. He did have more mosques built and permitted Islam to be practiced.

Generally, the non-Han Chinese people that came into China during the prior Yuan dynasty were encouraged to assimilate into the culture of the Han Chinese, which was, and still is, the largest of the ethnic Chinese population. In time, the isolation of the Ming necessarily resulted in the integration of non-Chinese into China.

European Contact

The Portuguese were renowned for being traders, and they had made contact with almost all of the significant countries in the East and the West. In 1517, a merchant vessel visited the city of Guangzhou, and King Manuel I of Portugal sent a delegation to the court of the Zhengde Emperor, who ruled from 1505 to 1521.

Malacca, in Indonesia, which Zheng He had visited during the treasure voyages, sent their ambassadors to see the succeeding Jiajing Emperor. The Indonesians were jealous of the Portuguese and started circulating rumors that the Portuguese kidnapped Chinese children and ate them! Through fear, the Ming navy refused to allow the Portuguese to land at Tuen Mun (near Hong Kong) in 1521 and did so again in 1522.

The Ningbo Incident

In 1523, Japan sent a vessel into the harbor of Ningbo bearing gifts and products for the Chinese emperor and his people. They had made contact with the Zhengde Emperor prior to that, but he had passed away by the time the Japanese delegation arrived. Japan only made these tribute journeys once every ten years, but it was very profitable for the Chinese, so the Jiajing Emperor agreed to receive them.

However, a massive squabble broke out that accelerated into violence. It seems that two Japanese delegations—the Hosokawa delegation and the Ouchi delegation—both came. When the Hosokawa clan was received ahead of the Ouchi, they drew swords. The head of the Hosokawa delegation was killed, and his ship was set on fire in the port. The Japanese warriors then disembarked, overran Ningbo, and plundered randomly. They even commandeered a Chinese ship, kidnapped the head of a garrison in Ningbo, and made off to sea with him. They were chased by a fleet of Ming vessels, but the Ouchi managed to defeat them.

Only two more Japanese trade missions followed: one in 1540 and another in 1549. The Jiajing Emperor was on the throne by this time, and he was a very isolated person. His preference for privacy spilled over into his regime, and he discontinued the Chinese-Japanese trade. China had already been pursuing a policy of isolation, but it only increased under the Jiajing Emperor.

The problem became more critical when Chinese merchants started setting up illegal trade in some of the more remote islands in the South Pacific. This ceased when some of these merchants ran into debt, creating embarrassing incidents involving China and Japan.

The Wokou Raids

Wokou means "dwarf pirates" in English. It was an insulting term used by the Chinese to refer to the Japanese. The wokou (Japanese pirates) continued to conduct illegal trade with Chinese merchants as they had done during the regime of the Jiajing Emperor. Because this overseas trade was banned by the Ming dynasty, many Chinese and Japanese merchants moved their bases of operation to the islands off the coasts of China and Japan.

Xu Hai was one of the most notable merchant-pirates, and he operated out of Malacca, which was one of the Indonesian islands explored by Zheng He. Wang Zhi was another Chinese pirate who was bold enough to work off of the island of Kyushu, located off the coast of southern Japan.

In 1547, the Portuguese partook in the piracy when they plundered Zhangzhou. A general named Zhu Wan was then appointed as the Superintendent of Military Affairs, and it was his responsibility to put an end to the piracy and illegal off-land trade. In 1549, his commander, Lu Tang, grabbed two Chinese junks operating illegally in the waters off of Zoumaxi. Zhu Wan took it upon himself to execute 96 Chinese smugglers. The Jiajing Emperor was furious, as Zhu Wan had acted on his accord instead of following protocol, and called for his arrest. Zhu Wan, however, committed suicide rather than be taken captive.

The empire went through a succession of commanders and lesser officials in charge of eradicating the pirate activities, including Zhang Jing, Hu Zongxian, Zhou Chang, and Yang Yi. They achieved only limited success, and cruel executions resulted. For instance, in 1555, it was reported that 1,900 pirates had been beheaded. Despite this impressive number, the emperor was unimpressed by the delays in their attacks, and as a result, the chief commander, Zhang Jing, was beheaded.

When Hu Zongxian became supreme commander in 1556, he was in favor of opening up trade—a move that would reduce piracy. He sent envoys to Japan to enlist their cooperation. Hu Zongxian also contacted the pirate Wang Zhi, hoping to reduce violence through appeasement. Wang Zhi, however, refused.

While making an effort to change how things were done, Hu was outwitted by a rogue pirate, Xu Hai. In 1556, Xu disembarked thousands of warriors on mainland China, who plundered the city of Zaolin. The city's defenders were initially successful in driving them away, but their reinforcements didn't arrive in time, and China lost the battle.

Even though he was wounded, Xu Hai had his pirate raiders move into the city of Tongxiang and place it under siege. The city resisted strongly, and the fact that they had a formidable defensive wall kept them alive. However, morale was very low after a month had passed.

Hu Zongxian then contacted Xu Hai to make a peace agreement with him. As a show of goodwill, the pirate released 200 Chinese prisoners. The emperor and the pirate reached an agreement, and the pirates withdrew. Hu then convinced Xu Hai to change sides and then had Xu himself eliminate some of the Japanese pirates.

As Xu continued eliminating pirates, chaos erupted. Other pirates had arrived and were scrambling to confiscate each other's booty. The Chinese navy descended upon the pirates and wiped them out, with the exception of the pirate Chen Dong, who was captured. Chen Dong was brought to Jiaxing, where he was executed.

In the meantime, the Jiajing Emperor notified Commander Hu that no surrender would be accepted. Instead, he preferred not to take prisoners, and he also wished to maintain his isolationist policy. He had no wish to negotiate with pirates or with the non-Chinese people, and he did not want to inaugurate any form of foreign trade.

Hu Zongxian then realized he needed to change his position about making trade agreements with the pirates. Hu Zongxian decided to trick another major pirate, Wang Zhi, into thinking he had a peace agreement. When Wang Zhi arrived, he was imprisoned and executed.

Wang Zhi's followers then reorganized, moved south to Fujian, and continued with the raids. A large island base was created in the Kinmen island chain, but there were far fewer pirates than there had been.

General Qi Jiguang took over after Hu Zongxian. He developed a new military formation and even wrote about it in the *New Treatise on Military Efficiency*. Qi's strategy was extremely effective and totally unanticipated by the raiders, and due to his efforts, and that of Hu before him, piracy was no longer considered a major threat.

The Shaanxi Earthquake

In 1556, the deadliest earthquake on record hit Shaanxi province in central China. It reverberated in the neighboring provinces of Henan, Hebei, Hunan, Shandong, Jiangsu, and Anhui. Around 520 miles was destroyed by the impact, and current estimates indicate that it hit either a 7.9 or an 8 on the Mercalli scale. Many people in Shaanxi lived in artificial caves, called yaodongs, which were hewn in loess cliffs. Loess is sediment made up of wind-blown dirt. It has a very low clay content, making it unstable and prone to crumbling. Due to this, the cliffs collapsed when the earthquake struck. Around 830,000 people died in the Shaanxi earthquake. Because China had isolated itself, it alone had to carry the burden, and the catastrophe had a devastating effect on the Chinese economy.

Trade Concessions

After a long period of isolation and cessation of trade, China acquiesced to the gentle persuasion of the Portuguese, who returned again in 1553. They dispelled some of the rumors and attempted to repair their reputation that had been sullied, and because of their efforts, the port of Macau was opened up to Portuguese trade in 1557.

Due to the Wokou raids that haunted the islands and ports of southern China, relations between China and Japan were frozen. Japanese merchants used the Portuguese as intermediaries so they could obtain silk, which they exchanged for Japanese silver. Spain became involved in trade with China after that and purchased not only silver and silk but also the fine porcelain for which the Ming dynasty was noted. Porcelain became a major export to Europe and Japan.

Ming Porcelain

The Ming artisans were famous for their exquisite porcelain items, such as vases, bowls, urns, cups, and incense burners. It was more translucent than porcelain from other countries, as the Chinese used kaolin (a white clay) for the body of the object and secured coloring agents by using cobalt oxide from minerals. Other colors, which were used less frequently, were red, yellow, and green. By the 16th century, many pieces were multi-colored. Kilns around the country spewed smoke into the sky and even created a fog-like cloud over Jingdezhen, one of the towns recognized for its art community. Today, Ming porcelain is prized on the antique markets.

An Explosion Predicts the Demise of the Ming Dynasty

On May 30th, 1626, Beijing was rocked by a massive explosion. Naked bodies fell from the air, their clothes obliterated by the blast. Uprooted trees landed miles away. The sky went black, and body parts of people and animals rained down upon the ground for miles around. The roof tiles of the Forbidden City and nearby residences became lethal projectiles, shooting into people on the streets and in their houses. About 20,000 people died.

The cause was reportedly an explosion at the Wanggongchang Armory, which manufactured gunpowder, weapons, and munitions. It was also a storage facility for hundreds of explosives. However, it should be noted that the exact cause of the explosion has never been determined. While the most likely theory is that it was started by the facility, that doesn't explain the lack of damage around the facility itself or the fact that people's clothing just flew off their bodies.

Many believed the explosion was a sign from the gods that they disapproved of the current Tianqi Emperor and his administration. The fact that the emperor also lost his son in the blast bolstered that opinion.

The Tianqi Emperor issued gold to be used for relief efforts. However, China was already in a state of financial collapse. Peasants were starving, and soldiers mutinied. Massive bands of rebels wandered the streets, no longer afraid of reprisals by imperial soldiers. The Tianqi Emperor died a year after the Wanggongchang explosion, and his brother took over, becoming the Chongzhen Emperor in 1627. Little did he know that a new dynasty was starting to form right before his eyes.

The Jurchens Return!

The Jurchens were now more sophisticated and had evolved from their nomadic roots. They had settled in Manchuria and were now called the Manchu. They were also referred to as the "red-tasseled Manchus."

While the last Ming emperor was still on the throne, the Manchu State flourished. Nurhaci, who grew up in a Chinese household, was the one responsible for uniting the various Jurchen tribes into the Manchu. He was learned but had the fire of youth and idealism. As early as 1616, he had united the Han Bannermen and the Eight Banners, which consisted mostly of Manchu people. He then proceeded to unite many of the Jurchen tribes. There were activist organizations throughout China, such as the Eight Banners, the Shun rebels, the Jurchens, and, in 1644, the Green Standard Army. Leaders rose and fell, as these groups culled out useless members and merged into more cohesive units.

Nurhaci was courageous, and he was dedicated to laying the foundation for a truly meaningful administration. To show his determination, he presented the Ming dynasty with a document called the *Seven Grievances*. This was tantamount to a declaration of war. The grievances are briefly listed here with explanations where needed:

1. The Ming slaughtered Nurhaci's father and grandfather without cause. (Nurhaci's father, Taksi, and his grandfather, Giocangga, were killed by Nikan Wailan, a Jurchen working as an operative for a Ming general.)

2. The Ming oppressed the Jianzhou (Jurchen clan) and favored two other clans, the Hada and Yehe.

3. The Ming violated the agreement made with Nurhaci in the past. (The Ming agreed to have marked borders between Ming lands and lands settled by the tribes, but the Ming ignored the agreement. The Ming also gave Nurhaci the power to regulate Jurchen activities and commerce but then undermined him.)

4. The Ming sent forces to protect the Yehe clan in their conflicts with the Jianzhou. (The Ming had agreed *not* to interfere with Nurhaci's duties. It was Nurhaci's responsibility to protect the Yehe.)

5. The Ming supported the Yehe and encouraged them to break their promise to Nurhaci. (The Ming saw to it that Nurhaci's fiancé was married off to the leader of the Yehe rather than to Nurhaci as they had agreed.)

6. The Ming forces forbade Nurhaci from harvesting crops from the lands he owned in three provinces.

7. The Ming garrison official, Shang Bozhi, was given free rein and abused his position.

In 1644, the Green Standard Amy, a paramilitary organization, was created. It consisted mainly of Han soldiers. All were required to adopt the queue, a Manchu hairstyle, by which a man has the top of his head shaven and braids the hair at the back of his head into a tail. Those who followed Confucius disliked it, as it says in Confucius's writings, "A person's body and hair, being gifts from one's parents, should not be damaged." Even though the Han

Chinese were averse to it, they did it because the punishment for not doing so was death.

Nurhaci's efforts spread to the Liaodong Peninsula, which contains Beijing. He needed as many supporters as he could get from that region. He attracted many Mongols, who had been suppressed by the Ming dynasty. Many Ming soldiers, who deplored the heartless practices of their own administration, defected and joined with the Eight Bannermen. The Jurchens, who were absorbed within this union, were never referred to as the "Jurchens" in the military records. This was because the name "Jurchen" conjured up the image of an unclean nomadic savage.

Nurhaci died in 1626 and was succeeded by his eighth son, Hong Taiji. Hong Taiji continued where his father left off, preparing for an armed assault of the Ming dynasty. One of his earliest accomplishments was the development of a cannon, which was fashioned after the European-style one. He used Ming metallurgists to build it and trained fighters to become accomplished artillerymen. Gunpowder weaponry was also made, along with muskets.

Hong Taiji also planned on having an organized administration, so he would have officials in place as needed. It was similar to the Ming form of government. Also, like the Ming, the new dynasty would use traditional protocols in order to gain the confidence of the people.

The Demise of the Ming Dynasty

The Chongzhen Emperor was naïve and grossly incompetent. The country's structure and government were, by then, only ghosts of what they once were. He didn't know how to handle the *Seven Grievances* of Nurhaci, and he knew he couldn't keep the Ming dynasty intact. Because the rebellions and various militant groups were out of control, the Chongzhen Emperor despaired. In 1644, he walked into his imperial garden and hung himself from a tree. His suicide note read, "I die, unable to face my ancestors in the underworld, dejected and ashamed."

Chapter 8 –The Rise of the Qing, 1636–1912

Hong Taiji died in 1643 before the Qing could entirely unite China. After his death, Hong's five-year-old son was looked at as the next successor, and a group of men declared that he had the Mandate of Heaven. He became the Shunzhi Emperor, but Hong Taiji's half-brother, Dorgon, held most of the power, as he was the regent.

His aim was conformity among the people, so, in 1645, he passed an edict dictating that the queue hairstyle was an obligation for all males. To him, it was a sign of loyalty, and Dorgon had a compulsive need for uniformity. Massive executions resulted from non-compliance with the queue requirement. Even some of the native Han Chinese carried these out, but they were done so under the orders of Dorgon.

In 1650, Dorgon died in a hunting expedition. Many hated him so much that they disinterred his body and mutilated it to pay for his "crimes." In 1662, after Dorgon's death, the Shunzhi assumed control. He had been very much aware of the hostility engendered by his predecessors and wanted a kinder, gentler administration to come about. He made attempted to ferret out the corruption, although it had long been entrenched.

To address the diverse ethnic groups within the Qing dynasty, Shunzhi's advisors had people use terms for him that coincided with their historical practice. For instance, in Tibet, he was called "Gong Ma"; in Mongolia, he was called "Bogda Khan"; in the Manchu regions, he was called "Huangdi," meaning "emperor," or "Khan," if people preferred that.

Revolt of the Three Feudatories

In 1655, there were three fiefdoms set up in China, the joint provinces of Yunnan and Guizhou, Fujian, and Guangdong.

Military commander Wu Sangui was placed in charge of the joint southwestern provinces of Yunnan and Guizhou. He was also assigned to serve as a liaison to the Dalai Lama, who lived in the region.

In Fujian province on the east coast, Geng Jingzhong was the ruler. Geng was tyrannical and, unknown to the emperor, established the practice of extorting money from his own people. His son replaced him in 1682 when Geng died. Unfortunately, he was very much like his father, so little changed.

Shang Zhixin was in charge of Guangdong province after his father, Shang Kexi, stepped down in 1673. Like Geng, the two of them were autocratic.

The Kangxi Emperor noted that those provinces, when put together, managed to spend half of the nation's treasure. In order to draw their attention to the fact that they might be monitored, the Kangxi Emperor reduced their powers and watched them carefully. The three generals, although they were quite capable, were all very headstrong and arrogant.

In 1667, Wu Sangui asked to retire. In 1673, both Geng Jingzhong and Shang Kexi followed suit. This was a curious coincidence. A conspiracy was afoot, but the Kangxi Emperor didn't suspect anything.

Civil War

In 1673, Wu Sangui declared a new dynasty of his own, the Zhou Dynasty, named after the former pre-imperial Zhou dynasty.

His call was for the restoration of the Ming rule, and he incited the Han Chinese to join him by promising to repeal the order about wearing the queues. Soon after this declaration, Wu Sangui attacked and captured Sichuan and Hunan in central China.

The following year, Geng Jingzhong took over Fujian, and Shang Kexi, along with his son, Shang Zhixin, annexed Guangdong. Then, Sun Yanling, Wang Fuchen, and Zheng Jing, who were also powerful generals, joined the revolt and confiscated the lands of Guangxi, Shaanxi, Tungning, Yunnan, and Zhejiang.

The Qing forces were loyal to the Kangxi Emperor and were tough warriors. The Han Green Standard Army, along with miscellaneous Manchu and Mongol forces, started dispelling the rebels in 1676. Wang Fuchen surrendered in the northwest regions. In 1678, Wu Sangui murdered his rival, Sun Yanling, and died that same year himself. His grandson, Wu Shifan, took over, but he eventually retreated and later committed suicide. Sichuan and Shaanxi were reclaimed by the Qing troops, along with Guangxi. Shang Zhixin survived the conflict in Guangdong but was forced to commit suicide in 1680. Zheng Jing's warriors were forced to withdraw and retreated back to Taiwan. Zheng died, and his son surrendered in his name in 1683.

The Qing dynasty acquired Taiwan by default because some of the rebels had annexed the island, although they hadn't set out to do that initially.

Because it was so widespread, the rebellion was very costly. During the rule of the Kangxi Emperor, he made allowances for the large landowners and also limited their ability to acquire more land. To finance the military, he passed a 30 percent gentry tax on the households of the elite. As a result, money rather than privilege became the means by which anyone could acquire land.

Regardless, the Kangxi Emperor had accomplished something his predecessors hadn't. He had united the Chinese. In the process, though, he did tend to make everyone act uniformly, which may have triggered the revolt in the first place.

A Peaceful Reign

Kangxi was succeeded by the Yongzheng Emperor in 1722. Yongzheng was trained in Confucianism and drew from that to set up an organized hierarchical administration. He also filled his posts with both Han Chinese and Manchu officials. When he viewed the financial situation of the country, he discovered that tax collection was lax. His predecessor had built up debt due to the prolonged revolt, and the treasury was depleting rapidly. The Yongzheng Emperor decided to mount a campaign to enforce the paying of taxes and also did some favors for his most influential supporters. Wisely, he put a lot of money into public improvements like irrigation, education, and the building of public roads.

As a result of this move, a deep financial crisis was avoided. Instead, prosperity was felt among the people. A side effect of this time of peace and prosperity was the growth of the population. China at that time didn't endure a heavy loss of life due to war, and smallpox was no longer a severe threat by the end of the 17th century.

The Fall and Rise of Maritime Trade

In the 16th century, China initiated a policy of isolationism due to piracy and conflicts that ensued because of international relations. Although maritime trade had opened up to some extent, China tended to minimize it. They limited their trading partners and even restricted them from visiting ports. In 1757, most of the legal trade was regulated by the Canton System. This policy restricted trade to Guangzhou (Canton) and a few ports in southern China. Only approved Chinese merchants were allowed to conduct foreign trade, including the British East India Company and the Dutch East India Company, which had been trading with China since the 14th century.

In 1735, the son of the Yongzheng Emperor, who took the name Qianlong Emperor, ascended to the throne. He continued the policy of limited trade with the outside world. In 1793, a British statesman named George Macartney wrote to him regarding opening up another island near Chusan to more trade. The emperor gave him an arrogant response, referring to Europeans as "barbarians," although he may not have intended to be so insulting. "Hitherto, all European nations, including your own barbarian merchants, have carried on trade with our Celestial Empire at Canton." The Qianlong Emperor later remarked in a letter to the king of England, "We possess all things. I place no value on objects strange or ingenious, and I have no use for your country's manufactures."

The Dutch ambassador, **Isaac Titsingh**, fared much better because he meticulously observed protocols and court etiquette when he visited the Qianlong Emperor at his palace.

China's refusal to open a new trading post for Britain impinged upon the British demand for tea, silk, and porcelain, which were demands that had increased exponentially over time. When the English couldn't get those products directly from China, they made arrangements with the Portuguese, who had a long-standing agreement with China to trade at Macao.

The Silver Wedge

Silver, which wasn't mined in China, was a prized commodity. It was used for currency and could be used to tempt the Chinese to trade with other countries. It is estimated that by 1800, China had imported so much silver that it possessed 30 percent of the world's supply of it. Japan was a primary exporter of silver, although political frictions prevented China from getting silver directly from them. Instead, Chinese merchants went to the Portuguese and the Dutch, who acted as intermediaries—for a profit, of course. If Japan didn't export silver, China might have fallen prey to merchants from the Americas or the Spanish colonies. The British and their love of tea drove England to take silver out of their country's treasury in order to get the precious commodity from China.

Population Explosion!

New products from the Americas had been traded with China in exchange for the luxurious silks and porcelain the country was noted for. Two of the most popular products from the Americas were the potato and the peanut. These products helped feed the growing populace of China. By the 18th century, the population of the vast nation numbered close to 300 million people. So much of the country was settled that the number of farms decreased. In addition, fertilization was never a real concern in China. By the time the Jiaqing Emperor assumed the throne in 1796, Manchuria and its environs had the largest amount of arable land.

A return to the discrimination of earlier eras occurred to control population growth and migration into China from other countries. The Han Chinese suffered most from that prejudice and weren't permitted to live in Manchuria, which is just one of many examples of what they had to endure. Many landowners, however, ignored that provision, as these people had the skills to run farms efficiently.

Religious Persecution: The Jahriyya Revolt

Toward the end of the reign of the Qianlong Emperor, there were conflicts and unrest among Muslim residents of the country over issues related to Ramadan and prayer practices. Much of the strife occurred in Qinghai, located in central China. In that area, local governors and judges from the Board of Punishment became involved when different sects of Islam conflicted with one another. Some Muslims became more vocal and complained about the Qing administration, calling the Qing dynasty an infidel regime. In 1781, two subdivisions of a Muslim sect called Sufism—the Jahriyya and the Khafiyya—erupted in violence. There was fighting on the streets and mob violence. The Qing had one of their most famous leaders of the Jahriyya, Ma Mingxin, executed. This only served to accelerate the rebellion. The Qing chose to aid the Khafiyya in the conflict, and subsequently, the Jahriyya Sufis were crushed. Those who were determined to continue to be religious activists were frequently exiled to Xinjiang, Guizhou, and Yunnan to serve as slaves in the military garrisons.

The White Lotus Rebellion of 1794

The name "White Lotus Rebellion" might strike a chord with readers, as an earlier rebellion had occurred during the Yuan dynasty. Although the White Lotus Rebellion of 1794 did bear a marginal resemblance to that earlier revolt, a splinter group from that, called the Wang Lun Uprising, adopted the term on occasion. Like the White Lotus movement of the 14th century, it did have a loose moral tinge to it. The members of the White Lotus Society promised eternal salvation for loyalty to their cause and proclaimed that they adhered to Confucian values.

The Qianlong Emperor and the Jiaqing Emperor both dealt with this rebellion, as it overlapped regimes, and they rejected that idea. The two rulers sought to squash the rebellion and rallied the Green Standard Army.

Local officials and police used this rebellion as a means to extort money from the people for self-protection. There was no proof that they did so, but the practice most likely did happen because of the chaos that permeated the local cities. This revolt lasted about ten years, from 1794 to 1804, and the Qing warriors were successful in eliminating this rebellion. However, there were spin-off groups from this rebellion, including the organizations that sponsored the Eight Trigrams, the Tiger Whips, and the Yihequan ("Boxers").

The Opium Wars
The First Opium War

When the Daoguang Emperor took the throne in 1820, he walked into an ongoing crisis. From the late 1700s, opium had been leaking into China. A maritime network of sea routes was already being used to ship porcelain, tea, and silk to Britain, mostly through third parties. In 1839, the trade with Britain, which was mostly handled in Canton, consisted of porcelain, tea, cotton, and silk. When cotton exports decreased, a trade imbalance occurred. Opium was seen as a replacement for it. Opium is addictive, and the British East India Company took advantage of that. The substance was harvested in Bengal, near India, and it would be purchased by the British, who then would trade it with the Chinese. Many eventually became addicted to the drug and needed it to cope with daily life or else suffer from withdrawals. Chinese smugglers brought it farther inland for distribution to the population, causing the problem to grow worse. Americans competed with the Bengal opium by buying it in Turkey and then offering discounted opium at Indian auctions. Chinese smugglers then bought it, and the British East India Company helped by making illicit agreements to distribute it farther inland. Around 40,000 chests of it were brought into the mainland in 1839 alone. Buyers paid silver for it, so the silver stockpiles in China decreased significantly.

The Daoguang Emperor had made the use of opium illegal and wanted it confiscated at Canton. When shipments of opium poured into Canton, he had his minister, Lin Zexu, blockade the harbor. In response, Britain sent in armed steamships and wiped out thousands of Chinese junks that were sitting in the harbor. The British ships were heavily armed, and so, the Qing forces surrendered. The Treaty of Nanking was signed in 1842, and it was the first of the "unequal treaties" that China was forced to sign. And the term was fairly applied to this treaty. Although the British had to withdraw their troops, the rest of the terms benefited them over the Chinese. The Qing had to repay the British for the opium Lin Zexu confiscated, release all British prisoners, and cede Hong Kong to the British. In addition to Hong Kong, four other ports were opened to the British.: Xiamen, Fuzhou, Ningbo, and Shanghai. The sale of opium, which was the cause of the war in the first place, was not even addressed in the treaty.

However, in China, the use of opium was still illegal. Chinese smugglers continued to distribute opium on the streets to be used at home or in dingy opium dens in secret sub-basements in crowded cities. Authorities were authorized to arrest these people but were generally unsuccessful, mostly due to the fact that local officials were bribed.

The Second Opium War

France complained about the preferential status given to Britain by the Treaty of Nanking and insisted that China open up ports in China for French merchants to use. In 1844, China acquiesced and signed the Treaty of Whampoa. Five ports were opened to them, and as compensation, China was allowed to charge a tariff. The

French also used that opportunity to persuade China to permit the presence of Catholic missionaries in China. In 1846, the Daoguang Emperor signed an edict allowing the Chinese to convert to Catholicism if they so wished. Despite that, a French missionary, Father Auguste Chapdelaine, was arrested by a Mandarin bureaucrat for causing unrest and was eventually executed. France was infuriated and sent out ships filled with forces.

Simultaneously, the British had been campaigning for the legalization of opium in China. The opportunity presented itself in 1856 when the Chinese seized a British ship, the *Arrow*, on charges of piracy for the illegal shipment of opium inside China. Ye Mingchen, the Chinese official, arrested the captain and the crew and took possession of the ship, saying that they only did so because the registration had expired.

Soon after this incident, the French allied themselves with Britain, and they attacked Canton. The Second Opium War officially broke out by this point, although it is clear that tensions had been simmering for some time. In 1858, the French and British managed to finally capture Canton. They also captured Ye Mingchen and exiled him to Calcutta, India. The Chinese attacked a US Navy steamer at the mouth of the Peiho River in Tientsin, and the Americans retaliated by attacking and capturing Chinese forts on the Pearl River. The Xianfeng Emperor was, at the time, embroiled in the Taiping Rebellion (see below), and his resources were becoming thin. He was forced to succumb to Western pressures and sought peace.

In 1858, the British and the French asked America and Russia to join them in drawing up the Treaty of Tientsin, which was another one of the "unequal treaties" in the eyes of the Chinese. This treaty granted foreign countries the right to use ten more ports in China to conduct trade, all foreign ships were permitted to sail on the Yangtze River, and foreign merchants were allowed to travel inside China. It also allowed Christian missionaries to spread their message across China peacefully, and perhaps worse of all, it legalized the import of opium. By the time the treaty was finalized in 1860, between 50,000 to 60,000 chests were entering the country every year.

Russia and China had border disputes in the prior century, but in 1858, China negotiated an ancillary treaty, the Treaty of Aigun, because they couldn't afford to start another conflict. By virtue of that treaty, China agreed to move the Russia-China border southward in order to give them access to a "warm water" port. That was important for Russia, as it would then be able to ship goods out even in the winter.

The Taiping Rebellion

Zeng Guofan, a military general, became a hero in the Taiping Rebellion of 1850–1864. It erupted when a deluded man by the name of Hong Xiuquan preached that he was the brother of Jesus Christ. Hong was a self-styled Christian with his own version of Christianity. He called his organization the Taiping Heavenly Kingdom. Hong had not only religious ideals but also very opinionated political views. However, he told his followers that they were fighting a "holy war." Hong's interest, however, was spurred by economic interests and power. That led him to command the lands in southern China below the Yangtze River. Despite the fact that Christianity doesn't promote violence, the Taiping Rebellion was one of the bloodiest in Chinese history. Boldly, Hong and his troops tried to annex Beijing but failed due to the efforts of Zeng Guofan.

When Hong Xiuquan died in 1864, his movement died with him. However, the contemporaries of that time remember that he was responsible for the deaths of ten to twenty million, including both troops and civilians.

The Great Qing Legal Code

During the Qing dynasty, the legal code contained hundreds of statutes, and many were applied during the religious persecutions. China had laws regulating government personnel, revenue, civil and religious rites, marriage, military affairs, homicide, and even construction. Offenses weren't split into civil or criminal as in other countries. Confucianism espoused an inextricable relationship between business and morals. Therefore, there was no civil code that didn't have a criminal component. Corporal punishment and even torture were among the penalties rendered if a party was found guilty. A confession was always perceived as an offense that merited punishment. Most people who filed charges over civil matters tended to settle their issues out of court, so the threat of harsh physical punishment acted as a prime motivator for conflict resolution. There were very harsh penalties for homosexuality, and adultery was strictly forbidden. Even widows had a difficult time remarrying, even though that would have been legal under the law, as the women couldn't prove they hadn't committed adultery. Many remained celibate, and some even committed suicide since they were unable to support themselves and their children. The Great Qing Legal Code lasted until the overthrow of the Qing dynasty.

Self-Strengthening

Zeng Guofan, like many of his Chinese compatriots, was humiliated by the country's defeats to the Western powers during the Opium Wars. Opium wasn't the issue; the issue was the fact that China didn't have enough military strength to be able to command respect and make demands of other counties in international crises.

In 1860, the British and the French had worked their way into Beijing, and China had little control over the unbridled freedoms these foreign powers were taking. Even the Christians, who had been granted the right to proselytize in 1846, were dodging tax obligations they had agreed to observe. While the Treaty of Tientsin was being finalized in 1860, the British and French were forcing China to accept more and more concessions by attacking the emperor's summer palaces. Zeng Guofan worked with noted Chinese statesman Li Hngzhang to manufacture more powerful weapons and put China on an equal military basis with the Western countries.

Li was instrumental in the attempts to upgrade China, setting up the China Merchants Steam Navigation Company in 1872, the coal mines in Kaiping in 1877, a telegraph network in 1879, and two factories that manufactured cotton in 1890.

Many of the more conservative and studious Chinese preferred to return to the past and secretly wished that the West would "go away." Li's and Zheng's efforts were heroic, as they had to convince Chinese authorities that the country needed to be nationalized. China needed to be united as a country and eschew factional conflicts, as they would only serve to weaken the country from within.

The Emigration Phenomenon

The population of China had increased substantially during the late 19th century, and the drain on resources was extreme. Female infanticide was on the rise, as there were very few opportunities for women to become wage-earners. Even young men couldn't find profitable work in China, and many emigrated to other countries. They went to Australia, America, Malaysia, Malacca, Borneo, the South Pacific islands, and Southeast Asian countries. In some Buddhist countries, like Thailand and Vietnam, the Chinese intermarried and virtually disappeared as a distinct culture. In Muslim countries like Java or in Christian countries like the Philippines, they lived in separate communities.

Unfortunately, many of these emigrants were hired by unscrupulous foreign employers and worked for very low wages. They were called "coolies," from the Chinese word *kuli*, meaning "bitter laborer." They were basically indentured servants who didn't earn enough to advance their lives forward in any way. In the American West, many were hired by railroad companies and treated very badly.

Preamble to War

In 1876, Korea and Japan signed a treaty, opening up trade between the two countries. Huang Zunxian, the Chinese ambassador to Korea, recommended that Korea maintain friendly relations with Japan. He felt that Japan would counterbalance any undesirable influence by Russia. At that time, Japan wasn't seen as a threat to the power of China.

Japan was also interested in a cordial relationship with the US to further balance any possible threat from Russia. However, when the Americans established relations with Korea, they overlooked the fact that Korea had a history of being a tributary state of China, which started back in 1637. The US felt that Korea should be considered an independent state. The skilled statesman Li Hongzhang was in charge of the Chinese-Korean policy and presented a compromise that would satisfy both the US and China. So, the Japan-Korea Treaty was amended to state that Korea was "an independent state enjoying the same sovereign rights as does Japan."

Li Hongzhang spoke with Korean representatives and recommended that they emulate the "self-strengthening" policy that China had started and introduce reforms that would help them relate to other countries from a position of strength—not overwhelming strength but at least equal strength. The Chinese then sent over a military unit to train Korean soldiers in warfare techniques and provided them with upgraded weapons.

The Japanese were ambivalent about Korea's interest in reform. Some were very much in favor of it and wanted to participate in helping Korea develop, but other Japanese preferred that Koreans focus on these improvements by themselves and thus be more passive on the world stage. Regardless of the differences of opinion in Japan, the Korean Prince Regent Heungseon Daewongun saw to it that reform efforts were started.

The Meddling Starts

Korea's relationships with China and Japan were tested in 1882 when a riot broke out in Korea during a drought. It started in Imo but inexplicably spread to the Japanese legation in Korea. Six Japanese were killed, and riots broke out throughout the city.

Japan then deployed four warships to Korea, and China sent in 4,500 troops. The two countries were now competing for control over Korean affairs. As a result of the Imo Incident, Korea made reparations and penalized the chief perpetrators of the rebellion, which had resulted in the deaths of Japanese representatives. When the Koreans blamed Heungseon Daewongun for the riot, the Chinese interfered by taking him to China, where he was confined.

Korea became a prize to be won or a pawn to be used. China wanted the Korean reforms to move along gradually, while Japan wanted them to make rapid improvements.

The Japanese dispatched a fleet into the Korean harbors of Pusan and Chempulpo, but they assured Li Hongzhang that they had no intention of attacking. They indicated that they simply wanted to balance off the Chinese forces already in the country.

King GoJong of Korea insisted that the Japanese depart. However, Japan adamantly refused.

The First Sino-Japanese War

In 1894, Japan and China reached a pivotal moment having to do with the nature of their relations with Korea. Emperor Meiji of Japan said, "Korea is an independent state. She was first introduced into the family of nations by the advice and guidance of Japan. It has, however, been China's habit to designate Korea as her dependency." The Guangxu Emperor of China retorted, "Korea has been our tributary for the past two hundred odd years. She has given us tribute all this time, which is a matter known to the world. For the past dozen years or so Korea has been troubled by repeated insurrections and we, in sympathy with our small tributary, have repeatedly sent her aid."

The First Sino-Japanese War was very short, lasting a little over eight months. Despite the fact that they had revitalized their military, China wasn't ready. In July, the Japanese vessels *Naniwa, Akitsushima,* and *Yoshino* captured and sunk the *Kowshing,* a British transport ship subcontracted by China to carry members of the Green Standard Army and Eight Banners Army into Asan, Korea.

The Japanese heavily outnumbered the Chinese, and at the Battle of Seonghwan, they defeated the Chinese, placing them within fifty miles of Seoul. The bulk of the Chinese shored up their defenses in northern Korea, sensing that the Japanese would make a strike there.

More Chinese were stationed in northern Korea than at the prior battle near Asan. Most were guarding the capital city of Pyongyang. The Japanese separated their forces into three divisions. Two engaged the Chinese at opposing diagonal corners of the city walls, and the third division attacked from the rear. After the Japanese won this battle, the Chinese pulled out of the north and withdrew toward the mouth of the Yalu River, which feeds out of the Yellow Sea, near the Chinese/Korean border.

At the Battle of the Yalu River, which took place in 1894, the Japanese navy's frontal formations proved to be superior to those of the Chinese. Although the Japanese made a number of tactical errors, the Chinese used an ineffective wedge formation, inviting broadside attacks. At the end of this one-day battle, China's Beiyang fleet withdrew.

The Chinese troops then moved to defend their own homeland in Manchuria when they saw the Japanese were moving toward their shores. However, the Japanese were able to capture the Chinese outpost of Hushan before moving on land to capture six towns in Manchuria.

In Port Arthur, the Japanese reported that they saw the decapitated head of a dead Japanese soldier on display. They retaliated with an indiscriminate massacre of thousands of Chinese soldiers and civilians. A Japanese eyewitness reported, "Anyone we saw in the town, we killed. The streets were filled with corpses...Blood was flowing and the smell was awful." The estimates of the number killed differ vastly. Some reported 1,000 were killed, while other media sources reported as many as 60,000 were slaughtered. Some have conjectured that the larger number was exaggerated by journalists for political reasons.

In the city of Weihaiwei in northeast China, Chinese soldiers stayed behind the fortification walls when the Japanese placed the city under siege. The Chinese abandoned the fort in the bitter cold of January 1895, and the battle moved to the Yellow Sea. After winning the Battle of Weihaiwei, the Japanese took over the Liaodong Peninsula, which borders northwestern Korea.

The ground forces of both parties were engaged in Manchuria and its environs, and the Japanese conquered six cities there. They then headed toward the Manchurian capital, Mukden. The Japanese captured the town of Haicheng on the Liaodong Peninsula. The Chinese made four attempts to retake the city but failed every time. As they were anxious to end the war, the Japanese decided they wanted to take either Mukden or Beijing, as losing either one would greatly cripple the Chinese forces.

The Japanese then surprised China and the international observers by capturing the Pescadores Islands in the Taiwan Strait. The Japanese wanted control of the Pescadores because that would be their key to gaining control of Taiwan. Those islands could have been used by Japan to prevent the arrival of Chinese reinforcements to Taiwan, as well as open the gates to gain Taiwan in a subsequent treaty.

Their strategy worked.

The Treaty of Shimonoseki

By virtue of the Shimonoseki Treaty, which was signed in April of 1895, Japan and China recognized the independence of Korea. Japan received Taiwan, the Pescadores Islands, and the Liaodong Peninsula "in perpetuity." The Japanese were also permitted to conduct trade on the Yangtze River.

The Qing Empire was humiliated. They had to pay 13,600 tons of silver in war reparations, and the Chinese inhabitants in Korea were forced to leave. Chinese settlers in Taiwan and the Taiwanese fought a guerilla-style rebellion against the Japanese. Many were slaughtered. Women were raped, and peasants were thrown off their lands unless they stayed on as tenant farmers.

Too Little, Too Late

In 1898, a brilliant politician and philosopher, Kang Youwei, obtained an audience with the Guangxu Emperor. He had a great deal of foresight and tried to encourage China to reform its antique approach to government. Even the Empress Dowager Cixi, who effectively ruled China from 1861 to 1908, was interested in his proposals. Some of them were:

1. Elimination of the civil service examinations, which only served to separate the applicants into the elites and the commoners

2. Education in Western liberal arts

3. Education of the imperial family abroad

4. Establishment of a constitutional monarchy

5. Introduction of some elements of capitalism to motivate people to work harder

6. Industrialization

7. Restructuring of the military

8. Construction of a railway system

These proposals were a part of the Hundred Days' Reform, a movement that the Guangxu Emperor promoted along with like-minded followers. However, too many people, including Empress Dowager Cixi, were consumed by dreams of the distant past and had difficulty accepting those propositions.

The Boxer Rebellion

Wrapped up in the nostalgia of the days when China was an isolationist country, a group of well-meaning but naïve young men trained in the martial arts felt that foreigners and missionaries needed to be expelled—all of them. So, in 1899, they started randomly killing foreigners and missionaries in Beijing and Tientsin.

The Dowager Empress Cixi sided with the Boxers. She complained, "The foreigners had been aggressive toward us, infringed on our territorial integrity, and trampled our people under their feet." The Boxers placed foreign legations and missions in Beijing and Tientsin under siege. However, 20,000 troops from other nations soon marched on Tientsin and Beijing, lifted the siege, and even looted the cities. The empress dowager and the emperor, who were hiding in the Forbidden City, fled.

Li Hongzhang was called upon to negotiate, but there was little he could do. He had warned China of the need to modernize, but China had been much too slow to respond to his call for action. By way of reparations, China had to pay 450 million ounces of silver; fortunately, Li was able to get his opponents to agree to an installment plan.

Beginning of the End

When the Empress Dowager Cixi was in her seventies, she announced that Puyi, the grandson of the emperor, would assume the throne after Emperor Guangxu. When the court heard that, they took two-year-old Puyi to see the empress. This was a traumatic event for him, and he once wrote about the meeting, saying, "I remember suddenly finding myself surrounded by strangers, while before me was hung a drab curtain through which I could see an emaciated and terrifyingly hideous face. This was Cixi."

The Guangxu Emperor died in 1908 "under mysterious circumstances." He was only 37 years old. A day later, Dowager Empress Cixi died. Many believe that Cixi, knowing the end was near, had the emperor poisoned. In 2008, a test was done on the body of the Guangxu Emperor, which found that his remains contained 2,000 times the normal amount of arsenic in a person's body. This leads historians to speculate that Cixi had the emperor killed so he could not continue advancing his progressive reforms.

Now, the throne of the Qing dynasty, which could never really break out of the shell of its isolationist fantasies, was now in the hands of a child, a child who was frightened by the face of an old woman. And while his father, Prince Chun, would become regent to the young boy, Puyi would grow up knowing nothing other than the fact that he was the emperor of China.

Chapter 9 – Revolutionary Madness

Wuchang Uprising

Toward the end of the Qing dynasty, some of the newly proposed administrative and national reforms were underway. One of them was the reorganization of the Chinese army, then called the Beiyang Army. It was mobilized to suppress violent resistors of the proposed railroad system. In 1910, the Qing dynasty made arrangements with a Western finance company to initiate the project. However, the diehard conservatives like the Boxers rejected these "capitalists." The man in charge of the project, Sheng Xuanhuai, nationalized the endeavor. Massive rallies and strikes took place, mostly in Chengdu.

This phase of the uprising was propelled by underground revolutionary groups such as the Tongmenghui, which was formed from several factions, including the Revive China Society. The Furen Literary Society and the Progressive Association supported them. The Tongmenghui was being funded by the wealthy Sun family, who owned thousands of acres in Hawaii.

Sun Yat-sen, who greatly promoted the cause of the Tongmenghui, believed in a revolutionary philosophy and raised money from many countries in order to sponsor some of the uprisings in China. When his intentions became known, he was essentially exiled, and he lived in a number of countries, including the United States, Canada, Great Britain, and Japan. When he heard about the Wuchang Uprising of 1911, Sun returned to China.

These groups were in the process of making explosive devices to be used for a large-scale revolution. When a supervisor named Sun Wu was injured while the explosives were being assembled, word leaked out about these rebel factions. Three of them were executed, but 5,000 dissidents escaped the Qing authorities.

Nearly one-third of the Qing defectors were military members, and they soon mutinied. In 1911, the army traitors attacked the garrison at Huguang, seizing the local Qing viceroy in the process.

The rebel commander, Xiong Bingkun, gathered together all the revolutionary forces he could and prepared to attack the Qing forces with 100,000 men. The highly motivated revolutionaries, composed of revolutionary cells and ex-military soldiers, conquered Wuchang.

The loyal members of the Beiyang Army under Yuan Shikai were called upon to suppress the rebellion. In the Battle of Yangxia, which took place between October and the beginning of December, fighting broke out at the cities of Hankou and Hanyang along the Yangtze River. However, the revolutionaries had inferior weapons and lost the battle at Hankou. The Beiyang Army then decided to burn the city. At Hanyang, there was fighting throughout the streets, even in houses. The Qing army took possession of the munitions factory and destroyed the rebels' artillery. As many as 3,000 revolutionaries died there. Despite those setbacks, many other provinces defected, including Sichuan, Nanjing, and Shaanxi. In addition, the entire Qing navy defected.

The Xinhai Revolution of 1911

The Wuchang Uprising kicked off what is known as the Xinhai Revolution. Sun Yat-sen, who would become the leader of the revolution, was still in the United States fundraising when this chaotic outbreak occurred. He wasn't aware of this revolt until months later, after which he went to England and contacted other Western countries in order to assure their neutrality and receive financing for a new republic. After this attempt, which proved unsuccessful, Sun Yat-sen returned to China, arriving there in late December 1911. However, when Sun Sat-yen was abroad, the Xinhai Revolution was in search of a leader. The people thrust the role upon Li Yuanhong, a military commander.

Thus, this revolution was truly "home-grown." Many dissident provinces staged their own attacks:

The Changsha Restoration, October 22nd

The Shaanxi Uprising, October 22nd

The Jiujiang Uprising, October 23rd

The Shanxi Taiyuan Revolt, October 29th

The Kunming "Double Ninth" Uprising, October 30th, so-named because it was the ninth day of the ninth month in the old Chinese calendar

The Nanchang Uprising, October 31st

The Shanghai Armed Uprising, November 3rd

The Guizhou Uprising, November 4th

The Zhejiang Uprising, November 4th

The Jiangsu Restoration, November 5th

The Anhui Uprising, November 5th

The Guangxi Uprising, November 7th

The Guangdong Independence, November 9th

The Fujian Independence, November 11th

The Shandong Independence, November 13th

The Ningxia Uprising, November 17th

The Sichuan Independence, November 21st

The Nanjing Uprising, December 3rd

There were two regions that deviated from this revolutionary pattern: Tibet and Mongolia. Their status was held in abeyance until order returned.

Last-Ditch Qing

The rebels, who were mostly from the military, took over Beijing. In a fit of desperation, the Qing dynasty proposed a constitutional monarchy with General Yuan Shikai as its new prime minister. The child emperor's adoptive mother, Empress Dowager Longyu, proposed that the emperor and his family assume only a ceremonial role.

However, when Sun Yat-sen arrived back in China in late December 1911, he was immediately appointed provisional president of the newly formed government, which was set up in Nanjing.

Yuan and Sun then negotiated a solution. Yuan Shikai would be the first president of the Republic of China, and the Qing emperor, Puyi, would officially abdicate with the understanding that the imperial family could continue to live in the Forbidden City.

Chapter 10 – The Republic of China to the People's Republic of China

The days of the dynasties were now over. General Yuan Shikai was inaugurated as the provisional president of the Republic of China in March 1912. He and his confidantes then moved to Beijing, and the new government received international recognition.

Financial Entanglements

Upon the launch of the new administration, China was in a financial crisis due to the expenditures of the many revolts. Yuan Shikai took out a number of loans from foreign parties. Although the investments were risky, foreign financial institutions extended loans to China. To protect themselves from financial risk, though, the investors charged an extremely high interest rate. The amount borrowed amounted to 21 million pounds of silver. Within three years, the government ran an annual deficit of two million pounds of silver.

Administration

In March, a proposed constitution was drafted, and arrangements were made for public voting. Only 10 percent of the male population were permitted to vote. Those who were bankrupt or addicted opium-smokers were excluded, along with women.

Sun Yat-sen, the initial leader of the revolutionaries, organized his own political party called the Kuomintang (KMT) after the Xinhai Revolution of 1911. Another party was created in 1912, the Republican Party, to which Yuan Shikai belonged. This party was a bit more conservative in nature compared to the KMT. In December 1912, an election was held, and Song Jiaoren was instrumental in ensuring victories for his party, the Kuomintang. It was widely thought that Song would become the next prime minister. However, tragedy struck.

In March 1913, as Song traveled to the railroad station to report to Beijing, a man approached him and shot him. Song died two days later. A commission investigated the assassination, but one by one, those thought to be involved were murdered. Due to the lack of evidence, Yuan Shikai, who most likely orchestrated the assassination, was never charged with anything.

It is thought that Yuan did this because of the popularity of Song and the KMT. In order to secure the support of those in Parliament, Yuan had regularly bribed them. Those who refused the bribes were dismissed. He also had the support of those who were still loyal in the Beiyang Army.

Second Revolution

In the summer of 1913, seven southern provinces rebelled because they felt that Yuan Shikai was responsible for the assassination of Song Jiaoren and because they felt he obtained his position through political manipulation rather than merit. In addition, the armies hadn't been paid. Members of Sun Yat-sen's Kuomintang participated but were defeated by Yuan's superior military strength under General Zhang Xun. Yuan then dissolved the parliament and appointed his own cabinet, which made him a president with dictatorial powers. His vice president was Li Yuanhong.

This wasn't Sun Yat-sen's vision for a new China. Sun attempted to rebuild opposition against Yuan and formed the Chinese Revolutionary Party. By this time, the Republican Party had been merged, along with other like-minded parties, into the Progressive Party. Although they supported Yuan in the Second Revolution, they didn't support his move to disband the KMT. They, like the Revolutionary Party, wanted to remove Yuan from power.

World War I

In 1914, World War I broke out. China declared its neutrality right from the beginning. However, there was some consternation over the fact that a German colony had been established in Shandong province back in 1897. Japan wanted the Germans out of there, and the Japanese used this as a wedge to involve China in the war. Yuan was in favor of expelling the Germans too, and despite China's declared neutrality, Yuan Shikai agreed to put 50,000 troops under Britain's control, provided they expelled the Germans in Shandong. Britain turned down that proposal.

Knowing that China didn't have a strong military force of its own, Japan simply annexed Shandong and ousted the Germans. Japan then sent China the Twenty-One Demands in 1915, which included granting Japan economic control of the railways in the north and give them long-term offices in Shandong, Manchuria, and Fujian. Yuan accepted those demands with some modifications. The Chinese population was livid.

After this, the Chinese joined the Allied side and mostly escorted troop transports and supply ships for the Allies in the Mediterranean.

To control the public opposition to his acceptance of the Twenty-One Demands, Yuan coerced journalists and writers to support him in their editorials and articles.

However, in 1916, he proclaimed himself the Hongxian Emperor and wanted to re-establish the monarchy. Provinces erupted in riots and rebellions. His governor Cal E and Tang Yiyao, governor of the influential Yunnan province, created the National

Protection War. Many districts declared themselves independent of the emperor. The Beiyang Army was sent in to quell the rebellions, but lacked little motivation, as they hadn't been paid in quite some time.

Yuan Shikai didn't suspect that reaction, and his rule as emperor only lasted 83 days, after which he ruled as president. When he died of a kidney condition in 1916, Vice President Li Yuanhong took over the government.

The Warlords and a "Coup"

Li Yuanhong and Parliament ruled in a vacuum. They had virtually little control over the whole country. In 1916, the petty leaders of the various provinces assumed control of their own "mini-kingdoms." They had no political parties to support them, however.

In 1917, Li Yuanhong's field marshal, Zhang Xun, rose up and announced a preposterous measure—the reinstatement of the former emperor, Puyi! He was now eleven years old. On July 1st, Puyi was set up in Beijing with a court and his handlers; however, he only ruled for eleven days. Soon after this, feuding warlords took over the city. Some were intelligent men, while others were just glorified bandits. Three of the strongest warlords were Zhang Zuolin, Wu Peifu, and Feng Yuxiang. Loyalty meant little to most of them. Feng, for example, once fought under Wu Peifu but then split from him to form his own group. There was constant pillaging of farms and shops, along with indiscriminate slaughter. Although the warlords only oversaw local areas, the chaos they produced threatened to continue for years to come.

One of the most troubling of the warlord groups was the Beiyang Army, which consisted of the loyal followers of the Qing dynasty. After the dynasty had collapsed, the Beiyang remained a threat because they were experienced and well-organized.

Rebirth of Unification Efforts

At the end of World War I, according to the Treaty of Versailles, Japan was allowed to keep the concessions they had in those regions, which the Chinese found astonishing. Sun Yat-sen collaborated with the southern provinces and resurrected the Kuomintang in 1917. He served as a "president" and again tried to get funds and the support of the Western countries. That attempt failed, so Sun sought Soviet support for the reunification efforts. Mikhail Borodin, an agent for the Comintern (Communist International), an organization promoting world communism, conferred with Sun Yat-sen in 1923. Together, they created the First United Front.

The First United Front was an alliance between the Kuomintang (KMT) and the Communist Party of China (CPC). The CPC had been founded in 1921 and was quickly growing in popularity. Chiang Kai-shek, Sun's lieutenant in the Kuomintang, and Sun Yat-sen didn't want to create a communist state. While Chiang Kai-shek had studied the Soviet system and admired its organizational aspects, he disagreed with the communist principles it promoted. Sun Yat-sen's vision was to develop a reunified China according to three phases: 1) reunion of China by force, 2) politically-based education in the new government, and 3) introduction of democracy.

In 1925, Sun died, and Chiang Kai-shek took over the reins. He created a military arm to support the Kuomintang, the National Revolutionary Army.

The Nanjing Decade

In 1926, Chiang Kai-shek launched the Northern Expedition. The purpose of this was to eliminate the threats from the rival Beiyang Army and warlords like Zhang Zuolin, Wu Peifu, and Feng Yuxiang. Under his leadership, the army wiped out the warlords and succeeded in controlling half of China.

In 1927, Chiang Kai-shek seized control of Nanjing from the local warlord, Sun Chuanfang. A problem arose when Chiang discovered that a heavily communist faction led by Wang Jingwei was set up in Wuhan province. That government, following orders from Soviet liaison Mikhail Borodin, tried futilely to strip Chiang of his powers. Wang met Chiang in Shanghai to discuss a power-sharing agreement. Wang indicated he would consider it and returned to Wuhan. However, the government in Wuhan rejected the compromise and prepared to go to Shanghai, where Chiang Kai-shek was currently seated.

In April 1927, the National Revolutionary Army reached Shanghai. Shanghai had a large majority of Communists, and Chiang was determined to rid China from Soviet influence. Chiang and his men tore through the city, arrested and executed known members of the Communist Party, and purged the government of them. As many as 12,000 people were killed. This event is known as the Shanghai massacre. Chiang didn't stop there, however. He initiated a large-scale massacre throughout all of China, known as the White Terror. Over 300,000 people were killed, and blood ran thick in the streets. The Communists who were still left in China mostly moved into rural districts where the Kuomintang wasn't present.

Chiang then worked to convince the provincial leaders to give up their independent local governments and turn them over to a central government. After hearing about the cruelty of Chiang's forces, the people were afraid and conformed.

Although total unification wasn't achieved, the country was divided into five realms: Nanjing, Guangxi, the Guominjun, another sector controlled by Yan Xishan, and the semi-autonomous state of Manchuria led by Zhang Xueliang.

Chiang Kai-shek then moved the Kuomintang government from Beijing to Nanjing and kept it there for ten years, which is why it was called the "Nanjing decade."

Modernization

Diplomatic efforts to build relations with the rest of the world were developed and continued after the Nanjing decade. Banking reforms were established, and public health facilities were upgraded and created. The legal and penal system was brought up to the standards exercised by other countries. In addition to these efforts, legislation against narcotics use and distribution were passed and enforced, and the manufacturing of agricultural machinery was increased.

While some characterize Chiang Kai-shek as a capitalist, he eschewed capitalism nearly as much as he did communism. He severely criticized the "imperialists," forbidding them from holding any governmental positions and coercing them into donating large portions of their money to the country, especially for modernization.

After all, neighboring countries had modernized—Japan, in particular. In fact, China made a business deal with Japan to build and manage the South Manchuria Railroad. It was a prosperous arrangement for both countries. However, in September of 1931, there was an explosion at the railroad. Japanese soldiers who were protecting the railway line at Mukden blamed the Chinese for causing it. They rushed over to a Chinese garrison nearby and attacked it. Hostilities accelerated, and a battle broke out in 1931. This event was called the Mukden Incident. This led to the invasion of Manchuria and the setting up of a puppet state there.

Mukden Incident of 1931

Chiang Kai-shek became alarmed about the conflict and appealed to the League of Nations, an international body that was intended to mediate such crises and stop pending wars. The League agreed with China and asked Japan to return Manchuria. Japan didn't agree with this ruling and left the League.

At that time, Chiang was in north-central China in the city of Xi'an with his National Revolutionary Army, and they were in the process of expelling the Communists. Chiang Kai-shek met with two of his generals, Yang Hucheng and Zhang Xueliang. Both men wanted Chiang to cease his hostilities against the Chinese Communists and had the great Chiang Kai-shek arrested. This was an outrageous act of betrayal.

Madame Chiang Kai-shek Intercedes

Chiang's wife, Soong May-ling, was politically astute and often advised her husband upon Chinese affairs. After hearing of Chiang's kidnapping in Xi'an, she advised him to shift his focus away from his obsession with the elimination of the Communist Party of China and turn his attention to the very serious Japanese threat. During negotiations with his captors, she advised Chiang to accept their terms, which were the cessation of hostilities between the Chinese Communists and to unite the Communist troops with the National Revolutionary Army forces in order to expel Japan from Manchuria and China. Once he agreed to those terms, Chiang was released, and he joined up with the Communist leader, Zhou Enlai.

In 1937, the Marco Polo Bridge Incident occurred. The Japanese, who were missing a soldier after a training exercise, demanded entry into a Chinese garrison to search for him. When the Chinese refused this, the Japanese attempted to force their way in, and tensions escalated until conflict broke out. Many consider this to be the start of the Second Sino-Japanese War, and some even consider it to be the starting date for World War II.

The Second Sino-Japanese War

Because Japan had been helping China upgrade its industrial base, it was well aware of the fact that China was behind other countries in terms of modernization. That made China very vulnerable. Japan craved the resources and opportunities China held so they could expand their own sphere of influence in the Pacific region. The Mukden Incident had presented them with a golden opportunity, as the Japanese could use Manchuria as a base in order to take over China.

This was a tenuous union, but one that was needed because Japan was their mutual enemy and a great threat to China. This merger of the Communist and Nationalist forces was called the Second United Front.

The Battle of Shanghai, August 13th–November 26th, 1937

This was the first major battle of the Second Sino-Japanese War. At first, Chiang's forces conducted an air war with Japan over the city. However, Japan's Mitsubishi A5M aircraft were far more superior than China's Curtiss F11C biplanes and shot them out of the sky. It eventually turned into a ground war in the city. The Chinese ground forces of 70,000 far outnumbered the Japanese troops of 6,300 marines, so their prospects for victory looked good. Shortly afterward, Japan sent in as many as 100,000 of their Imperial forces. As a result, the Chinese army was forced to retreat, leaving Shanghai in the hands of the Japanese.

The Capture of Nanjing (Nanking), December 1st–13th, 1937

In 1937, the Japanese captured Nanjing. While there, they killed not only soldiers but Chinese civilians. This event, known as the Nanking massacre, saw between 40,000 to 300,000 deaths. The sources conflict greatly on the actual number, as people debate on the geographical boundary of the massacre as well as the timespan of it. Some Japanese claim only several hundred died, and a small minority believe that the massacre never took place at all. In addition to the murder of innocents, widespread looting and raping occurred. Civilians fled to safety zones by the thousands, and China essentially lost control of the city of Nanjing.

The Battle of Taierzhuang, March 24th–April 7th

The Japanese army had a tendency to take matters into their own hands, and they often avoided getting permission from the Japanese government to continue the war. So, they marched into Jiangsu. The Chinese resistance was strong, and in April of 1938, the Chinese confronted the Japanese at Taierzhuang, which was located on the Grand Canal. Much to the surprise of the headstrong Japanese troops, they were beaten, making this battle the first major Chinese victory of the war.

The Japanese countered by attacking and capturing Kaifeng, the capital of Henan province, and threatened to take Zhengzhou as well. Chiang Kai-shek and his men knew the area well and understood its tendency to flood. In order to stop the Japanese rampage, the Chinese broke down some of the dikes on the Yellow River. Water gushed upon the Japanese troops, and Japanese soldiers died by the thousands. Chinese civilians reported that the rivers and streams were loaded with rotting corpses. Death and its insipid odor were everywhere.

Japan called for negotiations in order to stop the bloodshed, but Chiang Kai-shek delayed. The Japanese then launched attacks at Suixian–Zaoyang, Changsha, and South Guangxi. Messages running through Japan's line of communication had been delayed because of the immense amount of territory Japan was trying to control simultaneously. Therefore, they lost each battle.

The United States opposed this large-scale invasion of China, so they started sending supplies and money for China to support the war effort. With the Japanese attack on Pearl Harbor in December 1941, the Second Sino-Japanese War quickly merged into another conflict of World War II, opening up the Pacific theater of the war.

China in World War II

The United States declared war against Japan after the attack on its naval base, and China soon joined them. At the Battle of Changsha, which started on December 24th, 1941, the Chinese assisted the British forces in Hong Kong. The Japanese fended off the Chinese army and entered Changsha. However, they hadn't planned on China's next actions, as the Chinese forces outside of the city completely surrounded the Japanese in Changsha. After suffering heavy casualties, the Japanese withdrew on January 15th.

In 1942, in Burma, the British were surrounded by the Japanese at the town of Yenangyaung but were rescued by the large 38th Corps of the Chinese army. The Japanese swooped into Zhejiang and Jiangxi provinces, but they were forced out by the Chinese army. In Burma, Chiang Kai-shek worked alongside Lieutenant Joseph Stillwell of the United States to break a Japanese blockade. Chiang and Stillwell disagreed over tactics, as Chiang suspected that Stillwell wanted to use the Chinese to help protect the British territories rather than bring Allied forces into China to expel the Japanese. America decided to replace Stillwell with General Albert Coady Wedemeyer, who was more willing to cooperate.

In 1944, Chinese troops came in from India, and with others from Yunnan province, they attacked the Japanese in Burma, freeing up a critical supply route into China. In 1945, the Chinese successfully retook Hunan and Guangxi. The Soviets, who were on the Allied side, invaded the Japanese in Manchuria and freed it, giving it back to the Chinese. General Wedemeyer and the Chinese planned to retake Guangdong province and readied their forces to do so. However, the bombings of Nagasaki and Hiroshima put a sudden stop to the war.

The Japanese troops in China formally surrendered to Chiang Kai-shek on September 9th, 1945, at 9:00 a.m. This was the ninth day of the ninth month at the ninth hour. 9-9-9 was significant to the Chinese, as the number nine stood for "long-lasting." At the end of the war, China was regarded as a great power.

The Deadly Aftermath

The estimates of the Chinese killed or wounded in the Second Sino-Japanese War and World War II are staggering. Between fifteen and twenty million died, and fifteen million were wounded. There were about 95 million refugees. Many of them were from Guangdong province, as there wasn't anywhere for the inhabitants to resettle because of the widespread devastation. About $383 million was spent on the war effort.

The Two Chinas

The Second United Front in China, which had fought against Japan, was a precarious union between Chiang Kai-shek's Nationalists and the Chinese Communist Party. There was a tacit agreement that these two opposing political groups would suspend their differences during the course of the two wars, but as soon as World War II came to a conclusion, the tensions between the two arose once more.

Chiang Kai-shek had always had strenuous objections to the inclusion of communism in China, but he wanted some kind of peace after the fighting had stopped. So, he contacted Mao Zedong, the chairman of the Chinese Communist Party, as he was desirous of reaching a compromise. Chiang Kai-shek, Mao Zedong, and American ambassador Patrick Hurley conferred together. However, as soon as they held the initial private conference, conflicts broke out between the Communists and the Nationalists. Both walked away from the negotiations.

The US decided to send in George Marshall in December 1945 to coax the two groups to return to the negotiating table. They agreed to reorganize the government, convoke a national assembly, adopt a constitution, and make reforms in the areas of economics and the structure of military forces.

The meeting, as it turned out, was merely theoretical but not practical. In Manchuria, where the Japanese were still withdrawing after the war, there was a scramble for power. Nationalist troops rushed into Mukden, and Communist soldiers solidified positions in northern Manchuria. The fighting spread to Hebei, Jiangsu, Shantung, and Chengde. After Nationalist troops took over the city of Kalgan, the Nationalists set up the first meeting of a national assembly, without notifying Zhou Enlai. The assembly then proceeded to draft a constitution, without input from the Chinese Communist Party. Zhou was enraged, and George Marshall condemned the Nationalists for making this foolish move and left China.

One of Chiang Kai-shek's ministers, General Zhang Zhizhong, contacted the Communists and expressed a willingness to resume talks. He restated the initial conditions discussed at the beginning of the negotiations, but the Communists were no longer interested.

The Communists then took over the railroad in Mukden that led to central China. Mao announced, "The Chinese People's Liberation Army has carried the fight into the Kuomintang area. This is a turning point in history."

By 1947, the Nationalist forces had lost much of its military strength. They concentrated their efforts on Manchuria, but due to their military inferiority, they became a defensive rather than an offensive force. Under General Lin Biao, the Communist troops sought to strike weakened positions along the Nationalist lines and hammered away at them. The strategy worked well, and the Communists regained control of Manchuria in 1948. They then moved to other northern provinces and later regained control of Shantung, Yunnan, and Zhengzhou from the Nationalists. One by one, more northern provinces were controlled by the Communists. After they had essentially taken over northern China, Mao Zedong announced that his new government would soon encompass all of China.

Financial Crises

In order to keep financing his military engagements, Chiang Kai-shek simply printed more money. That inevitably led to inflation, and the value of the Chinese dollar plummeted. People saw their savings wiped out, and no help from the government was forthcoming. Price and wage controls were put into place to slow the inflation, but it was too late for that. So, Chiang Kai-shek called upon the United States, Britain, France, and the Soviet Union to help settle the differences between the Nationalists and the Communists. Because of these joint efforts, the Nationalists signed a non-aggression pact with the Communists. To help alleviate financial strains, the Soviet Union gave China credits for $250 million, and the other countries contributed $263.5 million.

The Communists again sent their list of demands to General Zhang Zhizhong, the representative of the Nationalist forces. Their demands included: 1) the punishment of "war criminals," 2) the abrogation of the constitution passed by the Nationalist-led assembly, 3) the abolition of the governments, 4) the reorganization of the army, 5) land reform, 6) the abrogation of "treasonous treaties," and 7) the creation of a national coalition without the Nationalists.

By 1949, Chiang Kai-shek and the Nationalists had lost their bid to control China. Chiang Kai-shek then resigned as the president of the Republic of China. His next in command, Li Zongren, took over. Chiang Kai-shek took $200 million in gold and US dollars from the Chinese treasury, which he said he was using to protect the Nationalist government. Li desperately needed that money to pay his troops and shore up the government, but Chiang refused to release it.

After some consternation over Li's proposed choice for a premier, Chiang finally agreed to accept the proposal proffered by Yan Xishan, a former warlord. Despite his shaky background, Yan had some finesse in diplomatic matters, and he became premier in June 1949. Li and Chiang argued about money, and Chiang expressed some of his ideas toward resolving the dispute between Mao and the Nationalists.

Yan had advised Li to move his government to Canton from Nanjing, as the Communists had tight control over the areas surrounding Nanjing. Finally, Li acquiesced and moved it. Li had difficulty organizing the Kuomintang military and gathered too many of his forces into the area around Canton rather than in other strategic areas in southern China where the Communists weren't strong. Li was hoping that the United States would send forces to help him there, but they didn't. Chiang Kai-shek decided to release some of the money he was holding from the Chinese treasury, but it wasn't enough to make a real difference. Chiang Kai-shek's constant interference made Li furious, and he started ousting strong Chiang supporters from the Kuomintang.

When the Communists suddenly conquered Canton in October 1949, Li was forced to flee to Chongqing. When he arrived, Li effectively surrendered the presidency and left for America for a medical procedure. Chiang tried to put up a defense with the forces left, but he was unsuccessful. He then was airlifted with his wife and family to Taiwan in December 1949.

After this happened, Mao Zedong announced that the new government of China was the People's Republic of China.

However, Chiang Kai-shek resumed his role as president of the Republic of China in 1950 from Taiwan. For years, he promoted a movement called Project National Glory, which was the attempt to regain mainland China from the Communists. Many Chinese émigrés who lived in Taiwan initiated various political groups, like the China Democratic Socialist Party, to support the return of the Republic of China. Chiang Kai-shek never set foot on his native soil again.

The People's Republic of China

Mao came into office and swept through the country like a cyclone. He promoted himself as a hero to the workers and the underclass. The society he envisioned was a society of the common man, speaking with one voice and thinking with one mind. He killed many of those whom he considered wealthy capitalists, as their existence and interference with affairs wouldn't create the society he dreamed of. He also encouraged workers to report on their employers if they were corrupt and distributed children's books that taught children to report on their parents, neighbors, and friends if they felt these people were criticizing Mao or the government. Thousands were arrested and were either sent to labor camps or shot.

Mao believed that intellectuals needed to understand how the common man lived, so he sent them to farms to be educated by the peasants about providing food for an entire country. This was called the Down to the Countryside Movement, which took place in the late 1960s and early 1970s. They were also required to work in factories. Having been suddenly transplanted from what they were accustomed to, they had difficulty adjusting. Suicides were common, and bodies fell from roofs in the cities. It even got to the point that pedestrians didn't walk on the sidewalks.

Sino-Soviet Split

A split occurred between Nikita Khrushchev and Mao Zedong over a period of time, but it finally culminated in 1961. The split had to do with their interpretations of communism. Mao felt that Khrushchev was too flexible in the application of communist principles. The Soviet system was "top-heavy," with numerous levels of management. Although it did lend itself to the obedience of a cult of personality, like that fostered by Mao, the Soviets had a multitude of agencies. Mao was a staunch Marxist-Leninist and believed in the succession of revolutions as leading to the creation of an ideal society under the leadership of one person and his vision. He felt that Khrushchev was too "revisionist" in his thinking and often softened or even altered his viewpoint in response to an international event or bend to persuasion by another country.

On another level, Mao objected to the intrusion of the Soviets into Chinese society, as it was too reminiscent of the vassal state structure. Mao believed that the Chinese and the Russians were two different peoples, and he believed that China had to arrange their society in such a way as to benefit the Chinese people.

A Great Leap Forward

Mao believed in a planned economy. In 1958, he created a program called the Great Leap Forward. Its aim was to transform China from an agrarian to an industrial, communist society. Grain distribution and the fruit of harvests were nationalized, requiring the growers to work in communes and huge commercialized farms. The objective was to create large amounts of food while decreasing the human labor necessary to produce it. Harvests were sent to the government for equal distribution amongst the people. Certain quotas were expected, so a family might be left with very little if their harvest was less than they'd hoped for. Because mechanization of huge farms lagged behind, farmers often couldn't meet their quotas. Food distribution efforts were unsuccessful, as there was a lack of organization, which led to grocery store shelves being half-empty. Between 1959 and 1961, there was a great famine in China, which occurred because of several factors: 1) the practice of close cropping and deep plowing reduced production, 2) as many as eighteen million youths moved to the cities by 1962, 3) Chairman Mao refused to accept international help and released incorrect data as to the depth of the crisis, and 4) the implementation of the "Four Pests Program." This program sought to eliminate pests like the Eurasian tree sparrow, which ate fruit and seeds. However, that sparrow also consumes insects. When the avian population diminished, locusts descended upon the fields and consumed the foliage, killing the crops.

Between 20 and 45 million people starved. By 1962, it was clear that the Great Leap Forward program was a dismal failure.

The Cultural Revolution

In 1966, Mao instituted the Cultural Revolution. He was convinced that anti-communist elements and capitalism were undermining the welfare of the common man or what was called the proletariat. Anti-communist elements had to be eliminated, whether they were a member of the bourgeoisie or a capitalist.

The Marxist-Leninist variety of communism advocated a class struggle in order to rid society of whatever was perceived as detrimental to the common good. As a result, capitalism was seen as the perennial enemy of the people. Mao isolated the Five Black Categories: landlords, wealthy farmers, counter-revolutionaries, bad elements of society—meaning those who didn't promote communism or Mao Zedong—and rightists.

People deemed to be in the Five Black Categories were persecuted, imprisoned, and/or executed. Universities were closed, and civil service examinations were abolished. Mao felt that education tended to produce capitalists who exploited the workers and peasants.

Mao didn't entirely subscribe to Marxism-Leninism, though. He was a megalomaniac who wanted his own brand of communism promoted. Toward promoting blind loyalty, he created a book of sayings casually called the *Little Red Book*, which were distributed to the people.

Bourgeois values were to be eschewed, as they were the antithesis of the socialist aspects of communism. Because the youth were more energetic in political endeavors, Mao encouraged them to chide their elders for promoting any bourgeois ideals. Children's books espousing his values were even distributed in food stores for youths to read, and they even recommended that children turn in their neighbors and even family members if they spoke out against the government.

Mao became very concerned that others in the government were trying to usurp him and attempted to purge his government of those people. The Communist Party President, Liu Shaoqi, became a target, and Mao dismissed him as president. Other members who were military commanders or government officials were also purged. They were labeled as "counter-revolutionaries," but Mao felt they simply stood in his way toward autocratic power and needed to find a way to push them out.

These purges were drastic. There were many massacres, and at times, due to the famine, cannibalism took place. It is impossible to know how many died during the Cultural Revolution. Estimates range from hundreds of thousands to twenty million people.

Richard Nixon Visits

After the failure of the Republic of China under Chiang Kai-shek, China went essentially silent. Because it was such a large and influential country in the East, Western countries were left to imagine how the Chinese perceived their role in international affairs. The United States and Chiang Kai-shek had often had face-to-face visits, in which each discussed their objectives and goals and created processes through which they might cooperate. But ever since Chairman Mao took office, that dialogue was non-existent.

In 1971 and 1972, US President Nixon and US Secretary of State Henry Kissinger met Mao in 1971 and 1972. These visits were very important, as the United States and the West, in general, felt that misunderstandings would inevitably develop if one party wasn't participating in discussions about issues that affected all the parties involved, like the possibility of trade.

Prior to the visit, Mao and Nixon decided their roles were not to argue ideologies but to focus on common interests. The United States was concerned about Mao's views on Korea and Vietnam. America also wanted to send a signal to the Soviet Union that issues about the region should include input from China as well. The meetings eventually led to the opening up of relations between China and the US.

Mao Zedong died in 1976 and was succeeded by Deng Xiaoping. Deng Xiaoping did not become the official leader until later, but for all intents and purposes, he ruled the country. Deng's first act was to reject Mao's Cultural Revolution. He felt that it created ignorance, fear, and chaos. He also reinstated civil service examinations and reopened the colleges.

Deng was very interested in international trade. He competed with other countries and campaigned for the export of manufactured products. It was very advantageous to the economy, and China was able to develop and produce its own goods efficiently and inexpensively.

Boluan Fanzheng

Deng wanted to reconcile with the intellectuals and elements that had been ostracized by Mao. In 1977, he proposed the idea of Boluan Fanzheng, the intent of which was to correct the unbalanced attitudes thrust upon the population by Mao. Once Deng became the paramount leader in 1978, he implemented the program.

Other Reforms

Term limits were then established, and Deng proposed that the country draft a new constitution, which was written in 1982 and is still in effect today. To reduce the confusion, he summarized China's society as based upon the Four Cardinal Principles: socialism, a dictatorship run by the people, support of the Chinese Communist Party, and adherence to the principles of Marxism-

Leninism. This technique presented the people with a structure upon which they could depend. However, not everyone agreed with it.

Tiananmen Square

In 1989, students rose up in protest when they objected to some of the effects of Deng's reforms. Nepotism and corruption reigned, and students felt they didn't have equal opportunities to attain jobs. Colleges focused on teaching only social sciences, and there was little opportunity to learn about and participate in politics. That was left to the purvey of favored elites. There was no freedom of the press and speech, and there were no democratic institutions.

When Hu Yaobang, a man who was for the reform of the communist government, died, students were upset, believing that his heart attack had been triggered by the forced resignation of his position as general secretary. Small gatherings appeared in Tiananmen Square on April 15th, the day after Hu's death. Thousands appeared in the square by April 17th, and at the height of the protest, there were nearly a million demonstrators.

The government couldn't agree on what to do with the protestors, with some wanting to open up a dialogue and others wanting to get rid of the problem with brute force. On the other hand, the protestors' goals varied greatly, making the opening of a dialogue hard to do. Deng, afraid the protests would continue to get out of hand and threaten the power of the Communist Party, declared martial law on May 20th. Tanks were sent into the square to clear it, along with armed soldiers. By June 4th, the protests were over, with thousands of people, mainly students, dead. Protests broke out around China in response to this, with some being brutally suppressed, causing even more deaths.

It is impossible to nail down a precise figure for those who died in the Tiananmen Square protests. The official number China gave was 300, but modern estimates put the number closer to 2,500 and 3,000 deaths. The world called this a massacre, and many countries cut off their arms shipments to China and imposed other embargoes.

President Xi Jinping

Elected in 2013, Xi Jinping is China's current president. He recognized the effects of nepotism and worked on eliminating that. However, his position is an autocratic one, as he eliminated the term limits placed by Deng Xiaoping during his term. Early on in his administration, Xi worked on consolidating his power. When he became president, he established a policy called Xi Jinping Thought. This ideology is meant to guide the Communist Party of China into a new and brighter future. An interesting note of this set of beliefs, which is part of China's constitution, is that it places Xi Jinping as the third leader of the People's Republic of China after Mao Zedong and Deng Xiaoping, essentially erasing Xi's two predecessors, Hu Jintao and Jiang Zemin.

For many years, China has nationalized its industries, including agriculture. However, Xi feels that its long-standing practices have produced bloated industries owned by the state and have stunted creativity and variety.

In order to promote trade, China established the One Belt One Road program. It promotes the use of the old trade routes of the past, supports upgrading them, and supports the creation of a network for the transportation of goods and products. China's economy has been slowing over the past decade, and the One Belt One Road project promises to spur the development of infrastructure.

Xi appears to be more sensitive to preventing corruption in the government and has penalized scores of government officials. In his campaign for the presidency, he promised to crack down on the "tigers and flies," which refers to both high-ranking and low-ranking leaders. Since he has taken office, over 100,000 people have been charged with corruption.

Centralization of Power

Soon after taking office, Xi created a series of Central Leading Groups. These groups are like consulting groups for society but with more authority. Among them are leading groups for cultural protection, energy resources, science and technology, environmental protection, marketing, and the stimulation of biotechnical research.

The Seven Dangers

Xi has indicated that there are seven dangers associated with Western values:

1. Constitutional democracy with separation of powers and judicial independence
2. Universal values contrary to Maoist principles
3. The belief that individual rights are paramount to the collective rights of the state
4. Liberal economic values and globalization
5. "Historical nihilism," meaning criticism of past errors
6. Media independence
7. Questioning of the Chinese style of socialism

In addition, Xi believes in internet censorship. Wikipedia has been blocked, along with some features of Facebook and Google. Blogging isn't forbidden, but the Chinese are warned to avoid talking about politics, controversial topics, or those that are contrary to communist principles.

Human Rights

Currently, the United Nations Human Rights Committee, Human Rights in China, Human Rights Watch, Amnesty International, and two non-governmental agencies have indicated that the current ruler of China has denied basic human rights to the citizens, such as freedom of speech and freedom of religion. Authorities in the People's Republic of China have registered objections to those assertions, however.

In addition, Xi has put ethnic Uyghurs in reeducation camps for purposes of indoctrination. In 2020, President Donald Trump signed the Uyghur Human Rights Act, imposing sanctions on officials responsible for these internments.

Republic of China

According to the Treaty of Shimonoseki of 1895, the Cairo Conference of 1943, and the defeat of Japan in 1945, the Republic of China is a political entity that is separate from the People's Republic of China. The Republic of China operates from Taiwan. Ever since it was formalized as a political entity, its status is controversial. Some say it is against international law, as the Republic of China lost its seat in the United Nations in 1971.

As mentioned above, the government of what would be the Republic of China was moved by Chiang Kai-shek in 1949. Chiang planned on moving it back to mainland China at some point but was unable to do so due to the victory of the Communists, who formed the People's Republic of China. Nonetheless, fourteen UN members still recognize it, as they want to keep all diplomatic channels open. The political status of the Republic of China is ambiguous because of the lack of a declaration of independence that is formally recognized by the international community.

The People's Republic of China believes in the One-China policy, which means that there is only one China, and since both governments have "China" in their name, only one of the governments is legitimate. There has been a push in recent years to either create the Republic of Taiwan or unite both governments.

Conclusion

China was and still is a country filled with people from many ethnic backgrounds who all nurture the guiding principle of unification. Throughout its entire history, other countries have attempted to intrude, such as the nomadic tribes from the north in its early history, Mongolia in the 13th century, Japan in the 19th and 20th centuries. Many countries have meddled in Chinese affairs, including the Russians, the British, the Portuguese, the Americans, and the peoples from the steppe regions of Asia. Pirates raided its shores from the South Pacific, and smugglers infiltrated its cities. However, in the end, the Chinese people learned to rely on themselves, although it was a very bumpy road.

After all, they weathered through a series of dynasties for centuries. China is said to have been born around 2100 BCE with the Xia dynasty, and throughout the years, the Chinese government was subject to internecine conflicts, sabotage, murder, petty jealousies, and internal corruption. The common people of the vast area of China, which is nearly four million square miles, although the area of the nation changed throughout history, had to deal with the fallout, which at times led to their deaths.

Despite this, the Chinese are people who have always told their stories, and their culture is still permeated with traditions and legends from long ago. Their tale is the story of revolution, of reaching for something better with each uprising.

Although Western audiences might not agree with the path China has taken, as their current government goes against democratic ideals, it is hard for anyone to argue the beauty of the art and writing that China has produced. Millions of people around the world imitate the beauty of Chinese silk paintings, porcelain, and poetry. Millions of people eat rice, and millions of people stir fry, deep fry, and steam their food like the Chinese did thousands of years ago. We credit the Chinese with the discovery of fireworks and gunpowder. Their history has inspired the creation of many video games and unique tales told over and over. The history of China is one that impacts all of us, and it is one that will continue to influence us for years to come.

Part 2: History of Japan

A Captivating Guide to Japanese History, Including Events Such as the Genpei War, Mongol Invasions, Battle of Tsushima, and Atomic Bombings of Hiroshima and Nagasaki

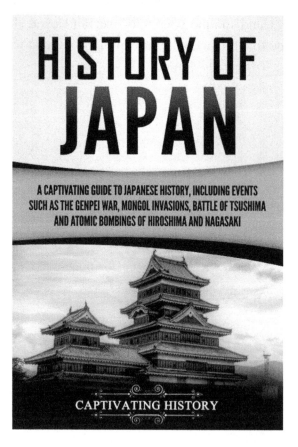

Introduction

They came from all walks of life, social classes, and religions, but they were united by their unquenchable thirst for freedom. Armed with unwavering courage, they came from southeast Asia, through China and over land bridges, into a new land. As with all primitive cultures, the first Japanese were divided into clans, clinging together for security, and built homesteads. They weren't alone. Already there was a collection of indigenous people, whose exact origin is unknown. Once the glacial waters receded, creating the Sea of Japan, the nascent country was alone and separated from China and the rest of Asia. In the first century, Japan developed independently from mainland China, but there were Chinese immigrations later on.

Japan is one of the most adaptable countries in the world. It is capable of very rapid change, even after crises that would halt the progress of other nations. When the shogunates collapsed in the 17th century, the feudal system disintegrated. Within time, though, railroads replaced ox carts. During World War I, a first-rate economy sprung up on deserted farmlands. During World War II, the modest islands of Japan burgeoned into an empire with one of the most powerful navies in the world. After the devastation of that world war, Japan emerged as one of the most modern countries in the world. The Japanese have survived frequent earthquakes and tsunamis and rebuilt their cities using enviable technologies.

The Japanese progressed throughout the eras because of the emperor, but they also progressed despite him. These are people who never let go of their sacred history, and their story is told and retold in art, film, literature, and even graphic novels across the entire world. Terms such as shoguns, samurai, haiku, anime, and manga are familiar to many in the Western world today. Westerners also learn flower arranging, martial arts, meditation, and enjoy a variety of visual and digital art forms because of the unique culture of Japan.

Chapter 1 – Children of the Sun

They trudged over to some of the 4,000 islands across Asian land bridges that floated on the seas toward the end of the glacial age. The archipelago that is Japan has only four sizable islands—Hokkaido in the north, Honshu (formerly called "Yamato") in the central region, and to the south, Shikoku and Kyushu. The northern wind is cold and dry, originating from the Asian mainland. Artifacts from the Paleolithic era some 20,000 years ago are similar to those found in Manchuria and Mongolia. The southern wind brings the typhoons, as they are conditioned by the Japan Current, or the Kuroshio, that comes from the tropics and the Oyashio Current, which is a cold current from Siberia that sweeps southward. Those that came to Japan found a hilly, mountainous country with five hundred volcanoes, though only about one hundred are currently active, the most famous of which is Mount Fuji, which dominates many Japanese paintings.

The Ainu people of Japan mostly settled in Hokkaido, as the rest of the archipelago was underwater during the glacial melting. Their appearance was proto-Caucasian or Mongoloid, and the males had full beards. Some of the Ainu people even had blue eyes. According to Japanese legend, "They lived in this place a hundred thousand years before the Children of the Sun came." The term "children of the sun" refers to the people of the Yayoi period in the third century BCE. That corresponds with the Chinese dynastic chronicle, the *History of the Wei Kingdom,* compiled in the year 300 CE. When Japan became more populous, the Ainu were discriminated against, as they were very different in their appearance and cultural practices. Today, there are about 25,000 of them left, but most are of mixed race due to intermarriages over the years.

The Jomon period spanned from around 14,000 to 1000 BCE. Some archeologists indicate that the Ainu people were the remnants of the Jomon civilization, though others indicate they preceded the Jomon period. It is possible that the Ainu originated from the northern steppes, while the Jomon came in from the South Pacific. The Jomon people were animists who worshiped nature, not out of fear but out of respect. That was because their survival depended upon the earth. They were shorter in stature and darker than the Ainu up north. The Jomon gathered nuts and roots, and they hunted and consumed shellfish. They lived in small settlements of round thatched homes sunken two feet into the ground. A fire crackled in the middle of their dwellings, and smoke billowed out a circular opening in the roofs. These people are known for "cord pottery," which was bulbous in form and impressed with cords that formed designs. Some clay pots were half-buried and were used for storage or cooking, while others used them for religious purposes.

The Yayoi period came next and is said to date from 1000 BCE to 300 CE. The people who came during that time most likely immigrated from China. They brought with them the knowledge of the irrigated rice paddy and lived in tight-knit units with distinctive leaders. While some homes were at ground level, most were elevated above the wet fields. They used bronze decorations and weapons, including spears, swords, mirrors, and bells. In central Honshu, huge bells were found, but they were without clappers, so they were most likely hit from the outside as part of a ceremony. Such bells weren't found south of there.

The Kofun period lasted from about 300 to 538 CE. These people were more aristocratic and more militant in nature. They had swords, helmets, and shields, as well as armor and horses. Some archeologists speculate that this wave of immigration came from Korea. The dead were treated with more sophistication than in earlier periods, where bodies were buried without coffins in the fetal position. The Kofun people interred their dead in huge earthenware jars and placed mounds above the graves. Later on, they dug stone tombs. Their leaders were called emperors, a term that was taken from China once they became acquainted with each other, which was retroactively applied to previous rulers. This position was hereditary, and the emperor was considered to be of divine origins. They used their powers of persuasion to unite the many clans under their purvey, and they also used their military might.

Society during this time was divided into hereditary clans or family groupings called *uji*. The *uji* of the more powerful clans were known as *omi* to distinguish themselves from the aristocrats who were more distantly related to royalty. Certain clans held a great deal of power in Japan, and it would be similar to the aristocratic families in Western cultures, who may not have been royalty but still wielded a lot of influence over the court and its decisions. In the future, the clans in Japan would have more power than even the emperor himself.

Asuka Japan

The Kofun period was followed by the Asuka period, which ran from 538 to 710 CE. The annals of old China called Japan the "land of Wa (or "Wei)." "Wa" is a derogatory word in Chinese for "dwarf," and the Chinese considered the people of Japan inferiors to themselves.

The *uji* were separated into occupational groups. For example, some groups were in charge of ritualistic ceremonies and priestly functions, while others were tasked with matters of the state. Labor forces composed the level below, consisting mostly of skilled craftsmen, fishermen, weavers, hunters, ceramic makers, and the like. The lowest groups were the commoners and slaves.

The commoners, as expected, were poor and uneducated and farmed the land for a living. However, monks traveled to China to proselytize and brought back rice paper to Japan. Young children weren't blessed with toys, so the art of origami was developed. A child learned how to make chairs, tables, people, birds, and the like. Then they played with those creations much like a child plays with their dolls in a dollhouse.

Most people grew their own rice and raised their own vegetables, along with some for their overlords, or the princes of the provinces and towns. Slaves represented only about five percent of the population.

In terms of marriage, all children were considered legitimate regardless of whether they were born by their father's wife or a concubine. Usually, marriages were monogamous.

Mythology

In Japan, the first gods were related, being sister and brother—Izanami and Izanagi. It was believed that they dipped their sacred spear into the waters and created the islands of Japan. Amaterasu was the sun goddess and Tsukuyomi was the moon god. A bronze mirror seen among the archeological artifacts signifies the sun goddess, and a round jewel stands for the moon god. Tsukuyomi was the enemy of the emperors,

who were said to have come into being in 660 BCE, but the date is very arbitrary as the creation myths underwent continual revisions. Japanese creation stories tend to explain natural events or occurrences in noted people, like the emperors.

The first emperor of Japan, according to legend, was named Jimmu Tenno. The seat of the imperial state was Yamato (Honshu). Around 270 CE, the people from Kyushu invaded and appointed Ojin as the emperor. He was renamed Hachiman, the Shinto god of war. This deification of emperors continued all the way until 1946.

Shintoism

The Shinto religion was the first religion in Japan. The members of that sect were animists and had an array of deities. Shintoism embraced many practices, including ancestor worship, fertility rites, and a reverence for nature. The spirit, called *kami*, resided in each person and even natural objects, such as a tree or a waterfall. It was like an essence that inhabited all living things. The Shinto religion had no founder, no sacred books, no saints, and no martyrs. Shinto shrines were simple, and they still exist all over Japan. A Shinto shrine is a structure with small ascending steps and a peaked roof. Inside there are symbolic objects like bronze mirrors or swords. There are bowls placed in front for washing, as washing is a way for one to be cleansed of impurities, including spiritual ones. Shintoism was and still is the most common religion in Japan. It did not conflict with other religions but rather blended with them.

Buddhism

Buddhism was officially introduced to Japan by Korea in 552 CE, although the origins of Buddhism go much further back. It is thought that Buddhism originated in India around the first millennium BCE and then traveled to Nepal. Buddhism was personified in Siddhartha Gautama, better known as the Buddha, meaning the "Enlightened One." Gautama wasn't a deity; he was human. Throughout his life, he brooded over the human condition and found that it was associated with suffering, which would give rise to desire. In order to reach a state of true happiness and peace, which is called Nirvana, it is necessary to rid oneself of earthly desires. One has to, therefore, follow an eightfold path consisting of right understanding, thought, speech, conduct, livelihood, effort, mindfulness, and concentration. It is a religion that emphasizes ethical conduct (*sila*), mental discipline (*samadhi*), and wisdom (*panna*). There are numerous Buddhist temples in Japan, but the temple of Horyu-ji is acknowledged as being the oldest wooden structure in the world. It is also one of the most beautiful temples in all of Japan. Today, it is a complex consisting of a monastery, library, lecture halls, refectory, and a five-story pagoda. Buddhism is the second-largest religion in Japan today.

The Japanese tradition of Buddhism is known as Mahayana Buddhism, and its adherents believe in the bodhisattvas, who are spiritual beings who have postponed their own state of eternal bliss in order to help humans along the path of salvation. At the end of time, they believe that a bodhisattva, named Miroku or Maitreya Buddha, will come to save humanity and bring it into a state of purity and paradise. This Buddha mirrors the Christ figure as taught in traditional Christianity.

The Soga vs. Nakatomi Clans

The *uji* in Yamato separated over the issue of adopting Buddhism or Shintoism. The Soga clan preferred to make the national religion Buddhism, while the Nakatomi clan preferred Shintoism. The debate started in 552 CE when the Japanese ally of Korea, Paekche, sent an image of Buddha to the imperial court. When an epidemic struck, Emperor Kinmei ordered the Buddhist images to be destroyed along with the Hoko-ji temple, also called the Asuka-dera temple.

In 585, another pestilence struck, and Emperor Yomei found out that some Korean priests had two images of the Buddha, and those were thrown into a moat. When the pestilence persisted, the emperor ordered the images to be restored, after which the plague then ceased. Korean priests and nuns arrived soon after, and Buddhism began to thrive. Empress Suiko, who reigned from592 to 628 CE and who was a devoted Buddhist, had a nephew, Prince Shotoku, who was a scholar and politician. Prince Shotoku was the son of Emperor Yomei, and he lived from 574 to 622 CE and wrote a commentary on Buddhism called *Śrīmālādevī Siṃhanāda*

Sūtra. A sutra is an aphorism or maxim based on a recognized truth. The term is also used in Muslim and Hindi teachings.

Confucianism

Confucius was a Chinese scholar who developed a practical code for right understanding, the second principle of the eightfold Buddhist path. Some people perceive of Confucianism as a religion, but it is more so a system of right thinking. It was from the studies of Confucius that Prince Shotoku created the first constitution of Japan in 604 CE. The Twelve Level Cap and Rank System of civil service was installed, and that was a major change for Japan. In this system, rank was based on merit and achievement instead of hereditary alone. This system inspired other cap and rank systems later on.

Relations with China

Prince Shotoku, who was an important politician during the reign of Empress Suiko, felt it was essential for Japan to establish good relations with China, so he sent fourteen missions to China. His faux-pas occurred prior to the first mission when he sent a letter to China. In this letter, he addressed China as the land of the setting sun while calling Japan the land of the rising sun. Chinese Emperor Yang of Sui took this as a deprecation, as he was accustomed to foreigners portraying themselves as subservient to China. However, the Buddhist monks and well-versed statesmen of Japan were able to overcome that drawback, so the two countries were able to share the knowledge and technology of the time. What's more, a paradigm had now been created for the maintenance of peace and understanding with China and other East Asian countries. Of course, throughout the years, hostilities occasionally arose that had found their footing in the politics and trade policies of other nations.

The Fujiwara (Nakatomi) Clan

One of the major clans in Yamato was the Fujiwara. The term "Fujiwara" was the revised name for the Nakatomi clan, and they particularly opposed the Soga clan because of its wholehearted support of Buddhism. In the year 645, they staged a coup, which then gave rise to a new imperial line. The first emperor of that line was Emperor Tenchi (or Tenji), and he seized power in 645 CE. Tenchi applied many reforms, called the Taika Reforms, to the hierarchical structure, and he reestablished heredity as the foundation of imperial lineage; however, merit was also honored and expected of the emperors and royal families. Buddhism was made the national religion, although Shintoism was tolerated. Imperial power was fortified, and the bureaucracy was sophisticated under Tenchi's rule.

The Taiko Reforms and the Taiho Code

In the year 645, the central government made many widespread changes that were based on Chinese systems. The central administration was subdivided hierarchically and abolished private land ownership. The land was nationalized in the name of the emperor and parceled out to able-bodied men. Taxes were charged on grain, rice, and other crops. The lower-levels who couldn't afford such taxes were given lots of land, which up to five families would till.

Under the Taiho Code of 702, the old tax-exempt status of the elite classes was eliminated, but the tax reform was very gradual in order to prevent rebellions. There were taxes on crops, crafts, and textiles. Military service was required, but more tax payments could be substituted for that. Despite the fact that the changes were gradually introduced, the taxes incurred by farmers were very burdensome and produced hardships. Taxes were usually paid in the form of rice or another crop and occasionally copper.

Nara Japan 710 - 794 CE

During this period, the capital was moved to Heijo, also known as Nara, located in south-central Honshu. As the Japanese learned more from the Chinese model of rule, they designed their new capital to resemble Chang'an (modern-day Xi'an), a city that ruled as a capital for many dynasties in China.

Politics in Nara were designed around court life. During this period, the emperors became progressively weaker. Interclan rivalries usually resulted in one clan or the other gaining dominance over the political scene, but the Fujiwara maintained most of the control, although it ebbed and flowed at times.

The nobility was absorbed with the maintenance of ritual ceremonies. They performed beautiful music and dance performances, some of which were imported from China. These performances were extremely elaborate, containing grandiose costumes and fanciful masks.

The Taiho Code of 702 was upgraded to the Yoro Code of 718. The Yoro Code was a revision of the basic code regarding governmental administration, but it also added on a penal code, a department of religion, and a declaration asserting the divinity of the emperor. Those departments managed the religious rites of the country and determined the penalties for crimes.

Local governments consisted of provinces, districts, and villages. Those who held higher offices were allotted larger tracts of land. As a result, there came to be landowners who owned huge plots of land. Many aristocrats and monastic orders were tax-exempt, and although they did reclaim unused land for agrarian purposes, it was labeled as state property and likewise wasn't taxable. These tax-exempt lands caused hardships for the rest of the population and placed even more of a burden upon the ordinary cultivators than it did during the Asuka era of the 6th century. This stimulated agrarian poverty and created a whole segment of vagrants, who were called *ronin*, although that term later evolved to mean something else.

During the period of Nara Japan, there was a series of natural disasters, in addition to a smallpox epidemic which, combined with the disasters, killed a quarter of the people. The emperor at the time, Shomu, blamed himself and felt that his lack of religiosity caused these calamities. He made up for it by constructing the Buddhist temple of Todai-ji. That shrine houses the world's largest bronze statue of the Buddha.

Chapter 2 – Warring Clans

Heian Japan 794 – 1185 CE

Again, the capital of Japan was moved—this time to Heian-kyo, or current-day Kyoto in south-central Japan. The main government of Heian times was obsessed with ritualistic observances. Costumes became even more elaborate, and there were even fastidious regulations regarding the colors of the robes the royal family was supposed to wear.

Throughout the Asuka period to the Heian era, tax-exempt property was increasing. The peasants could no longer shoulder the burden, so the administrators worked out a new system that resembled feudal times. Under this, the peasants were permitted to transfer their lands to a landowner in exchange for being placed under the owner's tax-free status, and with this, they also received protection against robbers and other criminals. This was done as a sheer matter of economic and physical survival.

From the 7th century to the 10th century, hostilities sometimes arose in the northern area of Japan, specifically in Mutsu Province where the Emishi tribes had settled. Ethnologists argue about their relationship with the indigenous people of Japan, known as the Ainu. Ethnologists have proposed that they are one and the same and date back to prehistoric times. However, those people had different racial characteristics than the tribes who came into Japan from Asia. For instance, Emishi males grew full beards and had skin tones that differed from that of the Japanese population. The Emishi were also among the most skilled horsemen in the Eastern world. Many of the Emishi people rejected the power of the emperor and resisted the pseudo-feudal structures that were emerging. After repeated conflicts, many of them fled northward and settled in Honshu, the largest island of Japan.

Other people on the islands of Japan followed the dictates of the emperor, who was the supreme head of the country. When he became older, he retired but maintained an impressive amount of power if he so wished. The emperors were often called "cloistered emperors," as they usually went to monasteries to retire.

As feudalism became more structured during the 12th century, the landowners and lords appointed warriors to guard their land tracts. The chiefs of these tracts were called "Commanders-in-Chief of the Expeditionary Force against the Barbarians," or *Sei-i Tashogun*. However, it is the shortened form of that name that has made its way into the collective conscious today—shogun. Their secondary warlords were known as *daimyo,* and they wielded power over the military function of the estates. Their warriors were called *bushi* but are commonly known as samurai to Westerners. *Ronin,* the term discussed above that means vagrants, also came to mean those samurai who had no lord. There were a plethora of reasons for why they had no master, for example, the death of his master, the loss of his master's favor, or the loss of his master's status. Some faithful samurai chose to commit ritual suicide, known as seppuku, as a sign of their ultimate loyalty to their master. Others wandered the country in search of new *daimyo* to follow. Usually, shogun and *daimyo* who hired *ronin* were considered to be less powerful.

While the general assumption was that the *ronin* were honorable men, this wasn't always the case. Because a samurai with no master had virtually no duties to perform and no other employable skills, he often became a criminal. Other ronin organized rebellions in order to carve out some territory of their own.

The population on these protected tracts were the peasants, who were divided into farmers, craftsmen, and merchants. Although the farmers were the poorest and dressed only in hemp, artisans or craftsmen were below them, and merchants were considered to be one of the two lowest classes. They were rated in a lower class because it was assumed they had a lower moral standing because of the greed, avarice, and dishonesty they often manifested. In time, merchants became very powerful because of their wealth.

The *burakumin*, on the other hand, was an outcast group at the bottom of the Japanese social order. These were people considered to be impure and were relegated to begging. The more enterprising among them became entertainers, such as musicians, dancers, or street performers. Others were hired as executioners or undertakers, as these occupations were considered to be tainted since they dealt with dead bodies. The *burakumin* actually lived in their own communities called *buraku*, and the status of being a part of this community was hereditary.

The Samurai

A samurai was a highly trained warrior who was a part of the military nobility. He lived according to Bushido, a set of precepts that dictated how to fight with honor, obedience, and dignity. The samurai was sworn to fealty to the shogun, the *daimyo*, and, ultimately, the emperor. A samurai warrior pledged his life to those authorities, and like the knights of the later medieval ages in Europe, they always strived to adhere to chivalrous conduct.

Eight virtues were specified in Bushido:

Righteousness – This meant justice and the support for their actions.

Courage – This was greater than a display of bravery. It was almost like blind obedience to a belief.

Courtesy – This wasn't superficial politeness. It meant a sense of genuine empathy and respect for the feelings of others.

Benevolence – This meant having mercy and sympathy for those who were in need.

Honesty – This meant forthrightness on all of their dealings.

Honor – A samurai was expected to do what was required but never to relish destruction or killing for its own sake.

Loyalty – Faithfulness to the *daimyo* and the shogun was expected, regardless of payment or reward.

Character – Every samurai was expected to manifest moral conduct in all aspects of his life, without exception.

The samurai learned Bushido from a very young age. Initially, they were taught the military arts from their fathers or other adult male members of the family. Then they were transferred to the mentorship of a fencing instructor and others with specific talents. They learned meditation and the martial arts, usually jujutsu. Each samurai warrior pledged his entire life to the defense of the leader of the province, even unto death. The ultimate purpose of such a strict code, of course, was the preservation of the shogun as the autocratic leader.

Clan Warfare

Basically, the Heian period was characterized by internecine warfare among the prominent clans—the Fujiwara, the Tairo, and the Minamoto. The Emishi people were always considered to be enemies by all of the clans. The best description of this period was the warrior era.

During Heian times, the central government progressively lost power because the nobles and the head of the clans seized more tax-free land, thus depriving the government of needed taxes to support the country. As the central government declined, so did the number of imperial military forces needed for defense. To compensate for that, each of the castles belonging to the clan leaders employed more and more samurai. There were three wars that were fought over control of the land and its people during that time—the Zenkunen War, or the Early Nine Years' War (1051 to 1063), the Gosannen War, or the Later Three-Year War (1083 to 1089), and the Genpei War (1180 to 1185).

The Zenkunen War took place in Mutsu Province on Honshu and was fought between the imperial army and the Abe clan, one of the oldest in all of Japan and a throwback to the former Yamato clan. This war was triggered by the Abe clan's harsh tax policy, as they ignored the wishes of the governor, the one who should have been overseeing the region and levying taxes. With the assistance of the Minamoto and Kiyowara clans, Emperor Nijo maintained control, and the Abe clan lost the war and was forced to alter its tax policy.

The Gosannen War was waged among three families from the Kiyohara clan: Masahira, Iehira, and Narihira. The governor of Mutsu Province attempted to negotiate with the families but to no avail. So, Governor Minamoto no Yoshiie was forced to use his own forces to stop the fighting, along with the help of the Fujiwara clan. As a result, there was severe devastation of the farmlands in Mutsu Province, followed by food shortages.

The Genpei War

During the late Heian era, clan rivalries were at its peak as each grappled for power, namely the Taira and Minamoto clans. In 1160, a war-mongering general by the name of Taira no Kiyomori of the Taira clan ruled Kyoto and had set up an entirely samurai-led government of his own making. Kiyomori wanted to expand his domains, so he placed his two-year-old grandson, Antoku, on the throne after the abdication of Emperor Takakura and moved the imperial throne from Kyoto to Fukuhara-kyo. In doing so, he was able to keep the royal family under his control. Kiyomori had a reputation for being a tyrant, and he was absolutely ruthless. Even many of the samurai under him had misgivings about him.

In the year 1180, the conflict came to a head. Former emperor Go-Shirakawa's son, Mochihito, felt as if he had been denied his rightful place on the throne and supported the other powerful clan of the time, the Minamoto clan. Minamoto no Yorimasa, a warrior and a poet, along with Mochihito, sent out for a call to arms, which Kiyomori did not appreciate. He called for the arrest of Mochihito, who took refuge in a Buddhist monastery. Many monks at those times were warrior monks; however, they did not prove to be strong enough to protect Yorimasa and Mochihito. So, they abandoned the monastery and took flight until they reached the River Uji. The bloody battle continued there, but the Minamoto forces were no match for the Taira, despite the fact that they had dismantled the wooden bridge over the river. Prince Mochihito initially was able to escape, but soon after, he was captured and killed. Minamoto no Yorimasa committed seppuku, ending the battle.

General Yoritomo of the Minamoto clan took over the leadership of the clan and persuaded more clans to ally themselves with him, the most influential being the Takeda clan. While Yoritomo and his men attacked from the front, the Takeda clan and others friendly to the Minamoto cause attacked from behind. This strategy worked, and the Minamoto clan finally managed to get the upper hand.

In September of 1180, the Battle of Ishibashiyama occurred. It was a surprise night attack against the Minamoto, who were joined by some of the disillusioned forces of the Taira forces, hoping to disrupt the enormous army of the Taira, which numbered close to 3,000. But their efforts failed, as the Minamoto only had around 300 men, and so, the overwhelming Taira army still won.

The fighting continued into the next year, but soon it would cease. In the spring of 1181, Taira no Kiyomori died, and around that same time, Japan was struck by famine. The Taira tried to attack a cousin of Yoritomo, Minamoto no Yoshinaka, but they were unsuccessful. This was the last course of action in the Genpei War for nearly two years.

At the Battle of Kurikara in June of 1183, the tide finally swung into the favor of the Minamoto clan. Minamoto no Yoshinaka and Minamoto no Yukiie cleverly set up their mountain forces in such a way that their numbers looked immense. Because the bulk of the Minamoto force appeared to be a desirable target, the Taira came raging up the mountain to attack. During the course of their ascent, two hidden divisions of the Minamoto army attacked the Taira army in the center and in the rear. The strategy was extremely successful, and it turned the war into the Minamoto clan's favor.

The Minamoto were having internecine disputes of their own that continued throughout this period. Minamoto no Yoshinaka, who was a strong commander at the Battle of Kurikara, was feuding with his cousins, Yoritomo and Yoshitsune, for control of the Minamoto clan. Yoshinaka and Yukiie conspired to set up a new imperial court in the north, away from the influence of the Taira clan, but before that could happen, Yukiie told their plans to Emperor Go-Shirakawa. As a result, the betrayed Yoshinaka took control of Kyoto. In the early years of 1184, Yoshinaka burned the Buddhist temple that the emperor was hiding in, taking him into custody. Yoshitsune soon arrived, along with his brother Noriyori and a considerable force, and at the River Uji, where an earlier battle had taken place, the cousins fought each other. Yoshinaka was defeated and killed.

While that was occurring, the Taira clan had gained custody of Kiyomori's infant grandson, Antoku, who still officially held the throne. He was accompanied by his grandmother, and they traveled with the Taira forces.

In 1185, on the southern coast of Honshu, the Minamoto tricked the Taira army into thinking the next engagement was going to be a land battle. The subterfuge was accomplished by having their scouts light many bonfires on the shore. However, the Minamoto were geared up toward a sea battle. As the Taira ships drew close to the shores of Honshu in the Straits of Shimonoseki, between the islands of Honshu and Kyushu, the Minamoto attacked them. Initially, the battle favored the Taira, but the tide changed, and the Minamoto ultimately ended up prevailing. Most of the Minamoto clan's success was due to a general named Taguchi defecting from the Taira side in the middle of the heavy action, as it was a vicious battle with a great deal of hand-to-hand combat on the decks of ships. The six-year-old Emperor Antoku and his grandmother perished, along with many of the Taira nobles. This battle, the Battle of Dan-no-ura, was a humiliating defeat for the Taira clan, and with this defeat, the Genpei War was all but won, paving the way for the establishment of the Kamakura shogunate in 1185.

The Emaki Scrolls

Japanese history was recorded on silk handscrolls called *emaki*, and they are held either horizontally or vertically. Some narrate the stories about the Zenkunen War or the Gosannen War, while others tell tales about notable figures. One of the most notable of the scrolls told the story about Sugawara no Michizane, a scholar who was engrossed with the studies of the Chinese classics. He was appointed to the governor of Sanuki Province, and during his time in this position, Michizane stepped in to help with the Ako Incident. This incident was between Emperor Uda, who reigned between the years of 887 to 897, and Fujiwara no Mototsune over Mototsune's role in the court after Emperor Uda gained the throne. Michizane assisted Emperor Uda in the affair, helping him regain power from the Fujiwara clan. Emperor Uda gave key positions in the court to those who were not from the Fujiwara clan, including Michizane. However, when Uda abdicated the throne, Michizane was surrounded by enemies from the Fujiwara. As a result, Fujiwara no Tokihira helped to demote Michizane, who died in exile. After his death, many disasters occurred in Japan, including famine and plague. The superstitious people then deified him and erected a Shinto shrine in his name called the Kitano Tenman-gu. The handscroll depicting Michizane's downfall is still in existence and is displayed at the Watanabe Museum in Tottori, Japan.

One of the most quoted poets of the Heian period was Ki no Tsurayuki. His poems were also recorded and illustrated on the *emaki*. His poems were semi-religious and reverent, and they were very popular in their day. They encapsulated facets of nature, romance, or a deeply emotional human experience. One such poem demonstrates the depth of the human experience:

> A dewdrop
>
> It is not, my heart, on a flower
>
> Fallen; yet
>
> With a breath of wind
>
> My concern grows deeper.

Women poets were equally respected and carried the same themes, such as this by Nakatsukasa: "Those cherry blossoms that I keep coming to see year after year, O mist do not rise now and hide them."

Kamakura Japan 1185 – 1333

The feudal system became more complex during the Kamakura period. Instead of merely the *daimyo*, there arose the constables or military governors who were called *shugo*, who served a judicial function, and the stewards of the land who were called *jito*. Emperors became less powerful during this period of time, as did their royal families. The shogun was essentially now the head of the central policy-making body, and a military-like structure permeated governmental bodies.

In 1192, the first shogun of the Kamakura period, Minamoto no Yoritomo, had his father-in-law, Hojo no Tokimasa from the Hojo clan, who had assisted in the Minamoto clan's win at the Battle of Dan-no-ura, as his advisor. Ironically enough, the Hojo clan was descended from the Taira, but they did not fight alongside their ancestors. Tokimasa's daughter, Masako, became the regent of their infant son, Yoriie, after Yoritomo died in 1199, which gave the Hojo clan great power.

The heart of this shogunate was in Kamakura, which is a picturesque seaside town outside of today's Tokyo. The actual capital of Japan at the time was Kyoto, however, and this was where the administrative functions were performed.

In 1266, Kublai Khan, the renowned leader of the Mongols, mandated that Japan become a vassal to their great empire. He sent emissaries to Japan with that command, but the Chinzei Bugyo, or the Defense Commissioner for the West, sent them away, and eventually, the Mongols sailed to Japan in order to start a war. The Japanese samurai won some decisive battles against the great khan, but a typhoon interfered with their conflict. The Mongols withdrew, but Kublai Khan swore he would return.

After the Mongolian withdrawal, the Kamakura military worked steadily and built an impressive sea wall surrounding Hakata Bay along present-day Fukuoka, on the island of Kyushu. In 1281, Kublai Khan did return. However, the great sea wall built by the Kamakura laborers confined the fighting to the narrow beach. The Battle of Koan, also known as the Second Battle of Hakata Bay, raged for 53 days, but a typhoon again interfered. Swollen streams flowed in from the sea, and thousands of Chinese and Mongolian sailors and soldiers and their mercenary Korean troops were sucked up by the drenched sand and sunk down into the depths of the sea. The khan never returned. This Kyushu port was very accessible to foreign invaders, but because of the sea wall, Japan was able to keep enemies at bay until 1945!

Arts and Religion

Although literature wasn't prominent during the Kamakura era, there were some artifacts and scrolls from that period. The scrolls were similar to the *emaki* of Heian Japan, but true likenesses of prominent individuals were adopted. Scrolls with those portraits were called *nise-e*. One such scroll, the "Hungry Ghosts," depicts the lessons of Buddhism about the levels of hell. These were moral sayings like, "The difference between passion and addiction is between a divine spark and a flame that incinerates," and "If the dreams I have on every blackberry-colored night were real, I would reveal my feelings to him."

Buddhism continued its dominance in the Kamakura age. Four branches of Buddhism emerged. The Pure Land sect indicated that fervent devotion to the Amida Buddha was sufficient enough to ensure salvation. The Jodo sect emphasized faith to bring about salvation, and the Nichiren sect stressed the chant "Hail to the Sutra of the Lotus of the Wonderful Law." The fourth sect, and one which is still very popular today, is Zen Buddhism. More effort is required of the followers of Zen Buddhism than the others, as they, for instance, emphasize the stages of disciplined concentration during meditation.

The fall of the Kamakura regime is characterized by the factor that accounts for the downfalls of many regimes—power struggles and factionalism among rival parties. The most common impetus for the domination of one regime over another is wealth. And as the elites and members of the royal families vie for larger portions of the wealth, societies can become corrupt and eventually are absorbed by their own indulgence. As the rise of the shoguns and the power of the *shugo* and the *jito* increased, imperial power decreased.

Chapter 3 – The Two Imperial Courts

Due to the turmoil incurred toward the end of the Kamakura period, resentment of the Hojo clan, which was the power behind the administration in Japan, rose.

In 1331, Emperor Go-Daigo conspired to overthrow the Kamakura shogunate, as it had made militarism so predominant in the country. He ended the practice of having cloistered emperors and clamored for control. Go-Daigo rallied some officials and members of the court to come to his support, and then he raised an army. This triggered the Genko War, which ran until 1333. Initially, Go-Daigo enjoyed some success, but the forces of the Kamakura shogunate came together, and Go-Daigo was forced to flee to a monastery at Kasagi. The Hojo clan themselves raided the temple, but Go-Daigo escaped. The Kakamura army under Ashikaga Takauji was then sent after him, but he changed loyalties and supported Go-Daigo. Kyoto was then established as the city that held the imperial power, and the Kamakura shogunate was dismantled.

Go-Daigo continued to be in control after this war and brought about what was known as the Kenmu Restoration. However, his ally, Ashikaga Takauji, became a turncoat and appointed himself shogun. He seized power in Kyoto and passed the imperial power to Kogon, a senior member of the imperial family. Go-Daigo himself was a junior member of that line and moved his court south to Yoshino in a mountainous area.

There were now two rival courts—Kogon in the north and Go-Daigo in the south.

Ashikaga Japan 1336 – 1573 CE

In 1392, the third Ashikaga shogun, Yoshimitsu, invited Go-Daigo back, promising to share power with him. However, Yoshimitsu never fulfilled his promise, and this period, the Ashikaga period, was characterized by political turbulence. Gradually, the factions that supported Go-Daigo faded away. The fact that the various factions traded control and power prolonged the lack of central leadership and stunted progress. The shogunate was the primary root of power in Japan, and the country was virtually a checkerboard of shogun power bases. Because of this, some historians have called this period the dark ages of Japan.

Greedy *daimyos* warred with each other and carved out larger and larger chunks of *shoen*, which were lands that were tax-free. In accumulating more of these lands, it only continued to undermine the emperor's power and contributed to the growth of the clans. In 1390, the Yamana clan owned as many as eleven provinces only to be reduced to ruling only two provinces after repeated conflicts with other clans. Such strife caused the country to resemble a piecemeal pattern of individual *daimyos*. The samurai and the people generally ignored the imperial court and followed the commands of their individual *daimyos*, leading the central power in the country to be decentralized.

Because of burdensome taxes and the dishonesty of money-lenders, the peasants revolted in 1428. This rebellion, called the Shocho uprising, had as its primary aim debt cancellation. The Ashikaga shogunate did not issue the debt cancellation, but due to the heavy looting, the peasants still achieved their goal since the proofs of their debts had been destroyed. In 1441, a peasants' rebellion, called the Kakitsu uprising, was also successful and contributed to the weakening of the Ashikaga regime. Again, its goal was debt cancellation.

Revolts weren't just reserved for the underprivileged class. Buddhist monasteries had structures akin to feudal divisions and even employed their own samurai warriors. During the 14th and 15th centuries, monks united with the peasants against the overwhelming power of the *daimyos* and shoguns. The Buddhist monks formed small leagues composed of themselves and oppressed peasants, called the *Ikko-ikki*, with *ikko* meaning single-minded. These *Ikko-ikki* groups were a frequent source of violent uprisings. The *Ikko-ikki* groups usually started out as mobs but became more sophisticated in time, wearing armor and toting weapons. They opposed samurai rule, as the shoguns and their warrior troops were responsible for most of the taxes.

The Onin War

The Onin War erupted in 1467 over the succession of the next shogun. In 1464, Ashikaga Yoshimasa, the shogun at the time, realized he had no one to succeed him as he had no heir. He convinced his brother, Ashikaga Yoshimi, to abandon the life of a monk and become his heir instead. However, Yoshimasa gave birth to a son the very next year, throwing the line of succession into question. Yoshimasa's wife, Hino Tomiko, did not want to relinquish the title of shogun to someone other than her son, and she had the backing of powerful samurai clans, namely the clan of Yamana Sozen. Yoshimi, on the other hand, had the support of a powerful clan, the Hosokawa clan.

In 1467, the war had become quite serious, as the Eastern Army of Hosokawa began to face off against the Western Army of Yamana. These armies were evenly matched, with both having about 80,000 men each. Several battles occurred, and even when

Hosokawa and Yamana died in 1473, the fighting continued. While the Hosokawa clan won and was able to place Yoshimasa's son as the next shogun, there wasn't much of Kyoto left to rule. As a result of the Onin War, a huge portion of Kyoto was destroyed. After that, looting occurred until the city was nearly in ruins. With the exception of the most powerful of the *daimyos*, poverty arose even in the imperial family. In fact, Emperor Go-Nara (ruled 1526 to 1557) was forced to sell his own calligraphy in the streets of Kyoto!

Commerce and Mercantilism

While political upheavals cropped up in various provinces in Japan, the lower classes had freedoms they had never before experienced. Small and large urban centers sprung up, and trade was initiated in this isolated country. There was international trade with China and Korea. The Ming dynasty in China opened relations with Japan after the Mongols were defeated, and as a result of this mercantile expansion, Japan imported silk, books, art, and porcelain products. They exported lumber, pearls, gold, sulfur, painted folded fans, and swords.

Art and Culture

While the samurai and shoguns were engaged in warfare, the people sought some kind of relief, and they found it in the theaters and the arts.

Noh, meaning skill or talent, refers to a specific art form that began in the 14th century and incorporates masks and costumes in a dance-based performance. The actors usually wear wigs and face masks, or they paint their faces white. Themes for these performances include religious and historical events, supernatural worlds, or some mix of both. The popularity of the *noh* theater faded during the Heian period, but it was revived during the Ashikaga period. In fact, *noh* theaters still exist today.

Another important aspect of Japanese culture at this time was Zen culture, which gave impetus to an expansion of the arts. These were often tangible arts like miniature landscape gardening, Zen gardens that stressed simplicity and minimalism, the cultivation of bonsai dwarf trees, flower arranging, and tea ceremonies.

Oda Nobunaga: A Tale of the Honorable and Dishonorable

Oda Nobunaga (1534–1582) was one of the most powerful *daimyos* during this warring period of Japan. He was single-minded, ambitious, and ruthless. He once said, "If the cuckoo does not sing, I will kill it!"

Despite his cruelty, Nobunaga was the right man to reunite Japan, which had become a country of mini-kingdoms. He was determined to rid the country of the Takeda, the Saito, Mori, Uesugi, Asakura, Asai, and Hojo clans. The Hojo clan was a holdover from Kamakura Japan, and the others were clans that built up strength throughout the years. Nobunaga wasn't a paragon of Bushido virtue. When he was in the process of conquering the castle of Takeda Katsuyori during the Battle of Nagashino in 1575, he forced Katsuyori out, which went against the Bushido code of courtesy and benevolence that should have been shown toward the head of a castle. Katsuyori then fled to the residence of Oyamada, his retainer, who was likewise among the dishonorable warriors of those treacherous times. When Oyamada refused Katsuyori entry, Katsuyori committed seppuku, thus demonstrating the Bushido principles of rectitude and loyalty. Similarly, Asakura Yoshikage of the Asakura clan was forced to commit seppuku when his cousin betrayed him after Nobunaga defeated his armies and tore apart his castle.

The Buddhists weren't simply monks absorbed in daily meditation. Their sprawling estates and defense forces were a viable threat to Nobunaga's power. In the year 1571, he and his troops entered the Enryakuji temple, destroyed thousands of buildings there, and slaughtered many of the monks.

In 1574, Nobunaga placed the great fortress of Nagashima under siege. This wasn't a shogunate fortress; it was one of the many fortifications built by the *Ikko-ikki*, that is, the Buddhist warrior/peasant alliances. Nobunaga's faithful samurai, Hashiba Hideyoshi, led the initial charges in the year 1576. He was supposed to be reinforced by Akechi Mitsuhide, another samurai who had allied himself with the *Ikko-ikki*. Hideyoshi was a samurai with an uncanny sense of battlefield strategy, and the Mori fortress, Ishiyama Hongan-ji, was taken over by Nobunaga with Hideyoshi's help. Eventually, Nobunaga was able to secure this fortress by completely cutting off the supplies for the *Ikko-ikki*, and then he set the whole building aflame. Akechi Mitsuhide never actually showed up to aid them as he had promised. Instead, he conspired against Nobunaga and wanted to eliminate him.

Hideyoshi was then dispatched to fight the Takeda clan at the Battle of Tedorigawa in 1577, successfully doing so. Nobunaga declared himself a minister and spent some time resting his weary warriors at Honno-ji, a temple in Kyoto.

In 1582, Mitsuhide attacked Nobunaga at the Honno-ji temple. He and his men separated Nobunaga from his men and cornered Nobunaga and his small group of men inside the temple. Seeing that he and his small unit were outnumbered by Mitsuhide's men, Nobunaga knew the end was near. He didn't want to be paraded in humiliation before jeering crowds, so he committed seppuku in one of the inner rooms.

Mitsuhide wasn't satisfied with the elimination of Nobunaga, however. Nobunaga's son and heir, Nobutada, was at the battle at the Ishiyama fortress when he heard about his father's death. Mitsuhide chased him and cornered Nobutada at Nijo Castle, but Nobutada committed seppuku, according to Bushido.

Mitsuhide then carried out a coup d-état over the powerful Oda clan. His treachery shocked the imperial court, who refused to back him.

Hashiba Hideyoshi, Nobunaga's samurai, rushed over to wreak revenge upon Mitsuhide and his men in the Battle of Yamazaki.

Instead of confronting him out in the open fields, Mitsuhide foolishly had his men climb Mount Tennozan. It was a dangerous climb, but he thought that the higher ground would give him the advantage. He was wrong. Hashiba Hideyoshi brought archbuses with him, which were devices that could shoot multiple arrows. Thus, he pommeled Mitsuhide's warriors, and they were forced to descend the mountain and move to an open plain to continue the battle.

When Hideyoshi began to conduct a full-frontal assault on Mitsuhide and his troops, the warriors scattered in panic, including Mitsuhide himself, who lived up to his bad reputation by deserting his own troops. He met his just fate when he fled toward the town of Ogurusu and was killed by bandits. Mitsuhide only ruled as shogun for thirteen days.

Toyotomi Hideyoshi (1537-1598)

For his courage, Hashiba Hideyoshi was given the clan name Toyotomi by the elite Fujiwara clan. He named his infant son, Tsurumatsu, as heir. Hideyoshi had a different approach than his *daimyo*, Nobunaga, and revised Nobunaga's famous cuckoo-saying with this: "If the cuckoo doesn't sing, I'll make it!"

The Osaka Castle was built in 1583 by Toyotomi Hideyoshi to celebrate his ascendancy. The site was built upon the grounds of the original *Ikko-ikki* temple of Ishiyama Hongan-ji. It covered 86 acres and had numerous decorated turrets and towers.

Like Nobunaga, Hideyoshi had Japanese reunification as his goal. In 1585, he seized the small island of Shikoku from the revolutionary leader, Chosokabe Motochika. He prized that island as it had the beautiful castle of Nishinomiya on it. Winning the battle at Nishinomiya was an easy victory as Hideyoshi had 113,000 troops against Motochika's 40,000.

One of Hideyoshi's samurai generals, who was also his nephew, was Hashiba Hidetsugu. Hidetsugu was Hideyoshi's heir-apparent after the death of his own son and his half-brother. Hideyoshi relied on Hidetsugu for his martial skills. However, when Hideyoshi's next son, Hideyori, was born, Hideyoshi considered Hidetsugu to be a potential threat to his rule as the imperial regent. So, in 1593, after Hidetsugu was accused of plotting against Hideyoshi and his family, Hideyoshi commanded Hidetsugu to commit seppuku. Obediently, Hidetsugu and some of his faithful samurai accompanied him to the top of Mount Koya, where they carried out Hideyoshi's orders. Hideyoshi was especially merciless, though, and ordered that Hidetsugu's entire family, including the children, be killed! Only two of his daughters were spared.

Hideyoshi saw threats everywhere, and his blind ambition for a dictatorial form of control made him very paranoid. He had at the Osaka Castle a master of the tea ceremony, Sen no Rikyu. Rikyu was also an accomplished poet, and he made many changes in the tea ceremony and influenced other cultural changes. Rikyu was very popular among the people, and Hideyoshi felt that this modest man was also a threat. In the year 1591, he commanded Rikyu to commit seppuku. As he was preparing the seppuku ritual, Rikyu held a tea ceremony and invited his closest friends to it. After they had finished their tea, he donated a tea bowl to each. He then took his own and smashed it against the wall, saying, "Never again shall this cup, polluted by misfortune, be used by man." He then recited a verse surrendering his soul to eternity through Buddha before killing himself.

Hideyoshi also felt threatened by the budding growth of Christianity and spoke out against it. Hideyoshi had been firmly rooted in the old traditions of feudal Japan, and he viewed any change in religion as another potential threat. As Japan was being opened up to commerce and the mercantilism of the Muromachi, or Ashikaga, period, some European missionaries came in from Spain and Portugal. Many of the mainstream Catholics fled underground during Hideyoshi's rule, but there were several noted individuals who were arrested by Hideyoshi's troops. In the year 1597, he executed 26 self-confessed Catholics by crucifying them at Nagasaki. They are called the "Twenty-Six Martyrs of Japan," and a memorial stone was placed where they shed their blood.

Another possible threat to Hideyoshi was Oda Nobunaga's younger son, Nobukatsu. One of the great samurais under Nobunaga was Tokugawa Ieyasu. Ieyasu, like Hideyoshi, had a firm belief in the reunification of Japan. Ieyasu actually outranked Hideyoshi and was his enemy, but this was only for a short period of time.

In 1584, at the Battle of Komaki and Nagakute, Tokugawa Ieyasu and Oda Nobukatsu waged war against Toyotomi Hideyoshi. The battle ended in a stalemate, but it debilitated the forces of Hideyoshi.

Ieyasu was a clever man and a patient one, and he didn't want Japan to disintegrate into a patchwork of small provinces once again. Therefore, he suggested that Nobukatsu and Hideyoshi resolve their differences, and Ieyasu submitted himself to Hideyoshi as a vassal.

Hideyoshi had an ill-advised dream of uniting China and Japan under his rule. He had engaged in two thwarted attempts to conquer Korea in order to forge the way to China, but he was forced to pull out of there due to illness, letting Ieyasu handle the troops, which he did in 1600 after Hideyoshi's death. To stabilize the future of Japan and avoid a succession crisis since his son was only five years old, Hideyoshi appointed a committee of five members of the most powerful clans, called the Council of the Five Elders, to make administrative decisions regarding the succession. At Fushimi Castle, located at the halfway point between Kyoto and Osaka, Toyotomi Hideyoshi died in 1598. Until they could determine who would be the best ruler to lead a unified Japan, they kept the death of Hideyoshi a secret until 1603. While Tokugawa

Ieyasu had been the de facto ruler of Japan since 1600, it wasn't made official until 1603.

The Battle of Sekigahara in 1600: A Humorous Affair

In 1600, Tokugawa Ieyasu had to engage in fighting with the Uesugi clan, whose lands were progressively shrinking. Craving more land, they engaged in rebellions, even after they had been put down multiple times. Ieyasu was residing at Osaka Palace at that time but had to lead his forces out in order to subdue the rebellious Uesugi clan. While he was away, however, the Mori clan along with their warriors, Kobayakawa Hideaki, a nephew of Hideyoshi, Mashita Nagamori, and Ankokuji Ekei, formed an alliance called the Western Army and seized Osaka Palace during Ieyasu's absence. So, Ieyasu formed an alliance with some of the more powerful *daimyos* and retainers like Fukushima Masanori, Ikoma Kazumasa, and Oda Nagamasu, along with his own faithful forces. This was called the Eastern Army.

The two sides were mismatched in terms of numbers. Ishida Mitsunari commanded the Western Army's 120,000 men, while Ieyasu only had 75,000 men. Therefore, this battle would require a great deal of strategy as the unity of Japan was at stake.

There were many misgivings among the fighters and a great reluctance on the part of some clans to fight at all. Some were confident in Ieyasu, while others weren't. Likewise, some of the members of the enemy army had mixed loyalties. As soon as the battle opened, the units under General Otani Yoshitsugu of Ieyasu's Eastern Army fought fiercely but were forced to retreat because they were so badly outnumbered. Mitsunari of the Western Army was a poor leader and had his troops badly formed. So, after Yoshitsugu retreated, it left a huge gap in Mitsunari's forces and essentially split the Western Army into two. That's when Ieyasu's units flew in to fill the gap.

Unfortunately, young Mitsunari had his left flank, mostly those from the Mori clan, placed in the mountains. One of those units, that of Mori Hidemoto, which was 15,000 strong, even sat down to dine! Thus, he didn't join in the battle.

Another Mori clan unit under Hosokawa Yusai deliberately marched so lethargically that they slowed all the other units following them. That gave the clans at the end of the marching column sufficient time to engage in minor skirmishes of their own, rather than staying together with the main Western force.

Kobayakawa Hideaki's unit had initially allied itself with the Western Army, but Hideaki was also wracked with indecision. So, he waited to see how the battle was going and switched sides when he saw Mitsunari's forces become confused and chaotic. As more units of Mitsunari's Western Army became separated, many more members defected to Ieyasu's side.

As could be predicted, Ieyasu and the Eastern Army won the battle.

Ishida Mitsunari, the general of the defeated Western Army, was beheaded in Kyoto. He makes appearances in Clavell's novel, *Shogun*, and the movie, *Sekigahara*, as well as in the video games *Samurai Warriors* and *Nobunaga's Ambition in Japan*.

Chapter 4 – Edo Japan: Part One-1603 to 1638

The Edo period, or the Tokugawa period, lasted from 1603 to 1868. It was during this time that the Tokugawa shogunate, which Ieyasu founded, ruled Japan. The shogunate was established in the new capital of Edo, which was later called Tokyo.

Ieyasu revised the cuckoo-quote of Nobunaga's and Hideyoshi's to be: "If the cuckoo does not sing, wait for it." Ieyasu was noted for his patience and timing. Like his predecessors before him, he wanted a united Japan; however, he always waited for the opportune time to attend to geopolitical matters. Hideyoshi and Nobunaga both entertained the goal of reuniting Japan and China. Ieyasu, instead, looked after the country and the happiness of its people before considering expansionist policies. He, therefore, postponed the employment of a more aggressive campaign to gain lands, which helped to contribute to the longevity of the Tokugawa era.

Ieyasu looked back at the Muromachi era, during which he had lived, and saw it as a vicious, warring time. It was a time when resentments, bitter rivalries, losses, and sorrows had been visited not only upon the military but also the people. He wanted to reunite Japan and focused his efforts on making that happen by the introduction of diversions and opportunities for cultural and literary advancements.

Even after the Battle of Sekigahara, Ieyasu felt that the private lands of the *daimyos* on both sides shouldn't be confiscated. That would only serve to reignite hostilities and trigger vengeance. So, instead, he divided Japan into domains run by the *daimyos*. Of course, the losing clans moved down a rung on the social hierarchy, and not every clan received what they wanted, but no one went penniless.

Ieyasu also felt that this was a time where arts and culture should be emphasized. He wanted his people to enjoy themselves once again without fear of military raids.

The Edo Pleasure Centers

In Edo, Ieyasu set up what came to be called the "Floating World," named due to the pleasure-seeking lifestyle of Yoshiwara, the red-light district of Edo. Geisha were very popular at this time, although to clear up the common Western misconception, geisha are not prostitutes. While some prostitutes (especially *oiran*, whose attire is similar to that of a geisha) might refer to themselves as a geisha, geisha entertain through dance, art, and singing, depending on more than just sex to entertain male visitors. Chaste teenage girls who danced for pay, called *odoriko*, were also present at this time, but sexual relations weren't permitted with them. Licensed prostitution was permitted, as it was in all of Japan, and homosexuality was also permitted.

Kabuki Performances

Kabuki was a form of theater and dance, somewhat more elaborate that the *noh* style. It was created by Izumo no Okuni, who was a very attractive woman. The actors—who were all female at the beginning—painted their faces white and put on musicals for the most part. Costumes were highly decorated and carefully constructed. Their headdresses were huge, and the players wore many kimonos and capes. Fans were always used and could convey a certain emotion. However, the color blue wasn't used, as it was considered to be negative. Stagehands wore black, so black worn by a performer meant that he was to be regarded as invisible. These performances were very popular in the red-light district in Edo, and women's kabuki was even banned at one point for being too erotic.

As time went on, men began to participate in kabuki. First, adolescent boys performed, but since they were deemed to be suitable for prostitution and often turned toward it, the shogunate banned this form of kabuki as well. So, by the mid-1600s, male kabuki became popular, with men playing both the female and male parts. Kabuki continued to thrive for many years and is still performed today.

Bunraku Puppet Theater

Although this performance uses puppets, *Bunraku* wasn't created for children. *Bunraku* tells a story with a theme that can really only be understood by adults. The puppets are called *ningyo* and have white faces. Chanting or music, either by itself or a combination of the two, is played in the background during these performances and is accompanied by the strumming of a *shamisen*, which is a three-stringed instrument. *Bunraku* is still performed today, and while performances dropped after World War II, it seems as if *Bunraku* has a long history still ahead of it, as more people are becoming interested in preserving this art.

Preservation of the Feudal Structure

The societal structure of Japan became rigid early on in the Tokugawa era, as the country failed to open up relations with other neighboring countries like Korea and China. The internal clan warfare had lessened, so the samurai had virtually little to do except enjoy the pleasure centers and entertainment. As a result, many became impoverished. In order to survive, many samurai slid into the entrepreneurial sector. Those samurai and *daimyos* who couldn't, however, fell into deeper and deeper debt.

The population also increased significantly around the main cities, like Kyoto and Osaka. Merchants took full advantage of that and often overcharged for their goods, thereby increasing the anxiety of the lower classes. Little was left for luxury and even essential items.

To resolve the problems created by the population surge and the money shortage, Ieyasu initiated agrarian projects, like irrigation and fertilization, and increased the amount of farmland available. Cash crops outpaced other crops, and tobacco, grain, sugar cane, rice, cotton, sesame, and spices spurred production. That, in turn, stimulated manufacture related to the use of those plant goods, like rice wine, clothing, weaving, and cotton clothing.

Arrival of Anjin

Ieyasu attempted to keep Japan as isolated as possible, but that principle was broken clandestinely by some of the merchants who traded with pirates. That wasn't the only time this isolation was fractured, however. In 1600, an Englishman by the name of William Adams arrived at the town of Bungo (present-day Usuki). Adams worked for the Dutch East India Company, which was engaged in international trade. When Adams arrived, however, he was sick and feverish, but Adams' presence alarmed the merchants as they didn't want any competition from foreign merchants. So, in an effort to dispose of the problem, the Japanese merchants told Ieyasu that Adams was dishonest. Ieyasu disliked foreigners anyway, so he believed the merchants and threw Adams into prison along with his sickly crew, who were placed in a different cell.

Later on, Ieyasu took Adams out of prison and asked him about the nature of his arrival. Having some familiarity with Asian languages, Adams replied, saying, "We are a people that seek friendship with all nations, and to have trade in all countries, bringing such merchandise as our country did afford into strange lands in the way of traffic." Tokugawa Ieyasu asked a few more general questions but reserved judgment. Concerned about the welfare of his crew, Adams then asked if he could see them. Ieyasu obliged him, and Adams was relieved when he saw that his crew was well and being fairly treated.

After that visit, Adams was thrown back into prison, but later on, Ieyasu asked to meet with him again. During the interview, the shogun asked Adams to build him a ship, as he had seen the remnants of Adams' ship and felt like it might be useful to own one. Adams explained he wasn't a carpenter, but he would do the best he could. With the help of some Japanese craftsmen, Adams built him a fine ship, and Ieyasu was very pleased. The shogun then raised him to the level of a samurai, saying that Williams Adams was dead and that Miura Anjin was born. *Anjin* means pilot and is the nautical term meaning seamen who guide larger ships into ports. This meant that Adams was free to serve the shogunate and made Adams a widow, leaving him no reason to not continue staying in Japan.

In 1605, Ieyasu retired in favor of his son, Tokugawa Hidetada, although he still retained a lot of power in the shogunate. This gave him some time to learn from the Englishman, and they had many discussions. Anjin taught the shogun some basic geometry and mathematics—education he hadn't been exposed to because of Japan's isolationist policies. After that, Ieyasu approved of his son opening up relations with the Dutch East India Company, and later on, in 1613, they opened up the port of Hirado not only to the Dutch but the English and Portuguese as well.

Hidetada permitted more international trading centers to open up in Kyoto, Osaka, Nagasaki, and Edo. Thus, more foreigners came to the country and conducted a great deal of trade. Hidetada and the shoguns who followed him constructed waterways, and eventually highways, to allow for the transportation of goods. Also, more pleasure centers were set up in other major cities.

The integration of the Dutch, English, and Portuguese with the Japanese people was difficult. The foreigners were loud and occasionally rowdy. What's more, they couldn't manage chopsticks and ate with their fingers. The Japanese were horrified at their manners and called them "bar beerean," meaning "barbarians," saying, "They eat with their fingers instead of with chopsticks such as we use. They show their feelings without any self-control."

To maintain peaceful relations and keep the prosperous trade continuing, Hidetada didn't permit the foreign merchants to mingle with the general population in the country, restricting them to the area around Hirado. However, the Portuguese also brought missionaries with them, who had already infiltrated other parts of the country. They did convert some of the Japanese, but they were not a problem to Hidetada until one of his *daimyos*, Arima Harunobu, a Christian convert, became involved in a conspiracy.

Christian Expulsion Edict

After he had lost some lands in the Battle of Sekigahara in 1600, Harunobu bribed an advisor to Ieyasu (who might not have the shogun when these intrigues was taking place but who held much power in the shogunate) to wield influence with the shogunate so he could retrieve some of the fiefs he once owned in the Hinoe Domain. The conspiracy became more entangled when Harunobu schemed with another Christian convert by the name of Okamoto Daihachi to bring that about. When Daihachi didn't follow through, Harunobu tried to get a Jesuit priest to help. That also didn't work, so Harunobu informed Ieyasu about the scheme. Ieyasu became incensed that these Christians were interfering with land redistribution without his permission. In 1612, Ieyasu had Daihachi arrested for his part in the affair and condemned him to execution. When many Christians came to the execution, Ieyasu became furious. This meddling in shogunate affairs caused Ieyasu to forbid Christianity in the entire country. Harunobu was exiled and ordered to commit seppuku after the whole investigation came to light. However, Harunobu indicated that his religion forbade him from committing suicide, so he was beheaded instead.

Ieyasu was especially baffled by the Christians' attendance at executions at which Christian criminals died. In 1614, he once said, "If they see a condemned fellow, they run to him with joy, bow to him, and do him reverence. This they say is the essence of their belief. If this is not an evil law, what is it?"

In June 1616, Tokugawa Ieyasu died, but his son carried on the policies his father had promulgated. More Christian executions followed that one.

The Christian Executions

In 1622, some Catholic missionaries and teachers entered Japan illegally from the Philippines under a Japanese Catholic captain, Joachim. The Dutch traders informed the Japanese governor of Nagasaki, and the ship was captured. They broke out but were captured yet again. The seamen were beheaded, and three more, including Joachim, were burned alive.

The governor then seized 52 Anglican monks who had been imprisoned, along with 30 other prisoners. They were beheaded in the city, including three boys. Thirty converts from Nagasaki were also beheaded or burned at the stake. The Christian persecutions continued from the year 1622 to the year 1637.

Martial Arts

Retired and unemployed former samurai soon realized that the foreigners in their country and even other Japanese wanted to learn martial arts. Dojos, that is, martial arts schools, sprung up around city and town centers. They taught two forms—jujutsu, which uses a short weapon or no weapon at all, and a modified form call kyudo, which uses bows and arrows. Kano Jigoro was a leader in the promotion of the martial arts, not for purposes of war but to highlight the concept he described as making the "most efficient use of mental and physical energy." He eliminated the torturous techniques of eye-gouging and the use of fish hooks to injure an opponent and instead taught his students to learn the art of disrupting an opponent's balance in order to win a bout. Sumo wrestlers, who were probably *ronin* (samurai with no masters) as they needed to find a source of income, also rose in popularity at this time.

Woodblock Art

Ukiyo-e is a type of art created by woodblocks. The term essentially translates to the "pictures of the floating world," the name given to the pleasure palaces. The process called for a number of artisans—the artist who designed it, the craftsman who copied the picture onto wood and cut it, the printer who inked and pressed it onto rice paper or cloth, and the publisher who printed and distributed the work. These beautiful prints were used a great deal to decorate the walls of the Edo pleasure palaces and in the homes of the elite. Japanese writer Asai Ryoi wrote about this art in glowing terms when he described its spirit as "living only for the moment, savoring the moon, the snow, the cherry blossoms, and the maple leaves, singing songs, drinking sake, and diverting oneself just in floating, like a gourd carried along with the river current: this is what we call ukiyo."

Early versions were monochromatic, but later on, color was introduced. Flora, fauna, and landscapes were typical themes. Sometimes the blocks were just of well-executed Japanese writing characters, but they could also be much more elaborate, with the introduction of forms such as women, warriors, and nature. The artisans impressed the blocks on rice paper or cloth and created many prints, even of the same picture. Woodblocks were also used to imprint fine designs on Japanese folding fans.

Ukiyo-e helped to develop the West's perception of Japanese artwork. They were particularly fond of them, so shops opened up around the trading centers.

Haiku

The most famous poet of the 17th century was Matsuo Basho. The haiku, a form of poetry, came into being during this time and was the primary form used by Basho, who is considered to be a master of it. Traditional haiku is composed of seventeen syllables divided into three lines of five syllables, seven syllables, and five syllables. Later on, poets developed variant forms of haiku to accommodate other languages, but they don't stray too far away or at all from the original form. One of Basho's poems follows below.

Furu ike ya

kawazu tobikomu

mizu no oto

(In English:

Breaking the silence

Of an ancient pond,

A frog jumped into the water –

A deep resonance.)

The Shimabara Rebellion

Peace had reigned during most of the reign of the Tokugawa shogunate, but in 1637, an uprising occurred. It didn't originate with the peasants, as might be expected, but with a group of *ronin* against *daimyos* Matsukura Shigemasa's son, Matsukura Katsuie, of the Shimabara Domain and Terasawa Katataka of the Karatsu Domain. The Matsukuras built a magnificent palace for themselves, with more construction soon to follow. However, the people and the samurai didn't have the money to finance such undertakings due to famine and over taxation. The Catholic peasants from the Arima clan, dismantled under Hideyoshi's former reign, also joined the rebellion under the leadership of Amakusa Shiro to protest the ban on Christianity.

The rebel forces stationed themselves at Hara Castle in the Nagasaki region of southern Japan. After more discontented people joined in, their forces grew to about 40,000 men. The Tokugawa shogunate was alarmed, as their own armies were beginning to be outnumbered, and the rebellion looked like it might drag on for many months. Therefore, the shogunate under Tokugawa Iemitsu, the grandson of Ieyasu, sought the support of the Dutch traders. The Dutch were mostly Protestants, who opposed the Catholics, and they could also provide armaments, gunpowder, and cannons. With this, the shogunate forces possessed an overwhelming advantage.

The rebels were forced to retreat to their headquarters at Hara Castle in April of 1638. They erected fortifications and redoubts to prevent entry. The shogun's forces tore down the fortifications and bombarded the castle, surrounding it. When the rebels ran out of supplies, one of their leaders, Yamada Emosaku, betrayed that fact to the shogunate, and the castle was overrun. Amakusa Shiro was beheaded, and his head was displayed in the predominantly Catholic town of Nagasaki. The castle was then burned along with all the bodies of the dead. Today, many tourists travel to this site to view the ruins of this once impressive castle.

Because many of the Portuguese traders were Catholics and their arrival included Jesuit missionaries, Portugal was forbidden to trade with Japan and had to leave. A huge population loss also occurred in Shimabara due to this revolt, and immigrants from other areas of Japan were invited into the region in order to save the rice harvest.

As could be predicted, the ban against Christianity was tightened, and the remaining Christians were forced to publicly renounce their faith. Many of the Christians, however, sought refuge underground, becoming what was known as "hidden Christians."

Chapter 5 – Edo Period: Part Two-1638 to 1868

Isolationism to Internationalism

After the Shimabara Rebellion, the Tokugawa clan receded within itself and made Japan an isolated country. They were oversensitive to foreign influence, and most broke relations with their trade partners within the country itself. Gradually, the shogun Tokugawa Iemitsu increased Japan's isolationist policy by passing a series of edicts between the years 1633 and 1639 called *sakoku*. Foreigners were not permitted entry into the country, and the common Japanese people were not permitted to leave under penalty of death. In fact, the Japanese merchants who were living abroad most of the year suddenly found themselves spending their lives in another country. This policy lasted for over 220 years, only ending after 1853 when trade was opened up to America.

As these mandates were being passed, the foreign traders were leaving, with the exception of the Dutch and the Dutch East India Company. They were told to relocate their trading houses to Dejima, a manmade island in the port of Nagasaki. For all intents and purposes, though, they were imprisoned there.

The Genroku era started in late 1688 and ended toward the beginning of 1704. The emperor at this time was Higashiyama, and the shogun was Tokugawa Tsunayoshi. The Japanese minister, Matsudaira Sadanobu, instituted many reforms. Under this leadership, agricultural, urban, and population growth increased and expanded. That set the stage toward internationalism and societal progress. One of the vanguard companies in that is the famous Mitsui corporation. Mitsui started out as a humble little clothing shop in 1673 under the name Mitsikoshi but exploded into a textile firm and then an international lending group.

All of the social classes had grown weary of their self-imposed suffering under outdated isolationism. The peasants were still highly taxed and couldn't share in the greater wealth created by a proliferation of crops. Merchants could conduct their businesses and amass great wealth, but they lacked political power and couldn't contribute to decisions related to their own function in society, which was to trade with the world. The larger landowners split their lands into smaller holdings farmed by one family or clan, and in time, each of the smaller landowners became more powerful. The *daimyos* and shoguns again became wealthy from the lands they were awarded by virtue of their military accomplishments; however, they but lacked purpose as there were no more wars to be fought. The samurai and military men had little cash flow and enormous debts. They were the most stagnant of all the social castes but were not quiet about it.

Edo Fires

Many *daimyos* chose to maintain a residence in Edo, as well as one in his own province, which also meant that a large number of samurai were housed in Edo as well. Not only that, but merchants and artisans moved to Edo in droves, creating a large population boom. Because of that, more residences, most of which were shabby, needed to be built for the people performing in the theater, as well as dancers, geisha, and other performers. Houses were built close together (although the *daimyos* and samurai enjoyed a bit more space than the other classes), and the paper and wood building materials made the spreading of a possible fire even easier. It would not take much heat to ignite a vigorous fire.

Also, at this time, it did not help that fire regulations were nearly nonexistent. They did have a crude city fire extinguisher, but it wasn't large enough to stop the spreading of a large blaze. There were no trained firemen. Actually, most of the firemen were steeplejacks, men who would climb great heights to carry out repairs, and they would use the fire to show off their skills, spreading the flames in the process.

The winds in Edo were changeable due to the meteorological conditions in the country, as they could carry the fires far and wide. The passageways between the buildings only enhanced this problem, as they were narrow enough to create "wind tunnels" between the flimsily constructed buildings.

In 1657, there was the Great fire of Meireki that destroyed between sixty to seventy percent of Edo. Legend has it that a temple priest had started it by burning a cursed kimono! However, it is entirely possible that it started by accident or was the cause of arson. The problem of arson was so severe during the 17th century that arson was punishable by death. However, as the shogunate grew more unstable, arson only increased.

Earthquake and the Great Eruption of Mount Fuji

Geological events broke the Japanese cocoon of isolation wide open during the Edo era because of the fires in Edo, a huge earthquake in Osaka in November of 1707, and the eruption of Mount Fuji in December of the same year. The earthquake, known as the Hoei earthquake, was the strongest earthquake in Japanese history until 2011. The quake itself, as well as the tsunami that it triggered, caused more than 5,000 casualties and destroyed 29,000 houses.

Besides starting the tsunami, some believe the earthquake also triggered the eruption of Mount Fuji by disrupting the magma layer underneath the ground, causing compression of the area containing the liquid magma. As the magma flowed underground, it mingled with the other magma already under Mount Fuji. The two magmas had different consistencies, thereby creating a more intense eruption called a Plinian eruption, which is named after Pliny the Younger, who described it in a letter after the eruption of Mount Vesuvius in 79 CE. Magma continued to collect under Mount Fuji, building up pressure before the pyroclastic expulsions caused huge rocks to spew high into the air, while the towns and buildings below were covered with deep ash. The air was full of this black smoke, making it so that even the sun could not be seen, and people had to evacuate.

There were a number of smaller intermittent quakes at first on the southeastern slope of Mount Fuji before the pyroclastic blast happened. Thousands of people and their homes were destroyed. In the end, the whole southwestern side of Mount Fuji was gone, leaving the Hoei crater in its place.

Survival Overcomes Stagnation

Recovery from geological disasters can be viewed as challenging interruptions in the ordinary course of life, and the eruption of Mount Fuji served as a wake-up call. Japan was practically asleep due to its isolationism, but the psychological impact of this eruption drew the people's attention to the fact that change was needed. Adaptation to changing circumstances was essential to Japan's survival as a nation in the ever-evolving world.

The Japanese during the Genroku era of the Tokugawa shogunate signaled the beginning of the end of the vestiges of the old Tokugawa era. Modern Japan was emerging, regardless of any of the efforts to hold onto feudalism. The peasants had staged uprising after uprising. The samurai, who found themselves virtually unemployed, rose up and destroyed their adherence to their previous way of life, shaking off the shackles of the military subcultures. They were impoverished by the lack of wars and no longer wanted to wage them anyway. Instead, they moved into other areas like entrepreneurship, the teaching of martial arts, and mercantilism. Some even became bureaucrats who had some power within the government.

Even the contemplative Buddhists moved into the world of social change. During the Shimabara Rebellion in 1637, monks fought alongside peasants and *ronin*, and commoners fought alongside samurai and Buddhists.

The infrastructure was also in place for the coming of modern Japan—there were railways, roads, and huge expanding urban centers. Farms were irrigated, and crops were produced and shipped not only within the country but outside of it as well.

Japanese Copper Cracks Opens the Japanese Door to the World

During the Edo Period, the Chinese and Koreans discovered that Japanese copper was far superior to that of China. In the interest of a source of newfound wealth, the sequestered shogunate broke its long-standing tradition of isolationism. The export of copper from Japan to China and Korea resulted in an exchange of learning that infiltrated Japan. This learning not only helped them hone their copper trade but other skills as well. In addition, Chinese texts and literature reached Japan, and commerce began to thrive.

The beginning of a large company started out investing in this raw material. In 1615, a Buddhist monk named Sumitomo Masatomo opened a bookshop to spread the teachings of Buddhism but then invested in the mining of copper. Today, it is known as the Sumitomo Group, which is a large financial investment firm.

The Forty-Seven Ronin

Japan's bond to each clan during the feudal times grew more intense due to their isolation. The samurai were expected to be loyal to their *daimyo* until they died. In the year 1701, Kamei Korechika and Asano Naganori, both shogunate officials, were ordered to prepare a reception for Kira Yoshinaka, a powerful official in the shogunate of Tokugawa Tsunayoshi. The celebration was held in the sacred town of Edo, and gifts were arranged, but they were judged to be inadequate by Yoshinaka, who complained bitterly. Naganori withstood this dressing-down stoically, but Yoshinaka continued to harass and insult him. At one point, Naganori lost his temper, drew a sword, and cut into Yoshinaka's flesh. The wound was only minor, but Yoshinaka took extreme offense. It was against the code of honor to draw a sword in Edo, and Yoshinaka was unforgiving and demanded that Asano Naganori commit seppuku.

He did so, leaving his estates to be divided up among the other lords and leaving behind 47 unemployed samurai, who would become *ronin* after his death. The leader of the *ronin*, Oishi Yoshio, who was usually drunk, swore revenge upon Kira Yoshinaka for this merciless killing. Oishi persuaded his men to attack, and for two years, they carefully planned an attack on Yoshinaka's residence with the intention of killing him as well. They found Yoshinaka, who was hiding in an inner chamber, and they told him their intentions, that they came as true samurai to avenge the death of their master, and offered Yoshinaka the death of a true samurai: seppuku. However, Yoshinaka was too scared to talk, and Oishi commanded his men to pin him down before he cut off his head.

It was illegal to carry out such an act of vengeance in Edo, but they did so anyway to avenge their master, Naganori, which was totally acceptable according to the precepts of the samurai. The shogunate officials met on the issue and sentenced the *ronin* to death. However, to come to a compromise, the *ronin* were asked to commit seppuku rather than undergo a criminal execution. They did so with great ceremony, which symbolized their loyalty, persistence, sacrifice, and honor. This tale had been told and retold throughout the centuries in plays, movies, and books.

Kyoho Reforms 1736

While Confucian teachings permeated the Japanese mind and spirit, Confucianism stressed the unimportance of money. Of course, money is essential to propel an economy forward, and those Confucian ideals in practice were unrealistic in a growing country with an expanding population. Wisely, the governmental administers made reforms that allowed for the greater growth of the merchant guilds, as well as the lifting of sanctions on reading Chinese and foreign books that could be used to expand skills, medical techniques, and the sciences. Attention was paid to more efficient agricultural methods, including the opening of the Dojima Rice Exchange. This gave rise to a securities market as well. It was, however, vulnerable to conditions in the market, and prices sometimes fell. However, that encouraged workers to develop other skills and products.

Monetization was introduced, especially since the discovery of copper gave the people an unbiased means of exchange. During this time, a rule was implemented that stated that every *daimyo* had to maintain two residences—one in his home community and one in Edo. That practice was eliminated, as it required not only the *daimyos* to maintain two homes but also carried the expectation that he must travel in style to Edo with long festive parades of followers carrying all the accouterments of celebration.

The Horeki River Incident

In 1754, a system of dams was proposed by the central government for the areas that tended to flood precious farmlands. Initially, the supervision of the project was awarded to the *daimyo* of the Satsuma prefecture. Clan rivalries erupted over that decision but were suppressed. Those who disliked the Tokugawa shogun, who was Ieshige, sabotaged the project, too. In addition to that drawback, the rising costs of this project led to severe periods of food shortages. Because of Japan's isolation, which deprived them of the knowledge of skills related to flood control, the project wasn't that effective. However, it did indicate the great need to make some improvements. Those were actually done during the next era, known as the Meiji Restoration period.

The Kansei Reforms

The Kansei Reforms were basically programs that set the course of growth in the reverse direction. They were engineered by a stateman named Matsudaira Sadanobu, the chief counselor to the shogun, Tokugawa Ienari. His program advocated a return to stricter obedience to the principles of Confucianism. Foreign books were prohibited, and foreign merchants were severely restricted. Japanese merchants who generally traveled abroad were prohibited from doing so. In fact, some of them were abroad at the time, and when these reforms came into practice in 1787, they were stranded in those other countries until the end of the reforms in 1793.

Isolation Broken

Japan was seen as an opportune location to conduct trade by the rest of the world. The fact that they had deep-water ports alone was tempting to foreign traders. The few foreigners who had gained legal entry for diplomatic and other reasons provided fodder for other countries to initiate projects to open up the country. Even Chinese pirates that illegally traded with Japanese junks off the coasts carried tales of the wealth of raw materials and products that could not only boost the local economy of southeast Asia but also boost the development of Japan.

"Black Ships of Evil Mien"[1]

However, the policy of sakoku, which denied foreigners entry to the country and common Japanese to leave it, didn't end with this opening up of trade. Many attempts were made throughout the years, but the ending of the policy was thanks to Commodore Matthew Perry of the US Navy, who arrived in Yokosuka, located south of Edo, with four warships in June 1853. The initial reaction of the startled Japanese sword-toting samurai in crude wooden ships was fear. They called this never-before-seen armada as "black" and "evil," which led to the ships being called the Black Ships. With the arrival of the Black Ships, the Japanese suddenly realized they had no defenses for such a force. It was a rude awakening for the shogunate.

The United States had just settled in the state of California and wanted some way to curtail the total European monopoly of the Pacific Ocean. Opening up Japan to world trade would be the best way to do so. Perry was sent by US President Millard Fillmore to do just that, even being given the authorization to use gunboat diplomacy if needed.

When Perry arrived in Yokosuka, he ordered his ships to turn their guns toward the city, ignoring any demands to leave or sail to Nagasaki, the only port open to foreigners. Attempting to intimidate them, Perry sent them a white flag and a letter which stated that if they chose to fight against his forces, the United States would destroy them.

At the time, Tokugawa Ieyoshi was sick, so there was no one in charge to make such a big decision. In July, a senior councilor decided to accept Perry's letter, who was allowed to land on shore a few days later. After giving them the letter, Perry told the delegates that he would be back the following year for their reply. The letter stated:

---

[1] *Mien*, when translated, means appearance.

Great and good friend: I send you this public letter by Commodore Matthew Perry visiting your imperial majesty's dominions. I have directed Commodore Perry to assure your imperial majesty that I entertain the kindest feelings towards your majesty's person and government, and that I have no other object in sending him to Japan but to propose to your imperial majesty the United States and Japan should live in friendship and have commercial intercourse with each other.

As a point of powerful persuasion, Perry's letter made mention of the fact that only China, Korea, and the Dutch were permitted to trade with Japan. As an incentive, the letter indicated that the United States had goods that were desirable in Japan, such as gold, precious stones, silver, and quicksilver. The letter also stated that the United States would be interested in buying coal from the Japanese for their steamships, along with water and provisions.

The shogun and the top leaders of the Tokugawa shogunate had already decided to accept the American offer. However, members of the ruling clans argued about where to hold talks with the Americans, thus delaying the entire process of negotiating a treaty. Finally, Yokohama was the site chosen, and a building was erected to handle the affair.

The Treaty of Kanagawa

Commodore Perry returned to Japan in February 1854, not even granting the Japanese the full year he had promised. This time, he arrived with a large fleet of ten ships and 1,600 men. After some initial resistance, Perry was allowed to land at Kanagawa, near present-day Yokohama, on March 8th. Hayashi Akira was the Japanese representative of the imperial court who spoke with Perry. After about a month of negotiations, the treaty was signed on March 31st, 1854, with the understanding that more treaties would follow. The treaty stipulated that Japan would 1) permit American access to the ports of Shimoda and Hakodate, 2) the Japanese would assist any shipwrecked American sailors if necessary, 3) American ships would purchase provisions from Japan exclusively, 4) America would open up a consulate in Shimoda, and 5) another official treaty would be drawn up delineating further details.

After the Kanagawa Convention, the United States gifted Japan with a model steam locomotive, a telegraph device, agricultural apparatuses, whiskey, clocks, stoves, and books about the US. The Japanese gave the Americans bronze ornaments, furniture decorated with gold lacquer, porcelain items, Japanese goblets, and a seashell collection in honor of Commodore Perry.

Although the negotiations ended peacefully, and Emperor Komei ratified it the following year, the treaty was not actually valid. The shogun, who held the actual power in Japan, did not sign the treaty nor did his representatives. However, that was a point that never really came up since more treaties were signed with the Americans and other foreigners.

The Harris Treaty

In 1858, Townsend Harris, an American diplomat, met with Japanese officials to negotiate a revised treaty called the Treaty of Amity and Commerce, also known as the Harris Treaty. This treaty opened up more ports to America in addition to Shimoda and Hakodate—Nagasaki, Kanagawa, Niigata, and Hyogo. The Americans were permitted religious freedom, duties on exports and imports of Japanese and American products were to be charged, Japan was granted a "most-favored-nation" status by America, and trade representatives were allowed to reside in the aforementioned port cities.

Within five years, Japan had signed treaties with other Western countries. However, these treaties were often unfair to the Japanese. For instance, the Ansei Treaties, which were signed with the United States, the United Kingdom, the Netherlands, France, and Russia, were seen by the Japanese as a way to force imperialism onto their country. Japan gave these nations control of the tariffs on the imports, and their diplomats were exempt from Japanese laws. Some Japanese chalked these unfair terms up to the use of gunboat diplomacy, which was the threat of war if a country did not agree with the more superior power.

End of the Tokugawa Shogunate

Horrendous disagreements arose between two domains, Satsuma and Choshu, when the Tokugawa shogunate failed to oppose the exposure of Japan to the outside world. Those two provinces delayed the signing of foreign treaties, and even some of the samurai were actively preaching a return to isolation in order to preserve their old system of individual shogunates and adherence to traditional practices. That only provoked the Japanese peasants and the tradesmen whose businesses could not expand without these treaties.

The more realistic samurai had come to the realization that it would be impossible for Japan to stop progress. When Sir Harry Parkes of the United Kingdom visited Japan in 1865 to negotiate a treaty, he deliberately avoided approaching the emperor's court and went directly to the country's judicial seat in Kyoto. When the counselors of the *daimyo* who held control of the ultra-conservative provinces of Satsuma and Choshu went to England, however, they reversed their position on isolationism. They realized that the traditional approach of the Tokugawa shogunate was ineffective in the 19th-century world.

In 1866, Tokugawa Iemochi died. He had wanted a return to tradition but was unable to make that happen, which shows that the shogunate was greatly weakened by this point. His successor was Tokugawa Yoshinobu, and many of the older traditional samurai expected him to follow their instructions and reinstate the isolationist policies of the past.

Yoshinobu actually seemed like he was headed the right way; he built up the shogunate, strengthening the army, navy, and government. But the Satsuma and Choshu Provinces, along with the province of Tosa, feared his growing power. It was clear that people were ready for a change, and even the emperor began issuing orders that the shogunate would have been responsible for in earlier years. For instance, Emperor Komei's "Order to Expel Barbarians" in 1863 was actually followed through, which even prompted attacks on the shogunate.

Although the shogunate might have seemed to be on the right path toward being the dominant power once again, the conditions in Japan just were not right for that to happen. The alliance of the three provinces wanted the shogun to be killed (although, to be fair, the Tosa Province just wanted him to resign). Yoshinobu actually did resign before any major trouble happened in 1867, leaving the power of the shogunate in the hands of the emperor.

Chapter 6 – The Meiji Restoration

The Meiji period, which lasted from 1868 to 1912, was a turning point in Japan. It was both politically and socially traumatic. After the conservatives from the Satsuma and Choshu Provinces had returned from their visit to England in 1866, a radical change had occurred. Reformers arose from within the Satsuma and Choshu areas, and their military advisors recommended that Emperor Komei and his son, Prince Mutsuhito, challenge the Tokugawa shogunate and restore prestige to the imperial line. After Komei's death, Prince Mutsuhito was renamed Emperor Meiji, and Edo was renamed "Tokyo."

A need to reform Japan's antiquated economic and administrative top-down structure was critical, and rapid political and social changes started to take place. Fukuzawa Yukichi, an accomplished scholar, visited Europe and founded Keio University, located in Tokyo.

Japan was a country that respected its heritage but didn't object to some extraneous modifications in areas that wouldn't revolutionize the country in all its facets, and in the 1870s, a more pragmatic approach prevailed. Confucianism supported the fact that the elites in society should be involved with the administrative functions and that the country should be run by senior bureaucrats who were more familiar with how the state should function.

Confucius also stated that mercantilism was a "dirty" but necessary profession, so those who worked in commerce were considered to be people who were not as bright as those who chose other professions. To rectify this, the finance minister, Matsukata Masayoshi, established some privatization of national industries. As it was, some were unprofitable, but private entrepreneurs could convert those organizations into useful entities.

Under these ideals, a new progressive government was formed. As part of the reforms, the Charter Oath was passed. It was designed to cushion the blow of sudden traumatic changes by incorporating more democratic ideals. The Charter Oath consisted of the creation of national assemblies, the involvement of all social classes in Japanese affairs, the search for international knowledge rather than just Japanese history, and the ceasing of "evil customs." "Evil customs" referred to the required customs, such as a topknot and a long braid, to distinguish between a samurai and a peasant, respectively. They were called "evil" to inform even the ignorant that these practices were from the past and would cause derision toward those who kept up with these old customs. Accouterments of that type were reserved for costumes, ceremonies, and historical depictions.

End of the Feudal System

The feudal social system was abolished in 1871 with the surrender of the *daimyo* estates. No one was locked into living in a particular class for their entire life. Lands owned by the *daimyos* were "surrendered" to the emperor in the form of nationalization. No longer were the domains controlled by the former Tokugawa *daimyos* considered their personal property; the land was instead divided into prefectures and subdivisions. The former *daimyos* either continued to rule over the lands, who were now regarded as governors, or they were given generous pensions and retired. The military was no longer driven by the samurai, and mandated military service was required of all able-bodied males in their twenties.

The merchants fared the best during this change, despite the fact that they were once considered the lowest class. They were enabled to grow their businesses, and many were financially stable, having granted loans to the samurai and other influential members of society. The Sumitomo Group, the aforementioned copper mining company established during the Tokugawa era, was now able to take advantage of Western technologies and extract copper more inexpensively. Not only that, but it later adopted processes for deriving silver from copper ore. The Sumitomo Group was also involved in the import-export business and opened up a silk business. The new freedoms established during the Meiji period helped the company expand into banking, coal, warehousing, and financial investment. The Mitsui corporation, which also found its origins during the Tokugawa period, opened a large bank during this period. Today, it has about ten corporate subsidiaries.

One of the reasons for the term "Meiji Restoration" refers to the fact that the emperor was "restored" to a supreme position in the country rather than a shogun, like Tokugawa Ieyasu or Tokugawa Hidetada, holding the power. A constitutional form of government seemed to be compatible with the country, which had been accustomed to a central government with a solitary leader and a workable system where everyone had some degree of representation. There were, however, a number of limitations on what is today considered to be democratic freedoms. In terms of voting, only males 25 years old or older who paid at least 15 yen in taxes were allowed to vote. That limited the number of legal voters to only one percent of the population.

Japan had a functioning system of justice since the Heian period but updated it through the establishment of the Ministry of Justice in the Meiji period. Criminal justice encompassed the administration of trials and the imposition of penalties. There were five different courts: the Supreme Court, high courts, district courts, family courts, and summary (martial law) courts. The new administrative government was composed of the office of Civil Affairs to handle internal affairs, foreign affairs, the army, the navy, the imperial household, the Department of Justice, public work projects, and education.

There had also been little attention paid to the important role of the military during the prior era, and there was very little instituted by way of technological improvements. For instance, transportation during the isolated Tokugawa period was primitive. The antiquated use of ox carts, palanquins (a litter carried by people), or boats on the water were the traditional ways to get from one place to another. To catch up with the rest of the developed world, a railway line was laid between Tokyo and Yokohama, as well as between Osaka and Kyoto. In 1868, Thomas Blake Glover, a Scottish merchant, introduced "Iron Duke," a steam locomotive, to Nagasaki. This innovation was extremely useful in getting products to and from international destinations, and British financiers provided the funding for the project. In 1871, Edmund Morei, a British engineer, was instrumental in the construction of another railroad on the island of Honshu. Hermann Rumschottel, a German engineer, supervised the construction of a railway system in Kyushu. Two more lines were financed by the Japanese government and connected the major cities of Japan to each other and were serviced by the Nippon Railway Company.

Education in the Tokugawa shogunate was limited to the elite classes, with schools devoted to the martial arts for the samurai. With the heralding of the Meiji period, education was made compulsory, and a new system was founded based on the American and French systems. In 1890, Emperor Meiji passed the "Imperial Rescript on Education," which presented the basic precepts of education for the country. Initial recommendations promoted

Confucian ideals of conformity and obedience to imperial authority, but the more liberal leaders modified it to allow for greater democracy, personal responsibility, and societal morality. With the aid of advisors, the Meiji administration set up schools in Buddhist temples, as well as other places for non-Buddhists. The old feudal schools to train the samurai were converted by the former *daimyos*, who were now functioning as governors, and became middle schools. During the Tokugawa period, there was an imperial school run by the shogunate staff, but this was transformed into what would become the University of Tokyo.

Reformation of the military was greatly enhanced by the recommendations of former samurai as well as civic leaders. Three years of military service was compulsory, and the Meiji adopted a Prussian model for its structure and even adopted modern weaponry. After some resistance, the samurai were coaxed to transfer loyalties they once felt for their shoguns to the emperor and the feudal landlords. A central office, the Imperial Japanese Army General Staff Office, oversaw the newly formed army. Shipbuilders were recruited, some of whom were foreign, and Japan worked diligently at building up a navy.

Governmental Reorganization

After the Satsuma Rebellion of 1877, which was really more of a civil war and will be discussed in more detail at the beginning of the next chapter, the government felt that they had exerted their control over the population. Emphasis was then placed on reinforcing internal stability, which set the stage for the establishment of governmental bodies. Modernization of industry, which had, to some extent, already started, continued to flourish. Cartels were formed to control particular industries, and

politics were relegated to the leaders supported by a staff of administrators. Because the Satsuma, Choshu, and Tosa people were the first to institute the break-up of the Tokugawa shogunate, they became the most powerful people in Japan, relegating many of the administrative posts to themselves. Since Japan was completely overhauling the government, early efforts tended to be directed toward eliminating the abuses of the Tokugawa era and designing a substitute framework for the social classes. Therefore, changes were disorganized and in the hands of a small number of people.

The "Freedom and People's Rights Movement" was a grassroots group, the purpose of which was to prevent the central government from becoming an association of a small group of people, mostly those from the Satsuma and Choshu Provinces. This movement was an effort to gain a voice in the formation of a new government.

New Trend: Political Parties

Various influential political leaders battled for supremacy in the formation of this new government. Of course, the entire country started out with no model for a coordinated approach. It was a collection of voices, each with its own agenda.

The Public Society for Patriots

To establish a direction, though, leaders arose, and political parties were formed. The first party was called the Public Society for Patriots, also called the "Liberal Party," and it was founded by Itagaki Taisuke, Chiba Takusaburo, Eto Shimpei, and Goto Shojiro.

Two of the political figures that initiated this party were Itagaki Taisuke and Chiba Takusaburo. One of the most important goals of this party was the writing of a constitution, with Chiba Takusaburo drafting one. Chiba wasn't the only person to advocate a constitution, though.

This party was formed in 1874 and can be considered to be the first political party of Japan. Although the party lost steam along the way, Taisuke revived it in the 1890s.

The Constitutional Progressive Party

In 1882, Okuma Shigenobu created a governmental structure similar to the British parliamentary system and also presented the

Meiji central body with a constitution. He called the central government a "Diet" with a legislative body that was bi-cameral, consisting of a House of Peers and a House of Representatives. The House of Peers were nobles or from the imperial family. The House of Representatives was restricted to males who paid a certain amount of taxes.

The Constitutional Imperial Rule Party

This party was conservative in nature and was founded in 1882 by Fukuchi Gen'ichiro. It supported a constitutional monarchy with a constitution, but they wanted to limit freedom of speech and the right to assemble freely.

The Rikken Seiyukai Party

This party, called "Seiyukai," for short, was a latecomer, being founded in 1900. Although Seiyukai ostensibly advertised itself as "liberal," it was relatively conservative. The origins of this party stemmed from businesses seeking to protect themselves by running pro-business candidates for offices in the Diet.

The Kenseito Party

In 1898, this party was formed under the leadership of Okuma Shigenobu, who had headed the short-lived Shimpoto party, and Itagaki Taisuke, who led the Constitutional Liberal Party (what was once the Public Society for Patriots). However, it almost disintegrated after Okuma failed to come through with his promises when he was made a prime minister. It managed to restructure itself, though, forming the New Kenseito with Itagaki at the head.

For the remainder of the Meiji Restoration, there was a proliferation of political parties and mergers and offshoots of them. For example, the Chugoku Progressive Party established in 1894, spun off the Liberal Democratic Party, the Constitutional Democratic Party, and the Democratic Party for the People, and it later formed the Shimpoto party.

The Meiji Constitution

Ito Hirobumi, a prominent Japanese politician, was commissioned by the central government to draw up a constitution in 1890. It was similar to Okuma Shigenobu's British-style model, and it also drew inspiration from the Prusso-German model. The Prusso-German facet of it utilized the concept of an absolute monarchy combined with a parliamentary structure. The emperor was the sovereign head of state. He had a Cabinet, a privy council, a judicial arm, a legislative group called the "Diet," and a military arm. It should be noted that while the emperor was seen as the head of state, the prime minister (who was voted in by the privy council) was seen as the head of government.

The emperor was considered to be of divine ancestry "unbroken for ages eternal." This was something that dated back to the beginning of Japanese history, and although the emperors lost power when the shogunates rose, they were still fairly well respected by the people. Now that they had gained the power back, the constitution wanted to ensure that there would be limitations to his power. They did this with two articles: he was limited to the provisions of the constitution, and he had to get the signature from one of his ministers of state before an edict or mandate could go into effect. However, the emperor had the right to dismiss a minister of state, so, in a sense, the emperor retained enormous control. This approach did have the effect of solidifying the power of the elites, though.

The emperor's people had some rights, including the freedom of movement, that is, the right to move one's residence; the freedom from unwarranted search or entry; the privacy of correspondence; the right to own personal property; and the freedom of speech.

First Elections

The Japanese had been acclimated to responding to the leadership of one person and his advisors. This trend continued into the Meiji period. Although there were many political parties, the Japanese tended to follow a particular leader and all but disregard the policies the parties advocated.

The first election was held in 1890. The most influential politicians of the time were Itagaki Taisuke and Okuma Shigenobu. Their parties won the majority of the votes in the House of Representatives, as expected. When the first prime minister, Yamagata Aritomo, recommended that the House support the central government in enacting meaningful change, it ignored him. Instead, they voted to cut the budget of the administration, starting with steep salary cuts. The central administration retaliated by resorting to intimidation, including threats from gangsters. Then Itagaki made a secret agreement with the prime minister and shocked his supporters by proposing a six percent, rather than a ten percent, cut in administrative salaries. When Yamagata left his position, it was filled by his protégé, and nothing new was proposed. Instead, more budgetary cuts were passed, including the expenses involved with forming a new navy and a shipbuilding program.

The central government was furious and dissolved the Diet. A special election was held in 1892, but it was violent, with four hundred people being killed. Stubbornly, the newly elected House didn't make any changes to the proposed budget. Because the budget was insufficient to build up the military, the emperor made a huge monetary contribution to military expenditures and recommended that other Cabinet members do the same. They did so, and the Diet then reinstated the original budgetary proposal and moved on from there to foreign affairs.

Economic Advances

Once the feudal collar had been loosened, the mercantile sector expanded more rapidly than the conservatives in government could control. The budgetary restraints after the first and second elections forced the central government to let the mercantile sector expand. Japanese conglomerates banded together, forming what is known as *zaibatsu*, in reaction to excessive governmental interference.

Although the term didn't become common until after World War I, their power started in the Meiji period, and they controlled significant chunks of the economy until the end of World War II.

Once the government realized that they could utilize these companies to assume duties in procuring military equipment and building ships for the expanding Japanese navy, they created agreements so the companies could do so.

The Meiji era had followed the model set down centuries ago, where a large number of people and entities were controlled by the few. For example, the Satsuma and Choshu prefectures had huge control over the entire company, much like the shogunates, who virtually ran Japan with a handful of powerful leaders.

Chapter 7 – Foreign Relations

Ganghwa Incident

Japan wanted to open up relations with Korea, so they sent a letter to the king in 1868; however, they used the incorrect Chinese characters to talk about the Japanese emperor. At the time, only the Chinese emperor was allowed to use those symbols, and Japan using them made it seem like they were claiming their emperor was equal to China's. The Chinese suggested the Koreans accept the letter regardless, knowing the power Japan now held, but the old school Koreans refused to do so, and tensions grew.

In September 1875, the Meiji administration sent over the *Un'yo*, a gunboat, to Korea. The crew stopped on Ganghwa Island, asking for water and provisions. Suddenly, the Korean gun batteries opened fire on them, and Japan responded with volleys of loud gunfire on their fort. The Japanese soldiers landed, and a skirmish broke out. Because the Korean weaponry was outdated, the Japanese were able to kill 35 of them. Once the causes behind the incident were straightened out, the Joseon dynasty in Korea quickly drew up a proposed treaty, as they could see the superiority of the Japanese equipment and its forces. The Treaty of Ganghwa was signed in late February 1876, and it contained an apology, just as the

Japanese had requested. The treaty opened up Korea to Japanese trade.

The Satsuma Rebellion

The most traumatic result of the abolition of the feudal system was the automatic loss of jobs for the samurai. Suddenly, they were robbed of a lifestyle they had had for the majority of their lives, and the short-sighted new government did a poor job of creating new employment opportunities for them.

In 1876, an activist named Saigo Takamori, a former samurai, concocted a scheme to trigger a war with Korea, thus creating a need for Japan to keep its samurai. Saigo was so committed to this cause that he decided to scapegoat himself by getting the Koreans to kill him. He did this by resurrecting an argument over a protocol faux-pas that occurred during the Ganghwa Incident. However, the imperial government discovered the conspiracy and prevented it from happening.

After that, Saigo built paramilitary academies full of highly motivated students. The Meiji government was concerned about Saigo's popularity and his following, so they had weapons removed from a local arsenal to prevent a raid. The students retaliated by removing weapons from a different arsenal, and sporadic skirmishes resulted. Saigo was astonished by the fervor of his following, and encouraged by this fact, he led a rebellion against the central government.

In 1877, his forces set siege upon Kumamoto Castle in Japan. When no significant headway was made by the rebels, more ex-samurai joined the ranks, and the Saigo supporters grew to be around 25,000 men. Under the leadership of Lieutenant General Tani Tateki, the imperial army, which numbered close to 100,000 (a vast difference between Saigo's forces, but Saigo had much more experienced men in his ranks), held off Saigo's warriors. When more imperial forces arrived, Saigo's supporters were forced to retreat. Saigo and his warriors then moved to Kagoshima in the southern prefecture of Kyushu. Despite the fact that Saigo sent a letter to the imperial forces offering to negotiate and end the hostilities, the government was determined to brutally suppress this rebellion. Instead of discussing terms, the Meiji government increased its numbers and backed the imperial forces up with a warship, pommeling the remaining rebels with volleys of firepower. Toward the very end of the fighting, only forty men remained under Saigo.

During the battle, Saigo was injured in the hip. Some accounts state that he committed seppuku or was assisted in his suicide, but some scholars think that Saigo actually went into shock from his wound and that his followers, upon seeing his impaired state, cut off his head. If this was the case, they would have later said that he committed seppuku to preserve his honor. Whatever the case may be, Saigo's death brought an end to the rebellion.

The Imo Incident

The Chinese indicated that Korea should exercise caution when Russia and the United States approached to open relations with them. In an unexpected move, the United States signed the Treaty of Peace, Amity, Commerce and Navigation, also known as the Shufeldt Treaty. However, the treaty identified Korea as an independent country, which wasn't China's understanding. When Korea definitively eliminated its status as a tributary state of China, this concerned Japan, as it meant that China might not rush to Korea's defense in case of an attack. Because Korea wasn't militarily prepared to defend itself against attacks, Japan felt like that would leave them vulnerable. They did send military advisors over to Korea to join up with members of the Japanese legation in Korea to help, but it was insufficient.

In 1882, when King Gojong of Korea heard that his garrison soldiers were underfed due to a famine, he appointed his staff to provide rice. However, corruption came into play by those who wanted him usurped, so the delivery of the rice was contaminated by food agents who used fillers like sand. Consequently, a mutiny came about. It started with attacking the home of Min Gyeom-ho, who they believed was the head conspirator. Gyeom-ho was the overseer of government finances, but he had assigned the matter of distributing the rice to his steward. Gyeom-ho wasn't completely innocent, as he had neglected his duties, but the blame does not rest with him alone.

After this, the massive force then stole ammunition and weapons from the arsenals. A separate group of 3,000 men raced to the Japanese legation, shouting out that they would kill their Japanese guests. Hanabusa Yoshitada, the minister to Korea and the head of the legation, ordered the occupants to evacuate, after which he had the building set on fire. They took refuge at Incheon first until their hosts gained word about what had happened. The Japanese, seeing that their hosts' attitude had changed, fled the city, being pursued by Korean soldiers. Six Japanese were killed, and five were seriously wounded. The survivors were able to board a British ship and escape to safety.

In the end, the Koreans paid reparations to the families of the deceased soldiers, and more money was donated to the Japanese government to help out with the food shortages.

Chinese Meddling in Korea

After the Imo Incident of 1882, China took advantage of Korea's ineffective military response to reassert its own influence in Korean matters. Chinese officers took over the training of the Korean army and provided more advanced weapons and ammunition. China and Korea then signed a treaty, in which Korea would permit itself to be classified as a dependent state of China. A Korean maritime service was created, administered by China, which was a boon to Chinese merchants. Chinese officials were also stationed in various sections of Korea under the rationale that they were protecting Chinese interests.

Both Korea and China were permitted to trade with each other, but China was the country that had a greater advantage as they had more goods.

Japan's Role in the Gapsin Coup

Kim Ok-gyun, a reformist activist, was a Korean who heavily supported the Westernization of Korea and introduced ideas for altering their society to adopt Western sciences, military equipment, and technology. He was also concerned that Japan might invade Korea, and under the guise of learning about new technologies, he went to Japan in 1884. There he discovered that Japan was not imminently planning to attack Korea. Therefore, the Japanese model might be a workable paradigm for Korea, and there wouldn't be any resistance to his explorations in this regard.

Kim also knew that while China's strength was declining, it was simultaneously trying to control Korea to use for its own purposes. Kim supported maintaining the independence of Korea but strongly believed that it would only be possible if reforms were rapidly enacted. Thankfully for him, Kim was a militant activist who was willing to go to the extreme to make that happen.

He and his followers returned to Korea in 1884 and planned a coup d'état to usurp the ultra-conservative King Gojong from his throne. Luckily for them, half of the Chinese soldiers who were present in Korea had been relocated to engage in the skirmishes between France and China over Vietnam. That reduced the number of Chinese forces Kim would have to face before he and his men could carry out the coup d'état. They began their coup at a banquet to celebrate a newly established post office. Kim and his followers approached the king, telling him that the Chinese were creating trouble and that he needed to go with them to a safe place. The group brought King Gojong to a small palace, where he was placed under watch by Japanese legation guards. Several of the Korean government officials who were in attendance at the banquet were either killed or injured.

Following that, Kim set up his fourteen-point reform proposal, which included the abolition of the elite privileges of the ruling class, the establishment of equal rights for all people, the restructure of the government as a constitutional monarchy, the revision of land taxes, the promulgation of free trade and commerce for all, and severe penalties for corruption.

It was a heroic effort, but it was unrealistic in terms of its practicality. The only defenders of the Gaehwapadang, besides the members themselves, were 140 Japanese soldiers from the Japanese legation. And even though half of the Chinese troops had left Korea, they still left a massive amount behind. For instance, the garrison they maintained at Seoul had 1,500 men.

Queen Myeongseong, requested that the Chinese descend upon the rebels, and they did so, killing forty of the Japanese fighters and burning down the Japanese legation building. The activists were then picked up by a Japanese ship. While the weak Japanese ambassador agreed to release them to Korean authorities, the captain of the ship countermanded his order. They were exiled to Japan, with some later moving to the United States. Kim Ok-gyun moved to Japan, living in Tokyo and later Sapporo, and had his name changed to an alias, "Iwata Shusaku." That isn't the end of his story, however.

Although Kim was paranoid about an assassination attempt, he couldn't turn down the chance to travel to Shanghai and meet the noted Chinese politician Li Hongzhang. As he was traveling to meet him, he was shot by a Korean activist. His body was turned over to the Chinese, who dismembered it and carried it through Seoul and several towns. This brutal mutilation triggered the First Sino-Japanese War.

The First Sino-Japanese War July 1894 – August 1895

This war between China and Japan was primarily fought over power in Korea, and the major battles and events are detailed below. It is interesting to note that China was breathing its last in terms of imperial rule. Despite their opposition to Korea and Japan, the last dynasty of China, the Qing dynasty, ended when the Meiji era faded into the sands of time.

Battle of Seonghwan

This was the first land battle of the war, and it took place south of Seoul near the city of Seonghwan, Korea. The Chinese forces were gathered there and had anticipated the arrival of the Japanese, building trenches and earthworks to prepare for the assault. Unfortunately for them, their reinforcements had been lost in an earlier naval battle, and all their supplies and reinforcements had to come by sea via the port of Aswan.

The Japanese, however, realized that most of this war would be fought at sea, as both Korea and Japan are surrounded by water, and the countries involved also had numerous rivers. Japan had been rapidly building a strong navy, and it was clear early on in this war that whichever country could control the water would win the war.

In a demonstration of the fact that the Chinese imperial government often had too much power, Empress Dowager Cixi embezzled some of the money targeted toward updating the Chinese fleets in order to build a sumptuous palace in Beijing. Most of the Chinese vessels were virtual relics; they were bulky and heavy in comparison to the quick-moving Japanese warships.

The primitive naval formation was predictable, as the Chinese warships tended to follow each other as if in a single file. This allowed Japan to form a blockade so that the Chinese garrison in Asan was deprived of reinforcements and fresh provisions.

The battle lasted a day in July of 1894. At the Seoul garrison, the Japanese and Korean land forces overran the Chinese, who were attempting to sequester themselves there. Five hundred of the nearly 4,000 Chinese troops were killed or wounded, and the rest were captured. The Japanese forces which numbered 4,000 suffered less than one hundred casualties.

Battle of Pyongyang

Quickly, China rushed between 13,000 to 15,000 fighters to the Pyongyang garrison. During the dark of night, Japanese warships circled Pyongyang on September 15th, 1894, before attacking on all sides. Three thousand Chinese were killed outright, and 4,000 were injured or missing. If one includes the 102 Japanese who were killed, that means 3,152 men fell within a 24-hour period.

Battle of Pungdo

If a non-combatant vessel was engaged in an act of war, such as aiding the enemy, it was considered to be a justifiable target according to the rules of engagement. At the end of July 1894, two Chinese ships were on their way to meet a British supply ship, the *Kowshing*. One of the Chinese cruisers escaped the attack of the Japanese flying squadron, but the other foundered on the rocks and exploded.

While the Japanese were in the process of guiding the English ship out of the action, the Chinese warriors on board threatened to kill the British captain. Negotiations ensued for four hours until the frustrated Japanese captain fired upon the *Kowshing*. His torpedo missed, but due to the proximity of the two vessels, the merchant ship was broadsided and sunk.

Battle of the Yalu River

On September 17th, 1894, the Japanese fleet met the Chinese Beiyang Fleet near the mouth of the Yalu River, which connects to the Korea Bay. The two most impressive vessels in the Chinese fleet were the *Dingyuan* and the *Zhenyuan*, German-built ironside warships. While they were formidable ships, they ran out of ammunition because they couldn't defeat the smaller, swifter ships of the Japanese navy.

Port Arthur Massacre

Japan had been successfully moving through Korea, and after winning a decisive victory over the Korean city of Pyongyang, they decided to try and capture Port Arthur in China, which was home to the Beiyang Fleet. In November 1894, they had made it to the port, but the Japanese army under General Yamaji Motoharu spotted the mutilated bodies of their fellow soldiers. Their hands and feet had been cut off, while others had been burned alive. This infuriated the troops, and after the city fell to the Japanese, a massacre ensued. A Japanese soldier wrote in his diary that the Japanese were filled with a desire to kill any Chinese soldiers they saw, but they also killed civilians.

> Anyone we saw in the town, we killed. The streets were full of corpses...We killed people in their homes, by and large, there wasn't a single house without three to six dead. Blood was flowing and the smell was awful.

Into Manchuria and Beijing

In January of 1895, the Chinese went into Manchuria, where there was a sheltered harbor at Weihaiwei. However, the Japanese laid siege on Weihaiwei, attacking them both from land and sea for nearly a month. After the fall of Weihaiwei, which was the last major battle fought in the war, the Japanese and Chinese engaged in minor skirmishes, including the Battle of Yinkou.

Although the Chinese sued for peace after the Battle of Weihaiwei, due to the fact that the Japanese could easily capture the capital of Beijing, the Japanese sought to capture Taiwan, making it one of their territories. Instead of attacking the island directly, the Japanese attacked the Pescadores Islands, which were nearby, in late March 1895. It took only three days of fighting for Japan to gain the coveted territory of Taiwan, placing it under Japanese rule until 1945.

Treaty of Shimonoseki, 1895

While the Meiji administration had its own internal problems, it scored a tremendous accomplishment with this war on two levels. First of all, the victory of Japan over the massive mainland country of China remains one of the most important events in its history. Through that victory, Japan proved to the world that it was truly a modern country and merited the respect of being looked upon as totally independent and a force to be reckoned with. Secondly, the territorial gains Japan had made were a boon to the likelihood that future Japanese businesses could become truly international, and Japan also earned a seat in all the international governmental bodies that dealt with Asian matters.

The most important territories it gained were Taiwan, the Penghu Islands, and the crucial peninsula of Liaodong, which gave it control of the Yellow Sea. Through the treaty, Japan gained the right to use the Yangtze River, and China also recognized the independence of Korea.

Russo-Japanese War (1904 to 1905)

After China's defeat in the Sino-Japanese War in 1895, Japan invaded Manchuria. It was particularly interested in gaining a stronghold with railroads that could access Eurasia. Japan feared that Russia might encroach on its territories, especially since Russia had been leasing Port Arthur, a naval base, from China. To settle the matter, Japan offered to cede control over Manchuria in exchange for Japan having influence over Korea, specifically North Korea. However, Russia refused. The Russian battleships were sheltered at the harbor of Port Arthur, and the Japanese began the war by attacking their fleet in February 1904.

The Battles of Port Arthur and Liaoyang

During the Battle of Port Arthur, one Russian ship was sunk, and two others were badly damaged. The Japanese attempted to blockade the port, so Russia couldn't use it, but two Russian battleships managed to slip out into the open waters. However, they struck Japanese mines, sinking one ship and heavily damaging another. Russia learned from the Japanese and their offense mining, and they also began to place mines in the area, damaging two Japanese ships. The bombardment continued and even moved on to land. Russia sent in reinforcements to protect its fleet, but it wasn't successful, as the Japanese artillery pommeled the moored ships. Every one of Russia's ships was disabled.

The first major land battle of the war was the Battle of Liaoyang, which took place from late August to early September 1904. The city was strategically important to the Russians to maintain a position in southern Manchuria. However, the Russians retreated, making it a Japanese victory, although it should be noted that the Japanese suffered higher casualties than the Russians.

Battle of Tsushima

In May 1905, the Japanese fleet made a punishing trip over the sea to reach the remaining Russian fleet of steel-reinforced battleships. The Japanese ship, *Mikasa,* was constantly hit with Russian gunfire from their ship, *Oslyabya,* and was badly damaged, but the Japanese gunfire prevailed until the Russian flagship sank. The Japanese continued their gunfire and set upon the Russian ship, the *Borodino,* until the ship exploded in a huge fireball. This was followed by the sinking of two more of the Russian battleships.

Nighttime brought torpedo attacks by Japanese submarines and destroyers. The destroyers attacked head-on, while the torpedo boats assaulted the Russian ships from two sides. It was pitch-black, and ships collided with one another. Every time the Russians turned on their searchlights, they revealed their position and were subsequently attacked. Three older Russian cruisers rushed in to help but were hit by torpedoes. The Japanese never relented during the entire night.

At first light, the Japanese fleet chased the Russians northward. The Russians hoisted a facsimile of a surrender flag using tablecloths, as they couldn't locate an actual one. That was deliberate, as Russia insisted its men fight to their deaths. Once the tablecloths were hoisted, they were ignored since they had tried to surrender in several battles during the Sino-Japanese War, and the Japanese now knew that it was a trick. Once the Russians brought their ships to a dead halt, Japan accepted their surrender. This battle was the last major battle of the war, although the peace treaty wasn't concluded until September 1905. The two Russian admirals were faced with charges upon their return home, but the tsar pardoned them from the death penalty. Despite that, the reputations of both men were ruined. Russia had no tolerance for failure, regardless of how justified it might have been.

This battle is notable for being the first decisive naval battle fought with modern steel battleships, and it was also the first naval battle in which the radio played an important role.

Chapter 8 – The Taisho Era

Between 1912 to 1926, Japan continued to modernize. This rapid modernization gobbled up the government's budget, leaving virtually little in reserve. The political situation was made precarious by the death of Emperor Meiji in 1912 and even more so by the cutting of Japan's largest expenditure—the military. Prime Minister Saionji Kinmochi made that decision, and it showed that Japan hadn't yet matured as a sovereign country. As a result of this traumatic change, the army minister resigned, with Kinmochi resigning shortly after. In essence, the country was still learning how to function effectively without looking upon a supreme authority to tell it what to do.

The new emperor, Yoshihito, Meiji's son, took on the imperial name of "Taisho" and responded to this crisis by appointing Katsura Taro as prime minister, who had been the prime minister before Kinmochi. Riots broke out, as Katsura was an elder statesman and the Japanese didn't trust him to propel them into the future. Katsura proved that fact almost immediately by attempting to solve the military crisis by doing the opposite of his predecessor. He restored the military budget but overextended it and virtually ignored the country's focus on its new constitution. In the midst of massive protests and the appointment of Katsura for yet another term, the political parties rose up to resolve the crisis. The Rikken Seiyukai promoted Yamamoto Gonnohyoe as Katsura's replacement, and the emperor approved. That was a mistake.

The Rikken Seiyukai party's interest was in business expansion, and it was later revealed that the Siemens Corporation had conspired to attract more business for itself by obtaining military contracts with the navy and paying a fifteen percent kickback to those who could procure those contracts. The people were furious when they found out, so they looked toward a shakeup of the legislative body, the Diet, to undermine the control of the Rikken Seiyukai and the Siemens Corporation. The scandal led to the collapse of the Yamamoto Cabinet. Hence, the Progressive Party won the majority of positions in the national Diet. Okuma Shigenobu, a leading member of that party, became prime minister in 1914.

Because of the political manipulations that took place from 1912 to 1914, the Japanese navy and military were powerful. When World War I broke out in 1914, Japan seized the opportunity to join the Allied Powers—Russia, France, and the United Kingdom—to subdue the Central Powers of Germany, Austria-Hungary, the Ottoman Empire, and Bulgaria from gaining control over the rich sea lanes in the Pacific Ocean. Japan's hidden agenda in creating agreements with the Allies was to expand its influence on China, whose international commerce depended upon the Pacific.

Japan in World War I

At the end of July 1914 and the beginning of August of the same year, the Allied Powers in Europe came together against Germany and Austria-Hungary over control in Europe. In order for the Allies to be successful, though, Germany needed to be weakened.

Germany had a number of colonies in the Pacific which their navy had to protect—the German colony of Qingdao on the Chinese mainland, the Marshall Islands, Papua New Guinea, the Solomon Islands, the Northern Mariana Islands, Samoa, and the smaller island chains of Micronesia in the South Pacific. It was tantamount to a mini-empire in the East.

The Allies were interested in eliminating the power of the Imperial German Navy in the Far East, and Great Britain, in particular, urged Japan to manage that area of the war. In the name of Emperor Taisho, Japan declared war on Germany.

Japan's first target was the German colony of Qingdao. Japan surrounded Qingdao and put it under siege. Several months later, Germany surrendered control of that colony. While in this area, Japan attacked Shandong Province via Jiaozhou Bay. That bay led out to the Yellow Sea, which Japan had coveted control over for years.

Docked in Jiaozhou Bay were an Austria-Hungarian sea cruiser, the SMS *Kaiserin Elisabeth,* and a German gunboat. Japanese efforts to evict them from the area were initially unsuccessful. With the aid of the British forces, though, it was overrun and occupied by both Britain and Japan.

The Japanese navy went on to seize the Mariana Islands and the Marshall Islands. There was no resistance on the part of the Germans, who were overwhelmed with events in the European theater of the war.

Twenty-One Demands

In early January 1915, Prime Minister Shigenobu and Foreign Minister Kato Takaaki presented 21 demands to China divided into 5 groups: 1) confirmation of Japanese control over Shandong Province, along with its railways and the Chinese coast along there; 2) exclusive ownership of a section of southern Manchuria and access to the raw materials in Inner Mongolia; 3) Japanese control over a metallurgical complex in central China; 4) a prohibition on China to allow foreign countries to have concessions to the Chinese coast and its islands; and 5) Japan could have advisors in China who could take over their finances and its police. Demand five was kept secret until absolutely necessary because it would essentially make China subservient to Japan.

After discussions with China, Japan reduced the number of demands to thirteen. Fearing war with Japan, China conceded to the revised demands and signed a treaty with Japan in late May 1915.

Although Japan and China made peace regarding the Chinese mainland, there were more issues that were left unsettled. In 1916, Great Britain indicated that they would support Japanese claims to the German colonies in the Pacific if Japan was willing to use their navy to assist with the ongoing war in the Western Hemisphere by escorting British battleships and performing rescues in the Mediterranean.

The United States entered the war and joined the Allies in 1917, although they were not officially an ally, instead preferring to be an "associated power" to avoid future wars. They knew of Japan's interest in controlling the Pacific and wanted that modified, but the needs of the Allies superseded that interest, at least until the end of the war.

In 1917, Japan's second squadron escorted and defended British transport vessels and provided manpower to aid in the anti-submarine warfare in the Mediterranean Sea. They also provided invaluable rescues at sea, including that of 3,000 people from an American ship, the SS *Transylvania*, which was transporting troops to the front lines.

The British were very pleased with the rapidity of Japan's response to sudden requests and crises on the seas due to warfare. France was also appreciative of the fact that Japan was able to secure twelve destroyers for its use in the war. Due to its modernization efforts, Japanese businesses and its military were experienced in import-export operations, and that impressed the other Allied countries. Japan was also experienced in obtaining war materials and provisions for the troops. They benefited a lot during this war, as they learned a lot of military techniques and absorbed some new technologies from Europe.

In 1917, the Bolshevik Revolution occurred in Russia, and Japan sent troops there in 1918 along with the United States. They were ordered to go to the harsh cold area of Siberia in order to strengthen the armies of Admiral Alexander Kolchak, who was waging a war against the Bolsheviks who were attempting to control much of the territory there. One of the reasons for the US entering the war was to halt the spread of communism. That was the brainchild of the Bolshevik Revolution essentially, but it did serve the purpose of helping to put an end to World War I. War weariness crept in as the war threatened to spread from country to country. Already the Ottomans and the Turks in the Middle East were fighting. In Russia, the struggle between the White Army and the Red Army of the Bolsheviks was a civil war. Austria-Hungary was dealing with dwindling resources to keep up the fight. The only reason Japan was involved was to aid in the Siberian front to aid the Americans. Later, in 1922, Tsarist Russia fell, and the Bolsheviks prevailed.

Treaty of Versailles

As a result of Japan's contribution toward the victory of the Allied Powers, Japan joined up with the "Big Four." The Big Four refers to the four major powers of the Allies who were at the peace conference to draw up the treaty. Japan was later included in that circle.

The Treaty of Versailles granted Japan the right to administer the islands they had conquered at the beginning of the war. Japan also received rights to Jiaozhou Bay, which would finally give Japan access to the Yellow Sea. The German-owned islands south of the Pacific were awarded to Australia, meaning that Micronesia, formerly controlled by Germany, was now on the path toward becoming independent.

United States President Woodrow Wilson supported Japan's right to administer the islands north of the equator that they had annexed during the war. However, that didn't mean that Japan owned those islands. They controlled them under the mandates of the newly formed League of Nations, which was intended to resolve disputes among countries and avoid future wars.

Japan was also allowed to maintain their control over Shandong Province in China, which they annexed during the war. Later on, in 1919, a fierce dispute over Japan's annexation of the Chinese province of Shandong arose. China wouldn't sign the treaty if Japan was allowed to control that province, and the matter wasn't resolved until 1922. Japan, unfortunately, had to give up its right to Shandong; however, it was still permitted to retain economic control of the railway there.

Japan proposed a "racial equality clause" to the Treaty of Versailles. Japan wanted to be treated as equals, and although their proposal was considered to be for universal racial equality, Japan just wanted it for those members of the League of Nations, of which it was a founding member. The Japanese knew they had been forced to sign unequal treaties after Matthew Perry opened the door for the rest of the world to enter Japan, and they wanted to prevent that from happening. But the idea of universal racial equality, which was what most of the peace conference assumed Japan wanted, was not really possible at the time, mostly due to the Western powers seeking more and more domains of non-white people to add to their empire.

Through several machinations, it was determined that a unanimous vote was needed to pass it. The United States, the United Kingdom, Portugal, and Romania didn't vote for the inclusion of the racial equality proposal, and as a result, Japan was inclined toward not cooperating with the Western nations.

The issues arising from the exclusion of the racial equality proposal weren't resolved until after World War II.

Effects of World War I on Japan

Prosperity descended upon Japan after the war. The corporate conglomerates and the *zaibatsu* organized during the Meiji era expanded during the Taisho era. The Allied Powers' need for military provisions, the use of ships from the Japanese navy, Japan's facility in the import-export business, and their banking sector created a boom in their economy. Later on, Japan became a creditor nation because of its dependence on imports. Japan even made agreements with Taiwan and Korea to grow rice.

Inflation was one of the fallouts of the war. Wages hadn't kept pace with the rising prices, which caused the Rice Riots of 1918. This didn't only affect the poor, as middle-income families also struggled with the rising prices. Because of the disparities in social classes, it encouraged the founding of the Japanese Communist Party in 1922. Socialism was attractive as it was felt that it would provide a solution to the many problems the lower classes faced. The Japanese Communist Party, though, had distinct differences from the Bolsheviks, as it didn't rest upon violent revolutions as a means of control.

After World War I, Japanese troops continued fighting in Siberia until 1922. The country was concerned about the anti-monarchical stance of the Bolshevik regime in Russia, as that contradicted Japan's governmental structure. Furthermore, many felt that communists might infiltrate Japan's government. Japan had gone through a painful period in order to convert to a constitutional monarchy and couldn't withstand another major change. Japan lost about 5,000 men in the Siberian expedition and lost the battle to oust the Bolsheviks. What's more, it suffered a large economic loss financing the Siberian effort. Not only were there the expenditures of conducting warfare, but Japanese banks made loans to Russia for the Siberian expedition, which Russia defaulted on. The Siberian expedition also contributed in part to creating a shortage of rice because the government had to buy it for their troops.

The other factor that created the food shortage during this period was the Great Kanto earthquake in 1923.

Great Kanto Earthquake

The epicenter of this earthquake was near Tokyo, in the heart of Japan. It registered at 7.9 on the moment magnitude scale (the successor of the Richter scale) and is one of the most powerful earthquakes that Japan has ever experienced. Widespread damage spread over the capital city and the surrounding cities and towns, including Yokohama, a nearby port. Over 140,000 people died, and since the earthquake occurred during lunchtime, when fires were being used to cook food, some of those deaths were due to fires being spread throughout the city. The single greatest loss of life actually occurred due to the fires when 38,000 people lost their lives after taking shelter in a clothing store. The earthquake also triggered landslides and a tsunami, which devasted the homes and lives of the people. A rumor arose that the Koreans who were living in Japan at the time were taking advantage of the disaster, that they were looting and committing arson. As a result, a countless number of Koreans were killed by mobs, with some estimating the number to be between 6,000 and 10,000.

The government placed the Koreans into protective custody, and martial law was declared. Despite that, the rumor grew to implicate socialists. Historians indicate that this was a move fostered by the imperial government to rid the country of political dissidents.

As a result of the earthquake, Tokyo underwent reconstruction. This was a backhanded opportunity to replace poorly constructed buildings up to standard. Of course, the recovery was very costly.

Universal Male Suffrage

The rise of democracy in Japan was strong during the Taisho era. There were demonstrations regarding the requirement that voter eligibility depended upon income. Because of that, it was difficult for the general public to run their own candidates through the political parties. The government, therefore, was run by the few, even in the 1920s. That fact alone reminded the people of old Japan that the emperor and his advisors dictated policies to the working public. The pro-business political party, the Rikken Seiyukai, was extremely powerful, so smaller political parties experienced slow growth. They were often unable to get candidates elected who represented the rural interests and those of medium-level wage earners.

Gradually, a new Kenseito political party emerged upon the ashes of the old Kenseito Party, which had collapsed during the Meiji era. The Kenseito party proposed the General Election Law in 1925, and it was passed by the Diet. This law stated that all males 25 years of age and older were allowed to vote, regardless of income.

Women weren't allowed to attend political meetings until 1922, so they did not achieve the right to vote at this time. The women's suffrage movement continued to grow, though, and women finally were given the right to vote in 1945.

Chapter 9 – The Showa Era

Hirohito succeeded Emperor Taisho in 1926, taking the title Emperor Showa. In the West, emperors from this point onward are more often remembered for their birth names than their name as emperor, which is how they are referred to after they die in Japan (while they are alive, they go by "His Majesty" or "His Majesty the Emperor") so they will be referred to as such in this book. The Showa era lasted until Hirohito's death in 1989.

There was a financial crisis following World War I due to all of the expenditures associated with the war and the very rapid democratization movements taking place within the country.

The Naval Race

After noting the necessity of having vibrant navies, the major powers who participated in World War I engaged in vigorous shipbuilding. The mad pace of the construction of warships and aircraft carriers was alarming. The ultimate purpose of this was the control of the Pacific Ocean. America, Great Britain, and Japan all had competing interests there. Returning to some sense of rationality after this initial frenzy, these nations discussed limitations. In 1922, the issue was discussed and continued to be discussed by nine of the nations involved in World War I, at what was called the

Washington Naval Conference, but no agreement was reached with regard to ships other than battleships and carriers. All the countries, however, recognized the importance of balancing its naval programs.

Other treaties were introduced within the next decade or so, which sought additional limitations on the construction of battleships. The terms of the original 1922 treaty were modified by the London Naval Treaty of 1930 and then the Second London Naval Treaty of 1936. However, Japan did not sign the Second London Naval Treaty. They saw the limitations of how many ships they could have in their navy as another snub by the United States, which only added to the tensions between the two countries. By the end of December 1934, the Japanese government had given formal notice that it intended to terminate the naval treaties it was engaged with.

The Manchurian Incident

The National Policy Company of Japan, whose function was to operate railways in northeastern China, acquired the south Manchurian railroad in 1906. To guard Japanese interests, a division of the Japanese army called the Kwantung Army was stationed there. After World War I, the Chinese built their own railroad, which ran parallel to the south Manchurian one. To eliminate this competition and help Japan gain stronger control over China, the Kwantung Army blew up a section of their own tracks in 1931. They did that so they could blame the explosion on the Chinese and create a pretext for invading Manchuria.

The Japanese troops then clashed with the Chinese soldiers and forced them north into northern China. By 1932, the Kwantung Army controlled all of Manchuria, setting up a puppet state called Manchukuo. The general of the Kwantung Army placed himself in the role of ambassador. All of this was done without any permission from the central government, and Tokyo reluctantly accepted the Manchukuo state, as it had already been done.

Realizing the implications of permitting this branch of the Japanese army to gain control over Japan, Prime Minister Inukai Tsuyoshi attempted to restrain the Kwantung Army before being assassinated by rebels in the Japanese navy who wanted the military to control the government. The plot, known as the May 15 Incident, also included attacking other prominent politicians and even assassinating the famous film star Charlie Chaplin to incite tension with the United States; however, Chaplin was watching a sumo match with the prime minister's son and was able to escape.

Rise of the Right

After the prime minister was assassinated, more young radicals vehemently opposed any reduction in military spending and attempted a coup d'état in 1936 under the leadership of Shumei Okawa. Since Emperor Hirohito stood on the right politically, he resented the fact that these young leftist radicals were trying to manipulate him. He responded by quashing the coup and arresting the perpetrators. Some were executed, including Ikki Kita, a noted socialist who opposed imperial domination.

In 1936, the liberals assassinated Takahashi Korekiyo, a rather conservative member of the House of Peers. Takahashi was one of the politicians who supported a cut in military spending, as he was a member of the Rikken Seiyukai party, which backed the economic and burgeoning business interests of Japan.

Japan was then on the road toward autocratic rule. The Diet approved of unilateral military interventions and expansionism with the objective of establishing a Japanese empire. Political parties and clubs that promulgated this ideology proliferated, including the Imperial Way Society, the National Foundation Party, the Society for the Preservation of the National Essence, and the National Purity Society.

The Second Sino-Japanese War

Fortified by their conquest of Manchuria in 1931, Japan aggressively pursued all the rights it felt it deserved after World War I. Its leadership was clamoring for control of China without any concessions, as well as southeast Asia so as to set up the "Empire of Japan." The Chinese, in particular, wanted to maintain the sovereignty of their own country—control they had held onto for centuries. By virtue of the Treaty of Versailles, Japan had to surrender control of Shandong Province, which they occupied during the war. They resented that and considered the agreement forged at Versailles to be an unequal treaty.

Not only had Japan annexed Manchuria, but they also obtained the rights to the raw materials in Inner Mongolia during the Taisho era. On the other hand, Chiang Kai-shek, the chairman of the National Government of the Republic of China, spent his efforts attempting to develop the ideals of a nationalist China. He was opposed to the communists who advocated a united front against the Japanese. In view of the fact that he opposed Japan, Chiang Kai-shek tried to drive out Japanese influence from China. That exploded into the Second Sino-Japanese War, which melded into World War II.

It all started in 1937 when Japan gained control of the Marco Polo Bridge, which led to the main route into Beijing. In retaliation, Chiang Kai-shek had his forces place a siege upon the Shanghai International Settlement, which was a territory composed of British and American civilians. Although some have called the subsequent bombing accidental, the result was the same. Three thousand Japanese civilians were killed, and after that, the Chinese army attacked the Japanese navy stationed near Shanghai.

The Battle of Shanghai

After the destruction at the Shanghai International Settlement, Chinese aircraft bombarded Japanese ships in and near the harbor in 1937. Although the Chinese pilots waged a ferocious battle in the air over Shanghai, the Japanese were able to hold on to their defensive positions for a while, as the Chinese suffered heavy casualties in the face of the more experienced Japanese. After Japanese troops captured the Dachang district within Shanghai, the National Revolutionary Army of China was forced to retreat.

Japan initially wanted to stop the war early on and discuss terms, but its victory at Shanghai wetted Japan's interest in continuing, so further attacks were authorized.

The Battle of Nanking

In 1937, Nanking was the capital of China. After it conquered Shanghai, Japan then marched on this city. General Iwane Matsui counterattacked, and for two days, the two sides fought. However, Chiang Kai-shek abandoned the defense of Nanking, as his forces couldn't hold out because they were outnumbered two to one. Many of the Chinese soldiers shed their uniforms and disappeared into the non-combatant population.

Inflated by their victory, the Japanese army executed Chinese prisoners of war, massacred the civilian population, raped women, and looted stores and homes. This caused an international outcry and became known as the Nanking Massacre.

Battle of Wuhan

In 1938, Chiang Kai-shek had to move the capital from the conquered city of Nanking to Wuhan. The Yangtze and Han Rivers divide the city into three regions—Hankou, Hanyang, and Wuchang. Hankou was the commercial region, Hanyang was the industrial district, and Wuchang housed the government. The Japanese forces followed Chiang Kai-shek, who wanted to defend the railway stationed in Wuhan and have accommodations for his administrative offices. China placed a huge number of troops there, close to 800,000. The Chinese stubbornly defended the area against the Kwantung Army, so Japan—in desperation—launched a poison gas attack and then seized Wuhan.

The fighting continued into 1939, and the Japanese gained Wuhan, but their victory came at a high cost; it is estimated that 1.2 million casualties occurred with both sides combined. The offensive left the Japanese fairly weakened, and the battle only bought the Chinese extra time to move their forces and equipment farther inland, making this a tactical victory for the Japanese but a strategic one for the Chinese.

Battle of Suixian-Zaoyang

In April 1939, the Chinese army had their 77th Division defending this southeastern territory because of the Japanese harbor blockades. The Chinese were attempting to prevent Japan from landing there and moving inland. Of course, the Chinese were more familiar with the terrain, which was very mountainous, and Japan lost the battle in late May. This appeared to be a turning point in the war, as it invigorated the Chinese army who were inspired to continue resisting, hoping that this would become a war of attrition.

Battle of Kunlun Pass

In 1939, the Chinese had been receiving military provisions through French Indochina via the mountainous Kunlun Pass. Japan, who already had limited control of Kunlun, wanted to cut off any more shipments to China. The newly formed 200th Division of the Chinese Revolutionary Army was a vicious and determined fighting force. Under the guidance of Brigade Commander Dai Anlan, the Chinese were able to split up the defending Japanese ground forces at the pass early in 1940, killing Japanese Major General Masao Nakamura in the process. The Japanese could only rely upon their air power at this point, but they were unable to prevail. Hence, the Chinese successfully regained control of the Kunlun Pass.

After that, China moved is capital to Chungking. Chiang Kai-shek then kept moving his army westward toward the Yangtze River and continued presenting a fierce resistance. In 1938, General Iwane Matsui of China received a message that he was going to be relieved of his command, along with eight other members of his senior staff, so there was a shakeup of the command structure.

From 1939 to 1942, Japan attempted to blockade the Chinese ports along the coast.

The Tientsin Incident

In 1939, the Japanese army blockaded foreign concessions in the Chinese port of Tientsin because the British took custody of four Chinese men who killed a Japanese official. When Japan requested that they be handed over to the Japanese authorities, the British refused. The Japanese responded by outrageously demanding the silver reserves held in British banks; they also strip-searched anyone leaving the port and blocked the importation of food and fuel.

In view of the fact that this would accelerate and widen the war. Britain remanded the Chinese into Japan's custody, and they were summarily executed.

Battle of South Henan

In early 1941, the Japanese clashed with the Chinese Revolutionary Army in the province of Henan. The Japanese split their army into three divisions in order to attack the Chinese. However, the Chinese avoided full-frontal assaults and spread out their forces to coax the Japanese into thinning out into a line. The Chinese then maneuvered in such a way that they were able to outflank the Japanese and squeeze them like a vice. Before that move could occur, the Japanese withdrew, and the Chinese was still able to maintain control of Henan.

American Interference

Starting in the year 1938, America extended loans to China upon hearing about the deaths of unarmed Chinese civilians. In addition, the US was aware of the inferior military position of China and began providing China with arms and ammunition. Furthermore, the US objected to Japan's use of its manufactured military products, like airplanes, ammunition, and even oil for their ships and aircraft. Aside from some moral embargoes, which forbade the shipment of war materials to Imperial Japan, America didn't want to become too involved in the conflict in the Pacific. Since the US vehemently protested aggressive actions against China by Japan, the American and Japanese positions became irreconcilable. The US secretary of state, Cordell Hull, strove for an agreement between China and Japan, calling for the withdrawal of Japan from China, the recognition of the sovereign leadership of Chiang Kai-shek, and a non-aggression policy between Japan and the islands in the Pacific Ocean.

An imperial conference was held in Tokyo, and it was decided that the American solution was unacceptable. In 1941, Minister of War Hideki Tojo was appointed as prime minister and loudly advocated the expansionist policies of Japan in the Pacific. In November of the same year, Admiral Isoroku Yamamoto, who was actually strongly against the war in China to the point of receiving death threats, ordered an attack on the American naval fleet at Pearl Harbor, Hawaii, in order to preemptively strike against the US in the inevitable war between the two countries.

Cordell Hull sensed that there might be a Japanese attack on American battle cruisers but thought it would occur in the Philippines or Malaya. However, that was not to be the case. Early on the morning of December 7th, 1941, Japanese aircraft were launched to attack the naval base of Pearl Harbor. As a result, 188 American airplanes were obliterated, all eight battleships were damaged, with four of them sinking, and 2,403 Americans, both soldiers and civilians, were killed, with 1,178 being wounded. The Japanese losses were light in comparison with 29 aircraft being destroyed and 64 men being killed in action. It was an undeniable tragedy in the annals of American history, but it was a major victory for the Japanese, who announced war on the United States that same day.

Chapter 10 – Japan in World War II and Its Aftermath

Although the Japanese declared war that day, the message wasn't delivered until the next day, the same day Franklin Delano Roosevelt delivered his *Infamy Speech* and the US Congress declared war on Japan. Three days later, Benito Mussolini, the dictator of Italy, and Adolph Hitler, the leader of Nazi Germany, declared war on the United States. The United States then joined the European Allies—the United Kingdom, France, the Soviet Union, China, Australia, Canada, South Africa, among others, to fight in the European theater of the war, as well as the Pacific theater. Japan had joined up with what was called the Axis Powers—Germany and Italy, along with other less powerful countries—when they signed the Tripartite Pact with them in September 1940.

The Philippines Campaign

Nine hours after the attack on Pearl Harbor, Japan targeted the Philippine Islands. Japan launched its invasion from Taiwan, which they controlled at the time. The Allied defenders on the islands were members of the Philippine National Guard and other miscellaneous troops who hadn't expected to be involved in any decisive action in World War II. Even though their arrival was a total surprise, the American-Filipino forces managed to last until April, but guerilla resistance still continued against the Japanese occupants after that.

The Malayan and Dutch East Indies Campaigns

Since these islands were so close together, the losses inflicted on one territory affected the other. An hour before the attack on Pearl Harbor, the Japanese landed on Malaysia, battling with the British Indian Army that was located there. The airport located in Kota Bharu, where the fighting was taking place, was captured, followed by more airports being captured the following day. The British failed to reinforce their dwindling troops throughout this campaign, and coupled with the monsoon season, they were no match for the Japanese, who cleverly used bicycles to work their way through the heavy jungle terrain. They were able to push the British, Indians, and Australians back, winning battle after battle. By the end of January, all of Malaysia was in the hands of the Japanese.

On December 17th, 1941, the Japanese planned to attack Borneo, landing in Malaysia to begin their airstrikes on the island. After gaining some important areas in Borneo, they next decided to capture the oil resources in the East Indies, which would cripple the Allied war efforts in the Pacific. Since the ABDA (American-British-Dutch-Australian Command) had differing views on what was most important to protect, they were unable to stop the progression of the Japanese, who also held much larger numbers than they did. Although ABDA put up fierce resistance against the Japanese, the Japanese had managed to gain many airports in the Dutch East Indies and had decimated their naval forces by late February. On March 9th, the Dutch surrendered.

Battle of Hong Kong

On the morning of December 8th, 1941, Japan attacked the British colony of Hong Kong. There was a huge garrison there, with Chinese, British, and Canadian units occupying. The battle spread out from the garrison into many neighboring areas, and despite a large number of Allied troops, the Japanese forces outnumbered them significantly. This engagement lasted for nearly a month, but the Allied forces had to abandon Hong Kong, leaving it in the hands of the Japanese.

The Burma Campaign

In January of 1942, Japan invaded the country of Burma, mainly because of the Burma Road, which was a major supply route to China, and its control would cut China off from badly needed supplies. Burma also had minerals and a lot of rice, which could serve to feed the Japanese troops for the duration of the war. To bolster its potential success, Japan recruited many Burmese and recruits from the country of Thailand. Thailand and Japan actually created an agreement between them, and the Thai assumed much of the responsibility for conducting the battle.

The Allied forces—Great Britain, the United States, and China— briefly held on to the capital city of Rangoon, but they were forced back by the hardy Japanese. In the craziness, thousands of Burmese citizens were attempting to escape the country. The government was progressively unable to organize in the confusion and evacuate the civilians. The Japanese took this opportunity to successfully defeat the Chinese troops as they were trying to flee to India. With the aid of US Lieutenant General Joseph Stilwell, the chaotic Chinese were reorganized and returned for a counterattack. However, many of them died attempting to pass through a mountainous region. Although the British and American allies outnumbered the Japanese, they were poorly trained, and nearly 31,000 of them died.

The battle trolled on throughout the region and resulted in the Japanese occupation of Burma, although military actions occurred and reoccurred whenever the Americans and the British renewed their attacks. Because of its strategic role, the Allied forces never gave up in their attempt to control Burma. In 1943, Lord Louis Mountbatten took over the Allied command and placed Field Marshal William Slim on the ground. Instead of employing guerilla techniques that the British had used earlier in the campaign, they now had air support. That gave the Allied forces access to supplies, and they also didn't have to use strike-and-run tactics. Once that occurred, the Allies were now fighting on open northern land instead of the jungles, which allowed them to gain ground. Then, in 1945, the second-largest city, Mandalay, fell into Allied hands. The Allies crossed the Irrawaddy River and took Rangoon. Pockets of Japanese continued to struggle, attempting to escape into Thailand. However, Thailand had the support of pro-Allied rebels, which prevented the entrenchment of the Japanese. In July 1945, a few months before the war ended, the Allies occupied Burma.

Battle of Singapore

Between February 8th and 15th, 1942, the Japanese empire attacked the British military base in Singapore. This was a sizeable naval base, and it was considered to be the key to British success in the Pacific war theater. The Allies had already suffered severe losses from the previous campaigns, in particular, the Malayan one, but attempted to put up a fierce fight. However, they were no match for the Japanese. It was a major loss for the Allies, and the largest British surrender in history, with 80,000 British, Indian, and Australian troops becoming prisoners of war (along with the 50,000 taken during the Malayan Campaign). Not only that, but their battleships were decimated or sunk by the proficient Japanese navy.

Battle of the Coral Sea

At the beginning of May in 1942, Japan sought to establish a southern base from which to gain control of the South Pacific, coveting Port Moresby on the southern coast of New Guinea in particular. All the fighting was conducted by aircraft carriers at sea and included Australian participation. Both sides claimed to be victorious in this battle, as the Japanese won a tactical victory by sinking several US ships, including *Lexington*, which represented a good chunk of the US carrier strength in the Pacific. However, the Japanese failed to seize control of the port, which would have been a strategically located southerly anchor point in the Pacific. This was also the first time the Japanese invading force was turned back from their objective, which greatly boosted the morale of the Allies.

Battle of Midway

Midway is an island that lies northwest of Hawaii. In early June of 1942, Admiral Isoroku Yamamoto and his fleet sailed from the Aleutian Islands off Alaska (then known as the Alaska Territory) and attacked what he predicted to be the remaining functioning American ships in the area. However, US Admiral Chester Nimitz was in possession of the decryption codes for Japanese transmissions and was prepared. He attacked the Japanese ships from the land and from aircraft carriers, crippling them. Japan lost four of its aircraft carriers and retreated.

The Guadalcanal Campaign

It was now August of 1942. Not having gained its coveted position in the South Pacific, Japan needed to find something else that would be suitable. Because supplies were being pumped to the Allies in the Pacific by Australia, Japan was in the process of constructing an airbase in the northern area of the Solomon Islands off the coast of New Guinea. Those islands are located northeast of New Guinea and are filled with dense jungles. That geographical factor enabled the two sides to hide their activities. In fact, many of the islanders who lived there weren't aware of them, particularly of the Japanese base. The Japanese ships near New Guinea and the Solomon Islands shipped supplies and materials to the island of Guadalcanal and the surrounding South Pacific area stealthily at night via a route dubbed the "Tokyo Express."

The Allies were determined to prevent Japan from using its base at Guadalcanal to disrupt the Americans from staging operations in the South Pacific. They then launched an offensive attack and managed to seize control of the base, which they called Henderson Field. Admiral Isoroku Yamamoto had 1,400 soldiers and 500 seamen, whom he ordered to retake the base. In addition, Japan had warships in position along with a formidable carrier force. Ground and air attacks ensued, and the sea was filled with torpedoes and smoke from the bombing of the ships. One of the Japanese carriers, the *Ryujo*, was sunk by the end of August. The other two Japanese carriers, the *Shokaku* and the *Zuikaku*, though, weren't damaged. America had two carriers, the USS *Saratoga* and the USS *Enterprise*.

In October of 1942, the Japanese land troops tried to take Henderson Field. They conducted naval and ground attacks before sending out airplanes. The bombardment continued until the airfield was destroyed, but Japan didn't capture it. As soon as the haze cleared, the Americans initiated repairs and called for replacements of planes and ships.

In November, the Japanese attempted to take the airbase again. However, US aircraft saw the approach of Vice-Admiral Hiroaki Abe's force and alerted the Allies. Early on the morning of November 13th, 1942, US Rear Admiral Daniel Callaghan and his force intercepted Abe's force. In the dark, the two warship forces opened fire on each other, making the battle very chaotic. Abe managed to sink or seriously damage all but one cruiser and one destroyer in Callaghan's fleet. Callaghan also died in the battle, along with US Rear Admiral Norman Scott.

Although the Allies lost the battle, they did manage to inflict damage on the Japanese forces. Two Japanese destroyers were sunk, and the *Hiei*, a battleship, was severely damaged; the *Hiei* actually sunk later that day. Due to this destruction of his force, Abe ordered his men to retreat.

On the following day, November 14th, Vice-Admiral Gunichi Mikawa oversaw a cruiser and destroyer force that was sent to attack Henderson Field. They caused some damage, but they weren't incredibly successful in their endeavors. As they retreated, Rear Admiral Raizo Tanaka, believing that Henderson Field was now inoperable, began to head toward Guadalcanal. Throughout the day, aircraft from Henderson Field and the *Enterprise,* a US carrier, attacked the forces of both Mikawa and Tanaka, and they managed to sink one heavy cruiser and seven of the Japanese transports.

Tanaka continued his run toward Guadalcanal, and Admiral Nobutake Kondo began to approach Henderson Field to begin his bombardment of it. Admiral William Halsey Jr. sent out the *Washington* and the *South Dakota,* two US battleships, along with four destroyers to take down Kondo's force. Kondo made quick work of the Allied fleet, sinking three of the destroyers and damaging the fourth one. As they were concentrated on attacking the *South Dakota,* the *Washington* managed to sneak up behind and opened fire on the *Kirishima,* a Japanese battleship, causing major damage to it.

Kondo ordered a retreat, and four Japanese transports beached on Guadalcanal and tried to unload equipment. Shortly after, American air and ground support destroyed the equipment. There were still some Japanese troops on Guadalcanal, but shipments of food and supplies for them via the Tokyo Express were insufficient for the Japanese stranded there. Many died of malnutrition and disease. Finally, by December 12th, Japan abandoned any efforts to retake Guadalcanal.

Allied Air Raids on Japan

In the middle of 1944, the Allied forces—America, Great Britain, and China—decided to attack Japan itself. American B-24 "Liberator" bombers and B-29 "Superfortress" bombers flew out of the Mariana Islands, which lay to the southeast of Japan. There were bombing raids on the city of Osaka in March, June, and August. A total of over 1,700 bombs were dropped, and the city lay in ruins. In March of 1945, in Kobe, civilian targets were bombed, giving rise to severe accusations based on ethical reasons. In June of 1945, bombers attacked Fukuoka, destroying almost one-quarter of the city.

Battle of Okinawa

Okinawa is one of the islands in the Kyushu area of Japan located south of the country, just 300 miles north of Taiwan. The Battle of Okinawa began with an amphibious attack by the United States in early April 1945 in order to gain the airbase there to begin Operation Downfall, which would have the Allies invading the islands of Japan. The battle didn't end until late June, meaning that the war in Europe had already ended by the middle of this campaign since Germany surrendered in May.

This battle was an incredibly fierce fight between the two sides. Japan employed kamikaze pilots for ferocious attacks designed to destroy large areas and enemy equipment by slamming an aircraft loaded with bombs straight into the targets. That resulted in the death of the pilots as well, but they were fully prepared to make that sacrifice. There were huge numbers of Allied tanks on Okinawa that pounded the Japanese defenses for almost three months, not to mention the ships that surrounded the island. Due to the intense fighting, this was one of the bloodiest battles of the war, with around 160,000 casualties from both sides.

Perhaps one of the greatest tragedies of this battle was the loss of civilian life. Estimates indicate that around 300,000 civilians lived on the island, and by the end of the war, between one-tenth and one-third of them had died. Part of the reason was due to the Americans finding it difficult, or just didn't care enough, to distinguish between civilians and soldiers. One soldier reported, "There was some return fire from a few of the houses, but the others were probably occupied by civilians and we didn't care...Americans always had great compassion, especially for children (but) now we fired indiscriminately." Nevertheless, the Japanese also showed indifference toward civilians, often using them as shields, confiscating their food, and murdering those who hid food or who they thought could be spies. Many were killed by starvation and malaria, and others even killed themselves after the Japanese forces, knowing that their defeat was imminent, told them that the Americans would kill and rape them, as many believed in the stereotype that the Americans were barbarians who would actually commit such crimes.

The annexation of Okinawa was originally intended to provide a place from which a full-scale ground and air invasion of the island of Japan could be launched. However, that strategy was scrapped in favor of a plan to use two atomic bombs on Nagasaki and Hiroshima. The Allies contacted Emperor Hirohito of Japan and demanded their full and unconditional surrender, or else Japan would face "utter destruction." The emperor refused, and the plan went ahead.

Atomic Bombings of Nagasaki and Hiroshima

On August 6th and August 9th, 1945, the bombs were dropped on Nagasaki and Hiroshima by US forces. Between 70,000 and 80,000 people died in Hiroshima by the blast and the resultant firestorm. Since Japan showed no indication of surrendering after US President Harry Truman once again asked for it, the Allies agreed to drop the other bomb on Nagasaki, with 25,000 to 75,000 immediately dying. For months and years afterward, though, people continued to die from radiation illness and related injuries, with starvation also occurring. Over the next two to four months, it has been estimated that between 90,000 and 146,000 people in Hiroshima had died, with the estimates for Nagasaki being between 39,000 and 80,000.

The Kyujo Incident: A Coup?

On August 12th, 1945, Major General Kenji Hatanaka, Lieutenant Colonels Ida Masataka, Masahiko Takeshita, and Masao Inada approached the war minister, Korechika Anami, asking that he prevent any attempts at surrender. Anami was the most important man in Japan next to the emperor himself, but he refused and indicated that he planned to ask Emperor Hirohito to record the announcement that Japan would surrender unconditionally to the Allies.

Many of the military commanders felt that Japan should continue to resist the Allies. They were convinced that the Japanese would be enslaved by the Allied forces, although the preliminary agreements specified no such thing. The emperor made the recording of the surrender to be broadcast and put it in the hands of the commanders of the Imperial Guards, Lieutenant General Takeshi Mori and General Shizuichi Tanaka.

Kenji Hatanaka, a military officer, decided to put in motion a plan to stop the surrender from happening. He and a group of men managed to convince Colonel Toyojiro Haga to join their cause, although he only did so by lying to him. Hatanaka told Haga that the commanders of the Eastern District Army and the Imperial Guards Division were all in on the plan. He hoped that just by being inside the palace, others in the army would be inspired to join in and continue the war.

Once inside, Hatanaka shot and killed Lieutenant General Takeshi Mori, as he refused to join the rebels. Hatanaka also murdered Mori's brother-in-law, Michinori Shiraishi, who was in a meeting with Mori when Hatanaka and his forces barged in. Hatanaka then had his rebels cut the communication lines to the outside world.

At around the same time, another group of rebels went to kill Prime Minister Kantaro Suzuki. However, Suzuki had already been warned, so the building was empty. The rebels elected to burn it down and then headed to Kiichiro Hiranuma's, the former prime minister, house to kill him instead. He managed to escape, although his house was burned down.

Hatanaka's plot began to unravel around him, and he was informed that the Eastern District Army was on its way to put down the rebellion. He pleaded to have just ten minutes on the air to explain to the public what he was trying to accomplish, but he was denied. To make matters worse, Haga found out that the Eastern District Army had not supported Hatanaka's plans, and he ordered him to leave the premises.

Hatanaka attempted to break into the recording studio to give himself airtime, but it was to no avail. He left the palace grounds and threw leaflets that explained his actions onto the streets, as he could not find any other avenue to explain his motives for the rebellion. An hour before the emperor broadcasted Japan's surrender, Hatanaka shot himself.

Japan officially surrendered on August 14th, 1945. General Douglas MacArthur presided over the proceedings on September 2nd, where they signed the Japanese Instrument of Surrender.

Occupied Japan

Between 1947 and 1952, the United States occupied Japan. The goals during that period were reform and recovery, with the ultimate goal being to design a treaty and peace agreement. Shigeru Yoshida served as prime minister and can be credited as one of the people who propelled Japan from a devastated country toward one with a healthy economy that matched pre-war levels.

First of all, a more democratic set of laws was deemed necessary, one that didn't favor elites or the wealthy. The power of the *zaibatsu* was immense to the point that it virtually controlled the economy, and greater pluralism was necessary in order to give people upward mobility. The emperor's role was nearly godlike to the point that any error he might make would reverberate throughout all of society and could have unintended effects. The intention of the US occupation was to grant Japan its freedom to initiate its own tenants and grant everyone the right to participate in creating laws that would work for them.

Because the country had incurred the negative effects of having itself managed by a class of elites, the imperial house, or wealthy businessmen, there was a need to remove senior leaders who would simply repeat the mistakes of the past. A new generation of leaders was essential in order to preserve freedom. It was also felt that the military shouldn't hold political positions.

Besides establishing the basis for democracy, the economy was utmost in terms of the survival and integrity of Japan as a sovereign country. Joseph Dodge, a banker from Detroit, acted as a consultant in reconstituting the financial system and balancing the budget. He also established an exchange rate for the Japanese yen.

Constitution of 1947

The post-war constitution, which replaced the Meiji Constitution, provided for a parliamentary government with members of the Diet being elected. It guaranteed the Japanese their rights of life, liberty, equality, academic freedom, and collective bargaining. The Diet was the sole legislative division, and the judicial branch was made independent.

Treaty of San Francisco

On September 8th, 1951, this treaty was signed between the Allied Powers and Japan. It established peaceful relations with Japan and stated a willingness to accept the judgment of the International Military Tribunal regarding war crimes committed during the war, including compensation for civilians and others who had suffered because of them. Japan was to have rights to its main islands but had to renounce all rights and titles to the Pescadores Islands, Taiwan, and the islands which it had gained during World War II. Japan retained some residual rights to the Ryukyu Islands, pending future revisions. By virtue of the 1971 Okinawa Reversion Agreement, the Ryukyu Islands were returned to Japan in 1972 and became one of the Japanese prefectures.

Full sovereignty was returned to Japan, but its military was dismantled and the country disarmed. Later, in 1954, the military was reorganized into a defensive force called the Japan Self-Defense

Forces. Currently, that has changed with regard to participation in conflicts outside Japan that have an impact on Japanese security.

The Treaty of Mutual Cooperation and Security between the United States and Japan was created in 1951 and revised in 1952. It delineated mutual defense obligations and economic cooperation.

After the treaty was signed, the US continued to occupy Japan, and the Supreme Council of Allied Powers (SCAP) took on the task of rebuilding Japan and initiated efforts to revive its economy. Changes were instituted such as land reform, limitations placed on the power of the *zaibatsu*, reduction of the emperor's status in favor of the parliamentary system, granting women greater rights, renouncing its right to wage war by transforming it to serve a defensive function only, initiating tax reforms, and reducing inflation.

Inflation happened because Japanese industries were subject to the jolt of a sudden influx of contracts due to the international need for provisions for wars being fought abroad. Dodge had initiated an austerity program with price controls to help Japan prevent further inflation. SCAP, through his guidance, set up policies for Japan to avoid frequent governmental bailouts of failing companies since that would drain the national budget. In sectors like farming that were subject to intermittent losses, he recommended a system of controlled subsidies.

Korea

In 1910, Japan had annexed Korea, but after the war, the territory no longer belonged to them. Instead of placing the territory into the hands of one country, Korea was divided along the 38th parallel, with the northern portion going to the Soviet Union and the southern portion going to the United States. Although there were some attempts to unite the country after this initial division, by 1948, it was clear that it was not going to happen. North Korea, under the guidance of the Soviet Union, became communist in nature, leading some of the citizens to flee to South Korea, whose head of government was staunchly against communism. In 1950, North Korea attacked South Korea in the hopes of unifying both countries under one banner.

The war between North Korea and the United Nations forces, which were led by the United States, ended in 1953, with the war ending in a stalemate. The outcome is as yet unresolved, although discussions are currently underway to officially end the frozen conflict. The equipment needed by the United States, who fought heavily in the war, was provided by the Japanese "Model J" corporation, which is a corporation whose employees are trained specifically for their jobs. This sudden infusion of money was a boon to Japan, providing twelve billion dollars to its economy.

Chapter 11 –Heisei Era

In 1989, Hirohito died and was succeeded by his son, Akihito. When Akihito dies, he will be renamed as Emperor Heisei, meaning "achieving peace." The Heisei period spanned from 1989 to 2019.

Economy

After the rate of growth had exploded toward the end of Hirohito's term, it created what is called a "bubble economy." Bubbles predictably break, so lending institutions were in need of rescue from the national treasury. Predictably, the economy stagnated, and the banks and financial institutions then scrambled to recover their losses. As a stop-gap measure, low-interest loans were provided along with special tax-reduction incentives for lenders. This was unwise, as it became inevitable that weak borrowers were likely to default. This economic trauma forced Japan to turn from a "creditor nation" to a "debtor nation."

Some financial bodies sprung up because they assumed they could continue to be supported by the government because they were "too big to fail." The government, however, began to realize that this practice shouldn't continue, as it forced companies to provide loans at ridiculously low-interest rates and would force them to lower wages. Eventually, that reduced the money in circulation. Money was being hoarded in the hands of the very few who were "cash-rich," giving them nearly exclusive control. That, in turn, discouraged corporate investment, depleted the gross domestic product (GDP), and affected the stock market. From 1993 to 1996, there was a period of economic stagnation, and the cycle repeated again from 2009 to 2012.

Economic Planning

While Japan supports free enterprise, Japan isn't purely capitalist or socialist. For example, farmers receive subsidies, and the government often rushes in with monetary aid if any areas of the economy seem to be lagging behind others.

In terms of the labor market, only a very small segment of society was involved in the primary industries—mining, farming, and fishing. One-third of the population was in the industry sector, and a huge segment of society was engaged in the service sector. To prevent a segment of the population from sinking into absolute poverty, Japan felt that it had to monitor and control the economy to some extent. This function operates independently and is attached to the office of the minister of state. He, in turn, reports to the prime minister.

In 2001, an agency called the Ministry of Economy, Trade and Industry (METI) was established, consisting of multiple bureaus: 1) the Economic and Industrial Policy Bureau, 2) the Trade Policy Bureau, 3) the Trade and Economic Cooperation Bureau, 4) the Industrial Science and Technology Bureau and Environment Bureau, 5) the Manufacturing Industries Bureau, 6) the Commerce and Information Policy Bureau, as well as some other related agencies.

Environmental Planning

Because Japan is so dependent upon imports, a new ministry called the Environmental Management Bureau was created by reorganizing the 1971 Environmental Agency into a Cabinet-level ministry. In 2001, this was done by establishing a sub-Cabinet level called the Environmental Agency to reduce reliance on foreign sources through energy reduction. Japan looked toward creating a system of sustainable development. It was, in part, a reaction to the 1973 oil crisis that negatively affected Japan, as well as the rest of the world. Japan made an aggressive effort to build nuclear power plants and reduce electrical consumption. The other motivation for this had to do with safety protocols related to natural disasters such as earthquakes and tsunamis.

Art and Entertainment

Historically, during times of economic trauma, the entertainment industry tends to expand. When people become more stressful, companies take full advantage of that opportunity by providing a means of escape. The proliferation of art stimulated the industries that produced movies, video processes, TV, comics, and other media. The Japanese are well known for two very unique styles—anime and manga.

Anime, a particular animation style with a clearly recognizable character style, first appeared in 1917 but took root in Japan and across the world through the Heisei era. Large eyes with exaggerated emotions set in a disproportionately large head are characteristic of anime. In the beginning, this animated form consisted of a static background and figures on these backgrounds that were animated. The characters were drawn in ink, as the handier celluloid version required acetate that had to be imported from abroad. Once digital art was introduced, the celluloid animation cells were no longer necessary. Animation studios proliferated when Japanese artists were snapped up by the industry in many different countries. The subject matter was initially aimed at juveniles, but there arose a whole field of anime that appealed only to adults.

Manga refers to graphic novels and comic art using the Japanese language. Manga is said to have first been seen in scrolls dating back to the 12ᵗʰ century. Its character style was refined in the 19ᵗʰ century, and Oten Shimokawa developed it even further in 1917. During the Heisei era, it burgeoned into a multi-billion-dollar industry. The technique that was used was actually a reincarnation of a style created in the 19ᵗʰ century. Themes cover all the traditional fields, including action, horror, science fiction, mystery, history, and even adult pornographic content. Manga fired up the publishing industry as most of the material is in print.

Japan is very oriented toward preserving its historical roots, and manga presented a means by which Japanese history could be taught to the population. Eventually, this spread worldwide and provided Japan with an opportunity to become prominent on the international stage. The introduction of digital media created new markets for the spread of manga, and if a manga series is incredibly popular today, it is likely it will be made into a television series or movie.

The Role of Natural Disasters

Disturbances along geological fault lines in Japan have great significance because they are relatively frequent and affect the stability of the country. Japan lies on a fault line where two tectonic plates—the Pacific Plate and the Philippine Sea Plate—meet. As magma, the liquid core of the inner earth, moves, the upper solid layers, the earth's crust, shift. This movement results in widespread destruction of buildings and hundreds to thousands of innocent lives.

In 1995, an earthquake struck Kobe, which is located southwest of Tokyo. This earthquake reached 6.8 on the moment magnitude scale. Nearly 6,000 people died, and more than 400,000 buildings were severely damaged. The older buildings that had heavy roofs built to withstand typhoons collapsed from the top floor down in what is called a "pancake collapse." The port at Kobe was one of the largest container ports in the world, and this earthquake had disastrous effects worldwide, as thousands of international products were stored there, pending shipment. The Japanese economy had plateaued at this time, and the earthquake aggravated it. The stock market (the Nikkei Index) plunged, and Prime Minister Keizo Obuchi was criticized for not having effective measures in place to protect Japan.

There had been several building codes adopted throughout the years, beginning in 1950. This code, called *kyu-taishin*, was a revision of the old 1924 code developed after the Great Kanto earthquake in 1923. It called for a reinforcement of the walls in order to hold up the roofs and would have eliminated the "pancake collapses" that occurred; however, the 1950 standards weren't enforced. The older buildings in Kobe, which had the heavy roofs, would never have collapsed if the 1950 standards had been applied. The *kyu-taishin* was replaced with the *shin-taishin* in 1981. This was designed to protect buildings from major damage resulting from mid-size quakes. In 2000, the new code required that buildings needed to pass inspection for foundation stability.

In 2004, the Chuetsu earthquake in Honshu, the largest island of Japan, occurred. Partially due to the cooperation of real estate developers in adhering to the *shin-taishin* amendment of the building code, only 68 people died.

In 2011, the Tohoku earthquake struck off the coast of Tohoku in the Iwate Prefecture, which lies 232 miles north of Tokyo. It spread to the northern island of Honshu because it had a 300-mile-long rupture line along the Pacific Plate. This is the most powerful earthquake ever recorded in Japan and the fourth in the world since people began recording earthquakes, reaching a magnitude of 9.0 to 9.1 and shifting the earth's axis by ten inches. Over 10,000 people died as a result of this and the tsunami that followed.

The tsunami flooded part of Honshu's eastern coast, although the area arose again several years later, and a partial nuclear meltdown occurred because it impacted the Fukushima Daiichi Nuclear Power Plant, disabling its emergency generators. This triggered a deliberate release of hydrogen gas so as to prevent a far worse after-event. Some of the ocean waters were also contaminated, and they had to build a sea wall to contain the contamination in 2013 because contamination was still leaking into the water. In order to curb rumors and misunderstandings, the Environmental Management Bureau introduced a public education program aimed at releasing accurate information about the occurrence.

Population Problems

In 2005, the population of Japan started to decline and continues to do so. Hence, the number of foreigners working in the country has increased in order to keep the economy flowing. Between 2007 and 2019, the number of foreign workers has quadrupled. Birth rates declined due to urbanization, the higher costs of raising children, and the rise of the nuclear family. In addition, there is a movement toward what is termed "herbivore men," which refers to men who aren't interested in marriage and don't spend a lot of time pursuing romantic relationships. The herbivore phenomenon is unrelated to vegetarianism or homosexuality and is more comparable to men who are intensely interested in pursuing a career and don't want to juggle it with marriage.

The Emperor Passes the Torch

In 2019, Emperor Akihito abdicated due to his old age and declining health. He served as a spokesman for environmental protection and human rights, and he made a lot of imperial visits to areas in the Pacific that had been intensely involved in World War II, like Okinawa and the Philippines. During his term, he became very focused on transnational issues. The Heisei era was a peaceable era, but commentators have issued the warning that too much pacifism could harm the future of the country because there have been threats and attacks made to first-world nations, of which

Japan is one. There is an old Chinese proverb that asks: "Is it better to be a warrior in a garden or to be a gardener in a war?" That might well be applied to the next future era.

Akihito, who is now known as emperor emeritus, was succeeded by his son, Naruhito, in May of 2019. This initiated the Reiwa era, with Reiwa meaning "beautiful harmony."

Conclusion

Japan is about the same size as the US state of California and has a population of about 130 million people. For a country of modest size, it has one of the richest and most varied histories in the world. Like many other countries, it has run the gamut from primitive warring clans to a sophisticated and advanced culture. In the beginning, it was very much the product of one person whose family would control the country until another family came to take their place. Today, it has democratic institutions and promotes independent thought.

The Tokugawa shogunate was one of the most successful and prosperous administrations during a time when other countries were divided piecemeal among the power brokers of the day. Although isolation was its national policy during the 17th century, it created a unified national identity that other countries couldn't rival. This national identity helped Japan be very successful at the beginning of World War II, and although they ultimately lost the war, the following constitution and policies helped to create less of a gap between social classes, bringing the vast majority of the Japanese closer together.

The art and culture of Japan tie these people together even more and plays a prominent role in many other cultures around the world. Although they have been updated, art forms that were created in the 8th century still exist today. Japan is truly a wondrous place where modern thinking comfortably dwells with the ancient, creating a harmonious blend of ideas.

Part 3: History of Korea

A Captivating Guide to Korean History, Including Events Such as the Mongol Invasions, the Split into North and South, and the Korean War

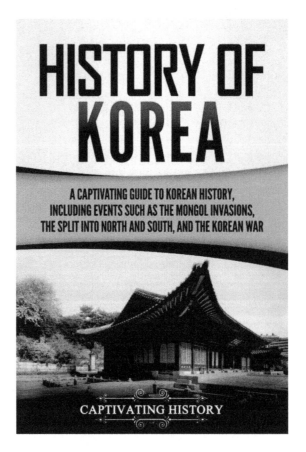

Introduction

The Korean Peninsula today is divided into two, but there was a time when this peninsula was divided into many states. Over the course of time, and besieged by expansive transient dynasties outside of this modest piece of land, many clans and tribes overran its regions. Of all those malicious and greedy potential overlords, none managed to prevail. The soil is rich with the blood of the people who made Korea happen, and it is the Korean people who rose victorious among the maelstrom of dead empires led by hated tyrants and wars fought by people in lands far beyond their own. The Koreans are survivors, known for their persistence and courage.

As Korea had long been seen as a gateway to other countries and the Yellow Sea, it was harassed for years by larger countries who were either on their way to somewhere else, like China, or who wanted a springboard to control the trade and colonization of the archipelagoes, smaller countries, and islands around the Pacific Ocean. The Western countries had interests in Korea, too, in order to curtail the full control of the Pacific to only one country, as well as to open Korea up to trade. As a result of these competing forces, Korea isolated itself during the latter half of the 19th century. In 1910, Japan annexed Korea and ruled it with an iron fist, even to the point of assimilating the unique culture of Korea into its own culture. In other words, they wanted to make it "disappear." The Koreans, however, fought long and hard to preserve their individuality as a nation. They eschewed control by other forces, even friendly ones, in order to preserve their unique cultural and political identity.

Even though Korea fought long and hard to remain one individual nation, they were eventually split into two. Western nations have made some overtures toward helping them achieve that unification and see an end to the Korean conflict. However, today, both North and South Korea want to lead that effort and do it their own way. Although Korea was granted its independence after two wars, the Korean people have it in their blood to be one undivided country, and they plan to work laboriously until that can be achieved in a way that is acceptable to both sides.

Chapter 1 – Land of the Bear

The Devil's Gate

In the cold dark cave of Chertovy Vorota, also known as the Devil's Gate, in northeastern Russia, lay her skull, long since abandoned by the ravages of Neolithic times from around 5700 BCE. No one knows her name, but she has achieved fame since she left geneticists with a record of the racial and ethnic origin of the hardy Korean people. The first people there fished in the frigid waters of the northern Pacific for salmon, cod, and hake. In addition, they hunted elk and moose. Unlike other primitive people, they were lactose intolerant, so they didn't milk any of the animals they hunted. Genome researchers also indicate that they raised agricultural products like rice and wheat to offset their high-protein diets. This was due to an influx of Neolithic people from southeastern Asia, where the growing season was longer. Later migrations show that the Han Chinese people from west of the Yellow River emigrated to the region, but there is plentiful evidence that many Chinese came to Korea much earlier (around 9,000 years ago). The Han Chinese were one of the largest ethnic groups in ancient China. They also brought the delightful mandarin orange plants with them for propagating. With the arrival of the agricultural people came the development of the "paddy-field," which was a step-wise segmented area flooded with water to foster the growth of rice.

Early people settling there lived in pit-houses consisting of a mud and straw roof over a dug-out pit. Or, as in the case of the woman from Chertovy Vorota, they lived in caves. They cooked their rice and grains in cups and bowls made of clay decorated with "comb-patterns." This type of pottery originated during the Mumun period, which lasted from 1500 to 300 BCE. Korea is actually the only place in the world where this unique style can be found.

Shellfish was originally plentiful along the coasts, but archeologists are quick to point out the fact that the supply of shellfish diminished because of overexploitation and population growth. They theorized this happened during the Late Mumun period (550 to 300 BCE).

The lack of shellfish resulted in the growth of farming activity. Farming was mainly conducted in southern Korea, while those who lived in the northern area of the peninsula favored meat and fish. To eat their food, as well as to make weapons, Koreans fashioned axes, knives, and cooking utensils out of bronze, which is made from heating copper and tin. These molten metals were then poured into clay molds.

Songguk-ri

Songguk-ri is an archeological site that contains only whispers about the civilization that lived in the central-western region of South Korea in the Middle and Late Mumun period (c. 850 to 300 BCE). Because of the arrangement of the pit-houses and the existence of large walls at Songguk-ri, it has been concluded that there were divisions among the tribes that lived there. Greenstones (primarily jade) and intricately designed bronze daggers found at burial sites seem to indicate that there were chiefs, who, along with their families, would have lorded over the rest of the common population.

The existence of the Songguk-ri wall indicates that there were competition and conflict between the various clans. In addition, there was a stratified social structure. As discussed earlier, the Chinese migrated to Korea. Between 475 to 221 BCE, the states of China were at war until the Qin Dynasty took over. Although most of the Korean migrants were from the state of Han, some were not. Those people brought their hostilities with them to Korea, and some of the settlements were burned and subsequently abandoned.

Within the individual clan societies, there is evidence that shows that the elites in the population controlled their subjects through the distribution of arable lands and labor demands. Most likely, the elite people had the subservient classes supply food for them, and they received more than enough to sustain themselves. Indications are that the food for the noble classes and royalty was of a higher quality. Researchers have found the remains of rice cakes and rice wine (*cheongju*), which would have been considered gourmet food. Because it was primarily an agrarian economy, control of the economy equaled control of the people, and so, the leaders provided incentives for food producers who had larger crop yields.

The other caste that emerged during this period was the one devoted to craft production. Besides household objects and weapons, Koreans produced beads made out of jade. These beads were often used as a sort of currency. Everyone had to pay tribute to the central leadership, and they used beads or barter to do so. The artifacts found of these crafts include mirrors, jewelry, and an assortment of weapons.

Later on, Korean craftsmen manufactured specialized swords. The most notable sword that has been discovered is the "Liaoning sword," or the seven-branched sword. Artifacts indicate that this type of sword originated in the northern peninsula and then became popular in other regions. Archeologists debate about whether or not it was used as a weapon, although the inscriptions on it would seem to indicate so. The characters are inlaid with gold, and on one side of the sword, it reads in part: "Using the sword repels 100 enemy soldiers. It is bestowed to the duke lord."

They Had Heat!

Korean winters are long and cold, especially in the north. To heat their houses, a fire would be built alongside the home in a pit, allowing heat to flow into a short basement under the floorboards. Rocks were fastened to the underside of the floor to help retain heat. There was an outlet on the opposite side of the house for a stove and, beyond that, a flue with a free-standing chimney that funneled the smoke out. The heating system was called *ondol*, and it would be built when the house was erected.

Since the fire was extinguished at night as a safety measure, the houses cooled and were very cold by late morning. Of course, they were relit, but it took a long time for the air in the rooms to heat back up. The room closest to the fire pit was very hot, while the room farthest away was much cooler. Even so, this heating system was incredibly sophisticated for a primitive culture.

Creation Myth

Ancient historians in 7th-century China wrote that a god by the name of Hwanung craved to live in the valleys and mountains of earth. He was the son of the "Lord of Heaven," Hwanin. Hwanung was granted the assistance of the spirits of the Rain, Wind, and Clouds in his quest to find land on earth, and he descended on Paektu Mountain with his followers. According to the legend, a tiger and a bear befriended him. The two animals prayed to become human, so Hwanung placed them into a solitary cave. Whoever would persist without food or water the longest would be the winner. In time, the tiger tired, gave in to his baser instincts, and left the cave to hunt. However, the bear persisted and did become human. She was named Ungnyeo, and Hwanung fell in love with her. They wed and gave birth to a son named Dangun Wanggeom. Dangun settled in the northern area of Korea with 3,000 followers and established the settlement of Gojoseon.

The Three Kingdoms: Goguryeo

By 18 BCE, Korea had been split into three prominent kingdoms: Goguryeo in the northern and central parts of the peninsula and Baekje and Silla on the southern tip.

Around 37 BCE, Goguryeo was first called "Gojoseon." They engaged in trade with the Han Chinese throughout the Bronze Age. Because of their language similarity with the native Japanese (Japonic language), they traded with Japan and even accepted some of them into their population.

In time, Gojoseon collapsed under a succession of rather weak descendants of Dangun. Under his descendant, King Dongmyeongseong, or "Jumong," the region was renamed Goguryeo (also spelled as Koguryo), and it became more powerful and larger after battles with the Chinese and nomadic tribes from Manchuria, Mongolia, and part of Russia. Jumong was a militaristic autocrat, and his successors followed in his footsteps. By 242 CE, Goguryeo had expanded north and doubled in size.

The use of iron for weaponry greatly assisted the monarchs of Goguryeo in conquering territory from China. Iron was plentiful in the rocks of Goguryeo. It could be melted down, but it could not be poured in molds like bronze. Instead, it had to be hammered into shape by a metalworker while still hot. Iron became more desirable as it was much stronger than bronze, which tended to bend or break.

The Three Kingdoms: Baekje

Baekje was the second of the three stable kingdoms. Legends tell a story about the son of King Jumong, Yuri, who was a troublemaker with poor manners. Yuri ran away from home when his father was away warring with the princes of the kingdom. When Jumong returned, he was furious. In order for his son and heir to be redeemed, Jumong buried half a sword and challenged Yuri to find the other half. It was Jumong's objective that Yuri learn how to start and finish a difficult task. When Yuri found the other half of the sword, he was reunited with his father.

After Jumong's wife died, Jumong took on a new wife named Soseono, and they had two sons—Onjo and Biryu. The two of them were always obedient and loyal. Since they would have no inheritance after their father died due to Yuri making up with his father, Jumong had them go southward and create their own state. The two brothers quarreled, as brothers often do, and each set up their own state in the southern part of Goguryeo.

Unfortunately, Biryu's segment, called Sipje, was totally unsuitable for productive habitation, as it was full of salt marshes. Humbly, he moved to his brother's neighboring state, Baekje, to the west. It lies beneath the shadow of the great Bukhan Mountain, which can be seen behind the current-day city of Seoul. Biryu couldn't handle this deep failure of his and committed suicide. However, his generous brother, Onjo, welcomed all of Biryu's relatives and subjects into his kingdom.

Onjo needed to expand his state to integrate all these new subjects, so he had to fight with elements from the Samhan confederacy farther south in order to create a larger state. The largest of these city-states was ruled by the kings of the Mahan confederacy, which was a part of the greater Samhan confederacy. When one of the Mahan kings committed suicide because he couldn't defend his territory against the forces of Onjo, he asked that Onjo treat his people with mercy. Onjo did so, and he gradually absorbed the Mahan region of the Samhan confederacy into the Baekje Kingdom.

While he was running the state of Baekje, Onjo's warriors had to continually defend the lands from nomadic peoples called the Malgal, or Mohe, a Tungusic people. They were originally from the southern districts of Manchuria and often pillaged Baekje around 5 BCE because it had become quite prosperous. Onjo proved to be successful in defending his lands, leading to a long line of rulers.

The Three Kingdoms: Silla

In 57 BCE, an ancient legend relates that a great light shone into a dark forest like a spotlight. A great "chicken dragon" pranced into the heavenly light and laid a large white egg. From that egg, a human baby hatched. His name was Park (also known as Bak or Pak) Hyeokgeose, and he founded the magnificent state of Silla to the east of Baekje.

The hills and mountains of Silla yielded much gold, and the area became a haven for craftsmen. Silla is known today for its intricate golden jewelry. The royal women of this state wore beautiful golden earrings, while the males owned golden ceremonial daggers in scabbards studded with jade and turquoise. The crowns were likewise delicate, consisting of a band of gold with two golden antler spikes and dangling golden beads.

Park Hyeokgeose wore such a crown until 4 CE, which was when his son took up the mantle. In time, a hereditary monarchy was established, and the state operated like a feudal society. It was a land of peace until there was friction between Silla and Baekje over territorial boundaries. Silla allied itself with Goguryeo for protection. In time, though, Goguryeo expanded southward and established a capital at Pyongyang. In 427 CE, Goguryeo started expanding even farther south. Due to the work of King Nulji of Silla, Silla and Baekje were able to resolve their differences, and the two states united their armed forces against Goguryeo. They drove the Goguryeo people farther north toward the Han River in the locale of South Korea's modern-day capital city of Seoul.

Silla, like the other Korean kingdoms, had a hereditary line of rulers. The system of inheritance of the throne was based on the bone-rank system, which was a caste system that segregated the levels of society. "Sacred bone" was the top rank, meaning that the ruler had royal blood from both their father and mother. The oldest surviving piece of the written history of Korea is the *Samguk Sagi* (or, in English, *History of the Three Kingdoms*), which was written in 1145 and is used today as a reference for archeologists and historians. According to the *Samguk Sagi,* Sol Kyedu, the son of an official, said: "In Silla, bone rank is the key to employment."

This system applied to women as well. Although it wasn't incredibly common for women to have power in Silla, it did happen on occasion, and the idea of "sacred bone" helped to work in their favor. In 632, there were no male descendants, so Seondeok ruled Silla after proving herself to her father, becoming the first queen of Silla. Initially, she was ridiculed by the nobles, and Emperor Taizong of the Tang Dynasty of China asked, "If you do not have an appropriate leader, shall I send you a king?" In time, though, the Korean people came to love her. She was concerned about the welfare of her people, and at the beginning of her reign, she sent out inspectors so she could be informed about the needs of her people, specifically the elderly, the poor, and the abandoned.

In the 1280s, another ancient historical tome was written called the *Samguk Yusa* (or, in English, *Memorabilia of the Three Kingdoms*). As opposed to the *Samguk Sagi,* the *Samguk Yusa* was a record of the legends and beliefs of the early societies of Korea. According to the *Samguk Yusa,* Seondeok had clairvoyant abilities. It stated that she saw white frogs croaking by the Jade Gate pond in the winter in a vision. Since frogs croak angrily like soldiers in a battle, Seondeok interpreted this vision as a sign that a great battle would occur between Silla and the people from the west (Baekje) and that Silla would prevail in the end. Queen Seondeok told her generals to search out enemy infiltrators who would be found hiding in the forests near Silla, preparing to attack. It happened just as she had said, and Silla engaged in war with the Baekje Kingdom. Having caught the Baekje warriors by surprise, the army of Silla slaughtered over one thousand soldiers.

After Seondeok's successor, Queen Jindeok took the throne, she wanted to court the favor of the Tang Dynasty in China. She sent a complimentary poem to Emperor Gaozong, which said, in part,

"Great Tang created the celestial empire...He rules over the whole creation and gives luster to everything—his deep benevolence is matched only by the sun and the moon." Gaozong was highly flattered by the beautiful poem, and so, the Tang Dynasty of China was favorably disposed toward Silla.

After Jindeok died in 654, Muyeol rose to the throne. King Muyeol was an accomplished strategist, and he made a military alliance with the Tang Dynasty of China. In 660, both conquered Baekje, leaving only Goguryeo to contend with.

Munmu, the next king who took over in 661, established an educational system to instruct all of his officials. They were also exposed to the Chinese classics. Munmu is also remembered for his military accomplishments. In 668, Munmu managed to defeat Goguryeo, meaning that Munmu was the first ruler to see the Korean Peninsula unified, which led to the Unified Silla period, also known as Later Silla. Munmu also had to deal with the Tang Dynasty during his rule. In 674, the mighty army of the Tang attempted to absorb Silla. However, they were defeated two years later in 676.

Silla, by this point, had become a great sea power, as it had a generous coastline along the Pacific Ocean. It conducted trade with local countries, including Japan. However, Japan became a threat to Korea during this period. They had a steady stream of pirates that attacked the port cities, and some of the Japanese forces raided the towns in Silla. Munmu set up defenses along its eastern coast, which did help to repel the invaders. As he aged, he asked that he might be entombed underwater. Korean beliefs in the 7th century indicate that he thought he could then become the "Dragon of the East Sea" by doing this and continue to protect his people. Today, one can see an impressive rocky island under which the body of the beloved king was interred.

Chapter 2 – The Dragon of the East Sea

The Great Ch'oyong

The *Samguk Yusa,* or *Memorabilia of the Three Kingdoms,* told a story about the Dragon of the East Sea. The people of Silla revered the royal family, especially King Munmu, and told stories of his accomplishments along with personal tales about his trials and tribulations. His story, as well as other stories, are peppered throughout this ancient text. Here is another one of the tales, which relates a story about the Dragon of the East Sea.

In the 9th century, the king of Silla, Heongang, failed to make his offerings to the great Dragon of the East Sea. Clouds shrouded the land and sea. Heongang was a humble king, and so, he asked his subjects why the great dragon frowned upon him. They told him he hadn't made his offerings and was negligent in his meditations. After making the expected offerings, the Dragon of the East Sea appeared before the king and his seven sons. There was a great celebration among the people, filled with music and dancing. After this tale, the *Samguk Yusa* goes on to tell of the misfortune of one of his sons, Ch'oyong.

Ch'oyong came home after the celebration to find that an evil spirit had possessed his wife and lured another man into their marriage bed. As related in the *Samguk Yusa*, Ch'oyong said, "Having caroused far into the night in the moonlit capital, I return home and in my bed, Behold, four legs. Two were mine; Whose are the other two? Formerly two were mine; What shall be done now they are taken?" Ch'oyong was heartbroken by this, but he spared the two and withdrew in silent resignation. After that virtuous act, the evil spirit appeared before him and said that he was impressed with Ch'oyong's response, which was not one of rage. The evil spirit then promised that whenever Ch'oyong's likeness is displayed, the evil spirit will not return.

Korean Buddhism

Back in the 4th century, Buddhism was introduced to Korea. It originated from India and was transported to China and then Korea. Buddhists believe in four truths: 1) existence brings suffering; 2) the cause of suffering is craving; 3) there is a way to end suffering; and 4) one needs to break one's earthly attachments. That will lead to the state of nirvana, or perfect happiness. The means by which one attains nirvana is to follow an eightfold path consisting of right understanding, right thought, right speech, right action, right livelihood, right effort, right mindfulness, and right concentration. Koreans added one more step to this path: the requirement to settle all disputes peaceably. The last step reflects the lessons derived from the historical struggle of the three kingdoms to unite.

Korean Confucianism

During the 4th century, Confucian beliefs were carried into Korea through the Han Chinese. Most of them were then living in the areas north of the Korean Peninsula. Confucianism is a humanistic belief system. It didn't conflict with other religions but was rather a structure for understanding how to live in a society with each other peacefully. It focuses on *ren*, which means that one learns how to live life in such a way as to promote order, peace, love for fellow humans, ethics, and respect for parents within society. Benevolence and compassion are virtues that flow from this paradigm and bring about wisdom. Its founder, Confucius, supported obedience to rightful authority figures and the observance of sacred rituals. He once said, "To master oneself and return to ritual propriety is human-heartedness."

Ancestor worship is derived from these beliefs, but it isn't "worship" per se; it is more a recognition of the contribution from prior generations that has formed a lasting imprint in the minds and hearts of the living. There were specific rituals created within extended families for memorializing the lives of the ancestors. Many are still practiced today and are not seen as a contradiction to other faiths, even Christianity.

The Golden Age

Korea, now united in 676, produced many great masterpieces of art and architecture. Many of these sites are still present today and manifest the distinctive beauty of Korea during the 7th and 8th centuries.

The Ansi fortress is an example of how architecture and the outcome of battles are related. Goguryeo in northern Korea had as many as 2,400 fortresses. Korean fortresses were built very differently than Chinese fortresses. Koreans used stones that were carefully shaped into oblong blocks; they were mostly made of granite quarried in the mountains, and these blocks were slotted together very carefully. The Chinese, on the other hand, used earthen-style fortresses, which were built of bricks, although sometimes they utilized mounds of earth. In 645, when Goguryeo battled with the Tang Dynasty of China in the Siege of Ansi, the Chinese built a giant earth mound from which to launch an attack. Because it was only made of earth, it collapsed. Thus, Korea prevailed against the Tang.

The Seokguram Grotto is another interesting piece of architecture. It was built in 774 and still contains a great statue of

Buddha that looks out to the sea. The position of the Buddha relates to the history of Korea since recurring threats to their land came from Japan and other seafaring peoples. The great Buddha statue shows Buddha with his right hand in the *dhyana mudra* position, indicating that the flow of energy from within is one of concentration. His left hand is in the *bhumisparsha mudra* position, symbolizing the earth. Thus, Buddha touches the spirit of life and shows unity, which is reminiscent of the Korean struggle to remain united. There is a central rotunda within the grotto with carefully carved sculptures of devas (angels), bodhisattvas (students), and disciples of the great Buddha. It is made of granite quarried in the eastern mountains.

The grotto is combined with the Bulguksa temple complex, which is made of gleaming white granite. There are three terraces with pillared railings of wood, and three pagodas are perched on top. The Bulguksa temple complex, rebuilt in 774, teaches through its architecture the journey of a Buddhist reaching nirvana. For example, within the temple, there are two halls, one of which is called the "Hall of No Words." This means that belief cannot be taught by mere words alone. This temple has undergone many embellishments throughout the years and is considered the foremost Buddhist temple in South Korea.

Two pagodas at the Gameunsa Temple Site, located on the eastern coast of Korea, were built in the 7th century to celebrate the victory of King Munmu over the Tang Chinese and the Japanese pirates. They were built from multiple oblong granite stones, and the stone structures have a three-tiered roof system. Originally, the pagodas were used for sacrificial rites. The Gameunsa pagodas survived the ravages of time and are featured today in many of the tourist brochures for Korea.

Pottery flourished during the Korean golden age as well. Pots and vessels from this period display natural themes, such as leaves or flowers. It is a simplistic, free-flowing, and open design, neither complex nor pattern-adherent. Potters painted each of their pieces individually, and they often used one or two colors. Pigments were made from the minerals found in the mountains.

Not all of the art had religious themes. In the fine tombs of the Korean nobles and kings, there are giant murals depicting the activities of daily life that feature the deceased couple. Other themes painted on the walls of the tombs show the occupations of the common people, like hunting, fishing, and farming. There are frescoes in these tombs that use exquisite decorative techniques to paint lotus flowers, fish, horses, tigers, deer, and dragons. Korean art shows a Chinese influence, but the themes draw it closer to the history of Korea because they use fewer pictographs.

Due to Chinese influences, woodblock printing was created during this time. Craftsmen carved characters in raised relief on blocks of wood, and ink was applied to the raised portions. The characters were to be read from right to left, like in a mirror image. The subject matters initially were about Buddhist *sutras*, or sayings. The Great Dharani Sutra is the earliest example of Korean woodblocks and was found inside the Bulguksa temple complex in South Korea. It is considered to be the oldest printed text in the world.

Balhae

To escape the earlier battles of the three kingdoms in Korea, many people fled to the north and settled there. They were ethnically related to the Manchurian and eastern Russian people. They despised the Tang rule and united with the nomadic Mohe people to free themselves from the government of Korea, which was heavily influenced by the Tang culture.

Dae Jo-yeong, a general from Goguryeo, had orders from the last king of Goguryeo to establish a new kingdom, and he chose the territory northeast of Korea to establish his new state. He and his Mohe allies had to defeat the Chinese who were occupying that region first. In 698, he and his army defeated the Tang Chinese at the Battle of Tianmenling. They called their new land Balhae, which is also referred to as Parhae in some academic sources.

In 732, the second king of Balhae, Mu, expanded the territory of Balhae even more. Once it was fully settled, Balhae opened up relations with Japan, an association which they nurtured for years. In addition to the officials of Balhae, poets, like Chongso and Injong, served as foreign diplomats. Balhae fostered the arts, and although only a few artifacts remain from that period, they are stately and imposing. The area is known for its two huge stone lanterns erected on huge pillars.

The last king of Balhae, Seon, greatly expanded Balhae and conquered some lands in today's North Korea. Balhae also encompassed portions of today's northeast China and Russia. Balhae was so strong at this point that Silla had to build a wall in 821 to prevent Balhae from encroaching on their territory.

However, there are no surviving records of Balhae after King Seon ended his reign in 830, so it is not known what happened next. His grandson did take the throne, but scholars don't have much information on him. What is known definitively is that the Khitans took over Balhae in 926. The Khitans were not a new problem; they had harassed Balhae throughout the years. Historians debate over their origin. Some conjecture that they came from Manchuria and Mongolia, while others contend that they originated from the Eurasian steppes. They were expert horsemen, wore furs, and were very skilled with the bow and arrow. They raised cattle and were meat-eaters, which horrified the vegetarian Buddhists, who called them "barbarians." The Khitans had formed the Liao Dynasty in 916 and were headquartered in China near the Yalu River, which borders North Korea.

Although Balhae did receive some aid from Goguryeo in the south, their culture and society were destroyed by the Khitans. Many of the people of Balhae migrated to Goguryeo, which protected them, and they were referred to as a "married country," meaning that the people of Goguryeo felt a kinship with them. Those who stayed in Balhae found themselves being ruled by the Khitans of the Dongdan Kingdom, which was later annexed by the Liao Dynasty in 936.

In 946, Paektu Mountain, a volcano, burst open, propelling a Plinian (hot gaseous) blast that sent steaming smoke and debris as far as the stratosphere. Following that was the pyroclastic (rock-spewing) explosion, which sent tremendous rocks and ash into the region. This eruption is one of the most powerful in history. Following that, the ancient records fall silent. Historians, therefore, conclude that this tremendous natural disaster wiped out most of the lands once known as Balhae.

The Later Three Kingdoms

Between 892 and 935, Later Silla started to disintegrate. Under the administration of Queen Jinseong (ruled 887 to 897), corruption had started to seep into the government. Taxes rose to supplement the money that officials were embezzling from the treasury, and because of the heavy tax burden, famines occurred. Simultaneously, political rivalries also arose within the administration. Revolts and decentralization took place as the regional people outside of the capital of Later Silla, Gyeongju, banded together to survive.

Taking advantage of the strife in the kingdom, some rebels sought to revive the kingdoms of Baekje and Goguryeo. The cultural differences between the three states also gave impetus to this separation. Goguryeo was allied with the Tang Chinese and showed the influences of that culture. Baekje resurrected itself and was primarily a trading region, but Silla was wrought with internal strife among the nobles and kings clamoring for power.

Later Baekje

The kingdom of Silla gave rise to powerful generals, one of whom was Gyeon Hwon. In 892, the peasants had been severely downtrodden and burdened with heavy taxation. Taking advantage of their dissatisfaction, Gyeon united them and formed a mighty army in order to overthrow the rulers and nobles. After conquering the large city districts of Wansanju and Mujinju, he declared himself king, and the area was then called Hubaekje ("Later Baekje).

In 927, Gyeon Hwon attacked the kingdom of Silla. He and his forces handily won, and the king of Silla, Gyeongae, chose to commit suicide over placing his fate in the hands of Gyeon Hwon. After that, Gyeon Hwon established a puppet monarch on the throne before turning his attention to Goryeo (which had previously been Later Goguryeo; see below). He led a full-scale attack there in the present-day city of Andong, located in the mid-eastern portion of Korea, but he lost. He continued to attempt to gain control, and sporadic battles ensued between Later Baekje and Goryeo.

While this was going on, internal strife was tearing the kingdom apart. Gyeon Hwon was deposed by his son, Gyeon Singeom, with the aid of some of his other brothers after Singeom had been passed over as heir to the throne. Gyeon Hwon fled to Goryeo, who welcomed his military experience with open arms.

Once Silla surrendered to Goryeo in 935, Gyeon Hwon was allowed to go after Later Baekje that same year. In doing so, he brought about the downfall of the very kingdom he founded.

Later Goguryeo

Like Gyeon Hwon of Baekje, Gung Ye, a one-eyed monk, was initially a Silla military prince. In 891, he united with the rebel factions and quickly rose in power. He was known as being a cruel and rigid leader. He was extremely self-centered and began referring to himself as the reincarnation of the Maitreya Buddha later on life; the Maitreya Buddha occupies the most prestigious place in Buddhism, even today. During the course of his life, he executed his own wife and two of his sons, whom he saw as rivals. When some of his fellow monks admonished him, he executed them as well. Gung Ye, who had a very changeable nature, joined with other warlords as time went on before amassing enough power to stage his own rebellion. In 901, he turned on the other warlords and proclaimed himself king of Hugoguryeo (known as Later Goguryeo). Due to his erratic nature, the name of the country was later changed to Majin, and the capital was moved to Cheorwon, a fortress located in a mountainous region.

In 911, the name of the country was changed yet again, this time to Taebong. Gung Ye appointed a prime minister named Wang Geon, also known as Taejo of Goryeo, two years later. Some of the nobles from the ruling families conspired with Wang Geon to stage a coup. While many historians indicate they did this because of objections to Gung Ye's tyrannical rule, they themselves were just as warlike when given authority. Wang Geon and the nobles usurped the throne from Gung Ye in 918, and he was killed by either one of his own soldiers or by peasants after having escaped the palace. Wang Geon was placed on the throne, and he renamed the kingdom as Goryeo, also spelled as Koryo, which is where the name Korea is derived from.

Later Silla

At the beginning of the 9th century, the nobles had grabbed a huge power base in Silla. The people were very unhappy over the tax burden and the constant conflicts that erupted in the different regions of Silla. There were famines caused by the high taxes the nobles collected, and there was no system for supplying the people with food and grain when their crops failed. As the nobles were warring with each other, the whole state of Silla was starting to disintegrate. As a result, Silla was losing many of their people since they moved to other parts of Korea, China, and even Japan.

A young man by the name of Jang Bogo arose from the population. He had integrity and mustered the favor of the Korean people. When Jang was studying his martial arts skills in China, the people from Silla who had fled from there were being poorly treated by the Chinese. Some of their women were abducted and sold into slavery, pirates raided their ships, and bandits roamed around the towns. When the Silla people met Jang Bogo, they were impressed with his chivalry and forthrightness. They even asked him to lead and defend them, which he did so in 825. He established a small private fleet, and in 827, he presented a petition to the king of Silla, Heungdeok, to construct a fortress along the coast to protect the fishermen. Due to his skills, a thriving maritime industry grew on the Yellow Sea. His fleet increased substantially, and the fishermen and merchants from Silla were conducting business not only with the legitimate Tang traders but with Persians and Arabians as well. Jang was a masterful negotiator, and his ships exploited what is called the "Maritime Silk Road," which ran down the coast of Korea and the coast of southern China, down along Vietnam, and around India, among other routes. Trade in aromatics and spices thrived during this era as a result.

In Silla proper, however, there were vicious succession battles. The reigns of the kings from 828 to 927 were very short-lived, as each made war on their predecessors. The territory was also frequently attacked by other forces, most notably those of Gyeon Hwon of Later Baekje and Taejo of Goryeo. Severely weakened by the wars, the last king of Silla, Gyeongsun, abdicated and surrendered the throne to Wang Geon, with Later Baekje soon following suit.

Thus, the three kingdoms were again reunited in 935. The greatest advantage of this reunification was the fact that the three cultural elements melded together and created the basis for the country of Korea.

Chapter 3 – Dynasties Rise and Fall

The Goryeo Dynasty

Once the Later Three Kingdoms all came under the control of Wang Geon, he established what is known as the Goryeo Dynasty. The power of the noble families had been a perennial problem on the peninsula. Wang Geon was a man of peace who looked toward unity in order to create an orderly society, making the country a fertile land for the arts and Buddhism. Cleverly, he married women from all the noble families and had 25 sons and 9 daughters by them. Wang Geon established a hierarchical system of administrators and passed reforms to strengthen monarchical authority. What's more, he freed prisoners of war from the tumultuous period of the conflicts among the old kingdoms. This was a strategic move, as it increased the tax base and helped to make the treasury healthy.

Wang Geon's third son, Jeongjong, formed a huge army of 300,000 men to defend the territory of Goryeo against the troublesome Khitans, whose empire was the most powerful at the time. Wang Geon's fourth son, Gwangjong, opened up relations with the massive Song Dynasty in China in 962 to aid him in keeping the nomadic Khitans out of Goryeo. Aside from that, Gwangjong continued making reforms and created a systematic bureaucracy by initiating civil service examinations to assure the country had capable and knowledgeable leadership with clearly defined job roles.

Seongjong, who inherited the throne in 981, focused upon education in Goryeo and founded the Gukjagam University in 992, which helped to promote Confucian philosophy. The university library was stocked with many Chinese classics, as well as texts on science and mathematics.

The Goryeo-Khitan War

During Seongjong's reign, the pesky Liao Empire reared its head again. In 993, they attacked the northwestern border of Goryeo. Seeing that his troops were heavily outnumbered, Seongjong asked to negotiate peace terms and sent his negotiator, Seo Hui, to meet with the Khitan commander, Xiao Sunning. Xiao then said to Seo, "I am a nobleman from a powerful country. You must bow down before coming into my tent." Seo objected, saying that such behavior wasn't appropriate for two envoys. Xiao was amazed by Seo's courage and suggested that the two sit down as equals and discuss terms.

Goryeo agreed to three terms in the treaty: 1) the cessation of relations with the Song Dynasty, 2) the payment of an annual tribute, and 3) the adoption of the Liao calendar. Goryeo abided by all but one of the terms in the agreement—the relationship with the Song Dynasty. This was a major problem for the Khitans, as the Liao Empire were enemies of the Song.

The treaty, signed in 993, lasted until 1009, which was when the Khitans again attacked Goryeo. The king of Goryeo at the time was King Mokjong. However, political intrigue in Goryeo polluted the leadership, allowing a coup to occur under General Gang Jo. He assassinated King Mokjong and established military rule in Goryeo. The devious Khitans attacked at this time, claiming that they were avenging the dead king but more likely hoping to gain something out of the internal turmoil. As a result of the conflict, the capital was destroyed. However, the Khitans couldn't obtain the desired foothold needed and were forced to retreat. Knowing that the Khitans would eventually strike again, King Hyeonjong, who had been placed on the throne by Gang Jo, attempted to enter peace negotiations with the Liao Empire. Since the Liao Empire demanded too much—they wanted key areas of the northern region in exchange for peace, which would have given them a foothold in Goryeo—hostilities reignited between the two powers. Successive attacks continued along the border regions in 1015, 1016, and 1017. Each time, the two sides withdrew and repaired their border fortifications. No resolution was reached, and so, the sporadic attacks continued.

In 1018, King Hyeonjong of Goryeo employed the military talents of General Gang Gam-chan, as well as that of the Mongols. Before the Khitan warriors had amassed at the border, he dammed the river up with cowhides near Heungwajin. The Khitans came storming through toward the river and the fortress located there. When they crossed the Yalu River, the Gang Gam-chan had his troops dismantle the dam, and thousands of Khitans were drowned.

Once the Khitans reorganized, they marched toward the capital of Goryeo. However, the Goryeo warriors put up a fierce fight, and they forced the Khitans back north. Gang Gam-chan waited at the fortress in Gwiju for the Khitans. Not many details exist about this battle, but it is known that the Khitans were almost completely annihilated. After this battle, the Liao Empire and Goryeo enjoyed peace with each other until the Liao Empire fell in 1125.

The Thousand-li Wall

A *li* is a traditional unit of distance in China, and it has been used by other Asiatic peoples throughout the years. Its measurements have changed over time, but it measured about 323 meters (almost

1,060 feet) when the wall was built, and it measures around 500 meters (about 1,640 feet) today.

After the Goryeo-Khitan War, Goryeo erected this immense wall, which was built between 1033 and 1044. It connected the northern fortresses of Goryeo, and a portion of it remains today.

The Invasions of the Jurchen People

The Jurchens were a tribe of agrarian people who settled in the Siberian/Mongolian tundra. They were also referred to as the "reindeer people." However, during the 11th century, they were vassals of the Liao Empire. At that time, the Khitans of the Liao Dynasty had been attempting to move toward Goryeo in search of warmer lands. Their "slash-and-burn" technique of agricultural destruction stunted the growth of their grain crops, thus giving impetus to the need to relocate. The Jurchens lived in areas of the Chinese mainland as a minority, but in 1104, the Jurchens grew stronger and amassed in force around northern Goryeo. They often raided the lands of northern Goryeo during the time of the Goryeo-Khitan War.

Once the Goryeo-Khitan War was over, the experienced military general, Yun Gwan, approached King Sukjong of Goryeo to reorganize a segment of the army into cavalry and ground forces, which would become known as the Byeolmuban, to expel the Jurchens. In 1107, he invaded Jurchen territory to the north of Goryeo. Initially, he was repelled by the battle-hardened Jurchens, but he returned and successfully erected nine fortresses on the northern border. In 1108, the fortresses were abandoned in exchange for a non-aggression pact.

The Jurgens then turned their attention to the Khitan Liao Dynasty, as they wished to overthrow their status as vassals. In 1114, the Jurchens attacked and subdued them, after which they took over regions of northeastern China, which eventually culminated in the establishment of the Jin Dynasty in China. By 1125, the Jurchens had managed to subdue the Khitans, ending the Liao Dynasty.

However, from 1189 to 1234 (the year the Jin Dynasty ended), the Jurchens were involved in battles with the Mongols. In the beginning, the Jurchens of the Jin Dynasty constantly raided the property of the Mongols, who dwelled in the southern steppes. The Jin destroyed the rice paddies and the families who grew the rice. The Mongols responded in kind, and in 1211, the great Genghis Khan came raging through after having united many of the various nomadic tribes from Mongolia into a giant force of warriors. In 1234, their powerful leader, Ögedei Khan, the third son and chosen successor of Genghis Khan, put an end to the Jin Dynasty, repeating the words of his father, "The eternal sky has promised us victory and vengeance."

The Mongol Sweep

During Genghis Khan's lifetime, the relationship between Goryeo and the Mongols was a fairly peaceful one. Goryeo had actually aided the Mongols in some battles with the Chinese farther north, and the Mongols helped Goryeo subdue the Khitans when they attempted to invade Goryeo as they fled from the Mongol horde.

In 1225, though, this changed. The Mongol Empire began to demand tribute, and when the Mongol envoy was killed, the Mongols prepared for war. In 1231, Ögedei Khan, actually ordered an attack on Goryeo. The Mongols conquered the town of Anju, while the forces of Goryeo defended themselves at Kuju, cities that would be located in northern North Korea today. Goryeo had adopted the use of the siege tower from the ancient Romans, which consists of a wooden tower with stairways inside that helped an army mount a city wall. Between that and the use of flaming carts and arrows wetted by wads of burning human flesh, the Mongols were forced to withdraw from Kuju. General Saritai of the Mongol army rushed southwest in response. They were experts with the bow and arrow and were an extremely mobile force using hardy Asian Akhal-Teke horses that were used to the cold. The Mongols next captured the capital of Goryeo, Kaesong. The king of Goryeo, Gojong, realized that the Mongols were superb warriors and that they presented an enormous challenge to his forces, so he sued for peace. However, the tribute the Mongols demanded was ridiculously high, so Gojong urged his men to continue the fight. Despite his king's pleas, the military general of Goryeo, Choe U, decided to move the king and his family, as well as most of the population, to the island of Ganghwa, as he knew that the Mongols were superstitious about the sea.

Upset with this move by Goryeo, the Mongols launched another attack. Wave after wave of Mongol forces blasted their way south through Goryeo, and although the Mongols did try on several occasions to capture the well-fortified island, they were unable to do so. At the city of Cheoin, located near current-day Yongin in South Korea, the two sides clashed. General Saritai of the Mongols was slain by a participating monk, Kim Yun-hu. After the death of Saritai, the Mongol forces went into disarray and withdrew.

Although they hadn't captured all of the cities they laid their sights on, the Mongols destroyed crops and farmlands, employing scorched-earth tactics. This meant that not only were farmlands set afire, but any ancillary buildings, including barns, stables, and houses were destroyed. The farmers and their families were likewise killed if they resisted, as well as their animals.

In 1238, King Gojong, who was stationed on Ganghwa Island, agreed to the Mongols' demand that he send members of his royal family as hostages to their court. However, he didn't follow through, though. Instead, the king sent an unrelated family member. His ploy didn't work, and the Mongols insisted that the administration on Ganghwa Island move to the mainland, along with handing over members of the royal family as hostages. King Gojong again refused, sending distant family members to the Mongols. So, in 1247, the Mongols sent one of their most ferocious warlords, Amuqan, to Goryeo. He and his forces then pillaged and ravaged as much of the Korean Peninsula as possible. Some of the officials of Goryeo did move to the mainland, but the king still refused to give in to their demands.

In 1251, Möngke Khan became the head of the Mongol Empire. The stalemate over peace negotiations with Goryeo, however, continued. After much resistance and attacks by the Mongols, King Gojong finally gave in to the Mongols, moving his court back to the mainland. King Gojong then sent his stepson, Angyeong, as a hostage, and the Mongols agreed to a ceasefire in 1254. Soon, though, the Mongols found out there were still Goryeo officials on Ganghwa, and once Möngke Khan discovered that the teen boy wasn't a blood relative, there was no way to stop the Mongols from attacking. Möngke killed a pro-Mongol Korean general named Lee Hyeong and his family in protest. His military general, Jalairtai, then destroyed lands and the buildings in Goryeo as punishment. Many of the peasants of Goryeo surrendered due to despair and famine.

In 1258, the Choe clan wanted to continue the war against the Mongols, despite the overwhelming odds. However, a political party within Goryeo called upon the literati party, which was against the war, to stage a counter-coup and assassinate the head of the Choe clan. The literati party was a group of scholars protected by clan members, and it was their function to render political advice based on their studies and wisdom. Upon their advice, the head of the Choe clan was assassinated, and a peace treaty was made with the Mongols. King Gojong sent his heir, Wonjong, as a hostage. Also, as part of the agreement between Goryeo and the Mongols, the king of Goryeo had to marry a Mongolian princess and be subservient to their Mongol overlords. For their part, the Mongols guaranteed autonomy to Goryeo with Wonjong at its head, as King Gojong died the next year in 1259. However, Goryeo had to agree to become a vassal state of the Mongols.

In 1271, the Yuan Dynasty under the fifth khagan, or leader of the Mongols, Kublai Khan, was established. They adopted a

Chinese-style administration but retained some of their Mongolian practices and were never totally Sinicized. The Mongolian aristocracy and the members of the Goryeo royal family intermarried over the years for the sake of unity.

In the late 13th century, the history of the Yuan Dynasty and Goryeo overlapped. Kublai Khan was expansionistic and sought to conquer the Song Dynasty in China and the islands of Japan.

Goryeo-Mongolian Relations

In 1274, after King Wonjong of Goryeo died, his heir, Chungnyeol, married Kublai Khan's daughter, Jangmok. That union brought the Korean Peninsula into a period of Mongolization, as the court system was now set up according to the administrative hierarchy of the Yuan Dynasty. The intermarriages continued throughout the imperial line. Ordinary, non-imperial people of Goryeo, the common people, along with the Han Chinese, was the largest subculture in China at the time.

The tribute Goryeo paid to the Mongols consisted of gold, silver, textiles, grain, ginseng, and falcons. In terms of personnel, the Koreans provided soldiers, eunuchs, palace women, and Buddhist monks. Goryeo concubines also serviced the Mongolian aristocrats.

The Mongols had already swallowed up mainland China in addition to Goryeo, but it was determined to spread its empire to Japan. In 1274, Kublai Khan demanded the skills of the Goryeo shipbuilders and weapon craftsmen to provide his forces with supplies to conduct an invasion. A large number of the Goryeo men were pressed into service as ground troops and seamen. Goryeo supplied as many as 770 ships, all fully manned, and 5,000 ground forces. That number increased to 10,000 infantrymen, and they were equipped with 900 ships to make an amphibious landing on Japan. However, the effort failed. Kublai tried again in 1281, but it failed due to a typhoon. In the same year, Kublai's favorite wife died, and he became despondent. In addition, the Yuan Dynasty ran into severe financial difficulties brought on by corruption and the perennial expenditures of wars. In 1294, Kublai Khan died. He was succeeded by nine short-lived khans until the ascendancy of Toghon Temür.

Much friction occurred when Toghon Temür fell in love with Lady Ki, a Korean concubine. Mongolian emperors were expected to marry only Mongolian women, so when he tried to promote Lady Ki to the status of secondary wife, it gave rise to much public resentment. In 1339, Lady Ki gave birth to a son, which allowed Toghon Temür to grant Lady Ki the status he wanted to give her. This son, Ayushiridara, was named as his heir. Lady Ki was politically manipulative and steadily worked toward getting not only members of her family into positions of power but also other people from Goryeo.

In 1354, one of the Mongol generals led an attack against the Red Turbans, a group that sought to curtail the power of the Mongols. Toghon Temür was terrified that this general would use his strength to crush the Yuan Dynasty, which had become weakened over the years, so he suddenly dismissed him. This might have helped him gain some power back, but it also meant that Toghon Temür had to rely on local warlords for assistance in military affairs.

When Toghon Temür lost interest in politics soon after, his son, Ayushiridara, known as Biligtü Khan, sought to gain power. He had become the crown prince in 1353, but despite his title, he came into conflict with Toghon Temür's aides, who held the real power of the empire. The Yuan Dynasty began to crumble at this stage, and it was overthrown by the Ming Dynasty of China in 1368, freeing China and Korea from Mongol rule. The Northern Yuan Dynasty was then formed, which was based in the Mongolian Plateau.

Red Turban Rebellion (1351–1368)

The Red Turban army was founded by Guo Zixing and included followers of the White Lotus, a religious movement that was popular among the Han Chinese. The rebellions were small and sporadic, at least to begin with, and they sought to wrest China away from the control of the Mongols. The country was being victimized by natural disasters, famine, and poverty, and so, the Chinese concluded that their Mongol overlords had lost the "mandate of heaven," meaning divine approval.

When King Gongmin of Goryeo noted the efforts of the Chinese to rid the mainland of the Mongols and the remnants of the Yuan Dynasty, Gongmin wanted to do the same in Goryeo. He removed all pro-Mongol officials, nobles, and military personnel who were pro-Mongolian. In 1356, his army annexed the provinces of northern Goryeo, which had been totally occupied by the Mongols. However, in 1359, the Red Turbans invaded Goryeo and retook the northern provinces, along with its capital city, Pyongyang. They were soon after pushed out of the city.

After this, the Red Turbans wanted to place the peninsula of Goryeo under Chinese control and subsume them into the future Ming Dynasty. In 1360, General Choe Yeong put down the Red Turbans. Choe Yeong became very popular when he appointed himself mayor of Pyongyang and increased crop production, staving off the hunger of the populace.

When she saw the growing strength of Choe Yeong, Lady Ki (now Empress Ki) of the declining Yuan Dynasty sent in troops under Choe Yu to overthrow Goryeo. Choe Yeong, however, defeated the Mongol troops, which were the last vestiges of the Yuan regime. Yeong thus established the independence of the Goryeo Dynasty by 1364.

In 1368, back in China, the Red Turban Rebellion was victorious, and their leader, Zhu Yuanzhang, established the Ming Dynasty.

Chapter 4 – The Joseon Dynasty of Goryeo

Having purged the government of the Mongols, King Gongmin of Goryeo sought to establish relations with the Ming Dynasty of China, but the bureaucracy faulted him for wanting to do so. They wanted an independent Goryeo because they were afraid of losing their status. In 1374, King Gongmin was assassinated by his wife and her lover. His son, U, also written as Woo, became the next king of Goryeo at the age of eleven.

In 1388, with the support of King U, General Choe Yeong decided to attempt to invade the Liaodong Peninsula, a peninsula in northeast China. Yi Seong-gye, also known as Yi Dan, who was a colleague of Choe Yeong's during the Red Turban invasion, strenuously advised against such a move, stating that the Ming were much stronger than Goryeo and that it was also against the Confucian way of thinking. In addition, Goryeo would be vulnerable to Japanese pirates and the upcoming monsoon season. Yi, who had been chosen to lead the invasion, refused to commit his troops and returned south.

Instead, Yi Seong-gye went to the capital and defeated the forces there that were still loyal to the king, which were led by Choe

Yeong. Yi enjoyed a lot of popularity among government officials and the general populace, so it wasn't too difficult for him to eliminate his opponent, Choe Yeong. Instead of seizing power for himself, Yi Seong-gye gave the throne to King U's son, Chang. A little over a year later, Yi Seong-gye poisoned both U and Chang, giving the throne to one more ruler, Gongyang, before seizing it for himself in 1392.

Yi wanted to keep the name Goryeo for the country but was persuaded to change it. Yi Seong-gye then chose the name Joseon for the new dynasty, which had been a name for a previous state, and he became known by the name of Taejo of Joseon—not to be confused with his namesake, Taejo, who ruled Goryeo in the 10ᵗʰ century.

The Vicious Dispute over Succession

As his first task, Taejo sent envoys to the Ming Dynasty of China, Japan, the Ryukyu Kingdom—an archipelago that lay to the south—and Siam (Thailand). His capital city was Hanseong, current-day Seoul.

As his second task, Taejo decided that the line of succession should be determined in view of the fact that he had eight sons. His fifth son, Yi Bang-won, would have been the most logical choice because he contributed a lot to establishing the organization of the new government. However, it was a well-known fact that Bang-won held animosity toward Taejo's prime minister, Jeong Do-jeon, so Taejo chose his youngest son, Yi Bang-seok, as his heir. Jeong Do-jeon supported his choice as well. After Taejo's wife died, Jeong Do-jeon sought to kill the other sons of Taejo in order to secure his position. However, Yi Bang-won heard of this plan, and in 1398, he killed Jeong Do-jeon, his followers, and two sons of the late queen, including the crown prince. Taejo was aghast that his son, Yi Bang-won, would kill his brothers, so he then chose his second son, Yi Bang-gwa, later known as King Jeongjong, as his heir apparent. Taejo retired soon after.

King Jeongjong was more easily intimidated by Yi Bang-won than his father had been, and he gave the crown to Yi Bang-won in 1400 after a successful rebellion by his forces. King Taejo, who was still alive, held on to the royal seal and refused to recognize Yi Bang-won, who assumed the throne under the name Taejong. This didn't stop Yi Bang-won from becoming king, though, and when King Taejo died in 1408, there was nothing left to stop King Taejong.

Administrative Changes

As one of his first acts, King Taejong abolished the private armies maintained by the aristocrats. This created a pool of trained soldiers with whom he could set up a national army. His second action was to reform taxation. During the process of determining land ownership, he discovered land that was hidden from authorities so the owners could escape paying taxes. Once that subterfuge was uncovered, it greatly increased the national treasury. In addition, Taejong closed many of the temples that were formerly constructed by the Goryeo kings, which increased the size of the treasury as well.

In 1399, King Taejong started converting Joseon into an absolute monarchy. He replaced the governmental body, the Dopyeong Assembly, with a state council that approved of the king's various edicts. Those who disobeyed his rulings were either killed or exiled.

Taejong also promoted a new brand of Confucianism and tailored it to emphasize government, military service, and civic responsibility. Neo-Confucianism promotes an orderly society guided by people whose positions are awarded on the basis of merit, not birth. During the 14th century, Buddhism had fallen into disrepute as corruption and greed grew among the Buddhist monks and their followers.

Gunpowder

For years, potassium nitrate, also known as saltpeter, was used as an elixir in China. During the course of developing medications using saltpeter, explosive properties were accidentally discovered during the manufacturing process whenever it was mixed with sulfur and charcoal. Flames and fire erupted, often burning the hands and faces of the alchemists. In time, they utilized the mixture for its explosive properties. During the Mongol invasions, it was attached to arrows, creating "flying fire." In 1350, it was put into rudimentary Chinese cannons, which would propel a projectile, helping to annihilate the Mongol troops. The Song Dynasty of China attempted to keep this invention secret, but soon, the process was replicated by troops in Joseon as well.

Between 1374 and 1376, a scientist by the name of Choe Museon visited China and bribed a Chinese scientist to give him the recipe for gunpowder. He then developed a technique to extract potassium nitrate from the soil, which is composed of decaying matter. Following that, he developed something called the *hwacha*, a device that was similar to the first modern multiple rocket launchers. The *hwacha* was used effectively in future clashes with the enemy, most notably during the Battle of Jinpo, which was against the Japanese.

Sejong the Great (r. 1418–1450)

King Taejong retired as king in 1418, but he still ruled as a regent with his son, Sejong. Following the Neo-Confucian philosophy of an organized and obedient society, King Sejong strengthened the military. In 1430, he established a new taxation system, but before doing so, he first distributed a poll to assess public opinion. It was a great way for him to provide equality throughout the land, and 57 percent of the respondents approved of the system he proposed. He also was one of the first to grant maternity and paternity leaves.

Agricultural Innovations

King Sejong commissioned two books on agriculture tailored to meet the needs of the soil and climate in Joseon. The most famous book is called *Nongsa jikseol*, or *Straight Talk on Farming*. The conditions that could be artificially created in order to raise rice under the different conditions in Joseon was elucidated. In his book, he talked about how to grow rice in irrigated lowland wetlands and the rainfed deep-water uplands, as well as the utilization of particular drought-resistant species of rice for growth in the dry uplands and the cultivation of rice during the rainy seasons. Trade with Ming China aided the two countries in establishing a market for the sale of seed varieties that were drought-resistant.

The writers also cover the most efficient uses of the ecosystems in Joseon for the production of two different kinds of millet—glutinous and foxtail millet—as well as the cultivation of soybeans, red beans, mung beans, barley, buckwheat, and sesame. The book also describes crop rotation as a means to permit the soil to replenish itself.

Sejong, who was very sensitive to agricultural disasters, such as droughts, extended allowances to farmers whose crops were affected by unexpected environmental occurrences. He also distributed food to those who were in need during times of economic stress.

Inventions

King Sejong appreciated skill and talent, regardless of one's social status. Around 1430, he promoted Jang Yeong-sil to a position that qualified him to work at the royal palace. In 1433, he developed a celestial globe, an instrument that could use the positions of heavenly objects throughout the year to predict the best growing seasons and to tell time. As he refined the design, Joseon astronomers were able to plot the course of seven visible planets as well as the sun, moon, and the stars. In 1434, the scientists at Jiphyeonjeon, a royal research institute, invented a better metal printing press, the first one having been invented by Choe Yun-ui of Goryeo in 1234. Jang also created sundials and a water clock, the latter being based on a crude Chinese model from the 11th century. Some of these inventions made during this time flowed from Sejong's focus on agriculture. Jang invented the *cheugugi*, Korea's first rain gauge, in 1441, which would later be used for gathering data on the precipitation in the country. Jang also invented the *supyo* in 1441, which was the world's first water gauge.

Language

King Sejong hired scholars on a regular basis and had them work in what was called the Hall of Worthies, also known as the aforementioned Jiphyeonjeon. One of his assignments for them was to develop the first Joseon alphabet, which is known as hangul. Before the creation of this alphabet, Koreans used Classical Chinese alongside their own native writing systems. This meant that many lower-class Koreans were illiterate, as there was a huge difference between the Chinese and Korean languages. In 1443, the institute created a manual for the new language, titled *Hunminjeongeum* (or, in English, *The Proper Sounds for the Education of the People*), and distributed it to all of the people. The language that King Sejong promulgated used far less alphabetic characters than the Chinese. Even the lower classes could master this new language, and they started becoming literate, much to the annoyance of the elites who wanted to be seen as in a class above and apart from the common people.

King Sejong himself was a poet, and the most famous poem attributed to him is *Songs of the Flying Dragon,* written in 1445. An excerpt:

The stream whose source is deep

Gushes forth even in a drought.

It forms a river

And gains the sea.

Death and Succession Crisis

In 1450, Sejong died after suffering complications from diabetes. He had appointed his eldest son, Munjong, to succeed him. Munjong was sickly, so Sejong accompanied that appointment with a further successor, his grandson, Danjong, whom he placed under the protection of the members of the Hall of Worthies. As Sejong had foreseen, Munjong didn't live long (only two years), and so, Danjong succeeded him. However, Danjong was only twelve years old, and that gave rise to a usurpation of the throne by his uncle, Sejo, in 1455.

Six scholars then wove a plot to have Danjong returned to the throne. However, one of the conspirators, Gim Jil, betrayed his associates from the Hall of Worthies and revealed the conspiracy to his father-in-law, who told King Sejo. Although he wanted to forgive them, even attempting to have them repent of their deeds and acknowledge his legitimacy, he realized they never would truly submit and had them executed. More than seventy people were put to death during this time, including Danjong. He also eliminated the Hall of Worthies altogether, but he did keep Gim Jil alive, whom he awarded with high-level positions. Eventually, Gim became the governor of Gyeongsang Province in southeastern Joseon.

King Sejo (r. 1455–1468)

King Sejo tightened the monarchy and further advanced legal organization by passing the Grand Code for State Administration, which was specifically designed for dynastic rulers to serve as a guide. The code contained laws regulating a system for the enforcement of a criminal code along with some portions devoted to contract law, finance, and civil matters. It wasn't actually put into effect until 1474 when it was completed under the reign of his successors.

The Joseon Dynasty and the Jianzhou Invasions

The Jurchen people had clashed with Korea back in the 12th century. In 1460 and 1470, one of the subdivisions of this tribe, the Jianzhou, intruded on the northern borders of Joseon. They crossed the borders of northern Joseon to obtain ginseng for trade, but they also attacked Joseon villages, mostly for the purpose of confiscating the red ginseng crop grown in that region. Red ginseng was highly sought after by the Chinese, who could only grow a limited amount.

Red ginseng has a long and illustrious history as a medicinal herb and was said to be an aphrodisiac, having properties that increase longevity, reduce stress, and increase vitality. The Joseon variety was a very profitable crop. It is no longer grown there, but single roots from which red ginseng were made from have been auctioned off in the modern day for as high as $50,000!

The Violent Regencies of the Joseon Queens

King Sejo died in 1468 and was succeeded by his son, Yejong, whose mother, Queen Jeonghee, the wife of Sejo, ruled in his place, as he was too sickly to rule. During her regency, farmers were granted many of the lands formerly owned by the military in order to increase agricultural production. Yejong and his mother only ruled for a year. Following his reign, Yeong's nephew, Seongjong, became the next king. He was also too young to rule (he was only twelve), and so, his grandmother, Queen Jeonghee, and his mother, Queen Insu, ruled in his stead until he was nineteen -years old.

King Seongjong added some improvements to the law of the land that was first developed by King Sejo. Despite some future revisions, this code was the longest-lasting legal code in Korean history.

Land ownership became extremely important during Seongjong's reign, not only as a source of taxes but also as an opportunity for leases and a way for peasants to produce crops. Status was now becoming attached to land ownership, and some larger estates were created. The legal codes were also expanded to regulate land ownership and rights.

Seongjong was a scholarly and religious man, and he restored Neo-Confucianism after Buddhism underwent a resurgence in 1462 due to Chinese influences; the resurgence was also influenced by his wife, Jeonghyeon, who was incredibly devoted to Buddhism. The

Hall of Worthies, which had been eradicated around 1456, morphed into the Hall of Leave of Study, which young scholars could attend. Due to King Seongjong's intellectual pursuits, there was a resurgence of literature and book publishing.

However, disputes did occur under Seongjong's prosperous rule. When Seongjong's first wife died, he married Yun. This made her Seongjong's second wife, and they had a son named Yi Yung. However, King Seongjong also had sexual relations with his concubines, which was, of course, permissible. Yun became insanely jealous of them. On one occasion, historians wrote that she had his concubines followed. Furious about these relationships, she attacked the king and even scratched his face with her sharp fingernails, leaving scars, and it is said that she even poisoned one of the concubines in 1477. Queen Yun was then deposed as regent and exiled. However, she didn't change her ways while in exile, and influential officials asked for her execution. She died in 1482, after having been poisoned.

In 1494, Sejong was then succeeded by his son, Yi Yung, now known as Yeonsangun. Upon his ascension to the throne, Yeonsangun discovered what happened to his mother and became wildly enraged. He opened an intensive investigation into her execution and interrogated all the palace personnel that served at the time. As his temper rose during these investigations, he transferred his hatred to many of the women and officials who were serving in the palace. When one of the scholars wrote a history that indicated King Sejo usurped the throne, it pushed Yeonsangun over the edge. He purged the government of scholars during the First Literati Purge in 1498, brutally executing some and exiling others.

The purges weren't over, however. In 1504, the details of his mother's death were revealed to him, which greatly upset him. He promptly responded to this news by beating two of his father's concubines to death, as well as ordering the execution of those officials who had supported his mother's death. At least 36 officials were killed by forcing them to drink poison, and eight of these bodies were mutilated. This number doesn't even include the families of the officials, who were also punished. During this time, he got into a fight with his grandmother, Queen Insu, and pushed her, killing her.

The rest of Yeonsangun's rule was very cruel, although it should be noted that the beginning of his reign before he discovered the truth about his mother was fairly stable. He converted the royal university into his own pleasure grounds, and he demolished a large residential area in the capital to build hunting grounds, displacing 20,000 residents. After the people began to mock him in hangul, he decided to ban the use of the alphabet. And his rough treatment extended to the nobility and government officials as well; he even executed a minister for accidentally spilling a drink when he poured it into Yeonsangun's cup.

Seeing that Yeonsangun's insane cruelty seemed to know no bounds, court officials conspired against him. In 1506, he was deposed and sent into exile on Ganghwa Island. His half-brother, Jungjong, replaced him. Jungjong wanted to return to the kind of Joseon Seongjong oversaw, but he was limited in his movements, as the coup leaders who placed him on the throne supervised his moves. Once they died, though, Jungjong began to assert his authority.

Jungjong very much favored the philosophies taught by the more liberal Confucian scholars, but very powerful political leaders within the government squelched what they considered to be improper philosophies. Jungjong, in particular, followed the teachings of Jo Gwang-jo, a scholar who promoted equality between the rich and the poor and who believed that officials could even be appointed from the lower classes. The older members of the administration were particularly afraid of the growing popularity of Jo's brand of Neo-Confucianism. Jo Gwang-jo quickly moved through the ranks, and officials who disliked him began to plant the seeds of doubt in

Jungjong's mind, saying that another coup could be possible with Jo Gwang-jo behind it this time. This started the Third Literati Purge, which began in 1519. Jo Gwang-jo did not see any of this coming and was exiled due to a massive outpouring of support for Jo Gwang-jo's innocence by his students. However, Jungjong wanted him dead, and in 1520, he was forced to drink poison. By 1521, 225 officials had been affected by the purge, and most of Jo's reforms, which promoted equality between the classes, had been rescinded.

The Three Offices

These offices existed in the earlier Goryeo Dynasty but were expanded under Seongjong's reign. It was Seongjong's hope that the Neo-Confucian scholars, called the Sarim, would check the power of the ministers, the Hungu. These two constantly fought with each other, and this conflict played a major role in the literati purges. Although the purges are thought to be due to these rival factions, some believe the kings of Joseon wanted to weaken the Three Offices, as they balanced out their rule. Below is a definition of the offices.

Office of Inspector General

This office was in charge of licensing inspectors and officials, impeachment, legal questions, and the proper behavior of the king's relatives. Additionally, it maintained Confucian order in the hierarchy of government. Admission to this office required a thorough background check.

Office of Censors

The Office of Censors had the delicate responsibility to advise the king if he wished to promulgate a policy or issue a decree. They didn't have the authority to pass a decree but could confer with the Office of Inspector General in terms of presenting a modification or preventing the passage of an improper mandate or decree. This group worked closely with the public press, especially in terms of the proper wording of official decrees.

Office of Special Advisors

This group monitored the content of the royal libraries and weighed the beliefs of Neo-Confucianism against the content of the documents present.

The Fourth Literati Purge

Jungjong died in 1544, and the crown prince Injong became king. However, he died eight months later, and the son of Jungjong's third wife, Myeongjong, became king. The chronicles seem to implicate Queen Munjeong in Injong's death, as they record that the queen was often visited by a spirit of the night and was haunted by the voice of the deceased child. She woke up screaming many nights. In mortal fear and terror, Queen Munjeong became so perturbed about it that she moved the palace.

Now, Jungjong's second wife, who had given birth to Injong, had a brother named Yun Im, while Queen Munjeong had a brother named Yun Won-hyeong. Each brother was very ambitious and formed their own political power groups. Yun Im's group was known as the Lesser Yun faction, and they were progressives. Yun Won-hyeong's group, the Greater Yun faction, was conservative. Geographically, members of the conservative faction mostly lived west of the capital, and the progressive element lived east of the capital. These divisions further split into subdivisions—the northerners, the southerners, and the eastern and western sections near the capital.

In 1545, there was an enormous shake-up of the political factions, and the Fourth Literati Purge took place. As a result, Yun Im was executed, along with some Confucian scholars. Many historians assert that the Yun Won-hyeong faction created a plot to have him executed.

The political feuds of the 15th and 16th centuries created military vulnerability because the size and strength of the army was often an item on the political agenda. During the reign of King Myeongjong's successor, King Seonjo, the conservative faction was in power, and reforms were slowed down. One of those reforms promoted an increase of the military to defend the country against the Jurchens along the border, as well as against Japan, which was becoming a formidable force in the area. However, the conservatives resisted a defensive buildup, and it led to their own undoing when other countries, like Japan, took advantage of that exposure.

Chapter 5 – Foreign Invasions

Six-Year War with Japan

In 1590, one of the most powerful daimyos of Japan, Toyotomi Hideyoshi, emerged as the primary military leader who united the clan factions within the country, allowing Japan to stand on its own. To keep the country from falling into civil war and to expand Japanese territory, Hideyoshi had plans to conquer China. He increased his military and naval strength in preparation. Then he contacted King Seonjo of Joseon, asking permission to enter into China through the peninsula. Through word he received back from the traders, Seonjo discovered this military buildup and wanted to determine Hideyoshi's real intentions for making that request. Therefore, Seonjo sent emissaries from both Joseon political parties to Hideyoshi to clarify the matter. They returned and reported to the king that Hideyoshi wanted to attack the Ming Dynasty in China. The letter Hideyoshi sent with the ambassadors asked Korea to submit to Japan and join them in the war against China.

Joseon had a long-standing, positive relationship with the Ming and realized that he shouldn't yield to Hideyoshi's demand, so he turned him down. However, Joseon had been weakened militarily during the prior years of internal conflicts. Seonjo's strongest naval commander, Yi Sun-sin, rushed to prepare for battle. He trained military forces and had warships built, including a newly invented ship called a "turtle ship," which was an iron-clad vessel equipped with artillery.

In May of 1592, Japan sent over 150,000 men to Pusan, also known as Busan, a port city on the southern coast of Joseon. At sea, the Joseon navy couldn't halt the initial advance but managed to scatter the naval reinforcement fleets. They also sunk 63 Japanese ships and blocked vessels carrying supplies.

The Japanese forces that did land raged throughout the southern regions, burning and looting as they moved northward toward Seoul. The people in Seoul virtually abandoned the capital, which included King Seonjo, who fled to Pyongyang, which is now the capital of North Korea.

The Japanese occupied both Seoul and Pyongyang before moving eastward toward the sea. Japan had planned not only on its supply ships but also on crops that could be confiscated locally. However, because of Joseon's amazing success at sea, that plan failed.

The Joseon people were furious at the government's failure to protect the country, so they organized a voluntary militia. What especially motivated them were the atrocities that the Japanese soldiers inflicted upon them. Scholars, civilians, and peasants were slaughtered. It was customary for the Japanese in those days to prove their valor on the battlefield by cutting off heads of those they killed. In the Korean invasions, due to the number of civilians killed, it was easier to transport noses instead of heads. The Mimizuka, or Ear Mound, is a monument in Japan that preserves at least 38,000 noses of the Koreans killed during the invasions.

In January of 1593, Ming China sent a force of around 40,000 men to join up with the Joseon forces; they attacked the Japanese stationed at Seoul and retook Pyongyang. However, when the Ming forces were defeated at the Battle of Byeokjegwan on February 27th, 1593, the Ming retreated, leaving the Koreans stranded. Regardless, the Joseon and the Chinese still had a mountain redoubt in Haengju in the north, and the forces there fought courageously, losing many men. The Japanese staged nine successive attacks there but were forced to retreat each time. This battle greatly improved Korean morale.

At the Siege of Jinju Fortress in July of that year, the Japanese broke down the dikes that held back the moat. They were met with punishing volleys of arrows and had to pull back, though. The Japanese then dragged in siege towers but were forced to back off because of the cannon fire from atop the battlements. It was a prolonged battle and lasted seven days. On the third day, General Kim Si-min was killed, along with many other Korean soldiers. Nevertheless, the hearty Koreans fought onward. The ladders the Japanese put up against the walls were smashed by the Korean defensive forces. Eventually, the Japanese mined sections of the wall. As it was raining intensely, sections of the wall weakened, and the Japanese were finally able to take possession of the fort. Today, there is an annual festival, the Jinju Namgang Yudeung Festival, commemorating the lives of the 70,000 Koreans slaughtered in this fierce conflict.

By this point in the war, the Japanese invasion force, which had started out with 150,000 men, were down to about 53,000. With more Chinese coming in every day as reinforcements, as well as the cold winter that brought about hunger and frostbite, the Japanese retreated to the coast. The two sides remained at a stalemate for several months, as both sides were unwilling to make any offensive moves.

The Japanese also lost a number of minor battles, and the Japanese general, Konishi Yukinaga, withdrew most of his forces and sued for peace. However, because the Ming had pulled out of Joseon, the deluded Japanese thought they'd won! The Ming felt the same way, as they had recaptured Pyongyang and the Joseons had taken the Haengu fortress and destroyed half of the Japanese fleet. Therefore, Ming China insisted Japan become its vassal state. An exchange of hostages was discussed but were never agreed to, and negotiations dragged on for three years with no resolution.

In February of 1597, the Japanese invaded Joseon a second time with around 141,000 troops. They landed at Pusan, as they had done in the previous conflict. This time, however, Joseon was much better prepared. The Ming also sent around 55,000 troops to help deal with the invasion. Initially, the Japanese were largely confined to Gyeongsang Province in southeastern Joseon. Because of their "slash-and-burn" techniques, virtually all of Gyeongsang Province became a wasteland. Thousands of Koreans were killed, with famine and disease followed that. The Ming were not much better; they did not distinguish between loyal Joseon civilians and those who supported the Japanese. The Joseon armies themselves often forcefully acquired food and supplies from civilians; as is typical in most warfare, the civilians got the worst of it.

Between 1597 and 1598, the Koreans demonstrated that they had become far more proficient in battle tactics than in 1593. In the Battle of Myeongnyang, the Joseon cleverly constructed multiple-level warships called panokseons, which used both rowers and a sail. The panokseons had flat bottoms, as the waters around Korea could be deceivingly shallow. The Myeongnyang Strait was especially tricky because it was incredibly narrow, and a sudden change of the tide could catch a sea captain unprepared. The Joseon, of course, used that knowledge to their advantage by luring in the clumsier Japanese warships. Joseon Admiral Yi Sun-sin was manning the flagship at the north end of the strait, and the numerous Japanese ships rushed in. Once the tide changed, however, the Japanese fleet started drifting backward, colliding into each other! As would happen in any narrow channel, the rapidity of the current can become treacherous, and many who tried to swim ashore in the chaos drowned.

The Siege of Ulsan, which lasted from January 29ᵗʰ to February 19ᵗʰ, 1598, represented a significant loss for Joseon, as they were overwhelmingly outnumbered by the Japanese once an unexpected contingent of reinforcements arrived. The Joseon wanted to capture the fortress of Ulsan from the Japanese, and the initial vanguard did manage to force the Japanese to seek shelter in the inner chambers as they were attacked by climbers. However, the fact that Ulsan was built on higher ground gave the Japanese a distinct topographical advantage. The Joseon troops had cannons, but the range was too short for the cannon fire to reach, so Inspector-General Yang Hao was forced to withdraw his men.

Joseon really craved another Japanese fort, though, and in the fall of 1598, they attempted to conquer the garrison at Suncheon. They tried tempting the Japanese commander, Konishi Yukinaga, and some of his forces out into the open under the pretext of negotiations. The Joseon troops miscalculated the timing and opened their cannon fire too soon, sending the Japanese scurrying back into the shelter of the fort. The Chinese allies, who weren't as familiar with the Korean waters, sent in ships. However, those ships became jammed in the shallow waters, and Joseon lost the battle.

Yi Sun-sin had been in charge of the navy, but he suspected he was being lured into an ambush after receiving orders to go after the Japanese, as the tip was from a Japanese spy. Thus, he held back from attacking them, but he displeased the king in doing so. As a result, he was removed from duty and replaced by Won Gyun. However, Won Gyun proved to be incompetent when compared to Yi Sun-sin, losing the Battle of Chilcheollyang and incurring a heavy loss of Joseon ships, as well as his own life. Quickly, Yi Sun-sin was reinstated. With only 12 ships and 200 seamen, he gained the advantage, utilizing his expert knowledge of the tides and currents. At the Battle of Noryang in December 1598, however, Yi Sun-sin was killed. Despite that, the Joseon/Ming fleet achieved a tremendous victory. The Japanese forces, which were heavily decimated, returned home to find out that the Japanese shogun, Toyotomi Hideyoshi, had died in September, his death being kept a secret so as not to squash the army's morale.

Following the Japanese invasion, the Joseon established a policy of isolationism. King Seonjo felt that trade with the Chinese was sufficient enough and that too much foreign interference only brought bloodshed and devastation.

Bloody Factionalism Continues

King Seonjo keenly felt the effects of the horrendous war with the Japanese, having to deal with the starvation of his people and the loss of acres of farmland. He gave free grain to families in need and tried to reconstruct Joseon but was thwarted by the terrible economic conditions. In 1608, he died, passing the crown to his second son, Gwanghaegun. Gwanghaegun took the throne during a particularly violent period of party politics. He also commanded little respect because he was the son of Seonjo's concubine, which was against Confucian beliefs.

As soon as he ascended to the throne, the small faction of northern conservatives conspired to stage a coup to make Gwanghaegun's brother, Yeong-chang, king. The plot was exposed, however, and its leader was executed. Yeong-chang was arrested and died the following year. The larger conservative faction, called the Greater Northerner faction, removed many officials from the opposing party from office. They also stripped Queen Inmok, Yeong-chang's mother, of her title and threw her into prison. His grandfather was also found guilty of treason and executed.

During his reign, King Gwanghaegun attempted to give members of all the factions representation in government but was unsuccessful. In 1623, he was the victim of a coup and was sent into exile. Injo, the grandson of King Seonjo, was then put on the throne by the ultra-conservative Westerner faction.

The Manchu Invasions

In the early 17th century, the more aggressive branch of the troublesome Jurchen people (the Jianzhou Jurchens) migrated to the northeastern region of China in the country now known as Manchuria. Their dynasty was called the Later Jin Dynasty, which eventually evolved into the Qing Dynasty.

In 1618, Nurhaci, the king of the Jurchens, declared war against the Ming Dynasty as well as those allied with them, that is, Joseon. Nurhaci wrote to King Injo of Joseon, condemning him for his association with the Ming Dynasty. Nurhaci justified himself by writing that Heaven had chosen him and his people as the rightful heads of both the Chinese and, therefore, the Koreans. He said:

> Heaven takes me as right and the Nikan, the Han Chinese people, as wrong. The Nikan emperor of the big kingdom also lives under the unchanging word of Heaven. However, the Nikan emperor violated Heaven's rules, going against Heaven, and making other nations suffer for it.

Nurhaci's rationale was rooted in shamanistic legend, which he used to his advantage. Historians, though, said that Nurhaci was actually seeking revenge for the deaths of his father and grandfather in an earlier battle with the Ming.

In 1627, Hong Taiji, who took over after Nurhaci, invaded Joseon. The Jurchen forces were composed mostly of Jurchen tribal warriors, and they first attacked the northern garrisons of Neunghan and Anju. Although Ming China sent some troops to help stave off the attack, those two forts fell, as did Pyongyang. The Jurchens then moved toward southern Joseon. King Injo fled from Hanseong (modern-day Seoul) and sued for peace. However, Hong Taiji complained that Joseon was still aiding the Ming people after a Joseon general, Mao Wenlong, provided food to the stricken Ming soldiers there. Furthermore, after the hostilities stopped, Mao and the Joseon in the north resumed trade with the Ming. The Jurchens insisted that Joseon break all relations with the Ming, and they did so. The Joseon authorities later executed General Wenlong for his "treachery." Injo's successor, Hyojong, honored the terms, although he sometimes wanted to take revenge.

In 1635, Hong Taiji changed the name of his people from Jurchens to Manchus in order to distance themselves from the Jianzhou Jurchens, who were ruled over by the Chinese. Since the Later Jin Dynasty was a reference to the Jurchen people, the nobles of the Manchus recommended that Hong Taiji establish a new dynasty in China. He did so in 1636, calling it the Qing Dynasty, with Hong Taiji as its first emperor. King Injo and many of the people in Joseon who were still loyal to the old Ming dynasty took that as an offense and agitated the people against the Qing Dynasty. In fact, when some Manchu delegates visited Joseon, the king refused to acknowledge them. The Manchu were incensed at that affront, as was the newly installed Qing emperor.

In 1636, Hong Taiji led Manchu, Mongolian, and Han Chinese warriors against Joseon. Manchu Prince Yu, also known as Dodo, led a huge division of 30,000 men, and Hong Taiji led the main division with 70,000 men. They attacked the formidable Namhan Mountain Fortress in order to prevent King Injo from fleeing to Ganghwa Island as other Joseon kings had done in the past. In prior months, however, the king was able to dispatch his consorts and his son to that island for their protection.

There, in the mountainous terrain of northern Joseon, the soldiers of Joseon successfully fended off the Qing invaders with heavy and persistent musket fire. This was only a temporary victory, though. In early 1637, a large force under the command of another Qing prince, Dorgon, assaulted Ganghwa Island, capturing King Injo's son and his wives. Joseon surrendered the following day.

Their agreement with the Qing army consisted of nine requirements:

> 1. Joseon would stop using Ming era name and surrender the Ming seal of investiture.

2. Joseon would offer his captured sons, Prince Sohyeon and Grand Prince Bontrim, also known as Hyojong, as hostages along with their wives and consorts.

3. Joseon would accept the Qing calendar.

4. Joseon would acknowledge the local Ming leaders as their overlords.

5. Joseon would provide men and supplies to aid the Qing army in future fights with the Ming.

6. Joseon would provide warships to the Qing.

7. Joseon wouldn't accept any Ming refugees into their country.

8. The noblewomen of Joseon would intermarry with the Qing.

9. Joseon wouldn't build any more fortresses or castles.

After the surrender of Joseon, atrocities occurred on account of the cruelty of the Qing. Joseon women were kidnapped and raped, and some of the Joseon princesses became concubines for the Qing princes. Because they had had intercourse with the Qing, they were alienated from their families.

While the Joseon prince, Hyojong, was living in Qing China with his wife, Inseon, he learned about many of the advanced military techniques from the Chinese and the Europeans who traded with them. Hyojong was very protective of his brother, Sohyeon, who was the heir to the Joseon throne. In fact, he even went on a Qing campaign to Russia in his brother's place.

It took around forty years for the new Qing Dynasty to assume control over mainland China because of the remaining Ming loyalists in southern China. Prince Sohyeon and Princess Minhoe returned to Joseon about eight years later, and several years after that, Hyojong and his wife did as well.

Since Sohyeon, who was King Ingo's first son and heir, had been in China for years, he returned with many Western scientific ideas and even entertained sympathy for Catholicism, which had grown in some areas of China. The king was horrified by his pro-Western ideas and was furious that Sohyeon had met with the Jesuit missionary Johann Schall von Bell in Beijing. Sohyeon died shortly after returning to Joseon under mysterious circumstances, and historical rumors indicate that the king killed his own son. When Sohyeon's wife attempted to investigate her husband's death, a story was concocted, possibly by Gwi-in, King Injo's concubine, about Princess Minhoe having committed treason. She was executed, and her three sons were exiled.

Hyojong succeeded Injo in 1649 and attempted to build up the Joseon army with the weapons he had seen in China, hiring some to manufacture muskets for them. However, economic conditions in war-torn Joseon were severe, and he spent much of his reign trying to rebuild and reconstruct his country and died before completing that task. His successor, Hyeonjong, continued that project.

Factionalism Fractures the Royal House

Even while the royal princes were held captive in Qing China, conflicts occurred in Joseon due to the political factions. Arguments and vindictiveness occurred over even the trivial issue about the required length of time for the wearing of mourning attire! When Hyojong died, the Western conservatives felt that only one year was necessary for the wearing of mourning robes by his second wife, Jangryeol, while the Southern faction felt that three years was necessary. In the end, King Hyeonjong made the final decision, which was the one-year period, allowing the Westerners to remain as the major faction.

The Musin Rebellion

In the early 18th century, small splinter groups grew out of the political factions. The Western faction split into the Norons, who followed the Confucian scholar Song Siyeol, and the Sorons, who abided by the teachings of Yun Jeung. In 1724, the Noron faction wanted King Gyeongjong of Joseon to step down in favor of his half-brother, Yeongjo, who favored the Norons. The Soron faction then plotted to assassinate Yeongjo. They didn't need to conspire, however, because Gyeongjong died of food poisoning that was due to the consumption of spoiled shrimp. In fact, historians support this idea, as they state that the king was foolish enough to have consumed seafood that was shipped to him in mid-summer and wasn't kept on ice.

Despite that obvious fact, the Sorons accused Yeongjo of deliberately poisoning the young king. In December 1728, the Musin Rebellion exploded between the two factions. Sim Yu-hyeon and Bak Mi-gwi stole gunpowder, planning to blow up the Hong-hua and Don-hua gates. The fighting between the factions raged on for three weeks, and the government lost control of many of the county seats of the Jeolla Province.

Another literati purge, the Shinim purge, occurred, in which almost all Noron officials lost their positions. Four lost their lives, and 170 were exiled. In 2017, secret letters written by Yeongjo were found, describing the purge. He detested the factional strife that had afflicted his country for years and attempted to put an end to it. He expelled the Sorons from the government and drew the country's attention away from politics. Instead of focusing on politics, King Yeongjo's letters to his people were compassionate.

The country at that time was inundated with frequent rainfalls, destroying many crops. To alleviate their suffering, Yeongjo reduced the taxes and set an example by reducing the size of his own meals. He also initiated many public works projects and encouraged mercantilism and the growth of guilds.

Chapter 6 – Merchants, Farmers, and Foreigners

During the 18th century, commercial wide-scale production of profitable crops, such as ginseng, tobacco, cotton, and, of course, rice, was introduced. New vegetables were grown, such as potatoes, tomatoes, squash, and peppers as a result of the mission spearheaded by Cho Om, who was sent to Japan as an envoy in 1764. Farmer markets became widespread across the countryside. Occupations related to transportation, warehousing, shipbuilding, inn-keeping, and banking flourished. The import-export trade also grew between Joseon and Qing China, and later on with Japan as well. Coins were minted by the thousands, but the upper classes sometimes hoarded them, creating coin shortages, or "coin famines."

Jeong Yakyong aka "Dasan"

The people of Joseon were highly influenced by the versatile thinkers of the age, like Jeong Yakyong, more commonly known as Dasan. He was noted for his Neo-Confucian philosophy, science, law, land reform structures, and government theory. Two of his most famous books, *The Mind of Governing People* and the *Design of Good Government*, focus on the role of government as the means by which a country's people could improve their economic conditions and direct their motivation along a path of righteous and generous behavior. Dasan always stressed the practical aspects of living, as opposed to the esoteric philosophic ramblings of those scholars who argued semantics and etymology. In 1805, Dasan outlined his theoretical methodology for the interpretation of the famous *I Ching,* or "Book of Changes," which is a text on divination that is still used today.

Dasan was exiled from late 1801 until 1818 when Korea discovered that they had as many as 17,000 Korean converts to Catholicism and was threatened by this creeping Western influence. Korea wanted to adhere to a Neo-Confucian philosophy and recognize no other leader than that of the state. In the Western world, the Catholic Church was already a strong political power, and while Dasan wasn't Catholic, his brother was.

The French Invasion

In 1863, King Gojong ascended to the throne. He was still a minor at the time, so his father, Yi Ha-eung, served as regent. His title was the Heungseon Daewongun, meaning "prince of the great court." He was very ambitious, and this was finally an opportunity for him to dominate the political scene. One of his first acts was to fortify the identity of Joseon as a self-determining Neo-Confucian state. Catholicism was considered to be a belief system that was in opposition to Neo-Confucianism, one that polluted the purity of Joseon ideology. Noting that there was a lot of interference in Joseon affairs from French Catholic missionaries, the Daewongun started out by forcibly removing the Catholic leaders and other Joseon Catholics, who had grown to number 23,000 in just a few years.

In January 1866, Russian ships appeared on the eastern coast of Joseon. The Korean Christians saw this as the perfect chance to strengthen their cause and suggested that Joseon join forces with France. The Daewongun seemed to be open to this idea and agreed to meet with Bishop Berneux. But it was just a ploy to get the bishop out in the open; once he arrived in the capital the following month, he was executed. After this, more French missionaries and Korean converts were rounded up.

Because of the execution of the French missionaries, the French consul decided to send a "punitive mission," to Joseon, saying, "Since the kingdom of Joseon killed nine French priests, we shall respond by killing 9,000 Joseon people." The consul made this threat without the authorization of the French government, but France, nevertheless, wanted to open up Joseon to trade.

In 1866, Rear Admiral Pierre-Gustave Roze set off with a small fleet and entered the Han River, which appeared to lead to the capital. Unfortunately, Roze noted that the waters were too shallow for French warships, so he attempted to occupy Ganghwa Island, which was located at the entrance of the Han River, and demanded reparations. The Daewongun was furious, and his fortress on the island held firm. The French troops did manage to invade the royal sanctuary on the mountain there and seized the royal histories and accounting books. Once Roze realized he couldn't make any further progress, though, he retreated.

The *General Sherman* Incident

In 1866, an American ship, the *General Sherman*, was shipwrecked along the Joseon shore. The Americans were concerned about the fate of the vessel but also wanted to use that as an opportunity to chart some of the waters near the peninsula and possibly develop a treaty to handle stranded American sailors. They dispatched the US ambassador to China along with five warships. In June of that year, a small contingent of the Joseon military opened fire upon the Americans. When the Americans requested an apology, none was forthcoming. The US then explained that they were on a peaceful mission, but still, no reply was offered. Like the French had done, the Americans responded with their own "punitive mission." They landed on Ganghwa Island and captured some of the fortresses there. The Joseon military had outdated weapons, and the Americans were able to capture the Joseon ship, the *Sugaki*. Over 200 Joseon troops were killed, along with the first mate of an American warship, the *Colorado*. After the Americans withdrew, the Daewongun further isolated Korea from foreign encroachments. Joseon, however, had very limited success with that, mostly because they were clearly outgunned by foreign forces.

The Tributary System

Ever since Joseon had sworn fidelity to the Qing Empire, Joseon had to pay quarterly tributes to China. It was delivered to the emperor by the Joseon king or his representative, and it consisted of 100 *piculs* (defined as shoulder-weight loads) of rice, 200 *piculs* of white silk, 100 *piculs* of red silk, 100 *piculs* of blue silk, 300 *piculs* of seal skins, 5,000 rolls of paper, and 10 swords. In a week's time, they were allowed to sell the goods to the Chinese public. Up until 1876, Joseon restricted most of their trade to China. Joseon did maintain a cursory relationship with Japan, however, at their outpost in Pusan on the southern coast. In 1854, word raced throughout Joseon about the landing of American ships in Japan that were commanded by Commodore Matthew Perry. These technologically advanced warships were clearly superior to those of Joseon, which intimidated them as the Japanese were forced to sign a treaty that opened up Japan to trade.

In 1873, at the age of 22, the heir to the Joseon throne, Gojong, announced that he was now the fully empowered head of Joseon. His wife, Queen Myeongseong, also known as Queen Min, also gained control over the court, filling high-level positions with her own family members. The Daewongun was upset by this, and he was exiled from the court. There is even a story that Queen Min bricked up his entrance to the palace. She was intelligent, politically astute, and had the tendency to interfere in state affairs. Min coaxed Gojong to initiate military reforms, and King Gojong and Queen

Min appealed to the US, which made other Western nations clamor to establish treaties with Joseon.

Japanese Intrusion

Japan sought Asiatic alliances after the American naval presence shook them up. Hurriedly, Japan sought to improve the condition of its own navy. In May 1875, they imitated Perry's arrival by sending out an iron-clad, steam-driven gunboat called the *Un'yo* to Pusan. These negotiations failed, however, and the Japanese returned back to their country.

Shortly thereafter, in September, the *Un'yo* sailed again, this time landing on Ganghwa Island to ask for water and provisions. The forts on the island fired on the Japanese, which they did not take lightly. After firing back, they torched houses and engaged Joseon troops on the island. As their weapons were more advanced, they made short work of the Joseon forces. After this incident, the Japanese navy blockaded the area, demanding an apology from Joseon. Joseon was forced into an unfair treaty with the Japanese in 1876, known as the Treaty of Ganghwa Island. Its stipulations included the following:

1. Joseon, later to be known as Korea, was an independent state.

2. The two countries would exchange envoys within fifteen months.

3. The port of Pusan and two more seaports would be open to unhindered Japanese trade within a year, along with space for the construction of ancillary buildings and land leases devoted to trade.

4. Mutual support of stranded Japanese or Korean ships on each other's shores would be offered.

5. The Japanese would receive immunity from prosecution for crimes committed on Korean soil.

This treaty essentially recognized Korea as a country independent from China, but it was considered an unequal treaty because Japan was afforded many more rights than Korea.

The Imo Incident

In 1881, King Gojong, who had become fascinated with the advancements the Japanese had and sought to make Joseon stronger, hired a Japanese advisor named Horimoto Reizo to help him update his military forces. Military training ensued, but the soldiers were not given their pay in rice for thirteen months. King Gojong, once he learned of the situation, ordered Min Gyeom-ho to pay them. However, he passed the duty onto a steward, who sold the good rice he had been given and gave the soldiers millet mixed with sand.

On July 23rd, 1882, a riot broke out over the matter. Soldiers headed for the home of Min Gyeom-ho, but he was not at home, having learned about the riot ahead of time. This didn't stop them from destroying his home, and after that, they looted weapons and freed political prisoners. Next, the rioters turned their attention on the Japanese, stabbing Horimoto one by one. They turned their attention to the Japanese legation, setting fire to the building. The majority of the people inside managed to make it out, although six Japanese were killed. After this, the rioters moved onto the palace, killing Min Gyeom-ho, as well as other high-ranking officials. They especially wanted to get their hands on Queen Min, but she had managed to escape. The riot was eventually contained, and several officials were executed as a result. However, this incident still damaged relations with the Japanese.

To restrict Japanese involvement in Joseon affairs, the Joseon government had Chinese advisors come in to help with the retraining of their troops. China, however, took advantage of that and started to regain control over Joseon. The Chinese sent in special military advisors and a trade minister, and China also worked out an agreement with Joseon, which resulted in the China-

Korea Treaty of 1882. The greatest difficulty with that agreement was the fact that it required Joseon to be a dependency of China.

The Joseon-American Treaty

About a month before the Imo Incident, Joseon had signed a treaty of amity with the United States. It indicated that Joseon was an independent country, that America would take Joseon's side on matters of foreign aggression, and granted Joseon a most-favored-nation status in terms of trade. They invited an American representative to set up a legation, and Lucius Foote was sent to Seoul as America's ambassador there. Upon Gojong's request, America was offered opportunities to invest in railroad construction, streetcars, and even a gold mine.

Aggressive Modernization Begins

Many members of the government were upset with Queen Min's influence; her family supported Chinese influence, something that many in the country were against. When a conflict between France and China broke out, some rebels saw this as the perfect time to stage a coup. In December 1884, a banquet was held to celebrate the opening of the new post office. King Gojong was approached by Kim Ok-gyun, the leader of the Gapsin Coup. He and his followers seized the king and secured protection from the Japanese at the royal palace. With the support of the Japanese, this rebel group issued directives in the king's name and created a program of reform. Some of the points they covered in their program were:

1. Elimination of their tributary relationship with Qing China

2. Cessation of the Confucian model of governance and the introduction of freedom for all classes.

3. A new tax system.

4. Establishment of free enterprise

They then executed six very conservative ministers and replaced them with more progressive statesmen. Their new government only lasted a few days, as the furious Queen Min assembled her own forces. She appealed to China for military support and freed her husband. The newly established reform party disbanded, but nearly all the rebels found refuge in Japan. Kim Ok-gyun was later entreated to come to China, where he was assassinated.

Since the Gapsin Coup was unable to stop the spread of Western influences, Joseon built Western-style hospitals and had consultants come from Western countries, who introduced new agricultural methods, in 1885. In 1886, Joseon obtained a loan from China to build a telegraph from Seoul to Uiju in the northern provinces and later obtained another loan from Germany to expand the telegraph to other major cities.

Russian Agreement

In 1884, Gojong and Queen Min also reached out to Russia for an agreement of amity and the establishment of commerce. China was displeased with that and even considered dethroning King Gojong in response. Joseon then worked on an overland trade agreement with Russia in 1885. Great Britain, alarmed that Joseon was involved in a secret agreement with Russia, then involved itself by making a deal with the Chinese to occupy the Joseon island of Geomundo and fortify it against any intrusions. This wasn't Chinese territory, though, and Joseon objected to this forcibly. Britain withdrew in 1887, but the area became a center of conflict among China, Japan, and Russia, all of whom wanted access to the Tumen River.

Prelude to War

In 1894, a short-lived revolt called the Donghak Rebellion broke out among the peasants, who were being crushed by the growing tax burden. The Japanese troops that were still in Korea moved to suppress the revolt. As they spread around Seoul, Queen Min became alarmed and then prevailed upon her husband to ask for Chinese aid, which he did. In June of 1894, Chinese troops arrived, but Japan asserted that they had violated the Treaty of Tientsin of

1885, which stated that China must notify Japan if they enter Joseon. More Japanese troops were then sent.

Now there were two foreign forces in Joseon—those of Qing China and Imperial Japan. They were on the verge of war, and the first battlefields of the First Sino-Japanese War would be in Joseon.

Chapter 7 – From Independence to Annexation

In July of 1894, Chinese and Japanese forces confronted each other at Aswan, east of Seoul. The Chinese were outnumbered and lost the initial conflict, so they retreated to Pyongyang in the north. By August, the Chinese were defeated in Joseon and moved farther north to the border city of Uiju. They then moved the war to Chinese soil.

Proposed Japanese Reorganization of Joseon

Japan was victorious after the First Sino-Japanese War and decided to control the politics and development of Joseon for the benefit of Japan. The Japanese minister to Joseon, Inoue Kaoru, compelled King Gojong to appoint two pro-Japanese officials to his Cabinet. He then prevailed upon Gojong to establish a new constitution under his guidance called the "Guiding Principles for the Nation." It had eight ministries: 1) foreign affairs, 2) finance, 3) justice, 5) commerce, 6) education, 7) defense, and 8) agriculture.

The Assassination of Queen Min

Japan's interference angered the king and Queen Min, as she always leaned more toward the Chinese. The king himself wasn't that strong, but Queen Min was. So, in 1895, she turned to Russia for help. Two powerful pro-Russian figures were placed on the Cabinet, and two other pro-Japanese ministers were thrown out. A Japanese man, named Miura Goro, had been sent to Joseon as Japan's ambassador with a secret assignment to assassinate Queen Min. Goro gathered a motley group of gangsters, and they killed Queen Min's guards, broke into her bedroom, and dragged her into the yard. There, she was hacked to death, and her body was burned. In fear of his life, King Gojong and his son, Sunjong, fled to the Russian legation, where they stayed for a year.

The Empire of Korea

In 1897, King Gojong returned. Responding to pressure from the Western nations, the country declared itself definitively independent from Japan and China. Gojong announced the establishment of the Empire of Korea, with Gojong as the first emperor.

Under Gojong's leadership, the Gwangmu Reform took place. It rejected the whole old-world order of hierarchical social strata, and its primary goal was social equality. Although many had surnames, those of the lower classes did not. According to this new system, the lower classes would use the names of their masters for themselves or adopt one of the common surnames in the area. The concept of citizenship was also introduced.

Military uniforms were Western-style and were an imitation of the Prussian styles. Diplomats wore Western-style suits, and even the police wore Western-style uniforms.

In 1897, land ownership was no longer determined by the landowners themselves but by outside subcontractors who used modern surveying equipment. In 1898, electricity came to Korea through a partnership between the United States and the Korean Hanseong Electric Company. A telephone network was already in place in 1896, with the first long-distance public phone being installed in 1902.

The educational system was also expanded under this reform, and many were manned by Western missionaries. The Catholic persecutions had ended, and Catholicism had been permitted in the 1880s. Secondary schools were also built by the government, including vocational schools, and private schools were erected as well. However, it wasn't until 1905 that universities were built. A health care system had been established when Korea opened its doors to the world in 1876. Under the Gwangmu Reform, three sectors were more fully fleshed out, which included public health, medical care, and the regulations for licensed medical practitioners.

Russia as Protectorate

Russia drew up a new agreement with Korea in 1898. They wanted Korea to conduct all state affairs through a set of Russian advisors, who would control the financial system and military affairs. The Russians trained the Korean forces and made economic deals with Korea for a long-lasting lumber contract and exclusive mining rights in the mountains. In addition, Korea devoted some of its ports to Russian ships and areas devoted to commercial buildings for Russian commerce. In exchange for those concessions, Russia provided monetary aid. Once any one of those privileges were withdrawn, Russia threatened it would withhold aid. This privileged status inflamed some of the people of Korea, giving rise to protests throughout the country.

Russia had made an agreement with China in late 1897, which allowed Russia access to Port Arthur, an important port city on the tip of the Liaodong Peninsula. Japan, who wanted access to Manchuria and Korea, saw Russia as a threat to their imperial ambitions. And they had good cause to worry because the Russo-Japanese War was looming on the horizon.

Japanese-Russian Buildup to War

In 1903, Russian troops swarmed into Manchuria and planned on using Korea as a bridgehead. Russia manipulated Korea into declaring itself neutral. Japan, however, wanted to keep up some of its influence in Korea, and so, there was a showdown between Japan and Russia over the issue of Korea's non-involvement because of the presence of Russian personnel in the country. Japanese troops were then sent into Seoul and occupied a few government buildings. Korea objected strenuously, so Japan responded by insisting that Korea expel its Russian representatives. As soon as Korea did so, though, Japanese companies bought land in Korea and built railroads from Seoul to Pusan to transport war materials for the anticipated battles with Russia. Little by little, the Japanese wedged their way into Korean affairs and forced the Korean emperor to hire a Japanese financial advisor, as well as advisors in police affairs, the ministry of defense, and the education ministry.

The Japanese came to use Incheon, located in modern-day northwestern South Korea, and other ports to launch naval attacks on Russian ships. In fact, Japan began to occupy much of Korea for its war preparations. Both sides engaged in bloody wars, mostly at sea. Even though they were victorious, the expense of the war nearly bankrupted Japan. Russia was in the throes of a revolution at home and was anxious to settle. In 1905, US President Theodore Roosevelt stepped in to mediate an end to the war and held the negotiations in Portsmouth, New Hampshire. However, in a secret discussion called the Taft-Katsura Memorandum, the United States agreed that Japan would keep its interests in Korea in exchange for Japan permitting the US to maintain its friendly relationship with the Philippines. It is not known for certain what happened during this meeting, as it was very secretive.

Once the Treaty of Portsmouth, the treaty that ended the Russo-Japanese War, was made public in 1905, Emperor Gojong and many of the Korean people staged protests. The Korean emperor said, "I declare that the so-called treaty of protectorate recently concluded between Korea and Japan was extorted at the point of the sword and under duress and therefore is null and void." In

1907, Gojong sent delegates to the Hague Peace Conference to protest the treaty, but his efforts were unsuccessful.

Prince Ito Hirobumi, who was made the Resident-General of Korea, proclaimed that the Korean emperor had acted against the treaty with his actions. As a result, Gojong was forced to abdicate his throne. Following that, his son, Sunjong, inherited the throne, but he was a minor and essentially powerless.

In 1910, a treaty of annexation was drawn up between Japan and Korea through the Resident-General, who handled Japan's role in Korea. Emperor Sunjong refused to sign it, so the prime minister of Korea, Ye Wanyong, did instead, raising questions about the legality of the document. However, despite these issues, Korea was annexed by Japan in 1910, dissolving the Korean Empire.

Government by Repression

After Korea had come so far in its efforts toward independence and more liberal attitudes that formed the basis for political parties, the Japanese overlords backstepped the country into a feudal-type status hierarchy. There was no free speech, and Korean representation wasn't allowed in the higher civil service positions. It was a militaristic-type of government; even the school teachers wore military uniforms and carried swords.

The Japanese plowed in and bought up as much land as they could because the Korean landowners couldn't pay the increased taxes that resulted from the expenses of the required irrigation, losing their lands that their families had spent so long trying to gain.

In 1912, the Governor-General, a position that overtook the Resident-General in late 1910 and was held by Terauchi Masatake at this time, had laws passed that essentially gave ownership of Korean land to the Japanese who were residing in Korea. The Koreans became tenant farmers and provided payments to the Japanese, leaving little for themselves. The Koreans were on the brink of starvation. Some of the farmers who weren't needed in

Korea were assigned to go to mainland Japan and many of the South Pacific islands to work for Japan in construction, mining, and shipbuilding. In the same year, Japan created the "Regulations for Fisheries Associations," which permitted not only Korean fishermen to work but Japanese fishermen as well. There were about 90,000 Japanese fishermen, and they depleted many of the fish that the Koreans had depended upon. In 1918, Japan passed the Korean Forestry Ordinance. Japanese lumber companies poured in and felled trees to provide lumber for Japan. The cleared land was then given to Japanese landowners to farm.

In terms of cultural identity, it was Japan's objective to "absorb" the Koreans into their way of life. According to a Japanese settler at the time, "The Korean people will be absorbed in the Japanese. They will talk our language, live our life, and be an integral part of us."

Within the next ten years, though, more liberalism was permitted, and political parties were able to form. The Koreans were even allowed to form labor unions and publish their own newspapers, but they were heavily censored.

Korean history books used in schools were edited to ensure that Japan was viewed in the most positive light possible. The histories were abridged in such a way as to eliminate any references to matters outside of the Korean Peninsula. Between 1910 and 1922, many private schools were closed, reducing the number from 2,000 to 600.

Japan was involved in World War I between 1914 to 1918 in an ancillary role. Korea wasn't directly involved, but Korean women and teenage girls were rounded up and forced to be "comfort women" for Japanese troops, in other words, sex slaves. Some of them were abducted from their homes, but most of them were lured by false promises of work or educational opportunities. A Korean survivor, Yun Doo Ri, stated this about her horrendous experience with a Japanese soldier, "He swiftly knocked me down and started pushing his thing inside me. It happened so fast. I found myself bleeding. I didn't know where the blood was coming from. I only felt pain. I was fifteen." These women and girls were badly mistreated, and later historians wrote that only a quarter of these girls survived.

In 1919, there was a huge Korean protest that demanded their independence. It was called the March 1ˢᵗ Movement, and although the demonstrations were peaceful, Japanese soldiers were called in to suppress the uprising. Around two million Koreans participated in the more than 1,500 demonstrations that took place throughout the country. Koreans believe that nearly 7,500 Koreans were killed, while Japanese officials at the time only reported 553 deaths; while it is not known for sure how many died, it is more than likely that several thousand did. Although many people died, the impetus for independence only grew among the Koreans.

Chapter 8 – Korea at War

Korea in World War II

In 1939, more than thirty countries were sucked into World War II, which started when Nazi Germany invaded Poland. When the Japanese attacked the US naval base at Pearl Harbor, Hawaii, in December 1941, America entered the war.

Japan had long craved mastery of the Pacific, along with its surrounding islands and the countries in Southeast Asia. The countries in the South Pacific afforded tremendous opportunities for trade and wealth. Elimination of most of the US Navy would have hindered the United States from engaging Japan in the Pacific theater. Japan had already annexed Manchuria, near the Chinese mainland, and installed a puppet government there. As part of their ambitions to expand the Japanese empire, they had allied themselves with the Axis powers of Germany and Italy in order to complete the conquest of China, along with the island kingdoms in the South Pacific.

Japan conscripted five million Koreans into their civilian war effort. Many of them were Japanese residents who had originally come from Korea during Japan's occupation of the country. They are called Zainichi Koreans, and, in fact, they comprise the second largest ethnic minority group in Japan today. These people worked in mines and factories that manufactured weapons and products for use by the Japanese soldiers on the front. The working conditions were deplorable, and as many as 60,000 of them died as a result.

About two percent of the Korean population was accepted from the 300,000 who voluntarily applied to join the Japanese Imperial Army. When Japan needed more soldiers in 1944, they inducted 200,000 more Korean men.

In early August 1945, the United States dropped atomic bombs on Nagasaki and Hiroshima. Although World War II had already ended in the European theater, this move ended the war in the Pacific one. The Allies, which included America, China, Great Britain, and the Soviet Union, among other countries, decided to strip Japan of all its conquests in the South Pacific, including Korea.

Before World War II officially ended, though, the Soviet Union invaded the Japanese puppet government in Manchuria, starting the Soviet-Japanese War a few days after the bombs were dropped on Japan. As a result of this war, the Soviet Union occupied the north of Korea, and the United States came in to occupy the southern part in September 1945, fearing Russian expansion. On September 12th, the People's Republic of Korea was established, which divided Korea into zones, with the Soviet Union in the north and the US in the south. The Soviet Union worked with the local People's Committee established there, passing sweeping reforms and redistributing the Japanese land to poor farmers. The old landed classes were not happy with this, and protests arose, with many fleeing south. The United States, on the other hand, refused to acknowledge the People's Republic of Korea, as it had communist elements in it, and outlawed it three months after its establishment. This led to people who supported the People's Republic to rise up; it is estimated that between 30,000 and 100,000 people were killed in the military campaigns against these insurgents over the course of a few years.

At the Moscow Conference in December 1945, it was agreed that the Soviet Union, the US, the Republic of China, and Great Britain would be a part of a trusteeship over Korea, which would end in five years when Korea would be declared independent and unified under one government. Although many Koreans wanted their independence, the trusteeship was put in place. A Soviet-US commission took place in 1946 and 1947 to work out the issues of a unified government but failed to make any progress. The Cold War tensions were already starting to seep in, and the Koreans were incredibly opposed to the trusteeship, making it hard to come to any conclusive agreements. As the commission bickered amongst themselves, the divisions between the two zones only deepened; in May 1946, it was illegal to cross the 38th parallel, the line that split the two zones, without a permit.

Since the commission wasn't making any progress, the issues were brought to the United Nations in 1947. The UN decided that Korea should elect a national assembly for the whole country and have the UN supervise the election. The Soviets rejected any form of election, and so, the elections were only held in the south. Koreans began to see this as the inevitable splitting up of their country, and protests against the elections began in 1948. However, the general election still took place in May. In August, the Republic of Korea took over the government from the US, with Syngman Rhee, an anti-communist and pro-American politician, as the president. In the north, the Democratic People's Republic of Korea was established in early September, with Kim Il-sung, a communist who had worked hard to get the Japanese out of his country, as the prime minister. Korea was officially split into two.

The Jeju Uprising

Jeju, a South Korean island, protested vehemently against the elections in 1947, a year before they even took place, as they knew it would lead to the splitting of Korea. The South Korean Labor Party (SKLP), or the Workers' Party of South Korea, a communist organization, led most of these protests, and as time went on, and as the election drew nearer, the protests became more frequent and more violent.

On April 3rd, 1948, 500 **SKLP** rebels, along with 3,000 other people who supported their cause, attacked the right-wing group Northwest Youth League, as well as police stations. Lieutenant General Kim Ik-ryeol attempted to solve the problem peacefully, but the two sides could not agree: the government wanted the rebels to completely surrender, while the rebels wanted the police to be disarmed, all government officials to be dismissed, the prohibition of paramilitary groups, and the reunification of the Korean Peninsula. The US sent forces to help squash the rebels, which worked for a time, as the rebels retreated. But at the end of April, the Korean governor of Jeju defected and joined the rebels, causing others in the military to do the same.

The fighting continued, picking up during the election week. The US feared that the rebels might be successful in stopping the elections from taking place and ordered a blockade of the island to prevent those sympathetic from the mainland in reaching Jeju. The rebels were not as active during the summer, but they picked back up once the elections in North Korea were about to take place, forming underground elections for those wanting to participate. The Republic of Korea (ROK) sent forces to help stop these activities, but they were unsuccessful, with one regiment deciding to assist the rebels once they arrived. ROK President Syngman Rhee was forced to declare martial law in mid-November, 1948. By the end of 1948, the ROK's harsh tactics had significantly damaged the rebel forces. They managed to launch one last offensive, but they were basically done.

Many civilians were killed during this uprising, most of them at the hands of the ROK and the US. It is thought that 14,373 civilians died, with some death tolls going as high as 30,000. The overall death toll goes up to as high as 100,000. About seventy percent of the island's villages were burned down, and recent discoveries have found mass graves of bodies.

This event was, for the most part, buried in history. For almost fifty years after the uprising, it was a crime for any South Korean to even mention the events of the Jeju uprising, punishable by beatings, torture, and/or a lengthy prison sentence. In the 1990s, though, the South Korean government openly admitted the atrocities that took place on the island, and in 2006, it issued an official apology.

The Korean War

When World War II ended, the Chinese Civil War resumed, which was between the government of the Republic of China, led by the Chinese Nationalist Party, and the Communist Party of China. In late September 1949, Mao Zedong established the People's Republic of China, and by August 1950, the Communist Party of China had won the war, placing Mao Zedong in charge.

Before that war fully ended, though, a new one had started. In March 1949, Kim Il-sung visited Joseph Stalin in Moscow and proposed a forcible reunification of Korea. Stalin agreed but wanted to wait to strike, as the time wasn't quite right. In the spring of 1950, Stalin believed the time was ripe; Mao Zedong had secured his final victory in China, and the US had withdrawn from Korea. Since the US didn't help in the Chinese Civil War, Stalin assumed they wouldn't come back to Korea to stop the spread of communist influence. As the Soviet Union had been supplying North Korea with arms, South Korea was becoming restless, knowing that war was imminent, and many clashes broke out along the 38th parallel.

On June 25th, 1950, the North Korean army crossed the 38th parallel and invaded South Korea. America, worried this could spread into another world war, wanted to move against North Korea, and they presented the issue to the United Nations. The United Nations condemned the invasion and decided to assist South Korea. The United Nations Command force (UNCOM) was placed under the leadership of US General Douglas MacArthur to expel the North Koreans and restore peace. The United States made up most of the force, but more countries volunteered to join the UN force or contribute in some way to the war effort.

First Battle of Seoul (June 25th to June 28th, 1950)

After North Korea crossed the 38th parallel, they marched toward Seoul. Using a blitzkrieg style of attacks, which the South Koreans could not stop, they easily took over the capital within three days. Seoul residents were advised to report on anyone who appeared to support South Korea and the UN. Former Korean newspapers were banned, and a photo of Kim Il-sung appeared on the front page of a newly published communist newspaper. The article in it blamed the war on Syngman Rhee, the South Korean president. It read, "Your bitter enemy is the traitor, Syngman Rhee, the tool of American imperialism."

Battle of Osan (July 5th)

At Osan, which is just south of the Korean capital of Seoul, a US task force moved in to repel the North Koreans. Unfortunately, the US force wasn't well equipped and only had 400 infantrymen, along with an artillery battery. The North Koreans, on the other hand, numbered to around 5,000 and had Soviet tanks to back them up. Although the US held them back, it was only temporary, and the North Koreans overran the Americans. This battle marked the first engagement between the US and North Korean forces.

Battle of Pyongtaek (July 6th)

The Americans retreated southward toward the city of Pyongtaek. They still didn't have the firepower they needed and regrouped there, as well as at Cheonan, also spelled as Chonan, which was farther south. Ammunition ran out, and communications equipment hadn't yet been sent in. In the face of the heavily armored Soviet-supplied T-34 tanks, the soldiers panicked and retreated in disorder.

Battle of Cheonan (July 7th to July 8th)

After receiving some ammunition and equipment, the US 34th Infantry Regiment and the 24th Infantry Division attempted to confront the North Koreans north of the town of Cheonan. The 3rd Battalion of the 34th Infantry set up a defensive perimeter on July 7th, and by nightfall, they were engaged with the North Koreans, who had moved in from the east and split into two columns. The 63rd Field Artillery unit, which was assisting the 34th Infantry, pelted the North Koreans and managed to hold off some of them.

It was at this point that the second column of the North Koreans arrived in the northwest, supported by the tanks. They destroyed motor vehicles in case any Americans were hiding in them. Colonel Robert Martin, the new commander of the 34th regiment, lost his life after being hit by tank fire. As the North Koreans kept pouring in, the troops up front were forced to retreat, and the back-up 1st Battalion withdrew under punishing mortar fire.

Battle of Chochiwon (July 10th to July 12th)

Forced to move even farther south, the newly assigned US 21st Infantry Regiment had orders to further delay the North Koreans in their southward advance until more men and equipment could be transported to South Korea. Much to the surprise of the American and UN forces, there were as many as 20,000 North Koreans but only 2,000 Americans and South Koreans to fight at Chochiwon. Airstrikes were carried on by US fighter planes called Mustangs, and they inflicted heavy damage on some of the powerful Soviet tanks.

The 1st Battalion, who had only held back-up positions at Cheonan, was now fully engaged with the North Koreans. The 3rd Battalion had a higher position on a ridge and regained some ground. They were also able to rescue some wounded men from the attacks that had occurred earlier in the day. The North Koreans had a multitude of machine guns and pommeled the UN positions heavily. Many of the infantrymen ran out of ammunition and had to engage in hand-to-hand combat. The UN troops lost 409 men, 140 were wounded, and 230 captured. Despite these losses, the 21st Infantry Regiment was praised for their work, as they managed to delay the North Koreans long enough for the 24th Infantry Division to set up defenses around Taejon.

Battle of Taejon (July 14th to July 21st)

American soldiers from the 3rd Battalion and the 34th Infantry were fired upon by the North Koreans from across the Kum River, which ran west then turned south. They didn't hit the American infantry positions, as they were on higher ground. Soon, though, the North Koreans crossed the river and fired mortar rounds and artillery. Because they had very little communication equipment, the North Koreans were able to surround the American infantry. The 1st Battalion, which was farther north, also came under heavy attack, and it was able to hold off the North Koreans until the men could find safety. More North Koreans crossed the river, managing to capture an outpost of the 63rd Field Artillery Battalion. They managed to destroy communication lines and vehicles, as well as inflicted heavy losses, with the survivors retreating south on foot.

Where the river turned west, the American forces were joined by the 19th Infantry to shore up the 34th Infantry line, which brought anti-tank weapons, such as RPGs (rocket-propelled grenades) to the fighting front. Just then, the North Korean forces sent in large numbers of fresh troops against the 19th Infantry, who weren't able to hold them off. In the melee, the American supply lines were blocked off. The 2nd Battalion then moved in to break up the roadblocks that were set up to stop their supply lines. However, they suffered heavy casualties and were unable to do so.

Part of this fight at Taejon was actually intended to set up a defensive line to halt the North Korean advance, sending them back by controlling the Nakdong River that fed into the Kum. Thus, Brigadier General William Dean, the commander of the 24th

Infantry, was ordered to hold the North Koreans back for as long as he could.

While Dean was defending that area, the North Koreans surrounded the city of Taejon, trapping the 24th and the 34th Infantry that were headquartered there. The North Koreans started occupying buildings, and there was intense house-to-house fighting for two days, with more North Koreans coming in, often disguised as farmers. Brigadier General Dean was there, as he had taken it upon himself to lead his men. He was captured, making him the highest-ranking prisoner during this war, but his identity wasn't known until much later.

Despite having fought bravely, the Americans were forced to withdraw once the North Koreans had the city nearly surrounded. Nearly 922 Americans were killed, 228 wounded, and 2,400 missing in action. It was later said by war historians that some of those soldiers who were missing or captured were immediately executed after the battle.

Although the battle was a loss for the Americans and South Koreans, it served the crucial purpose of buying time until their forces could set up a very strong defensive perimeter on the southeastern tip of South Korea, which included Pusan.

Battle of the Pusan Perimeter (August 4th to Sept 18th)

At this point in the war, Great Britain joined up with the UN forces. In the Battle of Taejon, the UN forces had to withdraw. However, a month later—in August—the UN was back to loosen North Korea's grip near the Kum River. This time, they focused on cutting the rail lines that were supplying the North Korean troops. Key railroad bridges were blown up, and more air attacks were inflicted upon them by the American bomber squadrons. The North Koreans lacked an adequate air defense, and at this point, many of their transport trucks had been destroyed. British ships, along with those of Australia, Canada, New Zealand, and the

Netherlands, unloaded not only 600 tanks but also more men and weapons.

Task Force Pohang cleared the North Korean troops out of the mountainous regions, and Task Force Bradley waged ground battles to defend Pohang and invade the North Koreans at Anjang-ni. They engaged the North Koreans at the Nakong River, where they had been prior to the Battle of Taejon.

In August, troops in the Korean People's Army (KPA) was increased by forces fed in by North Korea. However, their supply lines didn't keep up with the pace, and they found themselves thinning out their lines to cover the whole perimeter. That was a weakness that could be exploited by the UN troops. The KPA was able to drive the UN forces southwest toward Masan, thus surprising them.

Securing control over the Nakdong River was essential in determining the outcome of this battle. In mid-August, General MacArthur initiated a carpet bombing of the KPA positions. This was somewhat effective because it reduced the number of North Korean forces trying to penetrate the south and broke their perimeter.

By late August, the paucity of supplies caught up with the KPA, along with the loss of their equipment. At that point, the UN ground forces outnumbered the North Koreans. Regardless, they concentrated their forces and broke the Pusan perimeter in some places. Fighting was intense at Haman, Kyongju, the Naktong Bulge (a segment of higher land near the river), Nam River, Jongsan, Taegu, and Kasan. This was known as the Great Naktong Offensive.

While the confrontations were being brutally fought in the Pusan regions, the UN carried out their stealthily laid plans to create an amphibious assault at Incheon called Operation Chromite. That offensive was going to move southeast to squeeze out the KPA contingents between there and Pusan. The KPA was caught by this deadly surprise and started retreating northward to escape the Pusan area.

This battle was one of the first crucial engagements in the war, and it raged for ten bloody days. As one soldier, Corp. Roy Alridge, worded it, "If we hadn't held the lines at Pusan, there would be no South Korea today."

Once most of the supply routes for the North Koreans had been cut off, and the KPA was facing increasing offensives from the UN troops, they began a humiliating retreat. The Battle of the Pusan Perimeter was a resounding victory for the UN troops.

Casualties were extreme at Pusan. The South Koreans had more than 40,000 casualties, while the North Koreans incurred almost 64,000.

Battle of Inchon (September 10th to September 19th)

The North Koreans were falling back from the Pusan perimeter, so a counterattack was planned by Douglas MacArthur to retake the area of Seoul. This operation was an amphibious assault at the southern city of Inchon, which involved around 75,00 troops and 261 ships. The decisive UN victory not only boosted morale, but it also allowed the UN forces to recapture Seoul about two weeks later. In this bold push north, the UN forces were able to resist the Chinese and North Korean troops and even got as far as the Yalu River, located on the border of North Korea and China.

The Armistice

By mid-December, the US was looking to discuss peace terms to end the war. South Korean President Syngman Rhee was in favor of unifying the entire Korean Peninsula under his command and did not want the peace talks to happen. Kim Il-sung also did not want to enter these talks, but he was pushed to enter into them by the People's Republic of China and the Soviet Union, whose help he would need to win the war anyway.

The peace talks began in June 1951, and they proceeded slowly. On July 27th, 1953, the Korean Armistice Agreement was signed. This was not a peace treaty but rather a ceasefire, so peaceful relations between the two countries were not set. The armistice established the Military Demarcation Line and the Korean Demilitarized Zone (DMZ). The DMZ was designed to be a buffer zone between the two nations and is 2.5 miles (4 kilometers) wide and 160 miles (250 kilometers) long. Troops from both sides guard the DMZ, and in 2018, it was the most heavily defended national border in the world. Since there was no peace treaty, and since Syngman Rhee even refused to sign the agreement, the hostilities between the two nations still exist today.

Besides being known as the war that ultimately divided Korea, this war is also known for the numerous war crimes committed during it. In December of 1950, the South Korean president, Syngman Rhee, was furious about the fall of Pyongyang and executed communists and supporters of the opposition in what is known as the Bodo League massacre. It is estimated that at least 60,000 to 200,000 died. In July 1950, American servicemen killed an unknown number of South Korean refugees southeast of Seoul, believing them to be KPA soldiers. The South Korean side wasn't the only one to commit such atrocities, although they are better documented than the North Koreans. On June 28th, 1950, between 700 to 900 patients and medical staff were killed by the KPA in the Seoul National University Hospital massacre. The KPA has also been accused of beating, starving, and executing prisoners of war, although they deny such claims occurring on a widespread basis. One such massacre that they don't deny is the Hill 303 massacre, where 42 American prisoners of war were shot by the KPA, which led to KPA commanders enacting stricter guidelines on how to treat prisoners of war.

Chapter 9 – North Korea

Communism had undergone evolutionary changes during the 20th century and had split into Marxism-Leninism, Stalinism, Maoism (named after Mao Zedong of the People's Republic of China), and a flavor of communism promoted by Nikita Khrushchev when he was the premier of the Soviet Union from 1958 to 1964.

Stalin fostered a kind of "cult of personality" that Khrushchev abhorred. It promoted a kind of leader-worship, and Khrushchev preferred to return communism to the ideals of national collectivism and socialism. Stalin, on the other hand, flooded the country with self-portraits and controlled the press in such a way that it was his own personal mouthpiece. In his communique, "On the Cult of Personality and Its Consequences," Khrushchev called his process "de-Stalinization" and placed more authority in party leadership. Like Stalin, Kim Il-sung fervently believed in this cult approach. The history books published during his administration were revisionist, making it so that Kim's guerilla faction during World War II singlehandedly freed Korea from Japanese domination to impress upon North Korea his expertise in leadership.

When Kim Il-sung rose to power, there were four basic political factions: 1) the Pro-Soviet faction, who were Koreans who had lived in the Soviet Union since the 19th century; 2) the Domestic faction, which was composed of Koreans who did live in Korea but were vocally anti-Japanese, as many had been imprisoned by the Japanese during the occupation; 3) the Ya'an faction, who were Korean exiles who lived in China and joined the Communist Party of China; and 4) the Guerilla faction, who followed Kim Il-sung and who fought for the Soviet Army in Manchuria and later moved to the Soviet Union.

One by one, Kim eliminated his political rivals. In 1955, Pak Hon-yong, one of the main leaders of the communist movement in Korea, was arrested in a purge to rid North Korea of the members of the Workers' Party of Korea and was later executed. The real reason for his elimination, though, was his ability to attract huge numbers to his cause.

Three years later, Kim continued with his purge of potential rivals. In 1958, the leader of the Ya'an faction, Kim Tu-bong, mysteriously "disappeared." The leader of the Pro-Soviet faction was imprisoned in Pyongyang and murdered by the secret police in Korea in 1960. Members of the Pro-Soviet faction either joined Kim Il-sung's group or continue to live in the Soviet Union. Kim Il-sung merged the Workers' Party of Korea and the domestic faction.

Another noted individual, Li Sangjo, who was the Russian ambassador to North Korea, stated that the revolutionary struggle of the communist ideology was represented by Kim as being his own personal efforts to overthrow the Japanese overlords and that he exaggerated his own role in "liberating Korea." His campaign was dominated by presenting himself as "wise," a "genius," and an "iron commander."

Kim had absolute power in the country. North Korea, to this day, promotes self-reliance, or *Juche*, as a state ideal, indicating that North Korea is self-sufficient and truly independent. The *Juche* concept promotes economic sustainability through its own agriculture, and as a result, Kim isolated North Korea from the rest of the world.

The Songbun System

In 1958, Kim divided the population into three categories: 1) the core class, who were considered faithful followers of the regime; 2) the wavering class, who were perceived as being ambivalent toward Kim and his party's ideals; and 3) the hostile class, those who were openly hostile or had the potential to be hostile toward the North Korean government. The core class consisted of laborers in agriculture or factories, as well as high-ranking people who served in government posts. The wavering group was comprised of the ordinary Koreans who did not care much about politics or were uninformed. The hostile group consisted of former landowners and subversives, as they were the most likely to rebel against Kim Il-sung and the government. Files were kept on everyone and even included family backgrounds. With the exception of the core class, suspicion continued to be associated with those perceived as wavering or hostile, regardless of their future actions.

Agriculture in North Korea

Juche is at the center of agriculture in North Korea. A public distribution system was established in the 1950s, which required that farmers hand over seventy percent of their produce to the government for distribution to urban areas that could not grow food products. However, only seventeen percent of the land in North Korea can be farmed, as most of the nation is mountainous. The high elevations are rocky and uneven, which is unsuitable for farming, although some cattle grazing is possible at the lower elevations. The warm season is only three months long, and it is very rainy. Thus, there is the potential for flooding that can ruin crops. The flooding does, however, favor rice paddy farming if constructed on slopes and terraces. This is only possible in the southern areas of North Korea, though, as it is too cold farther north to do that. A lot of farmers fled the land in search of manufacturing, a low-level government or civil service job, or signed up for a career in the military. Many farmers and their families starved.

Farmers today work on state-run farms and collective farms, which are huge tracts of land cultivated by large groups of farmers. Unfortunately, it suffers from natural disasters, like floods and periods of droughts. The foodstuffs are then transported to the city areas and distributed there. Many of the crops are diverted for consumption by the elite and the military first and then to the factory workers and others in the urban areas.

Those who own some land around their homes often raise their own vegetable gardens for their families and neighbors. Mechanization is sparse, as are repairs and lack of spare parts, making farming a labor-intensive process. Fertilizers and biochemical elements that would enhance crop production is severely lacking but has improved over the years. The distribution system intended for a whole country is logistically very cumbersome, and there are significant delays in getting food to markets; thus, food is subsequently rationed.

In the 1990s, some mechanisms were introduced, and an irrigation system was put into place in the more arid areas. Rain and rice are more easily grown in North Korea now, but there is a lack of protein due to the lower intake of animal products, eggs, and beans. Protein deficiency is extremely severe, resulting in muscular weakness and even fluid buildup and edema. The areas of arable land are conducive to growing rice, potatoes, soybeans, sugar beets, mulberry, sorghum wheat, barley, and millet.

Food shortages are common in North Korea. The World Food Program estimates six million tons of grain are needed to feed the population, but only three million tons of grain are produced. In the mid-1990s, North Korea had huge food shortages. Between 1992 and 1998, it was estimated that nearly three million people died of starvation. In 2006, the production of wheat and barley decreased by nearly eighty percent, causing famine. This shortage was due to soil depletion and the fact that many farmers opted to work in the cities if they could.

The decline of the economy in North Korea is progressively getting worse. In 2014, North Korea passed the Enterprise Act, which permitted some foreign trade and joint ventures with other countries. Dr. Mitsuhiro Mimura, a Japanese research consultant, visited North Korea on numerous occasions and has called it the "poorest advanced economy in the world." Most of their money is devoted to nuclear development and defense instead of agricultural advancements.

Industrialization

North Korea operates on the principles of a "command economy," which means that the government determines what products are made, the quantity that needs to be made, and the prices that are charged for the goods. Following the Korean War, North Korea emphasized heavy industry. Tractors, bulldozers, and generators were manufactured and exported to the Middle East rather than being used for North Korea. Infrastructure and poor delivery system slowed the progress and movement of equipment and supplies.

North Korea has no oil or gas of its own. It does have anthracite coal, which is the hardest form of coal. That calls for the construction of mines and requires the construction of heavy-duty equipment to extract the coal from the earth and even more to transform it into acceptable fuel. They imported Western-style machinery and adopted some of the up-to-date management styles of those countries, including China, the Soviet Union, and even South Korea. Transportation systems were upgraded, along with automation. Education was expanded to train technicians and specialists in the fields of fuel, electronic, mechanical, and automation engineering.

By the 1970s, North Korea went into debt. The failure to maintain the equipment plus the lack of skills to do so shut down some factories. Because most of its money is spent on defense and the military, the economy stagnated. Estimates indicate that as much as forty percent of its revenue is spent on the manufacture of weapons. In 1993, North Korea established the Rason Special Economic Zone, which promoted foreign investment. There was some improvement in sales and income, but their structures are still undeveloped. Most of their trade is with China, which accounts for ninety percent of their imports. The per capita income of North Korea is only 1,700 US dollars.

Economic assistance came from China and the Soviet Union, but the Soviet Union started to demand hard currency for its imports, including oil. In the 1990s, China also reduced its imports. After the split of the Soviet Union in 1991, imports from them also decreased. Along with natural disasters, such as floods and droughts, North Korea was forced into an economic crisis.

By 1993, the North Koreans announced that it had completed a light-water nuclear reactor, capable of producing ten million kWh (kilowatt hour) of electricity annually. They then experimented with the light-water reactor to enrich uranium, which is needed for bringing it up to weapons-grade status. The process is slow, but a gas centrifuge is more efficient. There have been no reports of gas centrifuges in North Korea, though. The International Atomic Energy Agency wanted to inspect their facilities, specifically the Nyongbyon Nuclear Scientific Research Center, but Kim Il-sung declined. Pakistan, who possesses nuclear weapons, admitted in 2005 that they sold some nuclear technology to North Korea during the 1970s that could be used to manufacture nuclear weapons.

Lack of Electricity

In 1990, North Korea had some electricity, which was fueled by coal, oil, and hydroelectric plants. As political conditions changed in China and Russia, their electrical output severely decreased. The

North Koreans use solar panels to generate what electricity they can, but overcast and rainy days decrease the yield of those panels. Satellite photos taken at night reveal the paucity of electricity. The Korean Peninsula shows South Korea and China well-lit at night, but North Korea is almost totally dark.

Nuclear Armament

The armistice forbade the proliferation of nuclear weapons in either North Korea or South Korea. The United States made a statement shortly after the armistice that it wouldn't necessarily abide by the paragraph banning nuclear weapons. Between 1958 and 1991, the US stored nuclear weapons in South Korea.

South Korea again considered building new nuclear missiles and conducted a test. After revisiting the issue, South Korea decided against it. In 1968, South Korea and North Korea signed the Treaty on the Non-Proliferation of Nuclear Weapons. The US removed its nuclear weapons from the Korean Peninsula, but in 2003, North Korea withdrew from the non-proliferation agreement and have since started conducting nuclear tests.

In 2006, North Korea announced that it launched its first successful nuclear test underground. The explosion was confirmed by seismic readings taken in the West. The West vehemently reacted, but North Korea, who desperately needed oil shipments that had embargoes placed on it, indicated it was willing to shut down its nuclear research station at Nyongbyon. Meetings were conducted between North Korea, South Korea, China, Japan, Russia, and the United States. However, the talks were suspended when North Korea conducted another nuclear test in 2009.

In 2011, Kim Jong-il died of a suspected heart attack, and his death was followed by an elaborate funeral. Psychologists have labeled him as paranoid, anti-social, and narcissistic. He was later called the "Shining Star," and his body is preserved and displayed at Pyongyang's Kumsusan Memorial Palace. He was succeeded by his son, Kim Jong-un, who has carried on his policies.

In 2010, North Korea experimented with a different type of nuclear reaction. The traditional nuclear reaction is that of nuclear fission, where an atom is split by the bombardment of high-energy neutrons (non-charged) particles. This sets off a chain reaction, and the radioactive fallout is immense, like that which occurred at Nagasaki and Hiroshima during World War II. Fusion is another type of manipulation of the atom in which lighter atoms are combined. This produces a tremendous amount of energy and is similar to the kind of nuclear reactions in the sun. The reaction is huge, more so than that of an atomic bomb, although it produces far less radioactivity. Hydrogen bombs use the hydrogen atom for fusion. Experts who analyzed the purported fallout, though, doubt that the test was the result of fusion.

In 2012, under Kim Jong-un, North Korea agreed to suspend their uranium enrichment programs and was slated to receive food aid from the United States as an incentive. However, later that same year, North Korea armed a nuclear warhead on an antiballistic missile and tested it. In response, those food aid packages were canceled.

In 2017, China announced that it would suspend all oil shipments to North Korea—a fuel that they had used to generate electricity and create gasoline for the few cars it had manufactured. Shortly after this, North Korea launched four ballistic missiles, which landed in the Sea of Japan. Later the same year, North Korea launched two more, but they exploded shortly after they were launched. By the end of that year, North Korea was successful and claims that it now has the capability of launching a missile that could hit the United States mainland.

In 2003, six nations—China, Japan, the United States, Russia, North Korea, and South Korea—met to resolve the nuclear issue. No agreement has yet been formulated, but a framework for discussions has been laid out. They met again in 2009, but nothing was resolved. In 2018, Kim Jong-un announced that he was committed to the denuclearization of the Korean Peninsula.

As of 2019, the Bulletin of Atomic Scientists, a nonprofit organization concerned about global security issues, estimates that North Korea has between twenty and thirty nuclear weapons. In October the same year, Kim Jong-un, US President Donald Trump, and South Korean President Moon Jae-in held several meetings about the nuclear issue and the final resolution of the Korean War, but no agreement has been forthcoming yet.

Biological and Chemical Weapons

North Korea signed the Geneva Protocol, a treaty that prohibits the use of chemical and biological weapons in international fights, in 1989. However, North Korea never signed the Chemical Weapons Convention, which means it has no obligation to refrain from producing or stockpiling chemical weapons. Intelligence sources indicate that it possesses biological agents that can be easily combined to create a weaponized version of anthrax and smallpox, and reports also indicate that it has stockpiled mustard gas, phosgene, sarin, and V-type chemical agents. V-type agents cause its victims to lose muscular control, making them subject to seizures, uncontrollable urination, vomiting, and foaming at the mouth. Phosgene intoxicates the lungs, making its victims choke to the point that they are unable to breathe.

The Rulers

Kim Il-sung was the first premier of North Korea and ruled from 1948 to 1972. After 1972, his title was changed to president, and he remained in power until his death in 1994. Having been in the military most of his earlier adult life, Il-sung styled his country that way. It was austere and highly regimented. To wield his power, Il-sung remained as the head of the Korean Workers' Party for his lifetime and virtually made others join it. Although he upheld the principle of "self-reliance" and preferred isolationism, the country lacked the natural resources to supply all the food and oil it needed.

So, it became necessary to open up trade relations with other countries, but Il-sung restricted the number of those countries. In 1994, he signed the Agreed Framework, an agreement with the United States in which North Korea would refrain from producing nuclear weapons in exchange for an outside firm that would build two light-water nuclear reactors for the production of electricity. In 1983, North Korea attempted to assassinate President Chun Doo-hwan of South Korea and bombed Flight 858 to Seoul from Iraq, causing the United States and other countries to impose sanctions on North Korea.

Kim Il-sung was succeeded by his son, Kim Jong-il. Kim Jong-il didn't assume the title of president because that was reserved for the first president, his father, who is referred to as the "Eternal President." Therefore, Jong-il became the chairman of the National Defense Commission. His goal was a warming of relations between the two Koreas, and he met with South Korean President Kim Dae-jung to discuss those possibilities. In 1999, the United States agreed to lift some of the sanctions against the country in exchange for ceasing to test a long-range missile. By outward appearances, it seemed that Jong-il was abiding by the Agreed Framework his father had signed, but high-level intelligence reports indicated otherwise. In 2003, Jong-il announced the detonation of an underground nuclear weapons test. The US and North Korea attempted to write another agreement and came up with one in 2007, but it was left in abeyance over the issue of compliance. In 2011, Kim Il-sung died, and he was succeeded by his son, Kim Jong-un.

Kim Jong-un, like his grandfather, utilized the practice of eliminating his rivals or those within his administration who displeased him. When Kim Jong-un took power, his uncle, Jang Song-thaek, had been serving as a director of the Youth Work Department within the Workers' Party of Korea (WPK) Central Committee. He later became a member of the WPK Central

Committee and was spoken about as if he might be the next successor of North Korea after Kim Jong-il.

Song-thaek was seen again in March 2006 and later became the vice-director of the WPK and the vice-commissioner of the National Defense Commission. In 2013, he promulgated the construction of a bridge over the Yalu River but was glaringly absent at the dedication ceremony. Rumors from observers indicated that Kim Jong-un was displeased by what he perceived as cordial relations being discussed with China by Song-thaek. Then a dispute over control of the fishing rights between the Chinese and Korean fishermen occurred, which Song-thaek ultimately couldn't control. In addition, defectors to South Korea said that Song-thaek drank heavily at times and more than once made comments about North Koreans dying of hunger. In 2013, Kim Jong-un had his uncle arrested. He was tried by a special military tribunal and sentenced to execution. Song-thaek was dragged out into a yard and killed by antiaircraft machine guns, after which his body was burnt. Two of his deputies, Ri Ryong-ha and Jang Su-gil, were also slaughtered in the same fashion.

Many other influential members of the North Korean government have been killed in recent years. In 2014, O Song-hon, who worked for Jang Song-thaek, had followed his orders to create a separate arm for security for business purposes. He was executed by firing squad. A co-worker, Pak Chu-hong, was also executed. In 2015, Choe Yong-gon, one of the vice-premiers of North Korea and the deputy minister of construction and building, was reportedly executed after having got into an argument with Kim Jong-un over an issue related to forestry; he actually disappeared from public life, so it is unknown what happened to him. In 2016, Kim Jong-un's top educational official, Kim Jong-jin, was executed by a firing squad for being branded as an "anti-party and a counter-revolutionary" for showing a bad attitude during a meeting of the National Assembly.

Human Rights in North Korea

Freedom of speech is restricted, and the criticism of the government is forbidden. If one speaks out against the government or its leaders, they are sent to reeducation camps. Television, radio, and publishing are controlled by the government, as the praise and promotion of the country's supreme leader comes first before all else. Films and plays all circulate around the cult of personality, and criticism of the United States and other capitalistic countries appears in government-censored newspapers. Broadcasts from South Korea are also prohibited. North Korea uses a different coding system for broadcasting than South Korea, so it isn't even possible to view South Korean television programs in North Korea. Tampering with signals is a serious offense and results in a criminal penalty.

The practice of religion isn't technically forbidden, but there is no true freedom of religion in the country, as Christians, in particular, are targeted by the country. It is said that the Christians in North Korea are the most persecuted in the world. Christianity, as well as other religions, is practiced in secret. The only religions that are somewhat accepted are Buddhism and Confucianism.

All charity organizations and non-governmental organizations are carefully scrutinized. Anyone found to be proselytizing or practicing religions is imprisoned and subjected to harsh treatment. Estimates of religious prisoners are around 60,000 people. Some Buddhist temples remain but are mainly viewed as a part of the history of the country and do not actively engage in religious worship or practices. There are five churches in Pyongyang—three Protestant, one Russian Orthodox, and one Catholic. They are there for foreigners and for propaganda purposes.

Travel is severely restricted, and views of the cities from above show neatly laid-out but empty streets. Fuel is in low supply, and only the elite own vehicles. The people aren't permitted to relocate or move freely around the country, although people have managed to flee the country. Those who are forced back to Korea are often beaten and sent to prison camps, as they are deemed as defectors. Immigration and emigration are curtailed, and anyone returning from China, in particular, are punished.

Chapter 10 – South Korea

Just like any country, South Korea's history isn't picture-perfect. In 1949, just prior to the outbreak of the Korean War, several divisions of the South Korean army massacred unarmed civilians in the North Gyeongsang Province of South Korea, which is located on the eastern shore. The victims included women, children, and the people, all of whom were accused of being communist sympathizers. The South Korean government under Syngman Rhee, the newly elected president of South Korea, blamed Kim Il-sung's guerilla faction for being responsible. That wasn't the case, though. Many years later, South Korea admitted their involvement in the massacre, which resulted in the deaths of 75 people.

Rocky Beginnings

In 1948, Syngman Rhee was elected as president of the First Republic of Korea. Despite its announced commitment to democracy, Rhee was autocratic. He was also accused of corruption and of killing his political opponents. When he was elected for his fourth term in 1956, students in the port city of Masan rebelled, claiming the elections were rigged. Students staged an enormous revolt, which spread to the capital city of Seoul, and when the body of a student was found floating in the river along with 186 bodies, they were incensed. Martial law was then imposed, and Rhee resigned, fleeing to Hawaii to live in exile.

In 1960, Yun Posun was elected as president to the Second Republic of Korea, as the massive protests had established a new parliamentary government. Posun was more of a figurehead than anything else, as the real power was with the prime minister. Neither man could gain loyalty from any of the major political parties, leaving the government in a tough spot, especially since the economy was suffering due to the corruption of the prior government. Major General Park Chung-hee formed the Military Revolutionary Committee, aiming to overthrow the government. In May 1961, he staged a coup, overthrowing the government of Yun Posun and putting a military government in its place. This began the Third Republic of South Korea, which was, in practice, a dictatorship. It was ruled by the Democratic Republican Party and the Supreme Council, as well as Park Chung-hee, although Yun Posun remained president until 1962.

In 1963, Park was elected as president by a slim margin over Yun Posun, and in 1967, he was reelected for another term. The National Assembly, who, for the most part, favored Park, passed an extraordinary amendment allowing Park to run for a third term. He ran against Kim Dae-jung and won, again by a slim majority. In 1971, Park declared a state of emergency. He indicated that it was because of the "dangerous realities of the international situation," but more likely, it was an effort to reorganize the government in such a way that he could assume some form of dictatorial control over the country.

During this period of time, Park met with Kim Il-sung of North Korea to discuss the reunification of Korea. In anticipation of that, he called for revitalization reforms, starting with the forming of a conference consisting of around 2,500 elected members who would serve for six years. He announced the inauguration of the Yushin Constitution, but it was merely intended to give Park dictatorial powers. In 1972, after the passing of the constitution, the Fourth Republic of Korea was founded, granting him the powers he wanted. The Yushin Constitution forbade any opposition to the Yushin declaration itself and permitted Park to arrest anyone who opposed it. It also exempted low-income people from taxes and banned the known student protestor organizations and closed their schools.

In 1973, Park's former presidential opponent, Kim Dae-jung, was kidnapped from where he had been living in Japan and taken to Seoul. It was felt by those in power that this was triggered by his criticism of Park Chung-hee's attempts to seize dictatorial powers. Dae-jung's followers feared for his welfare, and the opposition against Park continued to grow among the people until it escalated into a major crisis.

In 1975, a large opposition group, who was trying to revive the People's Revolutionary Party, was arrested by the Korean Central Intelligence Service. They were accused of trying to set up a socialist state. One thousand twenty-four individuals were arrested, without warrants, and 253 of them were imprisoned. Less than five days later, eight of the leaders were sentenced to death, and eighteen hours later, they were executed.

In October 1979, Park himself was assassinated by the head of the Korean Central Intelligence Service. Martial law was declared the next day, and Choi Kyu-hah, the prime minister, stepped in as acting president and was officially elected as president in December. A coup was led shortly after by Major General Chun Doo-hwan, and by early 1980, the rebels basically controlled the government. Choi was made the head of the Korean Central Intelligence Agency in April 1980, and by May, he had dropped all pretense of not being the leader and declared martial law. Protests erupted, and the country was in chaos.

Gwangju Uprising

When martial law was declared by Chun Doo-hwan, universities were shut down. Around 200 angry students collected at the gates of Chonnam National University on May 18th, 1980. Suddenly, a unit of paratroopers arrived to disperse the crowd. The mob then moved down the main street and continued to grow until the crowd accumulated an estimated number of 2,000 protestors. More and more soldiers were sent in, and the episode erupted into violence. Troops beat demonstrators and even fired upon them. The protest spread not only to students but also to the general populace, which objected to the stringency of the new administration. Buses arrived loaded with demonstrators, and people flooded the streets. Citizens even seized arms from police stations and armories. A negotiation committee consisting of clergymen, lawyers, and professors reorganized the massive crowd into two groups, the Student Settlement Committee and the Citizens Settlement Committee. However, these groups were unable to make any progress in negotiating with the army.

The protest then spread to other provinces, such as Naju, Hwasan, Haenam, Mokpo, Yeongam, Muan, and Gangjin. Army forces were then sent to quell the insurrection in those sectors. On May 27th, after nine days of heavy fighting and protesting, the rebellion was suppressed in Gwangju. There is no universally accepted number of the dead for this tragic incident. The official figures released by the government stated that the death toll for the civilian population was a little less than 150. However, it has been argued that the death toll was closer to 1,000 or even 2,000.

Chun Doo-hwan Becomes President

After the intelligence chief, Choi, resigned in August, Chun Doo-hwan was recognized officially as president. In March 1981, the name of the government had changed once more, becoming the Fifth Republic of South Korea, which was a dictatorship and a one-party state under the Democratic Justice Party. Despite all of this political chaos, the economy expanded, and Chun altered Park's system of keeping economic decision-making in the top levels of government. Instead, he felt that economic decision-making should rely upon experts who were familiar with the market. An Economic Planning Board was established, although a lot of the traditionalists resented surrendering control. Because of that infighting, in fact, Dow Chemical, who had plants in South Korea, left the country. IBM had also considered investments in South Korea, but the political turmoil caused them to decide against it. Due to the pressure from conservative groups, Chun maintained a strong governmental presence in working with businesses but did insist upon American and European consultants in South Korea to aid in economic development.

In 1982, the Planning Board developed a five-year plan for expansion and hired a think tank, which had significant input from foreign business experts. Due to Chun's efforts to bridge the gap between the traditional and the liberal approaches to handling international business affairs, compromises were reached. In a CIA report released in 2018 about South Korea's economy in 1982, the conclusion was positive: "We believe the overall efficiency of South Korea's economic decision-making structure and the policies in place will enable the country to achieve a fairly good growth rate in the coming year." According to the Institute for International Economics, South Korea experienced what is called a "miracle economy."

Leading to Free Elections

Over time, the Fifth Republic slowly turned into a democratic state. In 1987, Chun Doo-hwan declared Roh Tae-woo to be the Democratic Justice Party, which effectively handed the role of president to him. Massive protests occurred throughout the country due to this, and Roh promised that a direct presidential election would occur, as well as a more democratic constitution. Chun resigned as the head of the party in July 1987, and the first honest election that South Korea had seen in twenty years took place in December, with Roh Tae-woo winning. This established the Sixth Republic of Korea, the current government in place.

Exploding Economy

Since the 1960s, South Korea expanded exponentially with some notable exceptions during financial downturns. Industries were initially springboarded by huge family-owned conglomerates like Hyundai and Samsung. Because of their potential financial resources, they were given tax incentives and interest-free financing. Workers' wages steadily increased, and their work conditions improved. South Korea's gross national product doubled in thirty years' time.

Because the country lacks a lot of natural resources, it mostly depends on exports. Foreign investment was greatly encouraged due to the low rate of personal savings. Industries and businesses were not only encouraged to update frequently, but they also had to in order to compete in the global market.

One of their largest businesses, even today, is the Hyundai Corporation. The founder, Chung Ju-yung, started the business as a repair garage during the Japanese occupation of Korea. Once it was replaced with a steel mill, he was forced out of business but had managed to save some money. After Korea was freed from Japanese control, he took advantage of foreign investments to establish the Hyundai Civil Industries Corporation in conjunction with American engineers. After the Korean War, the company helped reconstruct the country. Chung Ju-yung contributed his organizational skills, and his physical ones as well, into helping to construct the Soyang Dam in 1967, the Gyeongbu Expressway in 1968, and the Kori Nuclear Power Plant in 1972. In 1975, using consultants from Europe, he introduced his first car, the Hyundai Pony, following it up with the Hyundai Excel in 1986, a vehicle still sold today. In the 1990s, Hyundai had acquired eight financial affiliates.

In 1984, measures were adopted by the South Korean government that permitted Samsung to expand into the insurance market. In 1988, when Roh Tae-woo was the South Korean president, it initiated a credit card company and later purchased a securities firm. In the 1990s, also under Roh's administration, Samsung became one of the largest non-bank financial companies in the country.

A large competitor in the financial investment market was LG Corporation. It created Goldstar Investment in 1982, Konghae Mutual Savings Bank in 1985, and LG Investment Trust in 1988.

Loans were readily available to the larger companies, so Samsung, LG Corporation, and Hyundai all participated in the semiconductor industry during Roh's administration. Samsung had already done so years earlier, but the quality of their equipment wasn't up to par by comparison until they learned more about the industry.

Semiconductor Industry

While Park was still in office, Korea developed its own digital switching system, the TDX-1, and the government made it a proprietary product through its own research and development program, the Electronics and Telecommunications Research Institute (ETRI). The digital switching system is used for the construction of telecommunications networks. Under the administration of Roh Tae-woo and his successor, Kim Young-sam, the industry created the VLSIC (very large-scale interface circuit chips) in conjunction with the ETRI, called the ETRI-VSIC. Samsung, as well as smaller private manufacturers, added a fiber-optic cable to that system and thus secured a large portion of the global market once the business arm of Roh Tae-woo's and Kim Young-sam's governmental bodies liberalized trade policies and could license products across the world. Once they were freed from government constraints, Samsung, Goldstar, and Daewoo Electronics could market these products to the world. Their competitors on the world stage were AT&T, GED, and IBM. South Korea had truly proven itself as an accomplished first-world company.

In 1988, South Korea made a monumental advance in the semiconductor industry by adapting dynamic random-access memory (DRAM) to their TDX-1, making it compatible with their digital switching system. That technology wasn't unique to the South Koreans, but they were the first to make it adaptable.

The South Korean government had its hand in all these technological developments, unlike other countries with purely free enterprise. It was a benefit to South Korea, as they needed government-sponsored funding; however, that brought with it the problems of government regulations.

Non-Telecommunication Industrial Development

Besides the telecommunications industry, South Korea partakes in shipbuilding. The usual conglomerates were the first to enter the field: Hyundai Heavy Industries, Daewoo Shipbuilding and Marine Engineering, and Samsung Heavy Industries. Mining is a much smaller but important industry in South Korea because it can supply the prized minerals—tungsten, graphite, coal, and molybdenum, a silvery metal with a high melting point that is useful in the manufacture of metal alloys.

The Korea Railroad Corporation, Korail, is a high-speed railway system that is far improved from its ancestor, the Korean National Railroad, which was founded in 1963. In 2005, it split into the Korea Rail Network Authority and Korail. The railways are a complex network that operates intercity, commuter, and freight trains.

Obstacles to Trade Overcome

The government under Chun Doo-hwan, as well as the prior presidents, had a heavy hand in creating protectionist barriers to open trade. In the telecommunications market, in particular, South

Korea was very slow to remove those barriers, many of which had to do with the regulations that they had to use their own inspection teams.

From 1998 to 2003, South Korean President Kim Dae-jung emphasized the economy above all else. The growth rate was ten percent in 1999 and 9.2 percent the following year. The bigger companies were restructured to curtail monopolies, leaving more opportunities for other developers. Some free trade agreements were signed under Kim Dae-jung, including the Korea-Australia Free Trade Agreement.

During the recession period of 2008 to 2009, South Korea had a downturn, but so did the rest of the world. After some bankrupt industries left the market, South Korea was still able to recover.

Korea also underwent a financial crisis in 1997, but its fame as a well-developed industrial country aided in them being able to obtain a loan from the International Monetary Fund. This economic shake-up led to the loss of Kim Young-sam's reelection bid and the subsequent election of Kim Dae-jung in 1998. Kim Dae-jung received the Nobel Peace Prize in 2000 for his Sunshine Policy, which emphasized communication with North Korea, as North Korea was facing bankruptcy and starvation at the time. Kim Dae-jung is the only Korean to have won a Nobel Prize so far.

The Korean Wave

In the 21st century, South Korea became a major exporter of popular culture, giving rise to what is called the Korean Wave, which started its incline in the 1990s. The government of South Korea provides subsidies to its art and music, not only for the sake of entertainment but to publicize itself as an independent country. In 1999, South Korea's first big-budget film, *Shiri*, became a blockbuster and even surpassed the box-office record of *Titanic* in South Korea.

In 1999, K-pop music became incredibly popular on the internet, mostly via YouTube. In 2016, eighty percent of music videos circulated throughout the East were made in Korea and featured Korean artists. Outside of Asia, the United States became one of the largest consumers for K-pop music. Elements of Chinese and Japanese influences are present in this music, but it is a style unique to Korea.

The Korean Wave washed over China as well. In 2000, the Korean boy band H.O.T. (Highfive of Teenagers) was being sold out in China along with Super Junior. One of the most successful K-pop groups of 2016 was Big Bang, which was recorded to have earned nearly $44 million.

Korean romance dramas are shown across East Asia, including Nepal and Sri Lanka. In India, Korean films were forbidden, but they were squirreled in via the black market. This rage among the youth just could not be halted.

Korean restaurants became popular in other countries as well. Kimchi, a traditional Korean dish, was even served at the White House under US President Barack Obama. Korea has also bought numerous resorts in the United States and has some of the finest golf courses in the country.

Chinese consumers buy billions of dollars of Korean-manufactured cosmetics and skincare products. Korea has beauty products carefully constructed to suit the various shades of Asian skin, making it highly desirable.

Political Situation in the 21ˢᵗ Century

President Lee Myung-bak of South Korea met with President George W. Bush in 2008. Among the issues they discussed were solutions for the global recession that occurred during that time, as well as diplomatic relations. In their discussions, Lee and Bush had agreed to lift the ban on beef imports due to unfounded fears of "mad cow disease."

There were also controversies within the Cabinet, which Lee remedied by reshuffling his Cabinet officials and implementing industrial and administrative reforms. South Korea then reached out to the world by holding a summit in Seoul with other Asian countries.

Park Geun-hye served as president from 2013 to 2017. She was the first female president of the country, as well as the first president to be born after South Korea had been officially founded. After a series of scandals involving her and her administration came to light, she was impeached, and Prime Minister Hwang Kyo-ahn stepped in as acting president. Although his term of service was short, he focused upon security against North Korea at the Northern Limit Line, which clarifies the maritime border in the Yellow Sea between North Korea and South Korea, to prevent any incidents. After his tenure as acting president, Hwang Kyo-ahn joined the Liberty Korea Party, becoming the president of the party in early 2019. He opposes the Sunshine Policy, which helps to warm the relationships with North Korea and is seeing a revival under the current South Korean president, Moon Jae-in.

He was elected in 2017, and besides favoring the Sunshine Policy, he supports a proposal to build a natural gas pipeline that would originate in Russia and go through North Korea as well as South Korea. However, he is very concerned about North Korea's recent launches of intercontinental ballistic missiles. Prior to his election, Moon was opposed to a proposition with the United States for the use of the THAAD, the Terminal High Altitude Area Defense system, which was designed to destroy any incoming missiles. However, he changed his mind after the election and made an agreement with the US to set up a temporary system for South Korea's defense. His goal is the eventual reunification of North and South Korea and the non-proliferation of nuclear weapons. Moon and Kim have had two confidential meetings about reunification to date.

Although he is pro-American, Moon Jae-in has presented some reservations. "I'm pro-US, but now South Korea should adopt diplomacy in which it can discuss a request and say 'No' to Americans." He still recognizes the US as friends but wants to be sure that South Korea takes the lead.

Conclusion

Korea began as a humble little peninsula jutting into the Yellow Sea. They were home to many clans at the beginning, which brought about bloody rivalries that were only tempered by a hard-working population of independent and free-thinking people who wanted freedom from the grand and overwhelming dynasties of China. Although forced to seek the aid of such dynasties at times, the Koreans were very selective in terms of whom they chose to interact with. Trade was their initial goal, as well as freedom from the raging nomadic tribes seeking to overtake what was most precious to them—their farms and their unique cultures. They were practical people committed to survival who rejected intrusion by those who wanted to assimilate them into a people of their own making. Having been subjects to raids from other nomadic groups and aggressive nations in the Pacific, they took what they felt was valuable from those other cultures and rejected that which didn't suit their Buddhist and Confucian beliefs.

Koreans excel in intelligence and innovation, and South Korea is the third-largest economic force in the Pacific region after China and Japan today. They became isolated for a time but eventually compromised to accept help from other industrial nations without permitting themselves to become imitators of such cultures.

Currently, Kim Jong-un of North Korea and Moon Jae-in of South Korea are making overtures toward the reunification of the split country. In 2018, South Korea hosted the Winter Olympics, in which North Korea took part. In addition, separated families from both sides have had several reunion events, where they were able to socialize with members they might not have ever even met before. South Korean President Moon Jae-in has proposed that 2045 might be the year that the two portions of the country will be unified once again.

Part 4: History of Taiwan

A Captivating Guide to Taiwanese History and the Relationship with the People's Republic of China

Introduction

The history of Taiwan is astonishing. The societies of the Neolithic Era in around 3000 BCE seemed to have been determined by the topology of the island. The original ethnic identity of the indigenous peoples is most likely Austronesian, that is, from the Philippines, Oceania (South Pacific), Malaya, and Madagascar. Some of the Chinese from the Sui dynasty between the years of 581 and 618 came along later. This mixture of people settled on the lower highlands of the Central Mountain Range, the principal mountain range of Taiwan. There they farmed on terraces and hunted long-horned deer on the slopes. Along the western and southern coasts, the people fished. Oysters, in particular, are still extremely common, and it isn't unusual to find empty shells along the shore from the feasts of rodents and weasels. Some of the basin area was so wet that the bamboo houses were built on stilts. Today, oyster omelets are popular, and every tourist should sample them.

Politically, Taiwan— was a warlord culture. The Portuguese, when passing by the island in the mid-1540s, called the island "Ilha Formosa," which means "Beautiful Island." Then the Dutch came in the 1620s, searching for a base of operations for the Dutch East India Company. Relations between these strangely garbed, foreign-speaking white men and the people of this sub-tropic island were puzzling and difficult.

Then the Han Chinese came in the 17th century. Many of these Han Chinese were refugees from the wars in China. This influx caused an explosive reaction. For years, the relationships between the peoples on the island vacillated from beneficial to hostile, as it was a clash of civilizations. Many of the Dutch trading colonies eventually became lucrative for both native and immigrant populations, who did intermingle and intermarry. Chinese junks, an ancient Chinese sailing ship that is still used today, sailed the waters, along with the expected pirates that raided the shores and seas carrying opium to China and Taiwan.

The Taiwanese threw out their sea-serpent mythical gods in favor of the time-honored beliefs of Taoism and Confucianism, which many envious Westerners struggle to learn even today.

And then came the Japanese in 1894! Taiwan was subjugated to a Japanese program of inculcation. All the people of Taiwan had to learn Japanese, and Shinto shrines cropped up everywhere. The Japanese overlords were at times tyrannical, and the Chinese and Taiwanese people who lived there created stronger bonds with each other. That's when the rebellions started, and they continued for years until they merged into the period of the two World Wars.

Then came Chiang Kai-shek in 1949. He awakened the conflict between the vestiges of Japanese influences and the Republic of China. In fact, many of the Japanese who were living in Taiwan were repatriated.

Having been inflicted with so many cultural and political invasions, a new breed of Taiwanese people rose up, and they wanted freedom from the oppression they had faced for decades, although there were some who wanted socialism and communism. Taiwan is not even recognized as an independent sovereign by every country in the world today. Read Taiwan's story—a story of an island that walks a tightrope searching for its identity, balance, and fate.

Chapter 1 – Formosa: Beautiful Island

Around 3000 BCE, it is thought that people came to Taiwan from the islands and countries in Southeast Asia, such as Malaysia, Madagascar, and Polynesia. In those days, a land bridge was there, so flora and fauna likewise migrated over to Taiwan with them. Due to the existence of that land bridge, Taiwan wasn't an island. That didn't happen until the seas rose, engulfing the land bridge and turning it into what is now the Taiwan Strait. Yu Shan, or Mount Yu, looms over the northeastern area of the island at almost 13,000 feet. To the west of the Taiwanese mountain chain are the lowlands.

The Taiwanese were hardy tribes of indigenous peoples, which included the Siraya, a community that is still around today, who came to grow rice, sugar cane, and foxtail millet on terraces hewn into the highlands and raise their cattle on the lower slopes. There were also Plains Aborigines, or Makatao, who settled in the lowlands. The Taivoan people settled in the hills and basin area, and the Paiwan people lived in the southcentral mountainous area. The farms of these peoples were designed in concentric rings. The inner ring was for their homes and gardens, the secondary ring for a family's plantings, and the third ring for the family vegetables. The rest of the agricultural land was for the entire community. Their homes of bamboo and thatch were built on stilts, and the people made offerings to gods like *Shou,* also known as the god of longevity. He was the god to whom the people appealed to in order to keep the waters from rising too high and drowning out their homes and lands.

The women tilled the fields on the higher plateaus, and the men hunted for *gtsod,* a horned Tibetan antelope, or they fished. The men of the lowlands hunted the sika deer and the sambar deer. There was a wealth of marine life just off the western shore with oysters being the most popular. Their calcite shells could be carved into cutting tools. The aborigines also fashioned clever saw-like knives called adzes, made from stone and later on flint. The people drank rice wine, and the women made rice balls for their husbands to take with them on the hunt.

The Siraya is a matriarchal society, and women once served as priestesses and oracles. A woman's future husband married into her family, but this only happened after he was thirty years old when he no longer hunted. The aboriginal men from both the plains and the highlands were expected to be prepared militarily.

The Headhunters!

Except for the Yami people, a group who still lives on Orchid Island in the Taiwan Strait, and the Ivantan people, the aboriginal people of Taiwan practiced headhunting. The Yami people is simply another name for the Tao people. Their god was Simo-Rapao, and headhunting was a breach of the Tao belief in him as Simo-Rapao considered all life to be sacred.

The raids mostly originated from the people in the highlands. Once they slew their victims from the lowland tribes, they removed the victims' heads. It was a gruesome process. The skin would be removed first by making an incision behind the ear. Once it was separated from the skull, a small wooden ball would be inserted in order to maintain its shape after shrinking. The lips were sewn shut, and the flesh was boiled in water containing tannins. Tannins are plant-based mixtures or sap from oak bark that acts as an astringent, thus shrinking the skin around the ball. They then covered the skin with ash in order to keep the vengeful soul, called the *Muisak*, from escaping. Warriors carried the shrunken heads around as trophies, but they only did so temporarily as they were needed for future religious ceremonies.

It was believed that headhunting reduced the power of an enemy tribe. What's more, it was felt that the person who had been killed would serve his killer for the remainder of his days.

Coming and Going of the Chinese

An ancient historian, Ma Tuan-hiu, related that the Chinese people from the mainland raided Taiwan in the 7th century BCE. They landed on the southern coast, demanding tribute from the people in the lowlands for their leaders in the Chinese Sui dynasty. Stubbornly, the Siraya refused. The marauders burned their bamboo villages, and many were mercilessly slaughtered. Then their blood was used to make caulking for their boats, horrifying the survivors. But still, the survivors refused to pay the tribute. Some fled to the hills and mountains, but others stood their ground. Frustrated by these "wild men of the South," as they called them, the Chinese left without the demanded tribute.

Tahu Iron

The Taiwanese aborigines noticed the iron weapons and body decorations of the Chinese. The Tahu Culture, descendants from the aborigines of southern Taiwan, also wanted to learn the skill. Not only was it useful for themselves, but it could also be traded with other visiting peoples. From the year 400 BCE, they mined it in the mountainous regions, but the extraction process wasn't easy. The people built what were called "bloomeries," or clay furnaces. On the base, they placed charcoal and the ore, originally in the form of stone flecked with reddish streaks. The impurities were oxidized and left the oven through a small chimney. What was left after the other elements were mostly burned away was a crude form of iron. When it is hot, it is spongy, so the early blacksmiths were able to hammer it into their desired shapes. From the Tahu people, the practice spread to the Niaosung Culture, among others. Iron was also used for primitive coinage.

Chapter 2 – The Arrival of the Chinese and Their Religion

There was an influx of people from China into Taiwan starting in the 3rd century CE. During those early centuries, there were three main Chinese kingdoms competing for power on the mainland—the Cao Wei, the Shu Han, and the Sun Wu. The Shu Han people primarily based their livelihoods on agriculture, and many were fishermen. Their state was saturated by the Yellow River, a mighty river that brought bounty, but with it also came floods and drought when the river dried up. In those primitive days, the people of that age told their histories through myths and legends. They once told the tale of a great drought in the story of their mythical hero, the giant Kua Fu. He was kind and wanted to help his people who were starving in the sweltering heat while their plants died. He looked angrily upon the sun and felt that he should teach it a lesson. He decided he was going to chase and capture the great sun in the east. Hastily, he ran, but he stopped often to drink of the waters from the streams and rivers, including the Wei River. He kept running and running but became so very thirsty that he drank the Yellow River dry. Exhausted after days of running, he collapsed and died. From where his body lay, a great grove of peaches grew, thus feeding and quenching the thirst of the people.

In the 3rd century, the Three Kingdoms warred with each other. The Cao Wei settled in the north (where the Wei River of the myth is located) and then moved into what is now northern China. The Cao Wei then conquered the land of the Shu Han, where peaches were grown in abundance (it is also the location of the Donglin Forest). The Sun Wu (or Dong Wu) people settled around the Yangtze River in the eastern region. They were traders, and the people also mined crude metals and dried seawater for salt.

In 222, the Sun Wu managed to free themselves from the rule of the Cao Wei and became its own empire seven years later. A year later, in 230, the Sun Wu touched upon the shores of Taiwan.

Confucianism

The people of Taiwan sought to move beyond the myth and magic that permeated their culture, and they looked toward the Han people, a collective term that refers to the Chinese, and one of their religions, Confucianism, to help do so. As they were mostly tillers of the earth and seas, they saw their lives as cycles. For every day, there was a night, and the seasons fell into a pattern. Confucius was a religious scholar who looked upon the whole of the earth and heaven as a never-ending cycle of the yin and the yang, ever circling but spiraling toward unity. He also taught compassion as it brought peace. Too many bloody wars were fought that conflicted with the happiness that everyone deserved. It was the objective of all humanity to achieve unity, a oneness, with life. He spoke not of a personal god but the essence of love and of life.

Tian, in Confucianism, is the god of heaven to whom one owes respect and the performance of sacred rituals to demonstrate that belief. Tian is eternal and judges all the people, regardless of whether they are good or evil. According to the Confucian philosopher Xunzi, "Tian's course has regularities, which don't exist for the sage, Yao, and then disappear for the tyrant, Jie."

The five principles of this tradition are *Ren* (humaneness), *Yi* (righteousness), *Li* (rite), *Zhi* (knowledge), and *Xin* (integrity). Confucius eschewed the barbarity of the headhunters of the past and the greediness of those who led only by virtue of birth, responding with an alternative way to live. He called that way the "middle path." It is the road that leads between heaven and earth. It sprouts from the *li*, which is the interaction of all that lies between humans, objects, and states, such as laughing and mourning. A true understanding of the principles of *li* will lead to balance. Confucius valued loyalty to one's ruler but would recommend rebellion if that ruler was deemed truly evil—a little known fact of this teaching.

Ancestor worship is a misnomer often applied to the Chinese. It is not "worship" per se; it is more of a reverence for one's ancestors. Even today, Chinese Christians will have annual ceremonies respecting the memories of their ancestors. They still carve figures of their immediate ancestors out of soapstone or jade, and one can see stone figures of elderly men with canes, fishermen, women carrying leaves, and teachers with scrolls. It is still believed today that one's ancestors still protect and guide them. Soapstone is a metamorphic rock with a high talc content and is one of the softest of stones. Jade is a more expensive stone composed of aluminum and calcite. It has a green tint, which is the color of vitality and life.

Taoism

The Han people brought Taoism with them when they moved to Taiwan, which is a belief in the immortality of the human soul, but it is an immortality that can only be achieved by observing the precepts of the Tao, which literally translated means "the way."

The Tao is a belief in the universe and the oneness of life. It requires austerity and the practice of a virtuous life. Like Confucianism, it is about a balance as one is expected to live a life in harmony with the natural world. Taoism implies an afterlife exists but never focuses upon it as the Abrahamic religions do. Instead, it relates to a transformation from the corporal self to the enlightened spirit, what some refer to as the "soul."

The roots of Taoism go back to the 4th and 3rd centuries BCE, but its most famous spokesman was Lao Tzu. He exalted the idealistic leader as one who "is best when people barely know he exists. When his work is done, his aim fulfilled, people will say they did it themselves."

Taoism values simplicity and sees life as a process created by the yin and yang. The earth is viewed as a creative, dynamic progression. Taoists are pantheistic and believe in many deities. The highest deity is Yu Huang, who is never-changing and rules with compassion and understanding. Symbolically, he is represented by the sun, the moon, and the progeny of their union. Yu Huang is the god of the living and the dead, and he passes judgment on deceased souls and pronounces their eternal fates.

Yellow Turban Rebellion

Zhang Jue, the leader of the Yellow Turban Rebellion, wrote about it, saying, "The Azure Sky is already dead; the Yellow Sky will soon rise." The "azure sky" refers to the Han government, and the "yellow sky" was the term Zhang Jue gave to the peasants who were laboriously working along the Yellow River and were being crushed by their emperor, Emperor Ling. Between the years 184 to 205 CE, the early followers of Taoism under Zhang Jue rebelled on behalf of the rough and labor-hardened peasants. They wore yellow turbans or scarves. The Han government might have prevailed, but the fields went fallow during the war, and famine followed. Those who could emigrated to Taiwan.

This 3rd-century rebellion harkened back to the peaceful period of the Yellow Emperor, that is, Huangdi from the ancient period. Some believe he was a prominent leader who was later deified, while others believe he was a god that became incorporated into the list of historical figures. Huangdi was a cosmic ruler who brought peace and prosperity, and he was the legendary hero of the people suppressed by the succession of imperialist and autocratic dynastic leaders.

Buddhism

Buddhism was brought to Taiwan during the Ming dynasty in the 17th century when the Dutch ruled the island. The people came from southeastern China but had to keep their practices hidden, as the Dutch had mistaken their statues of Wusheng Laomu, the ancient mother goddess, and Guanyin, the goddess of compassion, not as the representations of the spiritual figures they represent but as the gods (idols) themselves.

The object of this religion is enlightenment, that is, a state of ultimate peace within the self and the union of the self with the world without its disruptive emotions and negativities. From this freedom flows wisdom. The noble truths that exist are existence in suffering (dukkha), the case of suffering which is earthly desire (trishna), the cessation of suffering (nirvana), and the path of righteousness that springs from those principles.

Buddhism grew after the Dutch were ejected, and it is now the largest religion in Taiwan.

Chapter 3 – The Dutch Trading Years

Trade via the Junks

Located in the Taiwan Strait are the Penghu Islands, a collection of islands which were settled by the Han people. Many of the early Taiwanese people established fishing villages there. They sailed the Taiwan Strait and the western Pacific in classic Chinese junks. The junk is a vessel built of wood with a bamboo interior. For a sealant, lime was mixed with tung oil, which was obtained from the tung tree. Tung oil has the characteristic of hardening almost upon contact. Later on, *ch-nam* was the tree resin used for caulking. Inside the junk, there was a multitude of inner compartments which served to hold off flooding. The American inventor, Benjamin Franklin, used chambers designed after the Chinese junks to keep the mail dry when he was shipping packets of it across the Atlantic.

Most junks have a centerboard which protrudes from the keel and helps stabilize the vessel. The maritime fishermen of the Penghu Islands and southern Taiwan created retractable centerboards because some of the waters were shallow. Later colonists who visited Taiwan adopted them.

After iron was discovered in Taiwan, iron tools, raw iron, silver, and white or blue/white porcelain pots and drinking vessels were shipped in mercantile junks. The products were shipped along a route called the Maritime Silk Road that connected China, Southeast Asia, India, the Arabian Peninsula, Somalia, Egypt, and Europe. In exchange, the junks carried spices such as pepper, frankincense, and dragon's blood, which was a reddish-colored resin used for varnish and even medicine, back to Taiwan.

Pottery

Archeologists found many beautiful pots and water and wine vessels made of clay dating back to the 9th and 10th centuries BCE in Taiwan. The background is light-colored, and linear and spherical designs appear darker when the clay is dried. The darker lines (or "red cords") are created by halting the firing process and covering the linear and spherical areas with ropes before reheating the pottery. Another technique they used was the impressment of coiled basket-weave over the vessel.

Chinese pottery was also manufactured in the kilns of Taiwan. The people had learned new techniques of heating their kilns up to 1400° Celsius (over 2550° Fahrenheit). That transformed the clay/quartz mixture and gave the pottery a translucent quality.

The Dutch vs. the Chinese and the Aborigines

In the early 1600s, Taiwan was mostly visited by Chinese fishermen, pirates, and smugglers. There were no permanent Chinese settlements other than those along the coasts. However, throughout the 1600s, maritime Spanish, Japanese, Chinese, English, and Dutch traders all wanted to convert Taiwan into peaceful trading colonies where herbs and metals could be produced and sold by the trading companies.

The Dutch East India Company was the first to try to do so, attempting to establish a post on the Penghu Islands in 1622, but they were driven off by Ming forces. Their ships, under the command of Marten Sonck, were forced to abandon the area after the brutal attacks of the Chinese and island warriors under Generals Yu and Wang Megxiong.

From there, the Dutch moved south and invaded a peninsula in the Anping District where they set up a huge fort called Fort Zeelandia in 1624. The Dutch and the original aborigine tribesmen were determined to pacify the hostile Chinese in order to establish a trading colony from which they could ship herbs, spices, iron, silver, and gold. In particular, Mattau, now the modern-day Madou District, in the lower hills and basin area of Taiwan where the Taivoan aborigines live, resisted the Dutch influx with great ferocity, killing Dutch soldiers and destroying their buildings. The Dutch sent in reinforcements and were finally able to subdue the people who lived there in 1635.

After successive attacks, the Dutch were able to control a number of villages, including Sakam, Soulang, Bakloan, and Sinkan. The people at the villages engaged in local trade with each other, providing their neighbors with venison, fish, and firewood, but they disliked interference. Eventually, the indigenous peoples established a working relationship with the Dutch, but it was short-lived. The tribes sometimes raided each other, started insurrections, and still went on head-hunting expeditions. To make matters worse, Chinese and Japanese pirates raided the towns from offshore.

In addition to the pirate raids, war erupted between the Chinese from the Ming Dynasty and the Dutch at sea. In 1633, the Chinese admiral Zheng Zhilong defeated the Dutch at the Battle of Liaoluo Bay. The inner revolts and rebellions continued until many of the people of Taiwan saw that those who had established relations with the Dutch were at peace. More and more villages came forward and offered peace in exchange for Dutch protection. That peace, known as the *pax Hollandica*, happened in 1636, and it showed that the Dutch East India Company now had firm control of the southwest of the island, which they referred to as Formosa. After that, the

Dutch leased their owned land to the native farmers and fishermen and taxed them as well.

The Dutch also promoted the migration of Chinese Han immigrants. However, the relationship between the two failed when Dutch officials raised taxes and were found to be corrupt, as some demanded sexual favors from aboriginal women as well as gifts of pelts and rice. As a result, an uprising occurred in 1652 called the Guo Huaiyi Rebellion. The Dutch put down the rebellion, killing 25 percent of those that participated and selling others into slavery. They also placed a ban on their provisions of iron and salt.

Fall of Fort Zeelandia and Dutch Colonies

Fort Zeelandia sat at one entrance to the U-shaped Liaoluo Bay, while a sister fort, Fort Provintia, was at the other end. In 1661, a Chinese leader by the name of Zheng Chenggong, better known as Koxinga, a Ming loyalist and warrior, wanted to establish his own kingdom in the highly prized Dutch Zeelandia area. He sailed from the sea south of Taiwan and attacked Dutch musketeers, defeating them. The Dutch then attacked the Chinese junks, but Koxinga prevailed along the shore and built fortifications right near the fort. Later, his many warriors, equipped with body-length shields of iron, plowed right through the Dutch defenders and utterly massacred them. The remaining Dutch soldiers were still holed up in the garrison at Fort Zeelandia while the Chinese attackers engaged in massive attacks against their vanguard forces.

Seeing that the Chinese were about to prevail, the Taiwanese people from Sakam, Soulang, Bakloan, Sinkan, and other Dutch colonies allied themselves with the Chinese, putting the Dutch in a precarious position.

Koxinga was also allied with escaped slaves who knew how to use muskets, rifles, and cannons. Other Chinese sent out volleys of arrows against the Dutch. The Dutch had seriously misjudged the strength and ferocity of their foes and were slowly shoved toward the sea. According to the historian William Campbell, Koxinga's men "continually pressed onwards, notwithstanding many were shot down; not stopping to consider, but ever rushing forward like mad dogs."

Retaliatory Strikes and Torture

Once the word of this humiliating defeat reached the Dutch in their headquarters in Jakarta (on the current-day island of Java), they sent out more warships. Koxinga's men had blockaded Fort Zeelandia, so only small-scale operations were attempted at sea, but they all failed. A month later, another assault was initiated, but it was also repelled. The Dutch soldiers bravely held onto the garrison, but since they were running low on ammunition and supplies, they fled in 1662.

Koxinga essentially then assumed leadership of most of the aboriginal and Taiwanese settlers. Two months later, an offensive assault was again staged by Koxinga to rid Formosa of the rest of the Dutch. General Frederick Coyett of Fort Zeelandia and General Valentyn of Fort Provintia were forced to surrender against the might of the great Koxinga. Koxinga then renamed Formosa the Kingdom of Tungtu in 1662. The name was later changed to Tungning by his son.

Chapter 4 – The Ming, The Qing, and Japan: The War Years

Koxinga died only a few months after the fall of Fort Zeelandia, and his son, Zheng Jing, took over. He promoted Chinese migration in order to recruit those migrants into military service. He also wanted to prevent a takeover by the Qing dynasty of China, which was established in 1636. Zheng Jing granted free ownership of land to the peasants who worked the land and performed military service. Education all but halted.

In 1683, the remaining Ming loyalists who had settled in Taiwan couldn't hold out against the huge forces of the Qing dynasty, and Koxinga's grandson, Zheng Keshuang, was forced to surrender to the Qing dynasty.

The Dark Period

Xuanye, the fourth emperor of the Qing dynasty and also known as the Kangxi Emperor, had little interest in Taiwan. He called it a "ball of mud." Therefore, he restricted migration from mainland China and erected earthen fortresses between the plains to the west and the highlands in the east. Those with aboriginal routes tended to settle in the highlands when the Qing dynasty was unsuccessful in converting them into taxpayers. Those who lived in the west paid taxes to the Qing imperial magistrates and leased their land, mostly for farming.

The Qing also discovered that Taiwan was difficult to govern, as the ethnic clashes continued among Han and Hakka people, as well as with the remaining aboriginal peoples and alienated peoples from other cultures like the Japanese. Even Han clans from the smaller districts warred with each other.

Despite the limit on emigration from China, disaffected Chinese gradually relocated to Taiwan. By the early 19th century, there were two million Chinese immigrants.

The Opium Wars

Great Britain saw the strategic advantage of using China and Taiwan as trading centers. They coveted Taiwan most of all as it was entirely surrounded by water and therefore accessible to shipping. However, Taiwan and China did not see the value in British goods and refused to trade. So, in order to get their foot in the door, the British smuggled in opium from India as a way to control and corrupt the government and its policies. Once China realized what the British were doing, they attempted to put a stop to it. In 1839, Chinese officials demanded the British hand over opium stored in a warehouse. Tensions rose to the boiling point, and the First Opium War was started, which took place between the years 1839 and 1842.

The Chinese then set up a blockade against foreign vessels in the harbor of Hong Kong, which permitted Chinese monopolies, like the Cohong from the Canton province, to control the import-export business. The British retaliated by bombing the port of Tingha along with some other ports. The Qing warriors proved that they were not up to conducting battle against the guns and cannons of the British warships and finally surrendered in 1842. Now, the British were in control of Hong Kong trade.

As a result of the Treaty of Nanking (or Nanjing) of 1842, the Chinese agreed to pay an indemnity to Hong Kong and ceded it to the British. After successive negotiations, other ports were designated for the use of British-Chinese trade.

The Second Opium War was fought between China and the forces of Great Britain, France, and Russia between 1856 and 1860. The issues stemmed over the legalization of opium, an eradication of Chinese piracy, the regulation of the coolie system, and more open trade relations. The coolie system was the importation of Chinese workers who were basically treated as slaves. They were paid less than the native population but were promised health benefits in return. Although that might sound somewhat promising, those involved in the coolie system were often lied to in order to get them to sign a contract. They would at times be sold to work on projects far from their homeland, such as the United States, and many of them died under terrible, back-breaking conditions.

So, in 1856, the Western countries attacked and occupied the Canton Province. The governor of Canton surrendered, and the British and French gained control of many of the Chinese forts and burned the summer palace of Prince Gong, an imperial Manchu prince and an important statesman in the Manchu-led Qing dynasty, in Beijing. The Qing dynasty lost the war, and as a result, many more ports were open to European countries, opium was legalized, compensation was paid by the Chinese for piracy, and the coolie system was systematized.

Due to this war, there was a migration from Manchuria into mainland China and Taiwan. The people from Manchuria are called the Manchu people, and they are an ethnic minority. This migration continued into the 1940s, and even though they represented a minority, the Manchu people changed the cultural character and identity of Taiwan as time went on.

The Sino-French War in Taiwan

Much of the focus of the Sino-French War was directed toward Vietnam, just south of China in the delta regions. The territory of Tonkin and Annam were French protectorates, and the Chinese attempted to gain control of those areas, as it was a lucrative region for fishing and agriculture. The Chinese also wanted the presence of European colonies eliminated from the peninsula. In addition, the Chinese coastal provinces were charging enormous taxes for the rights to trade, and it was a source of great wealth.

The French also wanted the northern ports in Taiwan and targeted Keelung and Tamsui in 1884. There were also rich iron mines in that area, some run by the British colonists. The British, who were already established in some of the towns, didn't want to become involved in this new war. The Qing dynasty heroically defended the area, putting most of his emphasis on Tamsui. It had the support of the Han people from the hills, who set up torpedoes and land mines and used long-range rifles called matchlocks. The Han were skilled marksmen, and they had been hardened by war. The Han incurred many severe wounds and mutilations during the battles, but the hospital there was excellent, so many of them left to fight another day.

At Tamsui, the French built a new fort, Fort Neuf, to protect the entrance to the Tamsui River. The French frigates moved into the area where they disembarked and moved inland to confront the Chinese defenders. The battlefield was full of natural obstacles—spiny plants, tall hedges, scrub brush, and deep ditches. Within that territory, the Chinese warriors hid. A huge firefight broke out in October 1884, filling the air with dust and gunpowder. The French companies became separated and were shoved back by the mighty troops of Sun Kaihua. The French fired and fired, sometimes just into the empty air, and since their bugler had been shot, they couldn't sound for a ceasefire. Thus, the troops continued to shoot until they were precariously low on ammunition. Finally, they heard a frantic call for retreat, and they raced toward the shore to board their waiting boats in the rough waters. Some of the French ships capsized in the process. The head of the forces, Captain Garnot, later said, "The courage and dash shown by our officers and sailors, who had not been trained for a land battle, cannot conceal the fact that we opened fire in a disorderly manner...that our troops lost our heads, firing wildly at the enemy and using their ammunition in a few minutes."

One of their most influential naval admirals, Amédée Courbet, called the French action in Taiwan "irrelevant." In view of the fact that France considered Tonkin in North Vietnam to be more valuable, they evacuated northern Taiwan and the Pescadores Islands just offshore. A preliminary accord between China and France was drawn up in 1884, followed by the Treaty of Tientsin in 1885. As a result of the treaty, France surrendered its interest in Taiwan and was allowed to retain their protectorate in Vietnam.

Gruesome Executions

In the Tamsui marketplace, the heads of the French fighters were displayed on pikes, along with body parts, including legs, arms, and hands. These barbaric practices were mostly inflicted by the hands of the Hakka warriors, that is, the native people from the hills. The Chinese general, Sun Kaihua, however, had them buried reverently where they fell. Sun Kaihua gave tribute to the goddess Mazu, and the emperor, Li Hung-Chang, said, "The goddess has been kind to people and kind to myself."

The Japanese Invasion of Taiwan

In 1894, Japan and China went to war. The Japanese craved many of the lands in northern China and attacked there, starting with Manchuria. The Japanese were quite successful against the poorly equipped Chinese troops there. Then their ambitions moved to the rich lands of southern China, wanting to gain these lands, which included Taiwan, in the peace treaty that would be signed to end the war. However, Taiwan and the Penghu Islands were excluded from the armistice. So, the Japanese attacked the Penghu Islands, managing to take it over in a matter of days. Once the main garrisons of the Penghu Islands were captured, there was little interest on the part of the Taiwanese to fight. Japan had control of much of China already and was quite strong. Prime Minister Hirobumi Itō and diplomat Mutsu Munemitsu of Japan negotiated with Li Hongzhang and Li Jingfang of the Qing dynasty, who was currently in control of Taiwan. Although the Qing representatives desperately tried to negotiate a truce, they didn't have the strength to prevail over the Japanese. Hence, they were forced to turn over all of Taiwan to Japan. In April 1895, Japan offered a treaty to Taiwan, the Treaty of Shimonoseki, which ceded control over Taiwan, and the government reluctantly signed it.

Uproar Over Taiwan

Qiu Fengjia, a Hakka patriot living in Taiwan, set up a brief republic in the country protected by a militia that he had spent his wealth on after the Qing dynasty had ceded its rights to Taiwan. However, an influx of nearly 10,000 Japanese soldiers descended upon the administration, terminating it and attacking the country, killing men, women, and children alike. They set fire to their homes and farms. The Taiwanese defenders fought a guerilla-style war and inflicted more damage upon the Japanese than would be expected. These Taiwanese were fiercely independent. Although the Japanese-appointed Governor-General, Kabayama Sukenori, reported to Tokyo that the "island is secured," it wasn't. Unrest fomented among the people. In the north, there were riots and rebellions monthly.

For inspiration, the local people told tales about Liao Tianding, a man who stole from the Japanese. Liao advocated continued uprising against Japanese rule, and legends about him cropped up everywhere in Taiwan. He was thought of as a "Robin Hood-like figure." Stories about healings that took place upon his intercession circulated. Others claimed to have seen his ghost and indicated he had saved the lives of ill people and reversed the fortunes of the poor. Shrines were built in his honor, and children's books were written with the theme of being courageous against oppression.

The short-lived Republic of Formosa lasted from May to October of 1895.

Chapter 5 – Japanese Taiwan

The "Gotō" Theory

Gotō Shinpei was a leading politician in Japan, and he was appointed as the head of the civilian affairs of Taiwan. Gotō believed in developing a theoretical structure that suited the personalities of the people, one that respected their histories and traditions and preserved their culture. He called this his "biological principles."

Gotō intensely disliked giving any conquered countries the appearance of a military state, wanting the people to feel that they were worthy of making contributions to society. His teachers and officials wore secular clothing, and the military police was replaced by a civilian-recruited police force. As heads of departments, he recruited the elder Taiwanese statesmen, as they knew the people well. There was a serious health problem on the island due to the rampant addiction to opium. Opium addiction was rampant in China and spread via the Han Chinese who settled in Taiwan. The government knew it would be impossible to eradicate opium entirely in the beginning, so they restricted its usage, and the authorities took over the opium trade. Albeit, that was a questionable solution because the government made a large profit on opium. Opium addiction was significantly reduced, though. There were anti-drug campaigns, and rehabilitation clinics opened, but opium wasn't outlawed until the mid-1940s. Gotō's ultimate objective was the total elimination of opium and with it the disintegration of all the criminal enterprises that sold the drug.

Industry

Gotō then laid the foundation for finance. Via the passage of the Bank Act of Taiwan in 1897, the island's first bank, the Bank of Taiwan, was founded in 1899. Gotō's purpose in doing that was to create a stable currency system in order to encourage investment by foreign countries as well as the citizens themselves. The bank also provided loans for people wishing to start new businesses. In the Bank of Taiwan, there was a national treasury, and its first currency was the Taiwanese yen. Unlike Western banks, the Bank of Taiwan was comprised of departments particularly fashioned to cater to various industries as well as those designated for government purposes. There were divisions for managing the finances for fields involved in precious metals, accounting, legal affairs, real estate, and even human resources.

Some of the largest corporations in the world found their histories intertwined with the Bank of Taiwan, which encouraged progress and development. Two of the largest are the Mitsubishi Corporation and the Mitsui Group.

China & Taiwan: World War I

In 1912, while Japan maintained colonial occupation of Taiwan, Chinese revolutionaries overthrew the last dynasty of China—the Qing dynasty. This development influenced the development of Taiwan in the years to come.

Sun Yat-sen was the vociferous leader of a new nationalist movement and established the Republic of China. This republic would have a president, with Sun Yat-sen being the first, and delegates from each of the provinces. A constitution was drawn up, as well as a bicameral legislature. Sun Yat-sen asked the provinces to set up a National Assembly, and he stepped down as president in 1912. The capital was then moved to Beijing. Two political parties were also on the rise—the Tongmenghui, the party led by Song Jiaoren, and the Republican Party, headed up by Yuan Shikai. The Tongmenghui reorganized and became the Kuomintang (also known as the Nationalist Party of China). However, the Republican Party did not last long, as it was only around for a little over a year.

During World War I (1914 to 1918), China and Japan provided supportive roles by keeping sea lanes open for the Allied Powers who were battling the Germans at sea. The Chinese didn't participate as soldiers but provided equipment maintenance, manned factories, and manufactured and shipped ammunition to the Allied countries. The war was won by the Allies, and Japan used that to gain some control in China. However, they were only able to get nominal control of the Shandong Province in northeastern China.

A happy result of World War I was the fact that it stimulated the economy of Taiwan. Their total farm production quadrupled, imports increased substantially, and so did its exports. The port of Keelung, built in 1896 in northeastern Taiwan, was updated and expanded to allow for increased marketing activities. Plans were then laid for the development of another port at Gaoxiong (Kaohsiung) in southern Taiwan. That, in particular, would help the Japanese colonial administration do business in Southeast Asia as well as with China.

With the additional money pouring in after World War I, education increased, the growth of a business class developed, and private enterprises rose, although every company was required to submit to oversight by the colonial authorities. Social reform took place as well.

The Japanese government made it a practice to incorporate the historical and religious beliefs of the people of Taiwan into its culture. Nevertheless, they gradually tried to fix the traditional Japanese social structure into the minds of the people. This brought about the "Dōka," meaning "integration," which lasted between 1915 and 1937. In this framework, a sense of equality was fostered.

The push and pull of various societal pressures gave rise to various idealistic political philosophies: 1) the colonial paradigm, under which the colonial authorities are seen as protectors who also dispensed justice; 2) the Taiwanese nationalists who saw Taiwan as a separate and distinct culture with its own set of laws and expectations; 3) the Chinese nationalists of Taiwan who saw themselves as a part of China; and 4) the group who wanted to be perceived as Japanese.

Gotō Shinpei then reorganized the economy of Taiwan by nationalizing agriculture, finance, and education. He also added a flood-control program. To accelerate growth that wouldn't depend upon subsidies from Japan, he encouraged shipping. He also introduced a railroad system, hospitals, roads, and infrastructure, which accelerated the country into the modern age. Gotō's nationalism efforts did run into problems due to popular uprisings starting with his nationalization of the railway system.

The Wuchang Uprising

This rebellion occurred when Japan was nationalizing the railway system. Originally, the railways were financed by private investors, including foreign investors, and some segments of the railroad were locally financed and run. However, the financial system that fueled this railway construction venture went bankrupt in 1911. That bankruptcy didn't affect all the portions of the system. Despite the fact that the bankruptcy didn't affect all areas of the railway system, the Japanese government came in and nationalized the system anyway under what was called the Railway Protection Movement. Financiers were furious, giving rise to this revolt in the Hubei Province in China. Revolutionaries took over the Viceroy's residence and assumed control of the city of Huguang and eventually the whole area. This helped to lead to the gradual decline of the Qing dynasty and the Xinhai Revolution which followed.

Xinhai Revolution

The history of China and Taiwan overlapped throughout the 20th century, although there were distinct differences. Also known as the Chinese Revolution, this rebellion, which started in 1911 and ended in 1912, shook up the area because it consisted of a series of smaller uprisings in various parts of Taiwan and mainland China. It resulted in the overthrow of the last Chinese imperial dynasty, the Qing. The government that took over called itself the Republic of China under Sun Yat-sen.

The Tapani Incident

There was, however, perennial friction between the aboriginal population, the well-settled immigrant population, and the Japanese overlords. In 1915, during World War I, the aboriginal people rebelled. They were members of the aboriginal tribe who had originally settled in the hills and basin areas of Taiwan. This rebellion, called the Tapani Incident, was one of the uprisings staged by the people of the island who had come to resent the sovereignty of non-native people from other countries. In particular, they were opposed to the nationalization of the sugar and forestry industries.

These people cross-bred their societal structure with religious beliefs. They believed that a new age was dawning in Taiwan. It was needed, they said, as there were so many criminals who preyed upon the weaker members of society, and the Taivoan people and the Han Taiwanese believed that included corrupt and greedy leaders. They felt that an apocalyptical event was on the horizon that would bring about a new Utopian age. Those who partook in this incident felt that violence was needed in order to trigger this new age of peace and harmony. It was like a religion, or perhaps it would be better described as a cult, but its significance evidenced what might be best described as a "clash of civilizations," and the

Taivoan occurrence was, in a sense, an omen of the transformation of Taiwan.

The Communist Party

In 1921, there were three separate governments in China, along with two minor breakaway entities. The only way that Yat-sen could establish a "One-China" policy, which would later include Taiwan, would be to delineate an understanding between his Kuomintang Party with the ever-growing Communist Party of China, which had been consuming the smaller factions. In 1923, he signed the Sun-Joffe Manifesto, which created a cooperative relationship among the various factions. Lenin, the head of Russia and the seat of the Communist Party, praised him for this move.

Musha Incident

In 1930, the Japanese government in Taiwan confiscated farmlands and rice paddies from the indigenous aborigine population in Taiwan. Men were gradually seized as slaves, along with their land. The women were molested and children maltreated. Taking advantage of a public event, the Association of Aboriginal People rebelled and killed about 130 Japanese soldiers, but only two Han Taiwanese were killed because they were dressed in Japanese clothing.

Japan treated the indigenous people differently than the later settlers in Taiwan. They considered them to be barbarians and took land from the indigenous farmers over the course of time. This land, by law, was reserved for the aboriginals, but the Japanese had little respect for the property allocations. "I think the Japanese incurred the wrath of our ancestors because they neglected the fact that we, the aboriginal people, have rights over land inherited from our ancestors," said Siyac, the leader of the aboriginal members.

Little by little, illegal land sales to the Han Chinese made it extremely difficult for the indigenous farmers to support themselves and their families because there wasn't enough land left for their farms.

The Mukden Incident/ Manchuria Incident

Even though this didn't take place in Taiwan proper, this takeover, which primarily involved the capital city of Mukden of Manchuria, affected Taiwan. In 1931, Japan was primarily concerned about expanding its occupied territory for the purposes of wealth and to create space for its growing population. A weak bombing of the Japanese-owned railroad was staged by Japan, which wanted to implicate China for the "attack." That way, they could use it as an excuse to go to war with China. As a consequence of this engagement, Japan took over all of Manchuria. They then set up a puppet government.

The Taiwan Exposition

In 1935, the transformation of Taiwan was exhibited in New Taipei City, which was formerly known as Keelung. It marked all of the achievements and advancements made by Taiwan to the world. Even the Republic of China admired all of the amazing accomplishments of the Taiwanese.

Members of the Taiwanese government began wearing civilian clothing rather than military uniforms, and finally, in 1935, the Taiwanese nationalists scored the majority in an election. Taiwan also gained representation in Japan proper in its administrative structure called the Imperial Diet. However, the Imperial Diet ended in 1947, shortly after World War II.

Chapter 6 – The Sino-Japanese War & World War II

The Shanghai Massacre–The Chinese Civil War

The Sun-Joffe Manifesto, which was agreed upon in 1923, was hardly enough to unite China and Taiwan. After the death of Sun Yat-sen, Chiang Kai-shek, a very powerful military leader of the Kuomintang (KMT), rose to power. He did so through armed uprisings, most of which were against the local warlords. Chiang Kai-shek's group was called the National Revolutionary Army (NRA).

By 1927, Chiang Kai-shek controlled the Wuhan, Nanchang, and Guangdong provinces. During that year, the Communists conspired to assassinate Chiang Kai-shek, but he discovered the plot and resolved to rid the country of the Communist Party. There were armed revolts and chaos in the area of Shanghai, which was led by student and labor leaders under Zhou Enlai and Chen Duxiu. As retribution for the planned assassination and the rise of the Chinese Communist Party, Chiang Kai-shek activated his KMT forces, and they tore through Shanghai in April 1927, beheading and slaughtering members of the Communist Party there. Some of the Communists were officially executed, and others went missing.

It is estimated that as many as 5,000 to 10,000 people were killed. Mao Zedong, who later became Chairman Mao, and his forces were defeated by Chiang Kai-shek. Mao then retreated to the countryside. In 1928, Chiang Kai-shek was considered to be the leader of the Republic of China.

The Marco Polo Bridge Incident and the Second Sino-Japanese War

Near Peking, China, the Marco Polo Bridge, or the Logou, is a great stone bridge built in 1189 and restored in 1698. On July 7, 1937, Japanese troops opened fire on the Chinese troops southwest of Beijing. The skirmish went on in fits and starts. These incidents triggered a declaration of war between Japan and China, also known as the Second Sino-Japanese War, which then slid into World War II in 1939. (The First Sino-Japanese War was fought between 1894 and 1895 over the control of Korea.)

After negotiations, an uneasy truce was signed. However, the terms weren't consistently observed, and subsequent battles broke out. This more violent conflict was called the Battle of Beiping-Tianjin, also known as the Battle of Beijing, and it started in July and ended in August 1937. The battle raged on from one area to another. The Chinese had traditional weaponry, but the Japanese brought in air and naval support, so it turned into a bloody massacre, with Japan winning the battle in Beijing. However, the anti-Japanese campaign continued. By 1939, the Japanese forces were scattered throughout mainland China and were becoming thin. The war reached a stalemate.

The Japanese had slowly been conquering the islands in the Southern Pacific along with sections of mainland China, starting with the conquest of Taiwan back in 1895. They had envisioned an expanded Japanese empire, so they continued their attacks in Asia and the islands in the Pacific. In 1941, the Japanese, who had already joined the fray in World War II on the side of Germany and Italy, attacked the base of Pearl Harbor, located in Hawaii. The

United States then formally entered the war. By 1942, four major counties had allied with each other—the United States, the Soviet Union, Great Britain, and China—as well as other smaller countries joining in. America sent aid to China, thus bolstering them against the Japanese invaders. Japan then turned to Taiwan for its manpower to continue fighting. Thus, the Second Sino-Japanese War merged into World War II.

World War II and Taiwan

Japan poured a lot of work into Taiwanese industries to manufacture materials for warfare. Japan recruited Taiwanese into their military forces and later conscripted them. There was a well-known unit composed entirely of aboriginal tribes called the Takasago Volunteers who fought in World War II. The aborigines were much more accustomed to the subtropical climate of Southeast Asia and were a tremendous asset to the Japanese war effort. The Takasago Volunteers fought in the Philippines, the Dutch East Indies, the Solomon Islands, and New Guinea along with other Taiwanese and Japanese soldiers. Some of them were even part of the Kaoru Special Attack Force, a force that was specifically designated to go out on suicide missions.

The Japanese Navy operated out of Japan, and the largest unit, called the South Strike Force, was based at current-day Taiwan University.

The Battle of Midway

In early June 1942, the Americans retaliated against the Japanese Navy for its attack on Pearl Harbor by breaking the cryptic code the Japanese used. Therefore, they were able to defend themselves against the air strikes from the South Strike Force upon their aircraft carriers. This happened in the northcentral Pacific under the leadership of American General Chester Nimitz. Many Japanese personnel were lost, and four fleet carriers were torpedoed. This severely weakened the Japanese Navy.

The Cairo Declaration

In 1943, three Allied leaders—United States President Franklin Delano Roosevelt, British Prime Minister Winston Churchill, and Generalissimo Chiang Kai-shek of the Republic of China—met at Cairo to announce their objectives in World War II. Some of the goals they presented included Japanese withdrawal from Manchuria, the Penghu Islands, and Taiwan itself. Those territories the Allies wanted returned back to the Republic of China. In addition, the Allies wanted Korea to become an independent country. Korea had been annexed in the First Sino-Chinese War. The declaration stated: "With these objects in view, the three allies, in harmony with the United Nations at war with Japan, will continue to persevere in the serious and prolonged operations necessary to procure the unconditional surrender of Japan."

The Formosa Air Battle

In 1944, the United States Fast Carrier Task Force and the naval and land-based forces of Japan battled each other in the vicinity of the base for the Japanese Navy in south Taiwan. The American fighter planes bombed during the day while the Japanese bombed at night. The South Strike Force at the Japanese naval base took on the American air fighters over Taiwan.

This battle, fought between October 12th and October 16th, utilized the Third Fleet of the U.S. Navy under Admiral William Halsey Jr. and four fleets of the Imperial Japanese Navy under Vice Admirals Ryūnosuke Kusaka and Shigeru Fukudome. The Japanese used the Philippines and the city of Takao, Taiwan, as their bases. The U.S. utilized aircraft carriers along with accompanying destroyers. This battle was primarily fought in the air and on the sea, and it included bombing runs on the island of Okinawa, southwest of Taiwan, as well as a major operation on the Ryukyu Islands near Japan.

On the first day, all four divisions of the U.S. task force engaged the anti-aircraft fire over numerous runs of Japanese fighter jets around dawn. The American aircraft carriers shot down about 100 Japanese fighter planes. The Japanese pilots weren't fully trained, and that put them at an extreme disadvantage. The battle continued throughout the day and into the night when an experienced Japanese fighter squadron staged a nighttime radar-assisted air group utilizing aerial torpedoes and shot down three U.S. fighter jets; eight more Japanese jets were also destroyed. The following day was overcast, but there were nighttime air attacks.

On October 14th, there were heavy engagements during the day. Twenty-five Japanese jets flew low and came tearing out of the cloud cover without much warning. Very few Japanese aircraft survived this first wave of attacks. In the late afternoon, the American task force was again hit heavily by Japanese bombers. Two torpedoes from a Japanese plane then headed for the USS *Houston*. One of the two hit its target, and the engine room flooded. There was so much damage that some of the men dove into the water that had been roughened by the vibrations of bomb blasts and exploding shells. The *Houston* sailors were picked up by the battleship, USS *Boston*, and it was towed to Ulithi. Other American carrier groups sustained minimal damage. Not many of the other Japanese fighter planes and bombers were able to evade the American fighter aircraft.

The Japanese decided to change their strategy and started fighting from dawn to dusk against American Task Force 38. On October 15th, nearly two dozen Japanese fighter planes were shot down. The largest Japanese fighter plane attack consisted of 75 planes, but the American aircraft gun batteries kept firing incessantly.

At the end of the battle, Vice Admiral Fukudome sadly commented, "Our fighters were nothing but so many eggs thrown at the stone wall of the indomitable enemy formation." Despite his remark, the Japanese promulgated the message that they were victorious.

Further Military Campaigns in the Pacific Theater

Between 1944 and 1945, battles in the southern Pacific continued with campaigns between America and its allies against Japan. In the Pacific, battles were fought in Japan, the Dutch East Indies, the Solomon Islands, New Guinea, the Philippines, Timor, and Borneo. Sixty-seven Japanese cities were destroyed, mostly by B-24 Liberator bombers. The B-24s were loaded with huge bombs which the soldiers rolled out through chutes. The men had to grasp handles on the side of the metal aircraft while they shoved the huge bombs out. The planes were very cold inside due to the high altitude, depending upon the season. There was one soldier who handled the upper turret with his huge gun, but he was virtually a sitting target for Japanese aircraft that defended the airspace. On the ground, U.S. war veterans, who formed the Japanese Occupation Force, indicated that there was virtually little left standing in those cities and that refugees were everywhere. They just couldn't understand why Japan wouldn't surrender.

Potsdam Declaration

In late July 1945, representatives from the United States, the Republic of China, and Great Britain proposed an agreement that would end World War II. Together, both sides lost about 36 million men in the Pacific theater and were anxious to end this war, which had been fought on two fronts, Europe and the South Pacific. The fighting in Europe had stopped in May 1945, so the only area left to be subdued was the South Pacific. The treaty proposal delineated the island of Japan and some of its nearby islands as the sovereign property of Japan, and it also stated that Japan was to withdraw its military forces from the other countries it had been occupying. Mutual withdrawal of foreign troops and equipment would be agreed upon by the Allies. The end of this declaration carried the threat of "prompt and utter destruction" to be visited upon Japan unless it was signed. This announcement was called the Potsdam Declaration, and Emperor Hirohito of Japan postponed signing it until the Soviet Union agreed to mediate it. According to one of the Japanese officials, the Japanese were responding to the proposal by remaining silent, which the Americans took to mean that they were just going to ignore it. Hence, they carried out their threat of "utter destruction."

Atomic Bombing of Hiroshima and Nagasaki

In 1938, nuclear fission was discovered, and through the efforts exerted during the Manhattan Project, a nuclear bomb was created which was capable of devastating the land for miles around the drop site. As a result of the Quebec Agreement, signed by the United Kingdom and the United States, the two countries' scientists worked together to build the nuclear bomb. By mid-July 1945, the bomb was created. On August 6th and on August 9th, the bombs were dropped on the cities of Hiroshima and Nagasaki, respectively. Most of those killed were civilians, and the total number of deaths has been estimated to be around 129,000 to 226,000 people. For months and even years afterward, the effects of nuclear radiation continued to kill people. The Japanese surrendered on August 15th, 1945.

Treaty of San Francisco

The Japanese Instrument of Surrender officially ended the hostilities of World War II. It was signed by the Empire of Japan, the United States, the Republic of China, the United Kingdom, the Soviet Union, Australia, Canada, France, the Netherlands, and New Zealand on September 2nd, 1945. The Allies still occupied Japan, marking the only time in Japan's history where it has been occupied by a foreign power. Emperor Hirohito still retained his position, though.

In September 1951, Japan and 49 Allied nations signed the Treaty of San Francisco. By virtue of this agreement, Japan was granted sovereignty over its own country and ended the Allied occupation of Japan. Japan was to allocate some money to Allied prisoners who had endured war crimes. The treaty also called for the release of prisoners of war on both sides. Japan was required to give up its assets in Taiwan, Korea, northern China, including Manchuria and other parts of northeast China, and portions of central China, including Shanghai. In addition, Japan was to compensate other countries in the South Pacific to which it did damage. America created a trusteeship for the use of the Ryuku Islands, which includes the island of Okinawa.

The political status of Taiwan was to be a renounced sovereignty according to this treaty, leaving their status as a country ambiguous.

Chapter 7 – Taiwan After World War II

John Foster Dulles, the United States secretary of state of the U.S. under President Eisenhower from 1953 to 1959, was in favor of total sovereignty for Taiwan, but allowances for that in the treaty weren't specified. Instead, it ceded the sovereignty of Taiwan to no one. Following the San Francisco Treaty, another treaty called the Treaty of Taipei was developed in April 1952. Since the Republic of China did not sign the Treaty of San Francisco, Japan was encouraged by the United States to make their own treaty with them. This treaty surrendered Japan's claim to Taiwan, and the treaty went into effect in August 1952.

Despite Taiwan not being given to any country specifically, the Republic of China had already formed the Taiwan Provincial Administrative Office in September 1945 to start the takeover process of the nation on behalf of the Allies. Chen Yi was established as the Chief Executive of the Taiwan Province in late August, and his rule was quite controversial. He had the air of an aristocrat and even refused to speak Japanese, even though the Taiwanese were fluent in the language, having learned it from their Japanese overlords. It is said he himself wasn't corrupt, but Chen was lax in terms of the people who served in the government under him. Thus, corruption did creep in, and it grew until it was rampant.

Because of the widespread corruption, the economy of Taiwan went into a tailspin. Many were unemployed. And to make matters worse, Chinese nationals poured into the country and took jobs away from the Taiwanese. Con men wandered the streets and tried to mislead locals into fantastic schemes, thus exploiting their need for support.

The 2/28 Incident

In 1946, Chen Yi tightened his control on the government and followed the nationalization formula, with the government controlling certain industries like mining and transportation. He wanted to lessen the control of the central government, but it is difficult to determine whether that was due to his rivalry with Chinese nationalist leaders or out of a concern for Taiwan. It also did not help that those loyal to Japan, who relinquished Taiwan after World War II, were stirring the pot, creating problems and pointing out the flaws of the newly established government.

The tobacco industry was one of the many industries controlled by the government. On February 27th of 1947, a woman by the name of Lin was selling contraband cigarettes but was intercepted by some agents of the Taiwan Monopoly Bureau. She demanded the return of her cigarettes; instead, one of the agents hit her head with the butt of a pistol, beating her until she died. That enraged a crowd of onlookers, and an agent fired upon them, killing one.

The following day, February 28th, the Taiwanese participated in a peaceful protest, demanding justice. They complained at the Monopoly Bureau, but their appeals were ignored. They next moved to the governor-general's office, where four of the protestors were shot and killed with no warning. The crowd became unruly, and angry Taiwanese took over the administration of the town, broadcasting demands for more autonomy over the local radio station.

Civic leaders then organized into the "Committee to Settle the February 28th Incident" and presented their demands to the government. Outside of Taipei, the rebellion spread. Some Taiwanese even traveled to China, looting and stealing. Other Chinese came over to Taiwan, engaging in the same behavior. The 27 Brigade, under the leadership of Xie Xuehong, stole arms and grenades. While Chen Yi proclaimed his love for Taiwan on the radio and proposed to meet with the Committee, he secretly called in military troops from China to put down the rebellions. There were headless and mutilated bodies littered all over the streets. No one knows the exact number of people who died, but there are wide ranges of estimations, so it is most likely somewhere between 5,000 and 28,000. The Nationalist Army continued to fight and conducted wholesale executions resulting in about 3,000 more deaths.

Chen stated that he did not call for military support, telling this to the American ambassador, John Leighton Stuart. However, Stuart uncovered that Chen had indeed called for them, and he informed Chiang Kai-shek, who was at the KMT headquarters during this time. Due to this, Chen was dismissed and replaced by Wei Tao-ming. Following his dismissal, Chen took up various political positions. In early 1949, Chen thought the KMT would not regain its foothold and attempted to defect to the Chinese Communist Party, attempting to induce one of the commanders of a garrison to join him. This commander told Chang Kai-shek, who was furious and stripped Chen of his position. He was escorted to Taiwan in April 1950, where he was imprisoned and then later executed in June of that year.

Chen was right, though; the Communist forces would be too great to go against. In 1949, the People's Liberation Army, under Mao Zedong, inflicted great losses against the KMT forces. On October 1st, 1949, the People's Republic of China was established. In early December, Chiang Kai-shek fled to Taiwan to escape whatever the Communist Party had planned for him, leaving the control of China in the hands of Mao (although Chiang would try to gain control of it back later).

The White Terror

Martial law was declared in Taiwan in May 1949, and it continued to be in effect until the government relocated there; in fact, martial law wasn't repealed until 1987. During the White Terror, Chiang Kai-shek initiated a brutal crackdown on intellectuals and the elite based on the belief that they would object to rule by the KMT or that they were Communist sympathizers. Political groups supporting independence for Taiwan, namely the Formosan League for Reemancipation and the World United Formosans for Independence, were persecuted or imprisoned for allegedly having ties to the Communist Party. Speaking about the 2/28 massacre was forbidden, along with any form of criticism against Chiang Kai-shek's KMT. Chiang also forbade travel to China altogether.

During that period, the famous Bo Yang, a social critic and political writer, was imprisoned. He had courageously recommended the reform of the KMT and promoted human rights. The paranoia against Chinese communism was acute in Chiang Kai-shek's government.

The Battle of Kinmen

Also known as the Battle of Guningtou or the Battle of Kuningtou, this battle in late October 1949 was waged by Chiang Kai-shek and Mao Zedong. At that time, there were two governments—the Republic of China under Chiang Kai-shek and the People's Republic of China under Mao Zedong. Chiang had already been withdrawing its forces from mainland China to Taiwan since the establishment of the latter party.

ROC garrisons, however, still remained on the islands of Kinmen and Matsu, and the People's Republic believed they had to be dealt with. On these two islands in the Taiwan Strait, the two armies fought a short but bloody battle. The Republic of China's formidable battleship, *Chung Lung*, was anchored off Kinmen and pommeled the inadequate People's Republic junks and fishing boats. Once they ran out of ammunition and supplies, Mao's navy fled back to mainland China.

Members of the government under the rule of the Kuomintang and Chiang Kai-shek fled to Taiwan in December 1949 along with many civilians. About two million people had descended upon Taiwan throughout the year to reestablish themselves, hoping that they could return in the future to control mainland China.

In 1950, Chiang Kai-shek then resumed his position as president of the Republic of China, with the government now based in Taiwan, and drew up plans to retake the mainland. He called that effort "Project National Glory," but it wasn't successful.

The Struggle of Democratic Movements

In time, the Taiwanese and members of the KMT started to cooperate and resumed work on the economic recovery of the country. This was due in large part to Chiang Kai-shek's son, Chiang Ching-kuo, who assumed power in 1978 after his father's death in 1975 (Yen Chia-kan, as vice president, served in the role of president until the next election). Chiang Ching-kuo was a wiser and gentler ruler than his father. The first onslaught of transistor radios and textiles were steadily manufactured and sold overseas, and a middle class evolved.

There were also other political parties that grew up without governmental interference like the China Democratic Socialist Party, the Chinese Youth Party, and the Tangwai Movement (later called the Democratic Progressive Party). The Tangwai Movement comes from the term "Tangwai," meaning "outside the party." It fostered the attitude that the government of Taiwan should view Taiwan as a sovereign state that practices civil rights and democracy for all of its citizens, regardless of ethnic background. It stood against the "Japanization" of Taiwan that occurred when they were occupied by that country.

Although political parties were officially illegal, Chiang Ching-kuo usually practiced tolerance toward them, with some exceptions, like the Kaohsiung Incident (see below).

The Taiwan Relations Act

This act, signed by U.S. President Jimmy Carter, was approved by the U.S. Congress in 1979, and its purpose was maintaining peace and stability in the Western Pacific and "extensive, close and friendly relations" between the American people and the people of Taiwan. Because America had also given recognition to the People's Republic of China on the mainland, there was no official recognition of the Republic of China in Taiwan. However, to close that gap, the United States established the non-profit organization under the executive branch called the "American Institute of Taiwan." That group was to be America's unofficial channel for issues related to Taiwan as well as trade privileges and the maintaining of peace in the area.

Among the principles listed in the bill is a large section related to the security of Taiwan, indicating that the United States "will supply Taiwan with defense articles and services for its defense against an armed attack." America will also regard any attempt to undermine the economy or peace of Taiwan as a serious threat to the security of the western Pacific. Furthermore, it declares that it will not recognize the domination of the People's Republic of China over Taiwan. This act has been reaffirmed by all the American presidents since it was signed in by President Jimmy Carter, and it is cited by the U.S. Department of State as needed when applied to various agreements signed under its auspices.

The Kaohsiung Incident and Its Aftermath

Formosa Magazine and other politicians held pro-democracy demonstrations commemorating Human Rights Day on December

10th, 1979. The government sent in the police. The police didn't react immediately but later clashed with the crowds. Family members of Lin Yi-hsiung, a leader of the democratic movement, were killed or wounded by the KMT forces, including his mother and twin seven-year-old daughters who were stabbed to death. Many well-known leaders were arrested, beaten, and imprisoned.

Despite this crackdown, opposition to the KMT grew, and the Tangwai Movement advocated many reforms to the traditional KMT. In 1987, the common people were granted equal seats in the legislature, and all were eligible to apply for governmental posts, regardless of their political party. During that same year, martial law was lifted.

Political liberalization flourished, and civil rights groups blossomed, such as the Taiwan Women's Rescue Association, the Teachers' Human Rights Association, the Taiwan Environmental Protection Union, labor and farmers' groups, and many others. From these movements sprung a new party—the Democratic Progressive Party. Those members were originally affiliated with the Tangwai Movement.

The government attempted to quell these grassroots protests, due to the efforts of the Premier of the ROC, Hau Pei-tsun, but during 1990 to 1992, his efforts were generally ineffective, and he resigned in January 1993. Through the late 1990s, many of these social movements secured some decision-making powers within the government, like the Gender Equity Education Committee and a number of labor unions who freed themselves from corporate control.

Chapter 8 – Nascent Democracy

Lee Teng-hui succeeded Chiang Ching-kuo as president. He continued the democratization project to some extent. He emphasized Taiwanese cultural identity as being separate from China and promoted efforts to create exclusively Taiwan-based foreign relations. Lee had originally been a member of the KMT but was expelled for his pro-independence stance. He then formed the Taiwan Solidarity Union (TSU). Lee was, furthermore, totally in favor of full democracy for Taiwan and supported free elections rather than heredity as the process for selecting the country's leaders.

However, his administration and the legislature were extremely slow in initiating reforms, so it appears that Lee was only paying lip service to the cries for more liberalization. Some also believe that since Lee enjoyed good relations with Japan, being of Japanese descendancy himself, he was slow to initiate such reforms because he would rather have Japan rule over Taiwan instead.

Taiwanization

Taiwanization was a national movement to isolate the identity of Taiwan as being distinctly different from that of mainland China. It was a movement to glorify the Taiwanese culture, history, and economy. Taiwan, from the very beginning, was different. The aboriginal tribes there weren't Chinese, and the migrations from various sectors of China and Manchuria and ethnic groups came later in Taiwan's history.

Literature and poetry flourished during this movement and usually tended to reflect the growing pains of achieving a Taiwanese identity. In Lee Min-yung's poem, "If You Would Ask," he said, "If you ask what is the past of the island of Taiwan/ I will tell you/ Blood and tears drop on the history of the island of Taiwan/ If you ask" and "If you ask what is the future of the island of Taiwan/ I will tell you/ Step on your feet, the road is open to you."

Tiananmen Square Incident & the White Lily Movement

In 1989, there were pro-democracy protests staged by students of Taiwan University who traveled to Beijing. They were peaceful in the beginning, but later on, the crowds grew to tens of thousands of members. Li Peng, the Premier of the People's Republic of China, wanted to strengthen the authority of the Communist Party and opposed reforms that might undermine that. Li saw student-led protests as a threat to the central government and his economic control of the country. Orkesh Dolet, also known as Wu'erkaixi, the leader of the protest, went on national TV stating that Li Peng was ignoring the people's needs. Li Peng was furious and declared martial law and then sent in tanks and troops.

Li Peng was embarrassed by the demonstrations and had his troops crack down heavily upon the protestors. Troops fired indiscriminately upon the crowds, and a massacre ensued at Tiananmen Square. Hundreds, perhaps thousands, of people were slaughtered, and many were imprisoned.

On June 5th, 1990, one courageous young man stood in front of a huge tank moving into the square. The tank stopped, and the man then climbed on the tank and spoke with its driver, after which it tried to veer out of the column. He was eventually removed by the police, and his fate is unknown. The British press later identified him as Wang Weilin, a 19-year-old student, but the newspaper noted that they weren't actually sure of his identity. He remains today a hero of democracy in China.

The event is memorialized annually in Taiwan, and Tsai Ing-wen, the current president of Taiwan, said in 1989, "Freedom-loving people in Hong Kong and China rest assured that, despite threats and subversion, Taiwan will unconditionally defend democracy and safeguard freedom."

Economic Cooperation Framework Agreement (ECFA)

This agreement, signed in 2010 by Taiwan and China, was an attempt to normalize economic relations between the Republic of China and the People's Republic of China and create guidelines for trade between the two entities. This deal was seen as an impressive agreement because the two sides did not recognize each other as "countries" after the Chinese Civil War ended in 1949.

When negotiators discussed the goals of the ECFA, it did result in some protests and even fistfights in the conference room, as there were some parties in Taiwan who feared that China would use it as a means to control Taiwan.

The economic cooperation portion of the ECFA includes investment, investment cooperation, customs procedures, and food safety, among other things. Tariff reductions were featured as a means by which both countries would develop. As many as 235 products were made exempt from tariffs, and others were granted tariff reductions.

Some services, such as accounting, airplane maintenance, computer-related services, and various maintenance and repair services, were given a number of mutual benefits subsidized by the governments. Chinese-Taiwanese partnerships were encouraged.

Banks and financial institutions were openly set up in the two countries. That included subsidiaries in each country which facilitated business in the other.

Technological and R&D agencies and companies are not only protected from interference but promoted as a valuable asset to conduct business around the world. Intellectual property rights are spelled out in this agreement, although there is more protection for Taiwanese intellectual rights than Chinese. Rules and regulations were established along with a mechanism for enforcement. Today, there is much editorializing and discussion about making the ECFA more open to some foreign countries, including the United States.

The Democratic Progressive Party

Founded in the year 1986, the Democratic Progressive Party (DPP) stood for Taiwanese independence, and it also advocated social welfare policies, education, and frameworks for increasing the financial advantage of the people. The DPP firmly rejects the "One China" policy, a policy which states that there is only one state under the name of China.

In the 2000 presidential election in Taiwan, a member of the DPP, Chen Shui-bian, became president. During his administration, he pledged what was called the "Four Noes and One Without Policy," which meant that—provided that the PRC doesn't go to war with Taiwan—1) he would not institute Taiwanese independence, 2) would not change the name of the country from the Republic of China to the Republic of Taiwan, 3) not include the doctrine of special states to state relations, and 4) would not promote an effort toward reunification or independence. Chen served two terms, but scandals rocked his second term, which helped to cause his party to lose in the next election.

In the 2008 election, Ma Ying-jeou was voted in as the new president. He was from the conservative KMT but wanted to warm cross-straits relations for economic reasons. Although he does favor reunification of China and Taiwan, he has reservations about it because of the Tiananmen Square incident. As for independence, he claimed that the final decision must be made by the Taiwanese people. Ma was re-elected for another term.

The 1992 Consensus

In 1992, the head of the security council under Ma Ying-jeou attempted to define the nature of the relationship and cooperation between mainland China and Taiwan. In this consensus, the Republic of China issued its own view on the "One China" policy. They agreed that there is only one China, but each side has its own views on which is the "one China." The People's Republic of China, who is in control of mainland China, argues that they are the "one China" and refuses to acknowledge the Republic of China in Taiwan. However, both sides agree that Taiwan belongs to China, although, as can be seen, no side can agree on which one is actually the "one China."

Members of the DPP took issue with the decision of the consensus. Since there was no agreement on which government represents the "one China," then there truly was no consensus at all. In the November 2018 issue of *The Diplomat*, a Taiwanese journal, states, "Unfortunately, there is no Taiwanese consensus on the definition of the 1992 Consensus." Hence, the readers of history and current Asian events are left in a pure fog. However, in their survey, *The Diplomat* indicated that 75% of the people of Taiwan want Taiwan and China to be perceived as two different countries.

In 2016, Taiwan elected its first female president, Tsai Ing-wen. She is a member of the Democratic Progressive Party and still is serving today. Tsai has ancestors who were aborigines from the Paiwan tribe.

Taiwan Today

President Tsai has rejected the 1992 Consensus. She perceives the People's Republic of China as being a communist country interested in "putting the squeeze" on Taiwan. The PRC has cut off their relationship since Tsai took office in 2016, and it has banned Chinese individuals from going to Taiwan. Beijing has also sent warships to the general area and conducted international relations in such a way as to cut off ties between Taiwan and other countries.

Within the last ten years, China has repeatedly threatened the "use of force" if Taiwan declares independence. The U.S. Seventh Fleet also patrols the area.

As of this writing, Taiwan has signed an agreement with United States President Donald Trump to purchase weapons from the U.S. through the provisions of the Taiwan Relations Act, which clearly states that the United States may sell them to Taiwan for defensive purposes.

The People's Republic of China vs. the Republic of China (Taiwan)

In the June 2019 U.S. Department of Defense Report, it was noted that the People's Republic of China has been placing obstacles in front of Taiwan in terms of participation in international forums and health organization councils. Jonathan Moore of the U.S. Department of State has said, "Excluding 23 million Taiwanese people from these efforts runs counter to the very ethos of the international organizations we support." Little by little, the People's Republic has been quietly trying to shut off channels of communication between itself and Taiwan. America has stayed relatively mute on the subject due to the fact that the U.S. is attempting to create some amended trade agreements, in addition to new ones, with China.

Conclusion

Since 3000 BCE, the island of Taiwan has endured enormous changes. Its economy, society, and government have changed faster than it can adjust. Hence, it is a "country" that is neither a "country" nor a "state" by strict international definition. Although the Taiwanese call this condition the "status quo," it isn't a "status quo" at all. Politically, Taiwan straddles the fence between democracy and autocracy. It exists in the fog of ambiguity.

Taiwan's political status today is so ambiguous due to all the pulls and pushes from the various outside and inside forces that manage this almost 14,000-square-mile island. Taiwan is officially called the Republic of China, but it is inhabited by many varied ethnic groups. Although it carries the term "China," it is separate from mainland China. It is a country torn between the political preferences for the unification of mainland China and Taiwan and for Taiwanese independence. The KMT is still operating, and the Democratic Progressive Party (DPP) is the second-largest party. The DPP has as its primary goal the total independence of Taiwan, while the KMT has as its goal the reunification of China and Taiwan. However, due to intense pressure from the international community, specifically the United States, Japan, and the EU, it hasn't been able to recognize Taiwan as an independent country or nation-state.

However, looking past the issue of their political state, one can see that the Taiwanese are hard-working, ambitious, and intelligent people. Taiwan is a haven for artists, poets, and political scientists. It encourages developments in technologically-advanced fields and maintains a fierce and loyal spirit. It is an island that is awash in a melding of many Asiatic ethnic groups all the way from Manchuria to the islands in the South Pacific. The tension of its political stance is extreme, though, because of its modest size and location. In 2018, the journal *China Power* referred to Taiwan as an "evolving democracy," an apt term for a country that most likely still has evolving to do.

Here's another book by Captivating History
that you might be interested in

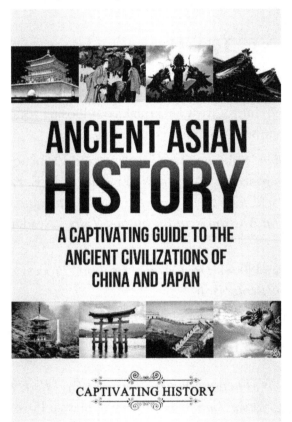

Bibliography

"Losing your Head among the Tattooed Headhunters of Taiwan," Retrieved from https://www.larskrutak.com/loosing-your-head-among-the-tattooed-headhunters-of-taiwan/

Blust, R. (1999) "Subgrouping, Circularity and Extinction: Some Issues in Austronesian Comparative Linguistics: In E. Zeithoun, P. K. Ki (eds), *Selected Papers from the Eighth International Conference on Austronesian Linguistics, Taipei.* Academia Sinca, pp. 31-94

Chiu, Hsin-hui (2008) *The Colonial Civilizing Process in Dutch Formosa, 1624-1662* Brill.

Jiao, T. (2007) *The Neolithic of Southeast China: Cultural Transformation and Regional Interaction on the Coast.* Cambria Press

Katz, P. (2005) *When the Valleys Turned Blood Red: The Tapani Incident in Colonial Taiwan.* University of Hawaii Press

Singh, G. (2010) "Kuomintang, Democratization and the One-China Principle," in Sharma, A. Chakrabarti, S. (eds) *Taiwan Today,* Anthem Press

Hsu, Wen-hsiung (1980) "From Aboriginal Island to Chinese Frontier: The Development of Taiwan before 1683," In Knapp, R.

(ed) *China's Island Frontier: Studies in the Historical Geography of Taiwan*. University Press of Hawaii.

Takekoshi, Y. (1907) *Japanese Rule in Formosa*. Green and Company.

Wong, E. & Edmonson, C. (2019) "Trump Administration Plans to Sell More Than $2 Billion of Arms to Taiwan," In *New York Times*, June 2, 2019. Retrieved from https://www.nytimes.com/2019/06/06/us/politics/trump-taiwan-arms-sale.html

"What does 1992 Consensus Mean to Citizens?" Retrieved from https://thediplomat.com/2018/11/what-does-the-1992-consensus-mean-to-citizens-in-taiwan/

"South China Sea: China Breaks from a Century of Humiliation," Retrieved from https://oxfordre.com/asianhistory/view/10.1093/acrefore/978019027 7727.001.0001/acrefore-9780190277727-e-157

Moore, J. (2019) "Taiwan at 'Cross-Strait Relations: Present Challenges and Future Developments." *U. S. Department of Defense Report, July 2, 2019*

McGovern, J. M. (1898) *Among the Headhunters of Formosa* Prabhat Prakashan.

"President Tsai Ing-wen Promises to Defend Democracy as Taiwan Marks 30th Anniversary of the Tiananmen Crackdown," In *South China Morning Post, June 4, 2019*. Retrieved from https://www.scmp.com/news/china/diplomacy/article/3013105/presi dent-tsai-ing-wen-promises-defend-democracy-taiwan-marks

Clements, J. (2010). *A Brief History of Kublai Khan*. Running Press.

"East Asia: Southeast Asia: China" Retrieved from https://www.cia.gov/library/publications/the-world-factbook/geos/ch.html

"Communist China's Painful Human Rights Story," Retrieved from https://www.cfr.org/article/communist-chinas-painful-human-rights-story

Guanzhong, L. & Palmer, M. (trans.) (2018 reprint). *The Romance of the Three Kingdoms.* Penguin Classics.

"History of Gunpowder," Retrieved from https://www.thoughtco.com/gunpowder-history-1991395

Hung, H. H. (2017). *The Brilliant Reign of the Kangxi Emperor: China's Qing Dynasty.* Algora Publishing.

Kim, S. (2017). *Ginseng and Borderland: Territorial Boundaries and Political Relations between Qing China and Choson Korea, 1636-1912.* University of California Press, 1ˢᵗ ed.

Levy, H. "The Bifurcation of the Yellow Turbans in the Later Han," Retrieved from https://brill.com/view/journals/orie/13/1/article-p251_11.xml

Man, J. (2004). *Kublai Khan: The Mongol Who Remade China.* Bantam Books.

Man, J. (2006). *Kublai Khan.* Bantam Books.

"Manchu Conquest of China," Retrieved from https://teachwar.wordpress.com/resources/war-justifications-archive/manchu-conquest-of-china-1618/

Melton, G. (2014). *Faiths across Time: 5,000 Years of Religious.* History ABC-CLIO.

Morgan, D. (1986). *The Mongols.* Blackwell Publishers.

Polo, M. (1918 reprint). *The Travels of Marco Polo the Venetian.* E. P. Dutton.

"Republic of China's Diplomatic Archives: Lessons of History," Retrieved from https://teachwar.wordpress.com/resources/war-justifications-archive/manchu-conquest-of-china-1618/

Sterling, C. "Visualizing Traditional China," Retrieved from https://zhang.digitalscholar.rochester.edu/china/tag/yang-guang/

Waldron, A. (1992). *The Great Wall of China: From History to Myth.* Cambridge University Press.

Werner, E.T.C. (2005), Retrieved from https://www.gutenberg.org/files/15250/15250-h/15250-h.htm#d0e1278

Wriggins, S. (2003 rev.). *The Silk Road Journey with Xuanzang.* Westview Press.

Wuyong, Q. & Novel, B. (trans.) (2019). *Fortune-teller Next to the Beauty: Vol 18.* Funstory.

"Zhu Qizhen: The Zhengtong Emperor," Retrieved from https://www.mingtombs.eu/emp/06zhengtong/zhengtong.html

Adiss, S., Groemer, G and Rimer, J. (2006) *Traditional Japanese Arts and Culture: An Illustrated Sourcebook,* Harvard University Press.

Buell, R. (1922) *The Washington Conference.* Columbia University Press.

Chikamatsu. K. "Edo's Transportation Network," Retrieved from https://web-japan.org/tokyo/know/trans/tra.html.

Costello, J. (1981) *The Pacific War.* Columbia University Press.

Farris, W. (1996) *Heavenly Warriors: The Evolution of Japan's Military: 500-1300.* Harvard University Press.

"The First Sino-Japanese War," Retrieved from https://www.thoughtco.com/frst-sino-japanese-war-1894-95-1894-95-195784.

Harries, M. and Susie (2001) *Soldiers of the Sun.* Random House.

Hibbett, H. (2001) *The Floating World in Japanese Fiction,* Tuttle Publishing.

"In the Realm of Hungry Ghosts," Retrieved from https://www.goodreads.com/book/show/617702.In_the_Realm_of_Hungry_Ghosts.

Jansen, J. (2002) *The Making of Modern Japan.* Harvard University Press.

"Japanese Law Research Guide: Legal System & Statistics," Retrieved from https://libguides.uchastings.edu/japan-law/legal-system-stats.

Irokawa, D. (1985) *The Culture of the Meiji Period.* Princeton University Press.

Meyer, M. (1993) *Japan: A Concise History, 3ʳ ed.* Littlefield Adams.

Ravina, M. (2011) *The Last Samurai: The Life and Battles of Saigo Takamori.* John Wiley and Sons.

Saskisaka, M. "Economic Planning in Japan," Retrieved from https://onlinelibrary.wiley.com/doi/pdf/10.1111/j.1746-1049.1963.tb00638.x.

Suzuki, D. *Zen and Japanese Culture.* New York University PreWatanabe, T. (1984) "The Western Image of Japanese Art in the Late Edo Period," In Modern Asian Studies, Cambridge University Press.

Choy, B. (2012). *Korea: A History.* Tuttle Publishing Company.

Ho, J., Gamarra, E.R. (2016). *The Globally Important Agricultural Wisdom in the 15ᵗʰ Century Choson Korea.* The Academy of Korean Studies.

Jho, W. (2013). *Building Telecom Markets: Evolution of Governance in the Korean Mobile.* Springer Books.

Kim, J. (2012). *A History of Korea: From "Land of the Morning Calm" to States in Conflict.* Indiana State University Press.

Kim, M. (2014). *Law and Custom in Korea: Comparative Legal History.* Cambridge University Press.

Kim, Bumsheol "Socioeconomic Development in the Bronze Age". Retrieved from https://scholarspace.manoa.hawaii.edu/bitstream/10125/55550/07_AP_54.1kim.pdf

"Korean Confucianism". Retrieved from http://intl.ikorea.ac.kr/korean/UserFiles/UKS3_Korean_Confuciani sm_eng.pdf

Lee, P. (ed.) (1983). *Anthology of Korean Literature: From the Earliest Era to the Nineteenth Century*. University of Hawaii Press.

Mintz, Gordon (ed.), Ra Hung Ha (trans) (2006). *Samguk Yusa: The History of the Three Kingdoms*. Silk Pagoda.

"The Miracle with a Dark Side". Retrieved from https://www.piie.com/publications/chapters_preview/341/3iie3373.p df "The Miracle with a Dark Side," 1980 From Reforming Korea.

Park, E. B., Jackson, B. (trans) (2017). *Letters from Korea,* Vol. 2. Cum Libro.

Pulsik, K. Shutz, E. (ed.) (2011). *The Koguryo Annals of the Samguk Sagi*. Academy of Korean Studies.

Rawski, E. S. (2015). *Modern China and Northeast Asia: Cross-Border Perspectives*. Cambridge University Press.

Shin, J. S. (2014) *A Brief History of Korea*, Vol. 1: "The Spirit of Korean Cultural Roots" (2005). Ewa Women's University Press.

Tang, L, Winkler, Dietmar (ed) (2017). *Hidden Treasures and Intercultural Encounters.*

Tennant, R. (2012). *History of Korea*. Routledge.

Made in the USA
Las Vegas, NV
12 December 2020

12907454R00233